AFTER THE DEATH OF NATURE

Carolyn Merchant's foundational 1980 book *The Death of Nature: Women, Ecology and the Scientific Revolution* established her as a pioneering researcher of human–nature relations. Her subsequent ground-breaking writing in a dozen books and over a hundred peer-reviewed articles has only fortified her position as one of the most influential scholars writing about the environment.

This book examines and builds upon her decades-long legacy of innovative environmental thought and her critical responses to modern mechanistic and patriarchal conceptions of nature and women, as well as her systematic taxonomies of environmental thought and action. Scholars and activists assess, praise, criticize, and extend Merchant's work to arrive at a better and more complete understanding of the human place in nature today. Their findings hold the potential for healthier and more just relations with nature and among people in the future.

Kenneth Worthy is Research Associate at the University of California, Santa Cruz and Lecturer at the University of California, Berkeley, St. Mary's College of California, and New York University.

Elizabeth Allison is Associate Professor of Ecology and Religion at the California Institute of Integral Studies in San Francisco, where she founded and chairs the graduate program in Ecology, Spirituality, and Religion.

Whitney A. Bauman is Associate Professor of Religious Studies at Florida International University.

Carolyn Merchant in her office in Giannini Hall at the University of California, Berkeley, shortly before her retirement in spring 2018. Photo by Kenneth Worthy.

AFTER THE DEATH OF NATURE

Carolyn Merchant and the Future of Human–Nature Relations

Edited by Kenneth Worthy, Elizabeth Allison, and Whitney A. Bauman

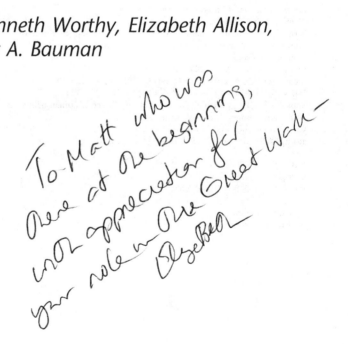

Routledge
Taylor & Francis Group

NEW YORK AND LONDON

First published 2019
by Routledge
711 Third Avenue, New York, NY 10017

and by Routledge
2 Park Square, Milton Park, Abingdon, Oxon OX14 4RN

Routledge is an imprint of the Taylor & Francis Group, an informa business

Cover Image by David Marcu, for more: https://www.instagram.com/marcu.
david/

Library of Congress Cataloging in Publication Data
Names: Worthy, Kenneth, 1961- editor.
Title: After the death of nature : Carolyn Merchant and the future of
human-nature relations / edited by Kenneth Worthy, Elizabeth Allison, and
Whitney A. Bauman.
Description: New York, NY : Routledge, 2019.
Identifiers: LCCN 2018019084| ISBN 9781138297302 (hbk) |
ISBN 9781138297319 (pbk) | ISBN 9781315099378 (ebk)
Subjects: LCSH: Human ecology. | Nature--Effect of human beings on. |
Merchant, Carolyn. Death of nature.
Classification: LCC GF503 .A38 2019 | DDC 304.2--dc23LC record available
at https://lccn.loc.gov/2018019084

ISBN: 978-1-138-29730-2 (hbk)
ISBN: 978-1-138-29731-9 (pbk)
ISBN: 978-1-315-09937-8 (ebk)

Typeset in Bembo
by Taylor & Francis Books

For our fathers:
Frank James Worthy (1928–2017),
Walter Lynn Bauman (1951–2017),
and Scott William Allison (1940–)

CONTENTS

PART III
The Politics of Landscapes, Embodiment, and Epistemologies

FIGURES

CONTRIBUTORS

Elizabeth Allison is Associate Professor of Ecology and Religion at the California Institute of Integral Studies in San Francisco, where she founded and chairs the graduate program in Ecology, Spirituality, and Religion. Her research and teaching explore connections between religion, ethics, and environmental practice, with particular attention to biodiversity, waste, ecological place, and climate change. Her articles appear in *WIREs Climate Change, Mountain Research and Development, The Journal for the Study of Religion, Nature, and Culture*, and in edited volumes on Bhutan, religion, and geography.

Whitney A. Bauman is Associate Professor of Religious Studies at Florida International University. He lectures on science and religion, religion and nature, and religion and queer theory. His books include *Religion and Ecology: Developing a Planetary Ethic* (Columbia University Press 2014), *Theology Creation and Environmental Ethics* (Routledge 2009), with Kevin O'Brien and Richard Bohannon, *Grounding Religion: A Fieldguide to the Study of Religion and Ecology, Second Revised Edition* (Routledge 2017), and with Lucas Johnston, *Science and Religion: One Planet, Many Possibilities* (Routledge 2014). He is currently working on a manuscript that examines the religious influences on Ernst Haeckel's understanding of the natural world.

J. Baird Callicott, who retired as University Distinguished Research Professor and Regents Professor of Philosophy at the University of North Texas in 2015, is widely known as a founder of academic environmental philosophy. He is co-Editor-in-Chief of the *Encyclopedia of Environmental Ethics and Philosophy* and author or editor of a score of books, among them *Earth's Insights: A Multicultural Survey of Ecological Ethics from the Mediterranean Basin to the Australian Outback* (University of California Press 1997), and author of dozens of journal articles, encyclopedia articles, and book chapters on environmental philosophy and ethics.

Dewi Candraningrum is an Indonesian scholar and activist who teaches at the Muhammadiyah University of Surakarta (UMS), Indonesia, and is a guest lecturer in Women's Studies (UI, UGM, SWCU). She established Jejer Wadon in Bentara Budaya Balai Soedjatmoko Solo. She also serves on the editorial board of the *International Journal of Indonesian Studies* (*IJIS*; Fac. of Monash University). She received her doctoral degree from the University of Münster, Germany, and her Master's degree from Monash University, Australia, and an S1 (bachelor's degree) from Universitas Muhammadiyah Surakarta (UMS). Her teaching, writing, and research are related to women's education and literature, sustainable development, ecological studies, ecofeminism, and gender.

Heather Eaton is Professor of Conflict Studies at Saint Paul University in Ottawa, Canada. Her current research includes ecological, gender/feminist, and religious dimensions of peace and conflict studies; theories of conflict, social justice, nonviolence and animal rights. She publishes frequently, including *Advancing Nonviolence and Social Transformation,* with Lauren Levesque (Equinox 2016), *The Intellectual Journey of Thomas Berry* (Lexington Press 2014), *Ecological Awareness: Exploring Religion, Ethics and Aesthetics*, with Sigurd Bergmann (LIT Verlag 2011), *Introducing Ecofeminist Theologies* (T&T Clark 2005), and, with Lois Lorentzen, *Ecofeminism and Globalization* (Rowman & Littlefield 2003).

Yaakov Garb is a tenured Senior Lecturer at Ben Gurion University where he holds joint appointments in the Department of Sociology and Anthropology and the Swiss Institute for Dryland Environmental & Energy Research. Trained at Berkeley and MIT, he has forged a deeply interdisciplinary approach to environmental issues, which fuses socio-analytic traditions (the sociology of science and technology, discourse analysis, political ecology) and applied technical expertise (environmental science, data and spatial analytics). His work in several environmental domains (transport, urban planning, building, waste) is reflected in a series of academic publications and research-based policy interventions in Israel, the West Bank, and the Czech Republic. Before joining the faculty of Ben Gurion University, Garb held post-doctoral positions at Harvard and Hebrew University, was a Fellow at the School of Advanced Studies (Princeton), and a Visiting Assistant Professor at Brown University.

Susan Griffin has, for over fifty years, through twenty books—one a Pulitzer Prize finalist—been making unconventional connections between seemingly disparate subjects. Whether pairing ecology and gender in her foundational work *Woman and Nature*, or the private life with the targeting of civilians by nuclear war in *A Chorus of Stones*, she sheds light on contemporary issues. Among her many awards and honors, she has been awarded a Guggenheim Fellowship, the Northern California Fred Cody Award for Lifetime Literary Achievement, an honorary doctorate from the Graduate Theological Union, a grant from the National Endowment for the Arts, and the Commonwealth Silver Award for Poetry.

Patsy Hallen is Associate Professor at Curtin University and a foundation member of staff at Murdoch University, both in Perth, Western Australia. She has published numerous articles and book chapters in the areas of Environmental Philosophy and Ethics, Ecofeminism and the Philosophy of Science. Her passions include teaching and dwelling in the 'more-than-human' world which galvanized her to take her Ecophilosophy students backpacking for prolonged periods in wild spaces as an integral part of their course, because the natural world is our most powerful educator.

Debora Hammond is Professor Emerita of Interdisciplinary Studies in the Hutchins School of Liberal Studies at Sonoma State University. Her doctoral work in the History of Science was published in 2003 as *The Science of Synthesis: Exploring the Social Implications of General Systems Theory*. She served as President of the International Society of the Systems Sciences and hosted the annual conference in 2006. In the fall of 2009, she assumed the role of Program Director of the Organization Development MA Program at SSU, which has broadened her interest and experience in the practice of applied systems theory.

Shepard Krech III is Emeritus Professor of Anthropology at Brown University and a research associate in the National Museum of Natural History, Smithsonian Institution. He has received numerous fellowships and grants, has served as a trustee of the National Humanities Center, and has authored or edited more than ten books and 150 articles and reviews, including *Praise the Bridge That Carries You Over*, *Indians, Animals and the Fur Trade*, *A Victorian Earl in the Arctic*, *Collecting Native America, 1870–1960* (ed. with B. Hail), *The Ecological Indian: Myth and History*, *Encyclopedia of World Environmental History* (ed. with J. R. McNeill and C. Merchant), *Spirits of the Air*, and *Indigenous Environments* (ed. with D. Gordon).

Carolyn Merchant's landmark book, *The Death of Nature: Women, Ecology, and the Scientific Revolution*, has shaped the fields of women's studies, environmental history, and the history of science ever since its publication in 1980. The subject of over 130 reviews, major symposia, special journal sections, and keynote lectures worldwide, it was followed by *Ecological Revolutions, Radical Ecology, Earthcare, Reinventing Eden, American Environmental History, Autonomous Nature, Spare the Birds!*, and *Science and Nature*, along with three edited books and over a hundred single-authored research articles. Merchant is Professor of Environmental History, Philosophy, and Ethics at the University of California, Berkeley.

Holmes Rolston III is University Distinguished Professor and Professor of Philosophy at Colorado State University. He has written seven books, most recently *A New Environmental Ethics: The Next Millennium for Life on Earth*. He gave the Gifford Lectures, University of Edinburgh, 1997–1998, and won the Templeton Prize in Religion in 2003. Rolston has spoken as distinguished lecturer on seven continents. He is featured in Joy A. Palmer Cooper, ed., *Key Thinkers on the Environment* (2018) and is Past and Founding President of the International Society for Environmental Ethics. He is a founding editor of the journal *Environmental Ethics*.

Sverker Sörlin is Professor of Environmental History in the Division of History of Science, Technology and Environment at the KTH Royal Institute of Technology in Stockholm, Sweden, where he co-founded the KTH Environmental Humanities Laboratory in 2011. He co-edited *The Future of Nature: Documents of Global Change* (Yale 2013) and has two books in press, *The Environment: A History* (Johns Hopkins University Press; co-authored with Libby Robin and Paul Warde) and *Grounding Urban Natures: Histories and Futures of Urban Ecologies* (MIT Press; co-edited with Henrik Ernstson). He advises the Swedish government on environmental and climate policy.

Mark Stoll is Professor of U.S. Environmental and U.S. Religious History at Texas Tech University. His new book, *Inherit the Holy Mountain: Religion and the Rise of the American Environmental Movement*, was published by Oxford University Press in May 2015. His first book was *Protestantism, Capitalism, and Nature in America* (1997). He has worked as the editor of the ABC-Clio book series *Nature and Human Societies* and co-edited with Dianne Glave *"To Love the Wind and the Rain": African Americans and Environmental History* (2005). Stoll also serves as Director of Environmental Studies at Texas Tech.

Nancy C. Unger is Professor and Chair of History at Santa Clara University. Her book *Beyond Nature's Housekeepers: American Women in Environmental History* (Oxford 2012) was a California Book Award finalist. She is author of the prize-winning biographies *Belle La Follette: Progressive Era Reformer* (Routledge 2016) and *Fighting Bob La Follette: The Righteous Reformer* (University of North Carolina 2000; 2nd edition Wisconsin Historical Society Press 2008). She recently co-edited (with Christopher McKnight Nichols) *A Companion to the Gilded Age and Progressive Era* (Wiley Blackwell 2017) and has published more than two dozen scholarly articles and essays.

Laura Alice Watt is Professor of Geography, Environment, and Planning at Sonoma State University, specializing in landscape history, management, and policy. Her book, *The Paradox of Preservation: Wilderness and Working Landscapes at Point Reyes National Seashore*, was published in 2017 by the University of California Press.

Norman Wirzba is Professor of Theology, Ecology, and Agrarian Studies at Duke Divinity School, and a Senior Fellow at Duke's Kenan Institute for Ethics. He teaches and writes at the intersections of religion, philosophy, and environmental studies, and is currently working on an account of humans in terms of their creaturely life. His books include *The Paradise of God: Renewing Religion in an Ecological Age, From Nature to Creation: A Christian Vision for Understanding and Loving Our World, Food and Faith: A Theology of Eating,* and (with Fred Bahnson) *Making Peace with the Land: God's Call to Reconcile with Creation.*

Kenneth Worthy is Research Associate at the University of California, Santa Cruz, and Lecturer at the University of California, Berkeley, St. Mary's College of California, and New York University. His book *Invisible Nature: Healing the Destructive Divide between People and the Environment* was published by Prometheus Books in 2013. He earned his Ph.D. at U.C. Berkeley in 2005 under the direction of Carolyn Merchant.

ACKNOWLEDGMENTS

This volume is truly the result of a collaborative process unfolding over several years and would not have come into being without the efforts of many. We first would like to thank our many contributors, who persevered through their own sometimes difficult schedules to respond to several rounds of revisions with us. Without their persistence and efforts, the book would not have materialized. We thank them for having patience with us. We thank also Routledge's three anonymous reviewers, who lent sound advice that has certainly made this a better work. Amanda Yee, our first editor at Routledge, early on saw promise in our project (and we hope we were not her reason for moving on!), and Dean Birkenkamp then took up the cause and graced us with his patience and guidance.

Quite clearly, none of this would make any sense whatsoever without the monumental persistence, dedication, and phenomenally hard work of Carolyn Merchant—teacher, researcher, mentor, co-conspirator, and friend, who created the rich tapestry of intellectual threads we reflect upon in this document. Her inspiring and important work could never be done justice by one retrospective and prospective volume such as this, but we hope it serves as a start. It was hard to resist getting Carolyn's views and advice on occasion, on various questions we encountered during certain stages of this project, and she generously complied. Nonetheless, we independently steered the ship and accept all responsibility for any faults in our work developing and editing the volume.

As scholars we are all embedded in numerous communities, at a range of scales from local to global, that support, encourage, and inspire our work. A fortuitous convergence of the three editors at the Association of Environmental Studies and Sciences (AESS) annual conference in New York City in 2014 led to the realization that we had all studied with Carolyn Merchant and wished to honor her significant influence and her impending retirement. Drafts of three of the chapters were presented on a panel on "Revivifying nature in the 21st century? The influence of Carolyn Merchant on the field of religion and ecology" at the 2016 American Academy of Religion (AAR) annual meeting. The chapters by Allison, Bauman, and Eaton benefitted from an excellent audience discussion and feedback in that session.

Elizabeth Allison would like to thank the two other editors of this volume, as well as Hekia Bodwitch and H. Max Pospisil for their helpful comments and discussions which strengthened her chapter. Elizabeth would also like to thank Eric and Emilia Grace for their good humor in tolerating work breaks during family vacations and (too) many pizza dinners, and the Sierra Nevada mountains, a source of sustenance and inspiration over many years.

Finally, let us not forget nature—our partner in all endeavors, quietly, often invisibly supporting us, engulfing us with sustenance and wisdom both.

FOREWORD

Susan Griffin

Great changes in the way we live are most often preceded by great changes in the way we think. The ideas of Voltaire, Rousseau, John Locke, Mary Wollstonecraft, and Immanuel Kant radically shifted the atmosphere of public perception in ways that inspired the American Revolution while allowing those who shaped a new and independent government to imagine that democracy was possible. As a young woman in the sixties, I participated in and witnessed several radical challenges to the status quo in American society: the Free Speech Movement that arose in opposition to McCarthyism, a growing Civil Rights Movement, a powerful Anti-War movement in response to American actions in Vietnam, a growing movement to protect the environment, and a movement for women's rights. And like so many other social and political movements, our rebellion against oppression and repression was deeply influenced by thinkers and writers from James Baldwin to Norman O. Brown, Herbert Marcuse to Simone de Beauvoir, Rachel Carson to Doris Lessing, who together created the conceptual ground for change.

Carolyn Merchant's considerable body of work belongs to this category of world-shifting thought, work that has had—and will continue to have—a profound influence on our shared futures. Steadily over almost four decades she has forged a link, both conceptually and through painstaking research, regarding the dominant society's ideas about women, the various roles to which women have been consigned in the past as well as the present, ecology, and broader issues of social justice. Her groundbreaking first book, *The Death of Nature*, shatters two of the most fundamental and destructive assumptions of Western culture: the idea that nature is dead matter, made up of things, to be manipulated and exploited at will, and that women, being closer to nature, are biologically inferior to men.

Although in American and European civilizations, a seemingly endless number of 'learned' dicta about women clearly and often purposefully mirrored ideas about nature, before the late 1970s, when the women's movement re-emerged, the connection between the prejudicial view of women as inferior and a reductive devaluation of nature was rarely, if ever, discussed. This was hardly because the socially constructed equation between women and nature was not believed to exist, but rather because it was so deeply believed to be true and so firmly anchored in consciousness that it was rarely, if ever, held up to scrutiny.

Through exacting historical research, what Merchant does in *The Death of Nature* is to show us that far from liberating women, in reducing nature to a mechanism without soul or intrinsic meaning, the Scientific Revolution and its accompanying technologies also reduced women's status in Western society, even to the extent of aiding the persecution and massacre of women who were healers. Yet her work is hardly against science. Rather, she challenges the philosophical assumptions, starting with the idea that nature or matter is dead, that lurk behind so many scientific pronouncements, providing justifications for countless forms of exploitation, especially given the rise of Capitalism in the same period that modern science emerged.

What we are seeing now from diverse sources within various sciences, such as the study of the way slime mold seems to make intelligent choices, or the study of communication and cooperation between trees by Suzanne Simard and Merlin Sheldrake, is the repudiation of the idea that nature is without meaning, intelligence, or consciousness. And it is hardly coincidental that at the same time many in Western society are beginning to acknowledge Indigenous wisdom and science, or traditional ecological knowledge (TEK).

Anticipating the contemporary use of the term "intersectionality," in several subsequent works, especially *Ecological Revolutions* (1989) and *Radical Ecology* (1992), Merchant shows how the suppression and denigration of Native knowledge was and still is, as we see in the recent and ongoing struggle over the Dakota Access Pipeline, inseparable from the destruction of nature. "The colonial ecological revolution in New England," she writes, "was externally caused and resulted in the erosion of Indian modes of relating to nature" (Merchant 1989:109). Over and over again, she locates her insights in specific places and times, in histories she explores through the radical lens of social justice as well as ecology, showing us how, for instance, the fur and timber industries disrupted and disabled hunter-gathering communities. Throughout her work, Merchant describes the ways that different inequalities and modes of domination support each other, making clear that oppression occurs from the correlation of many different identities and institutions, which produce, as Kimberlé Crenshaw argues, complexities beyond the overly simple categories and frames commonly imposed.

The ecological vision Merchant aims toward is neither opposed to nor divided from human communities. Rather, her work is centered in the understanding that nature and human society are interdependent, interlaced, and kindred, even when society becomes alienated from the natural world. In *Ecological Revolutions,* for instance, she cites Thoreau's warning that market economies enslave farmers to profits and property. "By the mid-nineteenth century," she tells us, most farmers had been touched by the market's demand "for efficiency and profit" (Merchant 1989:258). (This morally devolutionary process, one that only grew more intense in the twentieth century, warping communities, families and souls alike, has been movingly captured in Jane Smiley's great novel, *A Thousand Acres*).

Merchant also shows us how market economies, and capitalism, operating hand-in-hand with a mechanistic worldview, made countless efforts to demean and destroy Native American cultures. Because so many such cultures are grounded in a respect for nature, they could serve us well today. Her work anticipates significant work to follow, for instance that of Kimberlé Crenshaw in the practice of observing "intersectionality," or the work of Native American scientist and writer Robin Wall Kimmerer, who folds scientific knowledge into indigenous wisdom.

But Merchant does not reject Western traditions wholesale. We forget that, while the philosophies of various conquerors may in their turn hold sway over our shared consciousness, other varieties of thought and practice existed and many still endure. Tracing holistic thought in European cultures to earlier centuries, she corrects the notion we have inherited that the Renaissance delivered us from a worldview riddled with superstition. What arose, along with the artistic and architectural achievements we celebrate, was a mechanistic worldview that replaced a shared sense of the world as alive and connected, or, as she writes, "an organism," and along with that the belief that spirit is endemic to matter.

The separation of spirit from matter, which lies at the heart of mechanistic philosophies, was not challenged for centuries, until a new vision used the scientific method to travel far outside the boundaries of mechanistic views of nature. By that time, the word "spirit," no longer acceptable in scientific vocabulary, had been transubstantiated into the concept of energy.[1] So when the famous formula $E=mc^2$ challenged the division of energy (once spirit in Greek) from matter, both theoretically and experimentally showing that matter is indeed comprised of energy (and vice versa), the philosophical, political, and social implications of this new vision of nature were not pursued.[2] Instead a weapon with an inestimable destructive potential and toxic composition was developed that still threatens and poisons the world today.[3]

There are many paths to reclaiming not just the full significance of nature but our own existence, which is part of nature, from the jaws of division and meaninglessness. One is, of course, to retreat into fundamentalist religions that in their own ways rob nature and humanity of our infinite complexity and creativity, reducing life to the literal interpretations of ancient texts, often out of context and unjust (if not lacking in common sense altogether). Another is to reclaim traditional sources of wisdom, including those within Indigenous cultures that look to nature as a source of spirit and meaning. Another is to use science and technology to reveal more and more of the depth and breadth of nature's intelligence. Countless approaches can and do offer to lead us to a restoration of human intelligence about our home in the universe.

But, whichever path we choose, Merchant's work is crucial to each of these efforts. If we are to understand how we have managed to manufacture so many of crises facing us today—climate change, the erosion and disappearance of arable land, the poisoning of our rivers, the pollution of oceans, so many dangerous or murderous conflicts between peoples and nations—we will have to think about how we think, for along with nature and society, we have despoiled our own consciousness too. We will need to locate within our many histories the beginnings of practices, such as market economies, modern and post-modern colonial exploitations, and social constructs, such as racism and misogyny, that are inextricably related to the habit of treating nature as a thing to be used, mistreated, disposed of, or claimed at will.

For decades—with a painstakingly careful approach and an uncommon but steady percipience, documenting often overlooked histories, locating the genesis of destructive as well as generative ideas, deconstructing hidden assumptions, always connecting issues of social justice with events effecting ecologies—by preparing a conceptual ground, Merchant's work has liberated generations of scholars and thinkers to understand further what has brought us here and to imagine how we might begin to recover ourselves and the earth. This book is a testament to that process.

As I write, a small nation on the Korean peninsula, feeling threatened by larger powers, threatens death to millions of its neighbors, while at the same time, millions of residents in the U.S. city of Houston have lost their homes to the largest flood in recorded history ever to inundate an American city. If at this auspicious moment in time, we lack any positive voice or leadership from the administrative branch of government, Merchant's great body of work can summon that voice and that leadership among us and help us find ways to come together to save the lives and the earth that we love.

Susan Griffin
Berkeley, 2017

Notes

1 "What is the nature of light?" began as a religious question, for instance. In the late 12th and early 13th centuries, to cite one example, Robert Grosseteste, who was both a bishop and a theoretical scientist-philosopher, asserted that God is primordial light. As spirit became energy, questions about the nature of light persisted seamlessly, leading to the famous Michelson-Morley experiments in the 19th century that both disproved the theory of ether and contributed to Einstein's theory of special relativity.

2 See also Chapter 1 by J. Baird Callicott in this volume.

3 See also Chapter 9 by Debora Hammond in this volume.

Bibliography

Griffin, Susan. 1978. *Woman and Nature: The Roaring Inside Her.* New York: Harper & Row.

Griffin, Susan. 1996. *The Eros of Everyday Life: Essays on Ecology, Gender and Society.* New York: Anchor.

Griffin, Susan. 2017. "Sustainability and the Soul." Pp. 12–22 in *Ecological and Social Healing: Multicultural Women's Voices*, ed. Jeanine M. Canty. New York: Routledge.

Kimmerer, Robin Wall. 2013. *Braiding Sweetgrass: Indigenous Wisdom, Scientific Knowledge and the Teachings of Plants.* Minneapolis, MN: Milkweed.

Merchant, Carolyn. 1980. *The Death of Nature: Women, Ecology and the Scientific Revolution.* New York: Harper & Row.

Merchant, Carolyn. 1989. *Ecological Revolutions: Nature, Gender and Science in New England.* Chapel Hill: University of North Carolina Press.

Merchant, Carolyn. 1992. *Radical Ecology: The Search for a Livable World.* New York: Routledge.

Smiley, Jane. 1991. *A Thousand Acres.* New York: Alfred A. Knopf.

AFTER THE DEATH OF NATURE

Introduction

Kenneth Worthy, Elizabeth Allison, and Whitney A. Bauman

Professor Carolyn Merchant of the University of California, Berkeley stands as one of the most influential scholars in environmental studies. A pioneer in two fields—environmental history and ecofeminism—she has produced ground-breaking work in a number of other far-flung domains, including the history of science and religious studies. In more than a dozen books—with two new ones out in 2016 and one in 2017—and more than a hundred scholarly articles and chapters, she has contributed a remarkably coherent and compelling yet broad-ranging body of thought to environmental scholarship. Her work, pre-dating the rise of the environmental humanities as a field of inquiry, has been foundational for many in the humanistic environmental fields. This volume serves as a retro-spective of her work—one that is, as becomes clear below, necessarily incom-plete—while continuing the tradition of engaging with it and building upon it.

Long before the environmental humanities coalesced into a coherent field, Merchant's writings transcended academic boundaries to corral the fields that today constitute it. Her landmark 1980 book *The Death of Nature: Women, Ecol-ogy, and the Scientific Revolution* (hereafter *TDN*) (Merchant 1980) defined in important ways the necessity of studying links among science, nature, gender, and philosophy to understand environmental change in the Euro-American context. Bringing together environmental history, philosophy, and ethics with environ-mental sciences, geography, and religious studies, Merchant's impressive corpus connects seemingly disparate fields to analyze the ways in which the philosophical and religious inheritances of the European and "Western" canon, including the ancient Greeks and the Bible, have influenced human–nature relations in the industrial-capitalist modern world.

A pioneer in connecting religious beliefs with environmental ethics and his-tory, Merchant took seriously Lynn White's famous critique that religion plays a significant role in the environmental crisis. In *TDN*, she articulates the many ways in which Christianity and Judaism (among other streams of thought) helped to shape a metaphor of nature as feminine—at times a mother and at times an unruly force needing to be controlled and dominated. She has described how the Scientific Revolution transformed nature into "dead stuff" controlled and constructed through human (mostly male) agency. She further draws out the implications of metaphors used by scientists as the new priests controlling and torturing nature (based on language used in Christian Europe during the witch trials). Such an understanding brought new depth to the ways in which patriarchal structures materialized in the world and were adopted by the "enlightened" scientists of the sixteenth through eighteenth centuries. And Merchant not only critiques the dominant Western European paradigm's understanding of nature, but also recovers alternative, non-reductive conceptions of nature.

This type of analysis continues in Merchant's *Ecological Revolutions: Nature, Gender, and Science in New England* (1989), where she analyzes how Puritans and Protestants (more broadly) transformed the landscapes of the early United States in efforts to tame a feared "wild" nature into a civilized (read Christian) land. This approach extended to both agricultural and forestry practices, and to the "re-education," exploitation, and killing of Native peoples in New England. In *Reinventing Eden: The Fate of Nature in Western Culture (2003)*, Merchant builds on this account and provides a broader view to describe how Christian narratives of progress and decline have helped to transform the rest of the natural world, and how these narratives are taken up in some feminist and environmentalist metaphors of "returning" to a pure idyllic state or, alternately, a certain future apocalypse. In recent decades, Merchant has offered her own alternatives to these narratives of decline or recovery, based in chaos and complexity theory to better account for the agency of nature.

Merchant's tendency to cross disciplinary boundaries is no accident but is rather fundamental to her influential method, as is close attention to detail. As J. Baird Callicott outlines in Chapter 1 of this collection, Merchant cut her research teeth with a series of papers that doggedly pursued the myriad facets of several questions in the early history of modern science, including the *Vis Viva* controversy. At stake in the latter was whether any "life force" exists within nature down to the level of individual particles. In this question can be seen the kernel of *TDN*: Is the cosmos deemed alive or not, and what are the historical currents that precipitated the new conception of nature? Grappling with these questions, Merchant's radically interdisciplinary method received its earliest and perhaps grandest expression. She traversed a number of fields and subjects, bringing a range of perspectives and data to bear on her central question about the causes and consequences of the transformation from a living, organic cosmos, to a dead mechanistic one. Exhibiting the hallmark of much of her subsequent work, she draws on diverse fields including history of science, art history, gender studies, intellectual history, philosophy, cultural geography, colonial history, religious studies, theology, environmental ethics, and environmental history.

Much of Merchant's work arose out of this broad and (thus) stable foundation of fields, topics, and methods, like polycultures arising from fertile soil—and as this volume attests, so has much work by other environmental humanities (and other) scholars. Merchant further developed the theme of women and nature throughout many of her following works, including *Earthcare: Women and the Environment* (Merchant 1995). The theme of religion and the environment emerges repeatedly in her scholarship, most intensely examined in *Reinventing Eden: The Fate of Nature in Western Culture* (Merchant 2003) but forming a significant thread in *Ecological Revolutions: Nature, Gender, and Science in New England* (Merchant 1989), which follows through on some of the intellectual history set up in *TDN* as it heads West across the Atlantic. Cosmology and the history of science again become central themes in her more recent *Autonomous Nature: Problems of Prediction and Control from Ancient Times to the Scientific Revolution* (Merchant 2016a). Her books, together with numerous research articles in the history of physics, the history of women in science, environmental history, environmental ethics, women and the environment, and ecofeminism, together exhibit an interdisciplinarity often envisioned but rarely achieved in environmental studies.

Depth of Influence

Merchant's research and writing remain as relevant today for experts and others interested in any of these fields as they were when she began publishing four and a half decades ago. Although certainly not all of her works are greeted with universal acceptance, the connections she weaves between nature, gender, religion, and science must be traversed by any serious student of the environmental humanities. That level of engagement becomes evident from even the most cursory look at the bibliometrics of Merchant's published scholarly work. *TDN* has been reviewed dozens of times in the scholarly literature, and has been translated into half a dozen languages, including Chinese, Italian, and Swedish. It has been the subject of symposia in scholarly journals. Google Scholar reports over 4,600 published citations of *TDN*—an unusually high citation count for a text engaging with environmental themes. These counts do not even include her other, often influential, publications. She has given more than 355 invited lectures and conference presentations at universities in the United States, Europe, Brazil, and Australia. More than 230 reviews and discussions of all of Merchant's books have been published. The Web of Science lists over two thousand citations of Merchant's works in scholarly articles. Google Scholar's (somewhat less precise) accounting lists at least ten thousand total published citations of Merchant's books and articles. An issue of the journal *Organization & Environment* focused on Merchant's *The Death of Nature*, identifying it as a "citation classic" and a "foundational work" (Forbes and Jermier 1998:180). Similarly, a special feature section of the October 2005 issue of the journal *Environmental History* included a "Retrospective Review" of *TDN* featuring three articles by prominent scholars looking back over 25 years of its influence (Norwood 2005; Sturgeon 2005; Worster 2005). *Isis*, a journal of the History of Science Society, devoted five articles in its September 2006 issue to an investigation into the influence of *TDN* on the historiography of science (Cadden 2006; Merchant 2006; Mitman 2006; Park 2006; Thompson 2006).

In her ninth decade, Merchant shows little sign of letting up on her scholarly output. In the past two years, she has published three new books that, combined, further exhibit her impressive range as a scholar: *Autonomous Nature: Problems of Prediction and Control From Ancient Times to the Scientific Revolution* (Merchant 2016a), a look at how chaos and complexity theories help us understand the quest to predict and control nature; *Spare the Birds! George Bird Grinnell and the First Audubon Society* (Merchant 2016b), a history of the origins of the Society and the explorer and conservationist who launched it, including biographies of ornithologists John James Audubon and Alexander Wilson; and *Science and Nature: Past, Present, and Future* (Merchant 2017), which brings together Merchant's insights about the history of science, environmental history, and ethics. As we write this introduction, Merchant is Fellow in Residence at the Center for Advanced Study in the Behavioral Sciences at Stanford University, researching and writing a book on the Anthropocene and the humanities.

These several publications represent only the highlights to come out during the time we have been assembling this book. Her prodigious output, combined with the scope of her research and writing, complicate any attempt at a comprehensive assessment of her scholarship. And so none is offered here. Instead, this volume aims to offer a diversity of writings by scholars in a variety of fields that examine various aspects of Merchant's scholarship while assessing, praising, criticizing, and building upon it and acknowledging its breadth and depth. The approaches here range from the personal and particular to the purely intellectual and scholarly, with some chapters exhibiting a mixture. Although the subject matter herein focuses primarily on the United States and Western Europe—mirroring Merchant's own interests and areas of study—our contributors originate from three continents. Theory and history as well as current struggles over access to and protection of natural resources are included, along with stories of how Carolyn Merchant influenced and shaped careers and scholarly thinking.

Methodological Contributions to the Environmental Humanities

Merchant's work has been pathbreaking in defining the scope and possibilities of humanistic environmental studies, and helping this broad area of studies to coalesce into what is now known as the Environment Humanities. Several qualities define Merchant's approach. Her home discipline of History shines through in writing that is consistently grounded in the material particularities of the place and time about which she writes (from sixteenth-century Europe and North American colonies to the twenty-first-century United States). Painstaking attention to historical detail and an exhaustive search for sources, with data drawn from the visual arts, literary works, first-hand accounts, policy documents, and other primary texts, buttresses her arguments about the causes and consequences of environmental change. From her earliest published work, when she was writing under the name of Carolyn Iltis (as J. Baird Callicott discusses in this volume), Merchant's work is detail-oriented, intensive, and exhaustive. This assemblage of significant and descriptive details create what Bruno Latour characterizes as a "captation," giving the reader no clear option but to follow where her argument leads (Latour 1987). As referenced above, Merchant's work is also characterized by an expansive *breadth* that takes in the range of material conditions, practices, ideologies, and academic specialties that bear on the phenomenon under study.

Beginning with *TDN*, Merchant's scholarship has been ambitious—not content to address small historical moments but instead desiring to understand how those moments ripple through time and space to influence subsequent material and ideological relations on a larger scale. Her research has a broad scope that marshals wide-ranging evidence to answer major, pressing questions related to the mutual entanglement of humans and the rest of nature—and the sources of modernity's destructive relationship with nature. In addition to the influence of humans on nonhuman nature, Merchant also flips this dynamic, showing how nonhuman nature significantly shapes and constrains the possibilities of human actors.

A key aspect of the confluence of nature and culture as Merchant observes it is the role of race, class, and gender in the distribution of environmental burdens and benefits. In de-naturalizing these constructions of social location, and showing how social location is linked to particular concepts and practices around nonhuman nature, Merchant counters the prevailing neoliberal ideology that stridently claims There Is No Alternative (TINA) to existing social, environmental, and political structures, and shows that social relations are historically contingent, that is—they might have been (and can be) otherwise.

Narrative is a persistent feature of Merchant's method. Throughout her career, she has maintained a dual emphasis on deconstructing dominant narratives and uncovering hidden ones, both within and outside of the Western tradition, to aid this deconstruction. This dual focus has allowed Merchant to make powerful arguments about the ways that the subjugation of women and nature have been historically, economically, politically, and ideologically related, while offering emancipatory possibilities by locating alternative threads within the Western tradition that suggest alternatives.

As her concern with modernity's environmental predicament shows, Merchant is not an "ivory tower" academic. Her work cannot be considered detached or abstract; rather, it bravely engages with current political and economic realities to understand the causes of environmental change and to unpack ideologies, practices, and relations that contribute to environmental degradation. She does not shy away from pointing out those responsible for degradation. As J. Baird Callicott exclaims in this volume, "Amen, Sister!"

While tracing the causes of degradation, Merchant unearths alternate strands within the Western tradition that can help to overthrow relations of domination. She offers multiple viewpoints on, for example, emancipatory environmental ethics in *Radical Ecology: The Search for a Livable World* (Merchant 1992), allowing students and readers to find the path that best fits with their existing commitments and social location. At the same time, she offers the range of ideologies presented in *Radical Ecology* as a path to constructing an ameliorative environmental ethic needed for the twenty-first century. A similar, double-pronged approach helps her create her "partnership ethic," discussed by several contributors to this volume, which constitutes both an analytical critique of difficulties in current formulations of environmental ethics and a constructive alternative for the future.

Range of Influence

The range of scholars contributing to this book stands as a testament to Merchant's far-flung disciplinary travels: she influenced the anthropologist Shepherd Krech III in his interpretations of North American Indians; she prompted theologian Norman Wirzba to propose a "fidelity ethic" that builds from her "partnership ethic"; she inspired philosopher Holmes Rolston III to advance a new perspective on the Anthropocene; and she has lent some perspective to Indonesian ecofeminist activist-scholar Dewi Candraningrum's narrative of resistance in a landscape of Java. Some of the scholars writing herein were her graduate students, and are now faculty at diverse universities around the world. Some were personally and directly influenced in their scholarly directions and orientations by contact with Carolyn (e.g. Allison, Bauman, Garb, Hammond, Worthy). Others interacted with her professionally as senior scholars and thus have points of agreement and disagreement (e.g. Krech). Several have found both their personal lives and their work intersecting with Carolyn's in multiple surprising ways (e.g. Callicott), while others have been inspired intellectually, with little personal contact.

One scholar who was initially included in this volume (and suggesting another example of the breadth and influence of Merchant's work) is the religious studies and ecofeminist scholar Rosemary Radford Ruether. In many ways her work analyzing the religious roots of patriarchy and the ways that a monotheistic male God undergirds the domination of men over women and nature parallels Merchant's work in *TDN*. In the manuscript she submitted, she indicated that she had used *TDN* in her book *Gaia and God* (Ruether 1994), building on *TDN*'s close study of the rise of mechanistic science over and against the medieval model of nature as organic. In *Gaia and God*, this shift in science is connected with earlier shifts in Platonic thought that value reason above the material world and depends also on the invention of a monotheistic, male God who creates a hierarchical world in which elite men are above women and slaves, and humans are above the rest of the natural world.

As with many of this book's contributors, Ruether's intellectual cross-pollination with Merchant would also foster a personal relationship. After Ruether's retirement from Garrett Evangelical Theological Seminary, she took up a position at the Graduate Theological Union (GTU) in Berkeley. As a young graduate student, one of us (Whitney Bauman) and another graduate student (Greg Zuschlag) arranged a meeting between Merchant and Ruether to see if they might teach a joint course on religion, gender, and nature. The course became one of few cross-listed courses between the GTU and UC Berkeley, and it brought in a variety of guest lecturers as conversation partners, including Evan Eisenberg, Ted Hiebert, Steven Scharper, Fritof Capra, Mary Evelyn Tucker, and John Grim. This type of joint, interdisciplinary effort is representative of the type of work Merchant does, both in the classroom and in her scholarship. We are sad to say that Rosemary suffered a stroke during the production of this book and was unable to finish her contribution. We include this extended discussion of the Ruether–Merchant connection to provide a small glimpse of the types of connections Merchant has made in many corners of the academy.

As some of the following chapters attest, Carolyn Merchant has made deep and indelible personal and professional imprints on many people. For many ecofeminsts the personal, political, and professional can never be fully separated. Several of the essays cite her influence as a female and feminist professor in shaping younger scholars' perceptions of themselves as academics (see the chapters by Hammond, Unger, Watt, and Allison).

Scholars also describe how Merchant's teaching style and materials have influenced their own teaching practices as college instructors. As with her scholarship, blurring and transgressing boundaries across several disciplines, Merchant's teaching breaks down the boundaries between teaching and research, encouraging undergraduates and graduate students to engage with primary texts to become creators of knowledge themselves. Deborah Hammond notes the importance that Merchant conveys in her teaching for building social and political consciousness and developing concern among students for transformation within both the private and public spheres. She concludes, "Carolyn's teaching and writing clearly embody this transformative approach" (Hammond 2018:148). Authors' key insights into how their personal and professional relationships with Merchant shaped their own thinking, scholarship, and career trajectories add a unique dimension to the book that we find to be in tune with the ecofeminist ethic of *particularist* relationships. These accounts also provide valuable insights into how scholarship develops and proceeds in the academy and beyond.

Guide to the Book

The book is divided somewhat arbitrarily into three thematic parts corresponding roughly to three dominant themes in Merchant's work: Part I Environmental Philosophy and Ethics and Ecofeminism; Part II Environmental History; and Part III

The Politics of Landscapes, Embodiment, and Epistemologies. The boundaries between these parts are necessarily porous and somewhat artificial in light of Merchant's wide-ranging interests. Her feminist commitments influence her interpretations of environmental history; her commitment to engaging with real-world environmental issues influences her take on environmental philosophy and ethics. Nonetheless, these categories capture most of the dominant themes of Merchant's work discussed herein. Here we introduce the categories and the chapters they comprise.

Environmental Philosophy and Ethics and Ecofeminism

As an historian of ideas, Merchant has traced the sources of ideas about the environment, and the ideologies that guide human interaction with the environment, contributing to the fields of environmental philosophy and environmental ethics that arose in the 1970s and 1980s. The first part of the book surveys Merchant's contributions to thinking about human–nature relations in the context of environmental philosophy and ethics and ecofeminism, three fields entwined in Merchant's thought and writing.

Merchant's historiography of environmental thought in the West in *TDN* serves as a rich repository of analysis of the divisive thought that underlies modern fragmented living as can be seen in our co-editor Kenneth Worthy's book that builds upon it, *Invisible Nature: Healing the Destructive Divide Between People and Nature* (Worthy 2013). Merchant identifies the roots of ideas about human–nature interactions in the work of the ancient Greeks. Alongside J. Baird Callicott's explications of Aldo Leopold's "land ethic" (e.g. Callicott 1987, 1989, 2014) and Holmes Rolston III's accounting of value in the natural world (Rolston 1986), Merchant's analysis of the concepts undergirding human–nature relations in early modern Europe and North America is essential to constructing new environmental philosophies and ethics.

When *TDN* was published in 1980, it landed on the fertile ground of a blossoming inquiry among feminists about the links between women's biological cycles and cultural roles, between home economics and feminine virtues, between "the feminine mystique" and the larger roles that women might take on in the world. The discourse that became ecofeminism inquired into ways in which feminism could be applied to the protection of life on earth under the specter of nuclear annihilation. *TDN* joined such significant texts as Susan Griffin's *Woman and Nature: The Roaring Inside Her* (Griffin 1978), Mary Daly's *Gyn/Ecology: The Metaethics of Radical Feminism* (Daly 1978), and Françoise d'Eaubonne's *Le Féminisme ou la Mort* (d'Eaubonne 1974), which even names "ecofeminisme."

An ethic of caring for the natural world underlies all of Merchant's scholarship and surfaces in her work in environmental philosophy and ethics. *Radical Ecology* (Merchant 1992) surveys the extensive territory of environmental thought while

Earthcare (Merchant 1995) combines environmental history and ethics to understand the historical role of women in protecting and preserving nature. Through the feminist stance embedded in all of Merchant's work, she shows how attention to women's roles and social positions sheds new light on the genealogy of ideas about humans and nature. Environmental philosophy and ethics cannot be viewed apart from feminist critique and analysis, and ecofeminism inevitably becomes an environmental philosophy and ethic.

Merchant's trenchant analysis of the contradictions between production and reproduction in the capitalist system—which she fleshed out in greater detail in *Reinventing Eden, Radical Ecology,* and *Earthcare*—shows how control of women's bodies and the unpaid labor of those bodies are essential to the material, social, and cultural maintenance of capitalist society. Ecofeminism exposes the contradictions of production and reproduction in a capitalist, patriarchal society. While economic production depends on natural capital to generate its surpluses, biological reproduction is similarly backgrounded and obscured despite being essential for the maintenance of the system. The capitalist system both flagrantly exploits resources and produces a range of toxic wastes that assault living bodies and threaten the viability of reproduction through impoverishment of local environments (Merchant 1995:7).

Merchant has distinguished a range of ecofeminist positions: liberal, which seeks to "alter human relations with nature from within existing structures of governance through the passage of new laws and regulations"; cultural ecofeminism, which "analyzes environmental problems from within its critique of patriarchy and offers alternatives that could liberate both women and nature"; and social and socialist ecofeminism which, centered on analyses of capitalist patriarchy, investigate the ways in which "patriarchal relations of reproduction reveal the domination of women by men, and how capitalist relations of production reveal the domination of nature by men" (Merchant 1995:5–7). Merchant's brand of ecofeminist thinking has provided a robust critique of the connections between sexism, rationality, capitalism, science, technology, and colonialism. In many ways the instrumental rationality of western thought, perhaps modeled after an all-powerful monotheistic God who can create His own world out of nothing, helps to fuel the instrumentalization of the natural world through science and technology in conjunction with the resources made available in the process of western colonization. These were, of course, racist, sexist, and speciesist metaphors, and Merchant acknowledges this, making her analysis intersectional, long before intersectionality was called such.

To address the myriad challenges exposed by ecofeminist thought—problems of mechanistic science, rationality, capitalism, colonialism, politics, violence, and interspecies ethics—Merchant has proposed a "partnership ethic," in which humans of all genders, along with nonhuman nature, would be valued as equal partners inhabiting a flourishing earth (Merchant 2003). It arises out of her analysis of the destructive flaws in Western philosophy and science and asserts that humans must partner with each other and with nature for a sustainable future. The partnership ethic has become influential in environmental thought as an alternative to ego-centric, anthropocentric, and ecocentric approaches that place a singular element at the center of ethical concern and consideration. It instead places relation at the center of concern, following predominant ecofeminist principles. The famed eco-feminist environmental philosopher Val Plumwood (who would certainly have featured in our volume, but for her untimely death) judged Merchant's partnership ethic a necessary resolution to the dualistic thought pervading and fracturing Wes-tern and modern philosophy (Plumwood 2001:11–12).

In Chapter 1 noted environmental ethicist J. Baird Callicott, who in 2016 received the first-ever Lifetime Achievement Award from the International Society for the Study of Religion, Nature, and Culture, introduces us to the author of *TDN* before she was "Carolyn Merchant." Writing as a historian of science under the name Carolyn Iltis, she analyzed various abstruse arguments among early modern scientists over the nature of matter (and the matter of nature!). Callicott points out the emerging philosophical themes in these early papers, and connects them to Merchant's later arguments about the implications of scientific practice and ideology for nature. Kenneth Worthy, a former graduate student of Merchant and her current colleague at UC Berkeley, seeks in Chapter 2 to extend the argument of *TDN* by tracing its role in the divorce of humans from nature through the experiential "dissociations" in which people believe that they are separate from nature and act as such, cut off from phenomenal engagements with the larger living world that would inform and shape environmentally beneficial choices.

The ecofeminist scholar Heather Eaton offers in Chapter 3 a typology of the areas of study that arose from *TDN*. She identifies "launch pads" in Merchant's work that created the possibility for new areas of research and analysis to flourish. The next few chapters "lift off" from some of those launch pads. The theologian Norman Wirzba (Chapter 4) returns to the Garden of Eden, re-reads it, and brings in anthropologists and "new animists" to extend partnership ethics. In his estimation, the creation story calls forth a new "fidelity ethic." In "Bewitching Nature" (Chapter 5), Elizabeth Allison, a professor of religion and ecology, and former graduate student of Merchant's, also draws on the work of anthropologists and "new animists" to analyze the social, political, and epistemological conditions necessary to allow Merchant's partnership ethic to become broadly influential. She proposes that study of the traditional ecological knowledge practices and worldviews of Native and Indigenous peoples might provide models for re-thinking Western epistemological and ontological concepts. She concludes that significant changes in Western epistemologies are necessary if contemporary societies are to live in partnership with each other and nonhuman nature, as Merchant urges. The pioneering environmental ethicist Holmes Rolston III closes out the first section. In Chapter 6, he extends partnership ethics and dis-cusses how such an ethic should work in the new age of earth dominated by humans known as the Anthropocene.

Environmental History

Although Merchant's research straddles—and transgresses—several scholarly fields, she is most often identified (and identifies herself) as an environmental historian. Her earliest work in the history of science sought to unravel the intricacies of early modern science, for instance Leibniz's efforts to disentangle kinetic energy from momentum. Her growing expertise in early modern (seventeenth- and eighteenth-century) science gave Merchant a strong foundation on which to study the ways in which early modern scientists and philosophers re-visioned the cosmos from an animate and alive realm deserving respect to a mechanical one inviting manipulation. This insight forms the core of *TDN*, which established Merchant as a leading environmental scholar and a pioneer in the burgeoning field of environmental history. *TDN* became a foundational work and a citation classic in part because every subsequent study of the ideas that shape human–nature relationships in the modern world had to contend with its central thesis and with the astounding range of evidence brought to bear on it, from the writings of early modern philosophers to art of the period.

As towering as it is, *TDN* is far from Merchant's only work in environmental history. Her volume *Ecological Revolutions* (Merchant 1989) set forth a powerful framework for understanding environmental change, based in part on Marxist thought about contradictions between nature and capitalism, while presenting a wealth of information about Native American and early colonial environmental thought and practice in New England. Merchant's more recent book of environmental intellectual history, *Reinventing Eden* (Merchant 2003), complements *TDN* by showing the controlling power of the Biblical myth of Eden in shaping environmental practices to the present day. As a specialist in American environmental history, Merchant has also authored other important texts in the field: *American Environmental History: An Introduction* (Merchant 2007) and *The Columbia Guide to American Environmental History* (Merchant 2005) and, as editor, *Major Problems in American Environmental History: Documents and Essays* (Merchant 2011) (a popular textbook for undergraduate courses), *Green Versus Gold: Sources in California's Environmental History* (Merchant 1998), and *The Encyclopedia of World Environmental History, Vols. 1–3* (Krech, McNeill, and Merchant 2003). Merchant's sustained dedication to environmental history as she approaches retirement are evidenced by her publication of two new books in 2016, mentioned above: *Autonomous Nature* (Merchant 2016a) and *Spare the Birds!: George Bird Grinnell and the First Audubon Society* (Merchant 2016b).

Merchant's primary focus on environmental history is also shown by the numerous offices she has held in scholarly organizations, including President of the American Society for Environmental History, 2001–2003. She received the Distinguished Scholar Award from the Society in 2010. She was also named a Fellow in the American Association for the Advancement of Science in 2011 and a Fellow in the American Council of Learned Societies in 2012.

The chapters in Part II reflect Merchant's influence in the field. Significantly, many of the authors discuss Merchant's personal capacities as a teacher and a mentor, and the ways that her approach to the college classroom influenced their own. These observations testify to Merchant's ability to "walk the talk," and live her life in the ways that she advocates in her scholarly writings.

In Chapter 7, "Personal, Political, and Professional: The Impact of Carolyn Merchant's Life and Leadership," the environmental historian Nancy C. Unger reflects on how Merchant's example, as both a teacher and a scholar, inspired her own work, leading her to chart her path as a historian focused on the intersection of gender issues with environmental activism and issues. In Chapter 8, "Carolyn Merchant and *The Ecological Indian*," Shepard Krech, III traces the evolution of an interdisciplinary intellectual partnership between him, an anthropologist, and Merchant, a historian, and discusses how her approach to environmental history influenced (and did not influence) his writing of *The Ecological Indian: Myth and History* (Krech 1999), a groundbreaking book that challenges the conception of Native Americans as uniformly and universally benign toward their natural environments.

Debora Hammond, an historian of science and systems theorist, describes in Chapter 9 how exposure to Merchant's brand of environmental studies while working with her at Berkeley led her to connect systems theory with environmental philosophy to create a framework for social and environmental change. Hammond has also forged innovative connections among systems theory, environmental philosophy, and organizational development. Building on Merchant's insights about the role of beliefs and worldviews in shaping societal views of nature, the environmental historian Mark Stoll examines in detail in Chapter 10 the contributions of Calvinist natural scientists, and their understandings of God's presence in nature, to the rise of the ecological sciences of America and Britain.

In Chapter 11, "Carolyn Merchant and the Environmental Humanities in Scandinavia," Swedish environmental historian Sverker Sörlin recounts Merchant's longstanding association with environmental scholarship in Scandinavia, particularly Sweden. Merchant's connection to Sweden goes back to the early 1980s, when, not long after the publication of *TDN*, she was invited to become a visiting Fulbright scholar (she eventually went on to receive an honorary doctorate at Umeå University). Using bibliometric analysis, Sörlin assesses Merchant's outsized influence on environmental and other scholarship in Scandinavia. He also studies the political and social factors that may have made Scandinavia ripe for such influence and contemplates the influence that Scandinavian environmental scholarship may in turn have had on Merchant.

Together, these chapters address the dominant themes that have occupied Merchant as an environmental historian: gender, worldviews, philosophies, religion, and the relation of nondominant groups to dominant society. They also show something of the scholar as a person: a mentor who is generous with her time, aware of her influence on others, and passionate about her work—someone also who remains committed to her social and political convictions.

The Politics of Landscapes, Embodiment, and Epistemologies

Since the publication of *TDN*, Merchant's work has insisted on attending to the connections between theory and action, between concepts and praxis, and between the political and the personal. In drawing out the ties between precisely detailed historical contexts, documents, and institutions with the contemporary consequences of these legacies for the justice and well-being of both people and planet, Merchant shows that scholarship is never innocent or apolitical; rather, it always plants a stake in the ground and speaks for and from a point of view. Rather than letting others adopt her work to advance an agenda that may not be hers, Merchant ensures that her point of view and scholarly output serve a vision of a more just and flourishing world, in which the well-being of all of life is valued.

As a feminist scholar, Merchant shows the significance of embodiment and the implications of various ideologies for the ways that diverse bodies, human and nonhuman, are treated in Western society. This strand begins with her analysis of the economic, social, political, and ecological changes of the early Modern period that brought about the mechanistic view of nature, in which nonhuman nature was no longer a lively organismic matrix out of which life grew, but a storehouse of insentient stuff to be manipulated in any way humans saw fit. This analysis arose out of a concern for the human and more-than-human bodies of those exploited and degraded by such ideas. Merchant has carefully traced the threads that have been used to associate women more closely with nature through, among other attributes, their bodies; bodies that appeared (to men) protean, unruly, and uncontrollable compared with those more static-appearing bodies of men. The conflation of women and nature led, then, to the devaluation, exploitation, and degradation of both. Merchant's work helps us understand how we come to *know* and attach meaning to the bodies of human and nonhuman nature, how we identify their distinctiveness and individuality, and how these qualities have been both submerged and venerated across time (Merchant 1995, 2003).

In Chapter 12, "Landscape, Science, and Social Reproduction: The Long-Reaching Influence of Carolyn Merchant's Insight," Laura Alice Watt, embodies Merchant's concept of ecological revolutions by lending it a *spatial* element: historical changes in landscapes reflect shifts in intellectual frameworks and social relations in a society. Watt, who studied and taught with Merchant as a graduate student at UC Berkeley, muses on the process by which working with Merchant again recently—midway through Watt's career as a professor, as the two collaborated in organizing a conference—resulted in a new self-revelation about her own professional identity. Vitally, like Dewi Candraningrum and others in Part III, she provides an important contribution to this volume by grounding theoretical currents in the particularities of material existence, echoing (though not always explicitly) a key element of ecofeminist methods.

As bodies are always engaged in activity in the world, Merchant's work has been inspirational to and reflected in the work of activists and advocates who want to change the conditions of marginalized bodies. In Chapter 13, "The Spiritual Politics of the Kendeng Mountains Versus the Global Cement Industry," for example, the Indonesian ecofeminist scholar-activist Dewi Candraningrum examines the environmental activism of Indonesian women seeking to protect the karst landscape, biodiversity, and waters of the North Kendeng Mountain Range, running from central to eastern Java, against destruction and contamination by large-scale mining for the cement industry. She studies this movement from the perspective of *TDN* and *Radical Ecology*, and discusses it as another case of women caring for particular environments as Merchant describes in *Earthcare*.

Yaakov Garb's chapter in this section, "Toward a Political Ecology of Environmental Discourse" (Chapter 14), begins with a kind of embodiment on a large scale—the scale of planet Earth depicted in the *Whole Earth Catalog*, published regularly between 1968 and 1972. But he criticizes the embrace of the image by environmentalists for leaving out the particularities of everyday bodies on the planet. An environmental sociologist, Garb explores the development of his own environmental scholarship through his experiences as a graduate student at UC Berkeley into a critical reading of an essentialist yet embodied form of ecofeminism by contrasting Rachel Carson's "feminist mobilization of materialist tropes" with Vandana Shiva's recounting of the Chipko movement.

Whitney A. Bauman, a professor of religious studies and also a former student of Merchant's, shows in Chapter 15, "Environmental History and the Materialization of Bodies," how Merchant's work of deconstructing totalizing historical narratives serves liberatory purposes for bodies "abjected" by dominant narratives. He puts Merchant's work into conversation with queer theory, to show both that her efforts to deconstruct narratives can be aided by queer theory and that queer theory might benefit from taking account of Merchant's agential understanding of "nature."

In the final chapter of Part III, an endearing tribute called "A Mighty Tree is Carolyn Merchant" (Chapter 16), the Australian ecofeminist and environmental philosopher Patsy Hallen tells how *TDN* deeply influenced her own environmental philosophy. A collaborator, friend, and colleague of Merchant's, Hallen portrays the perspectival shift the book helped her achieve and calls the work "prophetic."

The authors in Part III explore embodiment at a range of scales, times, and places. They identify connections between humans and nonhumans, and suggest creative possibilities for an enlarged epistemology spacious enough to accommodate the valuing of a wider range of peoples, cultures, and species than the modern industrial paradigm has permitted.

At the conclusion of the book, Carolyn Merchant herself offers a retrospective Afterword in which she discusses what has happened historically after "the death of nature," reflects on the transition to the Anthropocene, and assesses what the foregoing chapters of the volume say about the possibilities for a new story moving forward. She concludes, "The New Ethic that accompanies the New Story is a Partnership Ethic."

Readers interested in exploring Carolyn Merchant's works further can find a complete list of her publications, including a full text of articles, at https://ourenvironment.berkeley.edu/people/carolyn-merchant

Bibliography

Cadden, Joan. 2006. "Focus: Getting Back to The Death of Nature: Rereading Carolyn Merchant: Introduction." *Isis* 97(3):485–486.

Callicott, J. Baird, ed. 1987. *Companion to A Sand County Almanac: Interpretive & Critical Essays*. Madison, WI: University of Wisconsin Press.

Callicott, J. Baird. 1989. *In Defense of the Land Ethic: Essays in Environmental Philosophy*. Albany, NY: State University of New York Press.

Callicott, J. Baird. 2014. *Thinking Like a Planet: The Land Ethic and the Earth Ethic*. 1st edition. New York: Oxford University Press.

Daly, Mary. 1978. *Gyn/Ecology: The Metaethics of Radical Feminism*. Boston, MA: Beacon Press.

d'Eaubonne, Françoise. 1974. *Le Féminisme ou la Mort*. Paris: P. Horay.

Forbes, Linda C. and John M. Jermier. 1998. "Language, Organization, and Environment: An Introduction to the Symposium on *The Death of Nature*." *Organization & Environment* 11(2):180–182.

Griffin, Susan. 1978. *Woman and Nature: The Roaring Inside Her*. London: Women's Press.

Hammond, Debora. 2018. "All Our Relations: Reflections on Women, Nature and Science." in *After the Death of Nature: Carolyn Merchant and the Future of Human–Nature Relations*, edited by K. Worthy, E. Allison, and W. Bauman. New York: Routledge.

Krech, Shepard, III. 1999. *The Ecological Indian: Myth and History*. 1st edition. New York: W.W. Norton.

Krech, Shepard, III, J. R. McNeill, and Carolyn Merchant, eds. 2003. *Encyclopedia of World Environmental History Vol. 1–3*. 1st edition. New York: Routledge. Latour, Bruno. 1987. *Science in Action: How to Follow Scientists and Engineers Through Society*. Cambridge, MA: Harvard University Press.

Merchant, Carolyn. 1980. *The Death of Nature: Women, Ecology, and the Scientific Revolution: A Feminist Reappraisal of the Scientific Revolution*. 1st edition. San Francisco, CA: Harper & Row.

Merchant, Carolyn. 1989. *Ecological Revolutions: Nature, Gender, and Science in New England*. Chapel Hill: University of North Carolina Press.

Merchant, Carolyn. 1992. *Radical Ecology: The Search for a Livable World*. New York: Routledge.

Merchant, Carolyn. 1995. *Earthcare: Women and the Environment*. New York: Routledge.

Merchant, Carolyn. 1998. *Green versus Gold: Sources in California's Environmental History*. Washington, DC: Island Press.

Merchant, Carolyn. 2003. *Reinventing Eden: The Fate of Nature in Western Culture*. New York: Routledge.

Merchant, Carolyn. 2005. *The Columbia Guide to American Environmental History*. Unstated edition. New York: Columbia University Press.

Merchant, Carolyn. 2006. "The Scientific Revolution and the Death of Nature." *Isis* 97 (3):513–533.

Merchant, Carolyn. 2007. *American Environmental History: An Introduction*. New York: Columbia University Press.

Merchant, Carolyn. 2011. *Major Problems in American Environmental History*. 3rd edition. Boston, MA: Cengage Learning.

Merchant, Carolyn. 2016a. *Autonomous Nature: Problems of Prediction and Control from Ancient Times to the Scientific Revolution*. New York: Routledge.

Merchant, Carolyn. 2016b. *Spare the Birds!: George Bird Grinnell and the First Audubon Society*. 1st edition. New Haven, CT: Yale University Press.

Merchant, Carolyn. 2017. *Science and Nature: Past, Present, and Future*. 1st edition. New York, NY: Routledge.

Mitman, Gregg. 2006. "Where Ecology, Nature, and Politics Meet: Reclaiming *The Death of Nature*." *Isis* 97(3):496–504.

Norwood, V. 2005. "Decaying Nature/Natural Beauty: How to Find Refuge Post-*The Death of Nature?*" *Environmental History* 10(4):812–815.

Park, Katharine. 2006. "Women, Gender, and Utopia: *The Death of Nature* and the Historiography of Early Modern Science." *Isis* 97(3):487–495.

Plumwood, Val. 2001. *Environmental Culture: The Ecological Crisis of Reason*. New York: Routledge.

Rolston, Holmes. 1986. *Philosophy Gone Wild: Essays in Environmental Ethics*. Buffalo, NY: Prometheus Books.

Ruether, Rosemary R. 1994. *Gaia and God: An Ecofeminist Theology of Earth Healing*. Reprint edition. San Francisco, CA: HarperOne.

Sturgeon, N. 2005. "*The Death of Nature: Women, Ecology and the Scientific Revolution*. By Carolyn Merchant. San Francisco: Harper & Row, 1980. Xx + 348 Pp. Includes Bibliographic References and Index." *Environmental History* 10(4):805–809.

Thompson, Charis. 2006. "Back to Nature? Resurrecting Ecofeminism after Poststructuralist and Third-Wave Feminisms." *Isis* 97(3):505–512.

Worster, D. 2005. "Carolyn Merchant's *The Death of Nature* at 25 Years." *Environmental History* 10(4):809–812.

Worthy, Kenneth. 2013. *Invisible Nature: Healing the Destructive Divide between People and the Environment*. Amherst, NY: Prometheus Books.

1

BEFORE *THE DEATH OF NATURE*

Carolyn Iltis, the Carolyn Merchant Few People Know

J. Baird Callicott

Why Feature the Work of Carolyn Iltis?: A Personal Introduction

I cannot distinctly remember the first time that I met Carolyn Merchant, but it must have been in the early 1980s. It was probably at the Second International Conference on Environmental History at Miami University in Oxford, Ohio, April 9–10, 1983. This I infer from an item on my CV, which indicates that I was in attendance to give a talk about "The Land Aesthetic." And because it was an environmental-history conference, Carolyn was also a participant. Whether on that occasion or another, I have a faint memory of an exchange with her at some conference round about then.

Later in that decade, I met and married Frances Moore Lappé. Frankie and I had been acquainted in the 1950s through the Unitarian Church. Then there were so few Unitarians in the South that our geographical section was bounded by my hometown, Memphis, on the east, and hers, Fort Worth, on the west. Every summer our families gathered for a Unitarian summer conference at a camp near Ardmore, Oklahoma. I had no idea that the Francie Moore, whom I knew when we were teenagers, had grown up to be the author of *Diet for a Small Planet*. I suppose, however, that there's only one Baird Callicott in the world and so did she. Frankie saw my name in the emerging environmental-humanities literature and looked me up. Our first marriages had by then ended; and we hit it off right away.

In the 1980s, Frankie ran an organization called Food and Development Policy (aka "Food First") based in San Francisco. She lived in Oakland-for-all-practical-purposes-Berkeley in the East Bay. I lived in Stevens Point, Wisconsin and spent my summers and school recesses with her; and she would swing by and visit me on her speaking jaunts as a public intellectual. Our marriage was brief. Long-distance relationships with no end in sight are doomed. But during that time, Frankie and I invited Carolyn over for dinner. As we chatted, I told Carolyn that I had been a fan of hers since she was writing under the name Carolyn Iltis. She expressed vehement incredulity. But no, I protested, it was true. So when Ken Worthy invited me to contribute to this book celebrating Carolyn's immense contribution to the environmental humanities, fondly remembering that moment, I proposed focusing on her early papers written under that name.

I was not a fellow specialist in the history of science. So Carolyn had every reason to doubt that I would have encountered work of hers on such abstruse topics as the *vis viva* controversy (more about that shortly) and Bernoulli's springs (the coiled kind, not the hot kind). Her work between 1970 and 1977, when she was writing as Carolyn Iltis, was squarely in the history of science, to be sure, but it was also just as squarely in the history of philosophy—for Iltis had a way of connecting the arcane technical issues, on which she focused, with the metaphysical and ontological issues in which I was interested. In twentieth-century Anglo-American Analytic philosophy, "metaphysics" had practically lost all connection with its ancient Greek and early Modern antecedents.[1] And Anglo-American Analytic philosophy of science was largely if not exclusively focused on scientific epistemology. And thus the metaphysical and ontological implications of science—both Modern and post-Modern—were almost entirely neglected. (In the undead corpse of that tradition, they still are.) The great exception is *The Metaphysical Foundations of Modern Physical Science: A Historical and Critical Essay* by E. A. Burtt (1924). I loved that book (and still do), but precisely because it does focus on the metaphysics and ontology of Modern physical science, it received but a sniffy reception in twentieth-century philosophy of science. My interest in Burtt's work led me to take an interest in the work of Carolyn Iltis, who was doing what her contemporaries in the philosophy of science were not. To what else was I to turn? And it's the work of Carolyn Iltis that laid the foundation for Carolyn Merchant's own great work beginning with the publication of *The Death of Nature: Women, Ecology, and the Scientific Revolution* (hereafter *TDN*) in 1980 right through to the publication of *Autonomous Nature: Problems of Prediction and Control From Ancient Times to the Scientific Revolution* (Merchant 2016).

Let me mention in passing a bit more personal history with Carolyn. I was asked to review the manuscript for *Autonomous Nature* that Carolyn had submitted to Oxford University Press. I was very positive in my referee report to the OUP acquisitions editor—with whom I had also worked on my book *Thinking Like a Planet* (Callicott 2013a). But I was also very critical and suggested a number of changes, along with a rationale for each. When I saw Carolyn at a conference in Paris in June of 2016, she told me that she had guessed who had reviewed her manuscript for OUP and very generously said that my comments and suggestions had been very helpful. And she insisted that there were other reasons having to do with timing for her decision to publish *Autonomous Nature* with Routledge instead. I still have my doubts though.

These bookends (pun intended) on Carolyn's literary corpus—so far! (one more is in the works)—epitomize, in my opinion, a return to natural philosophy, which was the first philosophy in the Western tradition going back to the Ionian Greeks of the sixth century BCE (Merchant 2018). I have made a plea for such a return in "A NeoPresocratic Manifesto" and in a forthcoming book titled *Greek Natural Philosophy: The Presocratics and Their Importance for Environmental Philosophy* (Callicott 2013b; Callicott, van Buren, and Brown 2018). The Second Scientific Revolution of the early twentieth century, including the advent of ecology, has upended the ontology and metaphysics that became established in the original Scientific Revolution of the sixteenth and seventeenth centuries.[2] Carolyn Iltis tells a fascinating story of how that—shall we say for short, "Newtonian"—metaphysics and ontology got established, for it was not without its seventeenth- and eighteenth-century opponents, as Dr. Iltis recounts sometimes in mind-numbing detail. (Okay, numbing to my philosophical mind, maybe, but such detail is the bread and butter of history and history was Dr. Iltis's academic discipline.)

The Nine Carolyn Iltis Papers, 1970–1977

(1) The first paper by Carolyn Iltis (1970), "D'Alembert and the *Vis Viva* Controversy," was published in *Studies in the History and Philosophy of Science*.[3] It's a straightforward history-of-science paper all about very technical questions—how to measure the "living force" and what nomenclature to use regarding what measurement—all embellished with some mathematical formulae. It is of minimal philosophical interest or significance, especially as D'Alembert entered the controversy in the middle of the eighteenth century after the much more philosophically interesting and significant metaphysical and ontological controversies of the late seventeenth and early eighteenth centuries had been, for all practical purposes, sorted out. While Iltis indicates what *vis viva* means—"living force"—she scarcely locates it in those larger issues in this, her first, publication.

(2) Reading them in chronological series, as I am doing now, my disappointment, from a philosophical point of view, in Iltis's first paper is somewhat relieved by her second, "Leibniz and the *Vis Viva* Controversy," published in *Isis* (Iltis 1971) With this paper, some of the themes with which we are familiar in *The Death of Nature* begin to emerge—in particular, the metaphysical and ontological differences between Descartes, Leibniz, and Newton.

Still, however, the discussion is very much down in the technical weeds; the math gets more complicated; and illustrative diagrams appear.[4] For example, Leibniz's "arguments with Descartes, beginning in 1686, were thus designed to establish the superiority of mv^2 over $m \mid v \mid$ not mv" (p. 23).[5] Lurking in the background, nonetheless, are bigger issues concerning such things as the role played by God in physics and "the essence of nature for Leibniz." Of interest especially to me, Iltis makes reference to "Parmenides and the pluralists" (that would be Anaxagoras and Empedocles) as having anticipated something like the conservation-of-matter law in holding that "'being' could neither be *created* nor destroyed" (p. 27, emphasis added). Foreign to Greek natural philosophy, however, is the concept of creation. In Greek mythology, the divine forms and forces of Nature are given birth to, not created. The subsequent Greek philosophers followed suit. Thus Parmenides, the Pluralists, and the Atomists (Leucippus and Democritus who should also be included with the pluralists as agreeing with Parmenides) thought that Being is neither generated nor does it perish—see Callicott et al. (2018) for a full discussion of all these matters. And of interest to everyone, I should think, is the revelation of Iltis's range as a historian of science, signified by this passing reference to the Greek natural philosophers.

Ultimately, though, the technical discussion in "Leibniz and the *Vis Viva* Controversy," opens out onto an expansive metaphysical vista: "What is real in nature for Leibniz is primitive force or striving, and this was developed by him in succeeding years as the essence of the monad. Motion and extension, the essence of Nature for Descartes, are to Leibniz merely relations and not realities" (p. 33). In the midst of the killing of Nature by Descartes and Newton, Leibniz becomes Iltis's and later Merchant's heroic defender of living (and even organismic) Nature with his *vis viva*, his *living* force. In *TDN* (p. 283), for example, Merchant writes, "Leibniz's dynamic vitalism was thus in direct opposition to the 'death of nature.'"

I cannot entirely agree with Merchant's reading of Leibniz in *TDN*, however—in particular, with her claim that his was a philosophy of "internal relations." In Leibniz's view, the living force is internal to the stuff of the world, to be sure; and all the stuff of the world has consciousness (however minimal in much of such stuff). But that very interiority makes *relations among the monads* external. That is, they are not mutually defining, such that one would not be what it is if not for its relations with others. Indeed, "They are impermeable," as Merchant says in *TDN*, and quotes Leibniz's famous declaration concerning his monads that "'they have no windows through which anything can enter and depart'" (p. 283). But that's beside my present point, which is that the groundwork for Merchant's *TDN* was laid down by Iltis, in the midst of the technical minutiae dear to historians, as early as 1971.

(3) In "The Decline of Cartesianism in Mechanics: The Leibnizian–Cartesian Debates" the metaphysical and ontological issues are foregrounded, as Iltis (1973a) begins with a summary of Descartes' "worldview"—a word that appears in the first sentence of the article indicating a comprehensive cognitive structure. Her outline of Descartes's worldview was revelatory for me, as I believe it would be for most philosophers not specializing in Descartes and even for some of those of us who do.[6] The distinction between philosophy and science became sedimented in the outlook of professional philosophers after the disciplination of philosophy at the turn of the twentieth century. And so Descartes's "philosophy" (represented by the *Discourse on Method* and the *Meditations on First Philosophy*) is familiar to all us philosophers, generally speaking, but his physics (contained in Parts II and III of his *Principles of Philosophy*) is not. Of course, there was no distinction

between philosophy and science prior to the twentieth century and certainly not in the minds of Descartes, his contemporaries, and his immediate successors.

What now especially strikes me in the summary of Descartes' natural philosophy that Iltis provides is how much it has in common with that of the Greek natural philosophers, including Aristotle, whose philosophy so greatly infected that of the Scholastics against whom Descartes cast his own. Like Parmenides, the other Eleatics (excepting the Atomists, whom I anomalously include among the Eleatics), and the qualitative pluralists, Descartes denied the existence of the void or empty space. Like Aristotle, Descartes thought that the sun and stars were composed of an unearthly "aether"—a concept common in Presocratic natural philosophy prior to Aristotle's appropriation of it for his own celestial mechanics (p. 357). And like practically all the Presocratics, Descartes thought that the earth was at the center of a vortex motion that exerted a centripetal force, which of course Newton later characterized as the gravitational *force*. But also somewhat as in twenty-first century physics, Descartes represented palpable matter itself to be spun from "primitive matter" or aether (his continuous physical plenum). The continua of contemporary physics are now called "fields," such as the ubiquitous Higgs field, recently confirmed with such fanfare, and the gravitational *field*, waves in which have recently been detected (O'Luanaigh 2013; Svitil et al. 2016). (The apparent action-at-a-distance force of gravity vexed Newton. Einstein's reinterpretation of gravity as a field might have vexed him even more, but at least it salves the action-at-a-distance carbuncle on his mechanical worldview.)

Iltis's title might give the impression that Leibniz and Descartes were the principals in a debate, as once were Descartes and Hobbes, but the debate actually took place between exponents of the two in the early eighteenth century. The lives of Descartes (who died in 1650) and Leibniz (who was born in 1646) barely overlapped. From the overview of the philosophical forest with which the essay begins, it quickly descends to the level of the historical trees and even the underbrush. Iltis first distinguishes the variations on the Cartesian theme by its individual champions, focusing on two in particular (Jean-Pierre Crousaz and Pierre Mazière) running on for several pages—complete with even more complicated mathematical equations. Then, quite methodically and at equal length, the discussion turns to the variations on the Leibnizian theme, focusing again on two in particular (those of Jean Bernoulli and Charles-Etienne Camus)—this section complete with yet more complicated diagrams. Next it turns back to the Cartesian counter attack (by Jacque Eugène de Louville and Jean Jacque Mairan). Then it all ends with a brief summary—and an ironic one, because it seems that the Cartesians wound up scoring points that ultimately supported the Newtonian worldview, not that of Descartes:

> To the extent to which their mechanical points were valid the results became united with Newtonian or Leibnizian mechanics. Thus Mazière and Louville used aspects of the Cartesian worldview to make Newtonian points;

Bernoulli and Camus strengthened Leibnizian concepts. However, Crousaz and Mairan, working within the traditional Cartesian framework, unsuccessfully attempted to retain a Cartesian kinematics. In this manner the Cartesian worldview declined in mechanics, for it could not produce a unique and adequate physics of the terrestrial world.

(p. 373)

(4) The next paper by Carolyn Iltis (1973b), "The Leibnizian–Newtonian Debates: Natural Philosophy and Social Psychology," continues the widening and deepening of Iltis's intellectual compass that began in her second paper—expanding herewith from mechanics to natural philosophy more generally and to the social psychology of science. And again "world view" (two words in this iteration) appears in the first sentence of the article. In this case, Leibniz and Newton are the principals in the debate, the latter via a surrogate, Samuel Clarke. After the deaths of the principals, the debate raged on among their respective exponents. Clarke was the author of "the bitterest attacks the controversy produced" and "[h]is fanatical devotion to Newton led him to make outrageous insults to those who opposed Newton" (p. 373). It all came down to

the fundamental differences between the philosophical interpretations of 'force' in the dynamics of Newton and Leibniz. For Leibniz 'force' was a substance, an inherent internal principle of matter, a tendency or striving toward motion. For Newton and his followers impressed forces were external, acted to change a body's state of rest or uniform motion, and afterwards no longer remained in the body.

(p. 374)

Iltis begins in a way that follows the lead of Thomas Kuhn (1962) regarding loyalty to a paradigm and its founder; and she anticipates the social construction of scientific "facts" later advanced most notably by Bruno Latour and Steve Woolger (Latour and Woolger 1979)—these being the social-psychology aspects of her title.[7] In words that could have been written by Latour, but before Latour might have written them, she claims that "This analysis ... helps to undermine the notion of 'objectivity' in the sciences, by showing how social factors can influence a scientist's perception" (p. 346). And with this paper, Iltis sustains attention to "the fundamental metaphysical dichotomies" of the two camps.

The range of Iltis's scholarship is again on display early in this essay as she reviews the theological differences between Leibniz (an "intellectualist") and Newton (a "voluntarist") tracing that dichotomy back to two other principals— Thomas and Augustine, respectively—and, along the way, she refers to "the Franciscans and nominalists, Duns Scotus and William of Ockham" (p. 347). As to their opposed philosophies of matter, Newton was a mechanist (matter was "dead"—or, less tendentiously, inert—and forces were external to it), while Leibniz was a vitalist (matter was ensouled) and forces were internal to it.

Leibniz's doctrine of force, according to Iltis, is traceable back to Paracelsus's thought in the sixteenth century.

After contrasting the worldviews—theology, metaphysics, and ontology—of the Leibnizians and the Newtonians, she gets down in the experimental weeds with more diagrams and more math. This goes on page after page. Iltis's thorough discussion of the experiments, designed by each camp to prove the validity of its own system, serves the social psychology thesis: Each camp reinterpreted the experimental results of the other to reinforce its own worldview. And only one person, William 'sGravesande (that's not a typo, it seems, as this spelling is consistent throughout this article and others), became convinced by the experiments of the other camp. He switched from being a Newtonian to a Leibnizian. Amusingly (to me anyway), Iltis reports that she did one of 'sGravesande's experiments safely at home and got results similar to his.

(5) While the "Leibnizian–Newtonian Debates" runs on for 34 pages, "Bernoulli's Springs and Repercussions of the *Vis Viva* Controversy" is a bare six pages long. It was written for presentation at a conference held in Moscow, USSR, in 1971 and eventually published in 1974 (Iltis 1974a). The Bernoulli's-springs paper, although written before the Leibnizian–Newtonian debates paper, completes Iltis's coverage of the experimental evidence for the existence of the *vis viva*. The latter paper covered "collision problems" and "free[-]fall problems," the former "compressed[-]spring" problems. It's all technical and mathematical; and except for the *vis viva* itself, no metaphysics or ontology is to be found in this paper.

(6) "Leibniz's Concept of Force: Physics and Metaphysics," is also a six-page-long paper written for presentation to another conference—this one held in Hannover, Germany in 1972—and also published in 1974 (Iltis 1974b). On the first page, I was happy to see that I was not alone in thinking that "seventeenth century mechanics is sometimes seen as a union of the Democritean tradition with the Pythagorean"—both Alexandre Koyré (1965) and Richard Westfall (1971) are credited by Iltis (1974b:143 and 148, n. 1). Had Plato not been hostile to material Atomism and had Aristotle not been a teleologist, the Scientific Revolution might have occurred more than two millennia before it actually did. That remark and others opening "Leibniz's Concept of Force" suggest the breadth of Iltis's thinking in this essay about the history and philosophy of science.

Seventeenth-century mechanics, she claims, was reorganized by both Leibniz and Newton in 1686–1687 around the concept of force. But their respective concepts of force (as by now we know) were radically different, Leibniz's being internal and alive, Newton's being externally impressed and "dead" (although again, I have reservations about that term for purely semantic reasons, for what is now dead was once alive). The Presocratics having been again invoked by Iltis, I feel I have license to mention that Empedocles's motive forces, Love and Strife, are to Anaxagoras's Mind much as Leibniz's *vis viva* is to Newton's *vis impressa*.

Empedocles's Love and Strife are internal and consciously felt, Anaxagoras's Mind is external and impressed (as Plato's character Socrates famously complains in the *Phaedo* 97b–98c).[8] From such expansive reflections on the history and philosophy of science, however, Iltis once more immediately descends into the minutiae of flawed experimental applications of the Leibnizian concept to pendula, springs, and such.

(7) "The Conservative Character of Science and Technology" was also originally written as a conference presentation for the meeting of the American Physical Society in Anaheim, California, January 1975 (Iltis 1975). It's also short (five pages), and develops themes that are only embryonic in the foregoing articles. It emerged out of a science and society course Carolyn had taught as a visiting lecturer at Berkeley in between stints at the University of San Francisco. Iltis writes, "I have become increasingly interested in the ways in which science is used to reinforce the interests of those groups and classes in positions of power in today's society and to militate against the concerns of the poor and powerless." Amen, sister!

The focus is still on the seventeenth century, but the angle of observation is political and far less microscopic:

> The mechanical view of nature generated [nicely put, as the Greeks would] in the seventeenth century was an interlocking complex of mechanical laws, a corpuscular [Newton's preferred terminology, in other words, atomic] theory of matter, and philosophical assumptions concerning the law of identity and the certainty of the mathematical method. Politically it functioned to legitimate the uses of machine technology by a rising capitalist middle class.
>
> *(p. 18)*

In addition to the usual suspects—Descartes, Leibniz, Newton, and their exponents—Galileo, Bacon, Mersenne, Gassendi, and Hobbes also come into the picture.

Further, the political background in which the Scientific Revolution took place is sketched, beginning with the reign of James I, who succeeded Elizabeth I, and went after witches and "women wearing the broad hats, pointed doublets, and short hair of the male citizenry" (p. 18). Much of the essay reads like a prospectus for *TDN*: in England, Bacon's epistemological metaphors of penetrating into nature's holes and corners and binding her into service of human ends reflected the "antifeminist laws" of King James; in France Mersenne and Gassendi revived Atomism—"dead, passive particles"—and the associated "mechanical world view," reflecting the "absolutism under Richelieu" (p. 19). Social upheavals and civil war led to a kind of collusion between "scientists" (actually, then, natural philosophers) and lawyers such that despotically imposed, putatively absolute and objective human laws were a reflection of the divinely imposed absolute and objective laws of Nature. The industrial machine system, into which fit the labor of human automata (machines), was a reflection of the world machine. This is the old macrocosm–microcosm hierarchy of Greek natural philosophy redux, in which humans and human societies reflected the beautiful-order (the meaning of *kosmos*) of Nature (*physis*). Except the imagined order of Nature, society, and the human body was not so beautiful in the seventeenth-century mechanical worldview. It all served to "maintain the stability sought after by the elites and to militate against social change and the assumption of control by the lower classes" (p. 20).

Iltis then turns her attention to the twentieth century, during which, despite a Second Scientific Revolution, the scientifically obsolete mechanical worldview still prevailed—alas, as it still does now on into the twenty-first. In the "Leibnizian–Newtonian Debates," as noted, she suggested that scientific "facts" were socially constructed, and she debunked the myth of scientific "objectivity," thus anticipating Latour's science studies. Similarly, in "The Conservative Character of Science and Technology," Iltis's relatively extensive discussion of the use of statistics to predict and control "the public" anticipates the rather ill-named concept of "biopolitics," which Michel Foucault (Foucault 2003) introduced the following year. It "renders democratic decision-making virtually inadmissible" (p. 20).

For all its freshness in some aspects, this essay also reveals how the technology ("calculating machine, punch-card machine, microfilm") and policy preoccupations (the "energy crisis") of the 1970s now seem quaint (p. 21). Much of the paper is devoted to the so-called energy crisis, which consisted of a perceived petroleum shortage. While then known to a few scientists, the looming prospect of "global warming" would not become a matter of popular awareness and concern until 1988. Of course, now the "energy crisis" is a matter of too much petroleum and other fossil fuels, rather than too little. To her credit, however, Iltis notes that demand for energy is artificially stimulated by "corporate growth" and "manipulation of the public into the need for increased energy [use]" (p. 21). One of the "All-of-the-Above" solutions to the present energy crisis is a revival of nuclear power generation. Iltis regards power generated by nuclear fission (she seems to consider controlled nuclear fusion to be in the realm of possibility) with horror, as also did I.

The article ends with a discussion of (i) the particulars of the course that inspired the paper, (ii) the new interdisciplinary concept of science and society, (iii) participatory and egalitarian pedagogy, and (iv) other educational innovations. Iltis suggests that those innovations can invert the macrocosm–microcosm relationship, such that a "holistic" macrocosmic worldview begins to reflect the holistic pedagogical microcosm (p. 22). For the first time in this series of papers, Iltis adds "the ecological environment" to her hitherto exclusive focus on physics (p. 22).

(8) The pièce de résistance of this collection of papers by Carolyn Iltis is "Madame du Châtelet's Metaphysics and Mechanics" (Iltis 1977a). It opens with a decidedly feminist complaint that "Gabrielle Émelie du Châtelet's historical

identity has all too often centered on her role as the witty temperamental mistress of Voltaire" (p. 29). And while Iltis generously acknowledges that she herself is not the only scholar to

> produce an evaluation of her science and philosophy … her mathematical achievements, her translation of Newton's *Principia*, her dissemination of the Leibnizian philosophy in France, her dissertation on the nature of fire … [Iltis will] present an analysis of her natural philosophy and mechanics as it appeared in the anonymously published *Institutions de Physique* [*Foundations of Physics*] of 1740.
>
> *(p. 30)*

I cannot honestly say that Dr. Iltis's account of the metaphysical foundations of du Châtelet's natural philosophy is any more understandable to me than her mathematically and diagrammatically embellished account of the *vis viva* controversy. It begins with du Châtelet's belief in free will and her desire to make room for it in her natural philosophy. But that initial concern seems to drop from sight as the discussion gets down in the metaphysical weeds concerning the differences between Descartes (a perennial favorite of du Châtelet's French audience) and Leibniz (whom she introduced to her French audience). While Descartes' cosmology and mechanics may be hard to understand, his metaphysics is clear and simple. There are two substances, (1) thought and (2) extension, each with its essential attributes—respectively: (i) sensation and ideas and (ii) shape, size, and motion—and the contingent modes of each. On the other hand, Leibniz's metaphysics, expressed in the *Monadology*, is a riddle wrapped in a mystery inside an enigma.

Personally, I think that the key to deciphering Leibniz's metaphysics is to regard it as an attempt to resolve the main metaphysical difficulty that Descartes had bequeathed to his successors: how there can be any causal interaction between his two substances. How can the blow of an errant hammer to one's thumb in the *res extensa* cause pain in one's mind in the *res cogitans*?; and how can a wish in one's mind cause a movement of one's hand? Geometrical points are unextended, albeit spatial—that is, inhabitants of the *res extensa*. So Leibniz endowed them with thought as otherwise they would be nothing—thus uniting Descartes's two substances, thought and extension. Thinking geometrical points are the monads, as I understand Leibniz. And because palpable material bodies are somehow composed of them (although Zeno showed how that led to paradoxes of the infinite), then palpable material bodies were composed of thinking things, solving the mind–body problem left over from Descartes, at least in principle.

Whether thinking of Zeno or coming up with the idea on his own, Voltaire—contrary to his mistress, Madame du Châtelet—thought that Leibniz was off his rocker: "Force is nothing but the action of bodies in motion and does not exist primarily in simple beings called monads which these philosophers say are without extension and yet constitute extended matter … . They can no more produce moving force than zeroes can form a number" (*Fide* Iltis 1977a:44). At the risk of pointing out the obvious, I will note that, unlike Gassendi and Newton, Leibniz was not an Atomist (or corpuscularist). Iltis quotes Leibniz in a footnote:

> I hold … that matter being divisible without end, no portion can be obtained so small that there are not in it animated bodies, or at least such as are endowed with primitive entelechy, and (if you will permit to use the word *life* so generally), with vital principle, that is to say, with corporeal substances, all of which it may be said in general that they are alive.
>
> (Fide *Iltis 1977a:44, n. 71*)

Descartes' aether (extended substance) was also an infinitely divisible continuum, but he created atom-like entities with micro-vortices in the macro-vortices traveling at warp speed around the earth, other planets, and the sun. Leibniz, to my knowledge, did not avail himself of Descartes' atom-like structures, so just how extensionless monads can compose extended bodies remains a mystery—at least to me and Voltaire.

But that's just my take on it—pretty much in line with Voltaire's—and my take takes no account of problems in physics, such as mv vs. mv^2. According to the better-informed and mathematically literate Dr. Iltis—who "grasp[s] the full subtleties of the Leibnizian doctrine"—the substance of the monads is not the Cartesian thinking thing (as the just-quoted words of Leibniz himself would suggest), but force, the *vis viva* (p. 38). And here's how she cuts to the chase regarding du Châtelet's synthesis of the natural philosophies of Leibniz and Descartes:

> [T]he main point of her philosophy was that force and matter must be placed on the same ontological level. Force is to be found in all matter; one is unknown without the other. Bodies cannot be described solely in terms of simple extension as Descartes and Malebranche had believed. It was therefore necessary to join the 'power to act' to extension. In insisting on the activity of matter she contributed to a new synthesis emerging from the older Cartesian philosophy long held in France.
>
> (p. 37)

So much for Section I. Section II is devoted to "Du Châtelet's Dynamics" and in it we are back to the *vis viva* controversy and related issues, with more detailed discussion about various experiments—thought experiments and actual ones—in hopes of settling the matter.

In the final section titled "Conclusion," Iltis credits du Châtelet with integrating the philosophies of the three most important natural philosophers of the seventeenth and early eighteenth centuries—Descartes, Newton, and Leibniz:

> In her metaphysics she adopted and unified arguments from the Cartesian view that extension was the defining characteristic of matter and from the Leibnizian philosophy in which force was viewed as the primary substance. In her mechanics she presented the Leibnizian position in dynamics along with a Newtonian exposition of basic mechanics.
>
> *(p. 46)*

But Iltis's discussion does not end there. Instead she briefly runs through the opinions of still more disputants (D'Alembert, John Theophilus Desaguliers, Roger Boscovich, and Thomas Reid) in the ongoing *vis viva* controversy, which continued for another century until "the emergence of the general law of the conservation of energy in the 1840s" (p. 47). Which makes me wonder whether Iltis's preoccupation with the *vis viva* controversy and her Leibnizian partisanship didn't finally upstage du Châtelet in a paper that began in such a way that it would seem that the spotlight would never stray from her. In *TDN*, du Châtelet is altogether shrouded in shadow. In a chapter titled "Women on Nature: Anne Conway and Other Philosophical Feminists," Carolyn Merchant mentions du Châtelet in passing only twice: (i) as "a principal expounder of Leibniz's system" and (ii) in a subsection on "Women as an Audience for Science."

(9) The last publication ever authored by Carolyn Iltis was a two-page book review of a 1973 English translation (by R. E. W. Maddison) of the 1960 presentation (by Pierre Costabel) of two previously unknown works by Leibniz on dynamics—basically, $m \, |v \,|$ vs. mv^2 (Iltis 1977b). Fine.

The Legacy of Carolyn Iltis

Of course the legacy of Carolyn Iltis is Carolyn Merchant, but the following is what I learned from Carolyn Iltis before I ever met Carolyn Merchant.

First, the so-called Scientific Revolution that begins with Copernicus's *De Revolutionibus* in the sixteenth century and culminates with Newton's *Principia* in the late seventeenth is a misnomer or, more precisely put, an anachronistic nomer. I don't know when exactly "science" took on the meaning that it has today, but it took it on much closer in time to us than to Copernicus or even to Newton. In the sixteenth, seventeenth, and eighteenth centuries what was going on was a revolution in Western natural philosophy. I have so far acceded to convention and identified her field as the history of science, but also, for the same reason, that nomer is anachronistic for what Carolyn Iltis was doing in the 1970s. She was, rather, a historian of natural philosophy and one of the best, despite her biases in favor of Leibniz over Descartes and Newton. (Hey, if science is not objective, why should we expect history to be?)

Second—and this comes out most clearly in Iltis's seventh paper—the Modern revolution in natural philosophy had a wide and long reach, touching practically everything else in the European and neo-European intellectual and cultural ambit—theology, ethics, politics, and economics—running on pretty much right down to the present. In the foregoing review of the papers of Carolyn Iltis, I called attention to her use of the word "worldview" (or "world view") early and often. More profoundly still, the "Scientific Revolution"—the revolution in Western natural philosophy—resulted in a full-tilt worldview transformation, which is at bottom what Carolyn Merchant's *TDN* is all about.

Finally, third, I learned from Carolyn Iltis that a Second Scientific Revolution has occurred and that its architects—Einstein, Heisenberg, Schrödinger, among others—were the natural philosophers of the twentieth century. Ours in the twenty-first—Brian Greene, Lisa Randall, Max Tegmark, among others—are ever advancing it. The metaphysics and ontology of the Second Scientific Revolution are no longer (i) atomistic, (ii) mechanistic, or (iii) dualistic.

Riffing on the Legacy of Carolyn Iltis

The Modern worldview was given palpable form in the mechanistic technologies of the Industrial Revolution and more subtly and thus more insidiously in the underlying mathematical structure of both painting and music (which neither Iltis nor Merchant explore). Galileo famously wrote that:

> Philosophy is written in this grand book—I mean the universe—which stands continually open to our gaze, but it cannot be understood unless one first learns to comprehend the language and interpret the characters in which it is written. It is written in the language of mathematics, and its characters are triangles, circles, and other geometrical figures, without which it is humanly impossible to understand a single word of it; without these, one is wandering around in a dark labyrinth.
>
> *(Drake 1957:237–238)*

The painters of the period were the illustrators of that grand book. The realism and naturalism characteristic of seventeenth-century landscape painting was achieved by the technique of linear perspective, which is an artistic application of projective geometry. In effect, the graphic artists were visually representing the emerging mathematized worldview of the then-new natural philosophy. And the music we call "classical" (including both Baroque and Romantic as well as Classical proper) is as different from Medieval music as seventeenth-century landscape painting is from the Medieval graphic arts, due primarily to its mathematical complexity and precision.

In her seventh paper, Iltis gives particular attention to the way Modern natural philosophy colonized moral and political philosophy and fostered the emergence of a capitalist economy. *TDN* tells the whole story, but on one aspect of it I am particularly keen to elaborate.

In *TDN* (p. 209), Merchant writes, "In his *Leviathan* (1651), Hobbes developed a mechanical model of society ... ." "The body politic was composed of equal atomistic beings united by contract out of fear and governed from above by a powerful sovereign." Let me reiterate and amplify Merchant's remark: the Modern individual is a social atom—clearly, if grotesquely, characterized by Hobbes. Furthermore, Hobbes and Leibniz have one thing in common—an internal endeavor, a striving (or *conatus*) within each individual being. Each social atom is driven on its inertial trajectory by an internal force that Hobbes called "Endeavor" with two polar charges (*TDN*, p. 209) and that Leibniz called monads which as "collections of confused minds" were perceived as extended bodies or "well-founded phenomena" (*TDN*, p. 279). Here is how Merchant puts it in *TDN* (p. 209) regarding Hobbes: "Found even in the embryo, endeavor was the first response of the animal to pleasure and pain, the first impulse toward motion 'for the avoiding of what troubleth it or the pursuing of what pleaseth it,' the two being called *aversion* and *appetite*," respectively. In Hobbes's social "state of nature," the social atoms are bound to collide. The social contract provides the rules of the road that minimize the collisions.

Note that in Hobbes's famous phrase, in the social "state of nature," human life is also "solitary," as well as "poor, nasty, brutish, and short." Society exists not by Nature (*physis*), but by law or convention (*nomos*)—to express that idea in the terms used by the Greeks in their version of the social-contract theory of the origin of both society and morality. The social contract merely aggregates and organizes the naturally solitary social "atoms"—it does not unite them. This vaunted Western individualism has become hypertrophic in the politics of the present, so nakedly expressed in the famous pronouncement of Margaret Thatcher (1987) to the effect that "There is no such thing [as] society. There are [only] individual men and women and there are families."

Hobbes was a thoroughgoing materialist. As noted, Descartes, with whom Hobbes corresponded, was a metaphysical dualist locating the "thinking thing" in the body—actually pin-pointing its location in the pineal gland in the center of the brain—the ghost in the machine. That the soul (psyche) is an independent entity was also an originally Greek idea traceable to Pythagoras; it was aggressively championed by Plato; it was adopted into a weird Hellenistic religion, featuring symbolic cannibalism, that somehow managed to seize hold of the European mind from the fifth century CE on; it was expressed in an especially clear and distinct way by Descartes; and it was thus baked into the Modern Western worldview.

So the Modern individual is an inner self, inhabiting a mechanistic body, fearfully apprehending an alien "external world" (a phrase all too common in Anglo-American Analytic philosophy to this very day). Our Modern social atoms, no less than Leibniz's monads, are externally related to one another, to the ambient aggregative society, and to the ambient natural environment. This metaphysical and ontological legacy of Western natural and moral philosophy and religion is both pernicious and dangerous. To be sure, it is the Modern foundation of our human rights and our liberties, but the price we pay is a pathological unawareness of the robust ontologies of the social and environmental wholes in which we are embedded and on which we depend for life itself and for our actual, not our fantasized, identities. Whether deliberately countering Thatcher or not, I don't know, but as biologist David George Haskell (2017:44) writes, "Perhaps the search for individuals, for the 'units' of biology, is misguided. Perhaps the fundamental nature of life may not be atomistic but relational."

The Metaphysics and Ontology of the Second Scientific Revolution

Twenty-first century physics is also well on the way to finally abandoning an atomistic ontology in favor of a relational field ontology. According to theoretical physicist David Tong, "Physicists routinely teach that the building blocks of nature are discrete particles, such as the electron or the quark. That is a lie. The building blocks of our theories are not particles but fields: continuous, fluid-like objects spread throughout space" (*Fide* Stenger, Lindsay, and Boghassian 2015) Apparently, today even in physics, as in biology, an ontology of individuals is a hangover from the Atomism invented by the Greek natural philosophers and revived by the Modern.

Surely, though, the metaphysics of the Second Scientific Revolution is mechanistic—we don't call quantum mechanics "quantum *mechanics*" for nothing. True, we don't. The name "quantum *mechanics*" is not a lie; it's not even a misnomer. But it is misleading. For there is nothing mechanistic about quantum mechanics. That is, there is no causation, at the quantum level of reality, via the contact of hard bodies—like the way a pool ball on a pool table causes another pool ball to move. Rather, in this context, the term "mechanics" functions as it does in hierarchy theory in ecology, such that the system (a) under study exists in the context of a larger-scale system (b) that constrains it; and its phenomena may be explained by reference to the smaller-scale systems (c)—"the mechanisms"—within it (Allen and Starr 1982). For example, the statistical oscillations of species populations (a) in a biotic community is constrained by the climate (b) of the biome in which those populations live; and may be explained by the mechanisms (c) of predation and competition, salient among others. But such mechanisms are not mechanical in the pool-table sense of the term. Organs— organs!—such as hearts and kidneys are mechanisms in the organismic wholes of animal bodies. Quantum mechanics is like that, it's about the invisible downscale phenomena underlying and explaining the up-scale phenomena that can be seen or otherwise perceived.

As Iltis indicates in her seventh publication (Iltis 1975), the ontology and metaphysics of contemporary natural philosophy is holistic—or "organic" sensu Merchant in *TDN*. Quantum mechanics exhibits genuinely holistic internal relations in the form of "nonlocality" or "entanglement" in which a change in one subatomic particle—a structure in the underlying fields, roughly similar to Descartes' micro-vortices in his aether— results in an instantaneous change in another, no matter how far apart the two are from one another (Popescu 2014). (That really should not be so shocking precisely because particles are in fact structures or excited states of the continua, the fields, of which Nature is ultimately composed.)

Twenty-first century physics has vindicated Leibniz, at least with regard to his difference with Descartes concerning the relationship of mind and body, thought and extension. Leibniz's physical monads were alive and conscious, while Descartes's physical world (the *res extensa*) was inert and unconscious; and Descartes's thinking things (in the *res cogitans*) were endowed with thought but were unextended. In twenty-first-century physics, Leibnizian panpsychism is consistent with and possibly derivable from contemporary quantum mechanics. An especially Leibnizian version, involving a gradation of consciousness from the quantum level to the human brain, has been developed by David Klemm and William Klink (Klemm and Klink 2008).

Indeed, the natural world we inhabit is holistic and internally related all the way from the quantum-mechanical microcosm to the universal (or maybe now the multiversal) macrocosm (Tegmark and Vilenkin 2011). It certainly is here in the middle-sized range of the cosmos, as the natural philosophers of evolutionary biology, ecology, and bacteriology tell us. Each species is shaped by its physical, chemical, and biological environments; each species is what it is because their environments are what they are (Wilson 1992). That's the meaning of "internally related." And the organisms that make up biotic communities are internally related through the flow of energy and materials through their bodies—they being but moments in ecological processes. And biotic communities and their associated ecosystems are transorganismic wholes. They are perhaps not as ontologically robust as they once were thought to be, but they are real nonetheless, as we discover to our regret and peril when they are compromised, diminished, or destroyed.

Frederick Clements (1905), the first dean of American ecology, portrayed what he called "plant associations" (later called biotic communities when the associated animals are considered) as "super-*organisms*." And by "super" he just meant big— reasoning that as tiny single-celled organisms associated to form much larger multi-celled organisms, just so did multi-celled organisms associate to form much larger super-organisms. That idea is no longer viable in ecology, but recently the worm has turned and we now regard multi-celled organisms as super-*ecosystems*. And here the word "super" doesn't mean big, it means in a higher degree. The super-ecosystems that are multi-celled organisms are more highly integrated than Clements ever imagined the objects of ecological study to be. In fact, the National Institutes of Health has initiated "The Human Microbiome Project," a program tasked to map the human super-ecosystem. According to DeSalle and Perkins (2015:ix), this represents a "recent paradigm shift in how we view the microbial world." We are constituted not only by our own cells, but by the microbial cells in and on us. They outnumber ours by an order of magnitude and represent thousands of species. Some are parasites, others commensals, and still others mutualists. Indeed, without the help of the mutualists, we would be unable to digest our food or ward off harmful invasive microbes. And while biotic communities and their associated ecosystems are not, by the lights of current ecology, super-organisms, the whole biosphere, Gaia, most certainly is, by the lights of Earth Systems science (Harding 2006).

So Why Are We Still Modern?

Bruno Latour (1991) claims that *"nous n'avons jamais été modernes"* because the distinctions between nature and culture, science and politics have always been blurry and are becoming ever more so. Au contraire! Iltis, Merchant, and I thoroughly disagree. The essence of Modernity is less Enlightenment rationality and much more the deeper worldview—the insidious and pervasive ontology and metaphysics—ushered in by Copernicus, Galileo, Descartes, Newton, and Hobbes: (a) the physical world is reducible to hard, inert, externally related, mechanically interacting material atoms, pushed around by various outside forces, and it is predictable and controllable; and (b) human beings and human society microcosmically reflect the physical macrocosm. Our bodies are essentially machines and the ego inhabiting the bodily mechanism is a psychic monad. Society is reducible to externally related social atoms/monads; and it is predictable and controllable with the aid of such social sciences as economics and psychology. This worldview is manifest in Modern medicine with its joint-replacement and transplant surgeries, in trains, planes, and automobiles; in railroads, highways, and airports; in factories; in steel and glass skyscrapers and strip malls; in advertising, consumerism, and capitalism; ... Indeed, we Europeans and neo-Europeans have been Modern for a long time—going back to the Industrial Revolution, which was ancillary to the Scientific Revolution. The question is: Why are we still Modern?

Why has the Second Scientific Revolution—the second revolution in natural philosophy that began more than a century ago—not profoundly changed the prevailing worldview, as did the first? Why do most Europeans and neo-Europeans still think of themselves as ghosts in machines, as externally related individuals? The very fabric of our being is in truth woven from our socio-environmental relationships and yet many people seem not to notice. And that fabric is severely imperiled and palpably unraveling. It's as though leprosy were eating away at parts of their bodies and as long as, say, their faces are unaffected the vast majority of Europeans and neo-Europeans don't seem to notice and don't seem to care. Many if not most of our technologies, from TVs to cellphones, are manifestations of quantum mechanics, just as steam and internal-combustion engines were manifestations of Newtonian mechanics. Why then is the prevailing worldview—and its associated politics and economics—still Newtonian with all that goes with it as Iltis/Merchant explains and as I embellish? Why is our worldview not responding as it did in the past? Where's the quantum-mechanical/relativistic/evolutionary/ecological politics, economics, graphic arts, literature, music, religion?

Maybe it's coming. There's an effort in religion to craft a new cosmological and evolutionary origin myth—a film version of which has been shown on public television, as well as in a number of theater and auditorium venues (Swimme and Tucker 2011). A sure sign that it may be gaining a foothold in the Zeitgeist is the searing criticism that it has attracted (Sideris 2017). Some people are experimenting with an economy of sharing—rides, homes, and such; some also with slow, local food, produced in a socially and environmentally ethical way. The ubiquity of mega-churches, roadside motels, fast-food joints, and traffic jams suggests that these alternatives are not transforming culture overnight. But perhaps these are bellwether phenomena. Further, a lot of people are outing their erstwhile inner selves from the closet of monadic consciousness and co-constituting their identities on social media—"an experience of the self that moves beyond the atomistic to be more reflective of interdependence and connection."[9] Social media may also be giving rise to field-like social phenomena such as simultaneous but unorchestrated reactions in a number of locales to a gratuitous police shooting here or a radical right-wing terrorist attack there.

History suggests that worldview remediation is inevitable as natural philosophy entrains its motifs in new technologies and new social imaginaries. So maybe the real question is not Why? Or Why not?, but When?. And that then leads to another: Do we have time for the Great Transition to cross a threshold, become irreversible, and develop rapidly, before a different threshold is crossed and global climate change becomes irreversible, develops rapidly, and brings civilization in any form to an abrupt end? (Boulding 1964; Korten 2006; Raskin et al. 2002). Thus are we called to the Great Work (Berry 1999).

Notes

1 I capitalize the word "Modern" (thus) when it is the proper name of the historical period following the Renaissance (just as we capitalize the proper name—"Renaissance"—the historical period preceding the Modern period). I also capitalize "Analytic" (thus) as the proper name of a now-historical movement of philosophy analogous to "Scholasticism" (a well-chosen comparison, I also mean to imply).

2 I also capitalize the phrase "Scientific Revolution" (thus) as the conventional name of an event in the intellectual history of the West—thus to avoid the implication that the phrase is an unproblematic description of that event—ditto "Second Scientific Revolution."

3 As many scholars do, Iltis mined her dissertation, *The Vis Viva Controversy: Leibniz to D'Alembert* (Madison: University of Wisconsin, 1967) for material suitable for publication as a series of articles, this one being the first, but, judging from her dissertation's title, adapted from its last sections.

4 This should be no surprise. Carolyn was a Top Ten Finalist for the Westinghouse Science Talent Search as a high school senior in 1954. Her baccalaureate is in chemistry, and she began her professorial career in the physics department at the University of San Francisco.

5 In the case of works written by Carolyn Iltis and Carolyn Merchant, I cite quotations simply by page numbers in the text when the work cited is unambiguous.

6 I use the past tense because my CV also suggests another forgotten detail. My book review of John Passmore's *Man's Responsibility for Nature: Ecological Problems and Western Traditions* (London: Duckworth, 1974) was also published in *Isis* 67 (1976): 294–295. Looking through back numbers of *Isis*, as I was preparing to tailor a review for its audience, may have been the occasion of for me to stumble onto the work of Carolyn Iltis. Certainly this paper would have attracted my rapt attention.

7 Iltis, however, does not cite Kuhn.

8 See Callicott et al. 2018 for a discussion.

9 Elizabeth Allison, personal communication (July 6, 2017).

References

Allen, Timothy F. H. and Thomas B. Starr. 1982. *Hierarchy Perspectives in Ecological Complexity*. Chicago: University of Chicago Press.

Berry, Thomas. 1999. *The Great Work: Our Way into the Future*. New York: Bell Tower.

Boulding, Kenneth E. 1964. *The Meaning of the 20th Century: The Great Transition*. New York: Harper Colophon Books.

Burtt, E. A. 1924. *The Metaphysical Foundations of Modern Physical Science: A Historical and Critical Essay*. London: Kegan Paul, Trech, Trübner.

Callicott, J. Baird. 2013a. *Thinking Like a Planet: The Land Ethic and the Earth Ethic*. New York: Oxford University Press.

Callicott, J. Baird. 2013b. "A NeoPresocratic Manifesto," *Environmental Humanities* 2:169–186.

Callicott, J. Baird, John van Buren, and Keith Wayne Brown. 2018. *Greek Natural Philosophy: The Presocratics and Their Importance for Environmental Philosophy*. San Diego, CA: Cognella Academic.

Clements, Frederick. 1905. *Research Methods in Ecology*. Lincoln, NE: University Publishing Company.

DeSalle, Rob and Susan Perkins. 2015. *Welcome to the Microbiome: Getting to Know the Trillions of Bacteria in on and around You*. New Haven, CT: Yale University Press.

Drake, Stillman. 1957. *Discoveries and Opinions of Galileo*. New York: Doubleday and Co., pp. 237–238.

Foucault, Michel. 2003. "Lecture 11, March 1976." Pp. 239–264 in David Macey, tr. *Society Must Be Defended: Lectures at the College of France, 1975–1976*. New York: Picador.

Harding, Stephan. 2006. *Animate Earth: Science, Intuition, and Gaia*. White River Junction, VT: Chelsea Green Publishing.

Haskell, David George. 2017. *The Songs of Trees: Stories from Nature's Great Connectors*. New York: Viking.

Iltis, Carolyn, 1970. "D'Alembert and the *Vis Viva* Controversy." *Studies in the History and Philosophy of Science* 1:135–144.

Iltis, Carolyn. 1971. "Leibniz and the *Vis Viva* Controversy." *Isis* 62:21–35.

Iltis, Carolyn. 1973a. "The Decline of Cartesianism in Mechanics: The Leibnizian–Cartesian Debates." *Isis* 64:356–373.

Iltis, Carolyn. 1973b. "The Leibnizian–Newtonian Debates: Natural Philosophy and Social Psychology." *The British Journal for the History of Science* 6:343–377.

Iltis, Carolyn. 1974. "Bernoulli's Springs and Repercussions of the *Vis Viva* Controversy." Pp. 309–315 in *Proceedings of the 13th International Congress of the History of Science, Moscow, Aug. 18–24, 1971*, Sect. 5. Moscow: Nauka.

Iltis, Carolyn. 1974b. "Leibniz's Concept of Force: Physics and Metaphysics." Pp. 143–149 in *Proceedings of the Second International Leibniz Congress, Hannover, July 17–22, 1972*, Vol. 2. Wiesbaden: Franz Steiner Verlag.

Iltis, Carolyn. 1975. "The Conservative Character of Science and Technology." *Interface Journal: Alternatives in Higher Education* 1(2):17–22.

Iltis, Carolyn. 1977a. "Madame du Châtelet's Metaphysics and Mechanics." *Studies in the History and Philosophy of Science* 8:29–47.

Iltis, Carolyn. 1977b. "Review of Pierre Costabal, Leibniz and Dynamics: The Texts of 1692, R. E. W. Maddison, tr. (London: Methuen, 1973)." *The British Journal of the History of Science* 10:176–177.

Klemm, David E. and William Klink. 2008. "Consciousness and Quantum Mechanics: Opting from Alternatives." *Zigon* 43:307–327.

Korten, David C. 2006. *The Great Turning: From Empire to Earth Community*. Bloomfield, CN: Kumerian Press.

Koyré, Alexandre. 1965. *Newtonian Studies*. Cambridge, MA: Harvard University Press.

Kuhn, Thomas. 1962. *The Structure of Scientific Revolutions*. Chicago: University of Chicago Press.

Latour, Bruno. 1991. *Nous n'avons jamais été modernes: Essai d'anthropologie symétrique*. Paris: La Découverte.

Latour, Bruno and Steve Woolger. 1979. *Laboratory Life: The Construction of Scientific Facts*. Princeton, NJ: Princeton University Press.

Merchant, Carolyn. 1980. *The Death of Nature: Women, Ecology, and the Scientific Revolution*. San Francisco, CA: Harper & Row.

Merchant, Carolyn. 2016. *Autonomous Nature: Problems of Prediction and Control From Ancient Times to the Scientific Revolution*. New York: Routledge.

Merchant, Carolyn. 2018. *Science and Nature: Past, Present, and Future*. New York: Routledge.

O'Luanaigh, Cian. 2013. "New Results Indicate That the New Particle Is a Higgs Boson," CERN Document Server, published 14 March http://home.cern/about/updates/2013/03/new-results-indicate-new-particle-higgs-boson (retrieved 17/06/17).

Popescu, Sandu. 2014. "Nonlocality Beyond Quantum Mechanics." *Nature Physics* 10:264–270.

Raskin, Paul, Tariq Banuri, Gilberto Gallopin, Pablo Gutman, Al Hammond, Robert Kates, and Rob Swart. 2002. *Great Transition to Planetary Civilization*. Boston: Stockholm Environmental Institute.

Sideris, Lisa H. 2017. *Consecrating Science: Wonder, Knowledge, and the Natural World*. Berkeley: University of California Press.

Stenger, Victor J., James A. Lindsay, and Peter Boghossian. 2015. "Physicists Are Philosophers, Too." *Scientific American*, published May 8 www.scientificamerican.com/article/physicists-are-philosophers-too/ (retrieved 01–17–17).

Svitil, Kathy, Kimberly Allen, Ivy Kupec, Fulvio Ricci, Susanne Milde, Terry O'Conner, and Benjamin Knispel. 2106. "Gravitational Waves Detected 100 Years After Einstein's Prediction." Laser Interferometer Gravitational Wave Observatory, published February 11 www.ligo.caltech.edu/ (retrieved 17/06/17).

Swimme, Brian and Mary Evelyn Tucker. 2011. *Journey of the Universe*. New Haven, CN: Yale University Press.

Tegmark, Max and Alexander Vilenkin. 2011. "The Case for Parallel Universes." *Scientific American*, published July 19 www.scientificamerican.com/article/multiverse-the-case-for-parallel-universe/ (retrieved 09/16/17).

Thatcher, Margaret. 1987. September 23 interview for *Woman's Own*, by journalist Douglas Keay, published October 31 www.margaretthatcher.org/document/106689 (retrieved 06–13–17).

Westfall, Richard S. 1971. *Force in Newton's Physics: The Science of Dynamics in the Seventeenth Century*. New York: Macdonald, London, and Elsevier.

Wilson, Edward O. 1992. *The Diversity of Life*. Cambridge, MA: Belknap Press of Harvard University.

2

THE DEATH OF NATURE OR DIVORCE FROM NATURE?

Kenneth Worthy

For three and a half decades Carolyn Merchant's 1980 book *The Death of Nature: Women, Ecology, and the Scientific Revolution* (hereafter *TDN*) has served as fertile soil in which to grow better understandings of the destructiveness of modern human–nature relationships. Its rich detail on early modern thought about nature provides seemingly endless opportunities for further analysis and interpretation about the ways modern culture and science approach the natural world. Merchant argues that the dual modern imaginaries of nature that depicted it as alternately machine-like and female render it a sphere at once open to manipulation and solicitous to a probing science. But the implications of the mechanistic cosmology promoted by modern natural philosophers extend beyond moral justification for unlimited exploitation and manipulation. Breaking down moral barriers was but a beginning.

In this chapter[1] I explain how the new mechanistic cosmology advanced humanity's "Great Divorce" from nature, as environmental historian J. Donald Hughes calls it (Hughes 2009:30), and in the process provided a powerful model for a range of fragmented and alienated conceptual and material relations that "run like a fault line" through modern thought and life experiences (Plumwood 1993:42). Positions of political and economic privilege encoded into influential threads of ancient Western philosophy inform and enable today's distancing from both nature and the consequences of our actions as they play out in the natural world. These *phenomenal dissociations*, as I call them, are grounded in conceptual dissociations that came to the fore in ancient Greek thought and were advanced by early modern philosopher-scientists. *Phenomenal dissociations* render us modern, industrialized people alienated and isolated from the intimate knowledge and experiences crucial to aligning our values and intentions with real-world outcomes. This "divorce" from nature thwarts our ethical subjectivity, as I explain below.

Early modern mechanism grew out of currents reaching back to a fifth-century BCE ancient world, a time when extreme Greek individualism, experienced as supreme autonomy and competitiveness, found its reflection in the atomic theories of Leucippus and Democritus, in which relation was insubstantial; instead, inert, unrelated particles bounced around like billiard balls (Sambursky 1960:105–131). But Bacon, Descartes, Newton, and their contemporaries, Merchant argues, synthesized atomism into a cosmological whole in which the detached and detachable parts were not simply those at the tiniest, invisible scales but were manifest at all levels. As it became increasingly prevalent in early modern daily experiences with the proliferation of clocks, watches, waterwheels, and other devices, the machine became a model for all Creation, with God as watchmaker and "man" as tinkerer.

Merchant characterizes the mechanistic assumptions founding this new worldview in the following now-well-known formulation (Merchant 1990:228):

1. Matter is composed of particles.
2. The universe is a natural order.
3. Knowledge and information can be abstracted from the natural world.
4. Problems can be analyzed into parts that can be manipulated by mathematics.
5. Sense data are discrete.

As God's proxy, "man" could disassemble and re-assemble nature at will. Whereas the prior organic cosmos demanded respect and care as a living other, as machine, nature *prima facie* became available for limitless manipulation. Alternately, as devious and solicitous female, nature invited probing and subjugation. Bacon wrote that (female) nature must be bound into service, made a slave, put in constraint, and molded by the "mechanical arts" (technology) (Merchant 1990:169). The new conception of nature as machine facilitated exploitation, but it also shifted human–nature relations in other ways. Living, autonomous nature[2] requires sustained thought and action to maintain a viable relationship. Dead, inert, mechanical nature is mute and unable to make such demands.

For four centuries the concept of nature as machine has prevailed in Western cosmological thought against challenges from the German Romantics, the American Transcendentalists, late-modern philosophers such as Alfred North Whitehead, philosophies of holism, and twentieth-century physics, including the holomovement theory of David Bohm. The idea plays out today in industrial monocultures that turn much of North America into a vast checkerboard of mechanical farmlands where the soil is treated as a dead substrate onto which seeds, water, and chemical fertilizers and pesticides are deposited. Mechanism drives also the quest to genetically engineer crops and human genomes alike by tinkering with genomes as a watchmaker might tinker with gears and springs. It treats living, sentient animals as if they were unfeeling egg, milk, fiber, and meat production machines. It shapes our rectilinear urban grids in which machines—cars, buses, elevators, refrigerators, ventilation systems—dominate, and it underlies our own objectified, reduced human status as passive consumers (of the products of the great machine of industry), buying what we are told to—rather than active shapers of our own civic lives.

The centuries-old mainstream context of Western mechanical philosophy makes it difficult to remember that one does not neglect one's living relations. Relationships demand work and must be maintained. Organic others require care and feeding; they have spontaneous needs that must be met. Although machines too need maintenance, they do not demand it of their owners; as a realm of instrumental value, they may be neglected until needed, with costs borne as a practical rather than moral consequence. In the technological West there is no inherent moral sanction against allowing a machine to degrade (though there may be other objectionable consequences of doing so, such as ecological ones). Thus neglect—not just exploitation—in the human–nature relationship is also sanctioned by mechanism.

Because the concept of nature as machine imposes an instrumental relationship on living nature, it invites comparison with the master–slave relational archetype. Val Plumwood's framework on the structure of dualisms makes an effective lens to understand the idea of mechanized nature (Plumwood 1993:41–68). Plumwood figures the master–slave arising in Western history as the archetype for a set of dualistic relations running through Western thought: human–nature, man-woman, culture–nature, mind–body, reason–emotion, subject–object, reason–nature, and so on. Her explanation of the techniques that maintain the power of the former in each of these pairs over the latter—the logic of colonization, as she calls it—is helpful in more fully understanding the implications of the death of nature. Several of these techniques are particularly relevant with respect to mechanized nature. *Backgrounding* or denial occurs when the master denies his dependency on subordinated others, such as denying the importance of the other's contribution and conceiving the other as expendable or insignificant. *Radical exclusion*, or hyper-separation, means that differences are emphasized and similarities downplayed. *Instrumentalism*, or objectification, conceives the slave or other object in relation to the needs of the master or self (Plumwood 1993:41–68).

Machines are radically excluded from humanity, they operate in the background, and they are our instruments—and so is nature conceived as machine. Rejecting nature as a living realm erases its agency and autonomy and thus obscures human dependence on this alive other, the technique of backgrounding. Radical exclusion functions when we envision nature as passive, dead, mechanical realm—what could differ more greatly from humans than machines? Seeing ourselves in nature, seeing the productive vibrancy and agency embodied not only in bears and acacia trees but in the landscape and ecological wholes, would make it difficult to deprecate nature as mere machine. Instrumentalism plays an obvious role in the mechanistic cosmology: the first and foremost aspect of our relationships with machines comes from our will to use them without restraint for our purposes.

The Great Divorce

Aside from the power implications of the mechanistic model of the cosmos, what other intellectual work is accomplished by conceiving of nature as machine? In the remainder of this chapter, I argue that mechanistic cosmology advanced the project of a divorce from nature growing out of ancient urban experiences of separation from the natural world, and, perhaps more important, it accelerated the adoption of an organizing principle that I call dissociation—various forms of disconnection, separation, isolation, and alienation—running through structures of Western thought. The concept of dissociation deepens and enhances the understanding of mechanistic cosmology elaborated in *TDN* by elucidating the effects of mechanism on relations of all kinds. As I describe elsewhere (Worthy 2013), in influential thought from classical Athens and through the early modern thinkers whom Merchant engages in *TDN*, dissociation emerges as a conceptual, perceptual, and experiential mode that distinguishes Western history from that of other places and drives forward environmental devastation and social abuses.[3] Dissociation undergirds an alienated, divorced relation with nature.

Dissociation as a conceptual organizing principle, in which objects and their characteristics are brought to the fore and relations are backgrounded, made its mark in classical Greek thought not just in the atomic theory. The environmental philosopher J. Baird Callicott (a contributor to this volume) writes that discontinuity and discreteness have typified Western thinking about nature for the last two and a half millennia (Callicott 1996:83).[4] The Greeks fragmented the world by imagining it and living in it as a profoundly disconnected place, by thinking of themselves as utterly independent of one another, and by behaving as if they were. An extreme social competitiveness manifests itself in winner-take-all debates and frequent conflict including war between the *oikoi*—Greek households, headed by men striving to elevate their personal fame and honor above all others (Gouldner 1965:9). Victory was not enough: total and conclusive wins against opponents in artistic contests, debates, inter-*oikos* competitions, and wars was essential. Competition was ruthless. Out of such conditions, in which relations and interdependence were derogated in favor of a focus on individuals and their attributes—fame, prestige, and property in the form of war booty and slaves—arose a conceptual regimen in which objects and their characteristics (perhaps modeled on the heroic Greek citizen, a native-born White male) took precedence over relations of any kind. Aristotle even wrote, "We deny that a genus of relations exists by itself" (Aristotle 1991:Metaphysics, Book I, Ch. 9, 990b15–20, p. 351).

One hallmark of the new Greek worldview, the atomic theory introduced by Leucippus and Democritus in the fifth century BCE, saw the entire physical world and even the soul as consisting of inert corpuscles—atoms—devoid of sensory attributes, interactions, and context (Gouldner 1965; Sambursky 1960). Atomism grounded an ontology that removes relation. Prominent classical Greek thinkers invented models of the cosmos consisting of independent, inert, autonomous parts. In different ways, Plato and Aristotle both dramatically extended this focus on objects and their characteristics in a relation-free metaphysics that would find its culmination in seventeenth-century Western mechanism.

Plato (428/7–348/7 BCE) developed his theories in an intellectual context that was, from his perspective, in crisis. Responding to the perceived chaos and flux of the material world, Heraclitus had famously declared, "No man ever steps in the same river twice" (Burnet and Whalen 1957:Heraclitus, Fragments 41–42, 136). Plato's teacher Cratylus took this metaphysics of change to its epistemological extreme by saying that if everything is constantly changing, no statement about anything could be true. Galled by the supreme skepticism implied by this perspective, Plato famously turned away from the material world. He concluded that the whole phenomenal world should be distrusted, held in suspicion. In his writings he resoundingly denounces the perceptible world, the whole physical world, as an unintelligible, turbulent realm that allows no knowledge.[5] His Ideas or Forms, where ontological stability could once again be achieved, was his solution to this dire metaphysical conundrum.

Plato gave his Forms ontological primacy above material reality with a series of statements scattered throughout his writings that judge the tangible world as a prison, a degraded realm, and so on (Plato 1961:Phaedo, 80e–81a, 64, Phaedo, 114d–e, 95, Phaedo, 81a, 118a, 64, 98, Phaedo, 82d–83b, 66). He denigrated sense data in the process, claiming that the senses distort reality and lie, and true knowledge only comes from contemplation of the Forms (Plato 1961:Symposium, 211–211e, pp. 562, 563).[6] To complete his break with the whole of physical nature, Plato also rejected Socrates' immanence theory of form, in which the Form is manifest in each phenomenal, material instance of it—that is, every chair expresses and contains within it the abstract Form of a chair (Collingwood 1967:66–67). He sought to rid the Forms of any remaining vestige of lowly physicality.

By aligning himself with the Pythagoreans and rejecting the rich, immanent, chaotic flux of material nature, Plato helped set the stage for the mechanistic worldview that would arise two millennia later during the second great efflorescence of Western cosmological thought, which Merchant examines in detail in *TDN*. His Forms can be seen as a forerunner of the dead, inert, interchangeable machine parts constituting the mechanical cosmos. Moreover, his stance toward material nature set up the moral ground for an exploitative relationship with nature. Although the physical world for the early modern philosopher-scientists was immanent, their transformation of nature from an alive and agentic sphere to a dead and passive one arguably required the Platonic deprecation of physical nature as a lower realm that, together with the senses, leads people astray.

Plato's metaphysics of transcendence also accorded with and intensified Hughes' "Great Divorce" of people from nature in the ancient world (Hughes 2009:30). Cloistered behind city walls in ancient Mesopotamia, Assyria, Persia, Greece, and later Rome, many priests, tradespeople, architects, builders, potters, and others experienced less and less direct participation with alive and active nature in their everyday experiences. While farmers and others working with natural resources outside the city still needed an understanding of natural processes, most elite decision makers and much of the public could remain somewhat innocent of the complex of natural processes of the natural world. For many of these people, like most of us in the modern industrial world, dependence on the natural world would have seemed to have abated. Yet the entire civilization in which they lived nevertheless depended decidedly on the rich productivity (and invisible labor) of fertile nature.

The Disembodied Privilege of Nature Disconnection

The ethereal and abstract cosmos that Plato envisioned in the Forms, combined with the degraded and lowly material nature he conceived, likewise must be understood as the imaginings of an elite urban citizen of powerful Athens—a person almost wholly dependent upon other people's physical labor and interactions with nature, including the woman and slaves of his household and farmers and craftspeople working with natural materials. The freeman's prejudice toward manual labor orients Plato's views. He likely performed little or none of it, and perhaps little craft besides writing. So Plato's metaphysics advancing the divorce of humans from nature must be seen as the product of his position of power and privilege, which envisions the truest and best work to be the contemplation of the Forms and which sees material nature and the senses needed to know it—and by extension those working with it—as inferior. The deepest historical origins of "the death of nature" thus lie in the power of the master who does no physical labor and has little necessary interaction with nature and thus relegates both nature and the slave (together with the women of the household) to a mutually subjugated sphere.

Like Plato's theory of Forms, his theory of the transcendent soul likewise reinforced the alienation of people from the realm of the material world—nature and the body. Plato *dissociated* the soul from the body in a dualistic construction that, as Plumwood argues, aligns the soul with the higher realm of the human, the male, culture, and the true ground of existence—the rational mind—while removing the unreliable, contaminating body to the lower realm of nature, female, and the senses. He makes it clear that the soul has no dependence on the body and both precedes it in life and persists after bodily death. The soul can only be "contaminated" by the body:

> When it [the soul] tries to investigate anything with the help of the body, it is obviously led astray.... Then here too—in despising the body and avoiding

it, and endeavoring to become independent—the philosopher's soul is ahead of all of the rest … . In fact the philosopher's occupation consists precisely in the freeing and separation of soul from body…true philosophers make dying their profession.

(Plato 1961:Phaedo, 65a–e, 48 and 67d–e, 50)

Plato has Socrates uttering these words shortly before the latter's death, which the elder welcomes. The body, and by extension the whole physical world, is merely an obstacle. Elsewhere, Plato considers the body a prison of the soul.[7] His worldview provides a way around this impediment even during life: the soul need not continue to associate itself with the burdensome body. The active disparagement and refusal of the body even becomes a requirement for entrance into heaven:

If at its release the soul is pure and carries with it no contamination of the body, because it has never willingly associated with it in life, but has shunned it and kept itself separate as its regular practice…then it departs to that place which is, like itself, invisible, divine, immortal, and wise, where on its arrival, happiness awaits it, and release from uncertainty and folly, from fears and uncontrolled desires, and all other human evils, and where, as they say of the initiates in the Mysteries, it really spends the rest of time with God.

(Plato 1961:Phaedo, 80e–81a, 64)[8]

In these chilling passages, Plato leaves no doubt about his contempt for embodiment and physicality—and their correlate, material nature. Only death can achieve the most desirable, greatest distance from the nature within and the nature without (Plumwood 1993:92). Life, as even the best live it, is a crippled thing. Death will release and fully heal the soul: "For is not philosophy the study of death?" (Plato 1961:Phaedo, 81a, 118a, pp. 64, 98)[9] The dissociation of people from nature, of the soul from the body—arguably a prerequisite for the death of nature—finds perhaps its most enthusiastic expression in Plato.

Et Tu, Aristotle?

Aristotle's (384–322 BC) doctrine of immanence clearly emerged as a countervailing wind to his teacher Plato's theory of Ideas. But dissociations nevertheless orient much of Aristotle's thought. Although for him knowledge is grounded in lived, observable, phenomenal reality, his science and philosophy tend to create conceptual dissociations—artificial divisions not essential to observable phenomena—by de-emphasizing or ignoring relationships. Unlike Plato, Aristotle promoted the acquisition of knowledge through observation and use of the senses (Aristotle 1991:Metaphysics, Book I, Ch. 1, 980a, 334). But like Plato, Aristotle valorized and reveled in abstraction, universalizing, and theorization more than empirical study. A's and B's abound in his writing, as do statements such as "*X* is a man." He writes about "every man" and "every kind of pleasure."[10] Particular things, beyond particular thinkers, do not seem to attract his interest, as he is concerned with producing a systematized and thus necessarily abstract accounting of the phenomenal world. He appears to have been obsessed with classifying things and only seems to want to know enough about a thing to place it into one of his categories. Once it is categorized, its qualities, especially those not used to assign it to a category, become moot. Aristotle's approach to classification reduces the living, pulsing landscape to an "automobile-parts warehouse" (Callicott 1996:29).

Aristotle's tendency to hyper-distinguish objects—to emphasize difference and ignore similarities based on selected qualities—as he worked to arrange the whole world into categories may have inspired early modern projects to set humans apart from all other animals (Soper 1995:53). In truth, we resemble and overlap with other animals, particularly other great apes, far more than we differ from them. Only in the past few decades has modern science rediscovered the conclusion intuited by most indigenous, animist cultures (including those alive during Aristotle's time): no single capability such as consciousness, reason, or upright walking separates humans from the rest of nature. But like Plato's Forms, Aristotle's abstraction and systematization seem motivated by a desire to wash one's hands of the messy flux and complexity of the natural world—literally, by rising above particularity, as is the freeman's privilege.

Aristotle's enthusiasm for formal categories sometimes seems to erase similarities and relationships among things, and his logic does likewise. His three logical principles—the law of identity, the law of non-contradiction, and the law of the excluded middle—infuse divisions into truth-seeking. And they represent only one way among many of introducing new knowledge: reasoning styles throughout much of the non-Western world contrast sharply with Aristotle's precepts. The law of identity, $A = A$, advises us to conceive of things frozen in time, dissociated from the flux of the material world. But is identity not a practical matter more than a logical one—are you really who you were forty years ago? The law of non-contradiction, which says that a statement cannot be both true and false, seeks to make clear-cut distinctions where none may exist. Perhaps Joe is a baseball player because he plays often, but not really a baseball player because he's not very good at it or has other identities more relevant to his life, such as accountant. So Joe is and is not a baseball player. Similarly, the law of the excluded middle, which says that every statement must be either true or false, denies the grey areas of truth in the complex tumult of physical reality. It urges us to ignore processes by which things come into being, change, and decay. The middle condition—Joe is neither a baseball player nor not one—must be excluded. Our sensual experiences reveal a full spectrum of truths. The sky is blue, but it's also painted a pale magenta by some sunsets. By denying the flux and continuity of the actual material world, Aristotle's logic divorces us from it, and that divorce sets the stage for death.

Aristotle's de-contextualizing logical principles are challenged not only by non-Western logics but also by more recent developments in formal logic by Western philosophers, including intuitionist logics, relevance logics, sociative logics, and "other systems that deny bivalence or the principle of non-contradiction or both" (Fuhrmann 2003:138; Sylvan 2000:53, 54). Sociative logics demand, for instance, that there be some actual connection between the antecedent (the fact being assumed) and the consequent (the conclusion) beyond the abstract rules of logic that bind them. That is, context and real-world situations must be considered. These non-Aristotelian logics do not fragment worldviews quite the way Aristotle's laws of logic do.[11]

Oppositional Aristotle

The modern opposition between alive, agentic humans and the dead mechanical nature that Merchant describes in TDN may be grounded in Aristotle's intense focus on opposition as a mode of relation. It stands as further evidence of Aristotle's tendency to create divisions. In the *Physics* he declares the importance of opposition: "In a sense all thinkers posit contraries as principles, and with good reason" (Aristotle 1991:Physics, Book I, Ch. 5, 188a25–30, 172). That is where he also arranges various qualities of nature into fundamental oppositional pairs such as Solid-Void, Rare-Dense, and Hot-Cold. In *Book I* of the *Metaphysics* Aristotle builds on the Pythagorean table of opposites to arrive at his own fuller set of oppositions out of which relationships arise: Finite-Infinite, Odd-Even, One-Many, Right-Left, Male-Female, Resting-Moving, Straight-Curved, Light-Darkness, Good-Bad, Square-Rectangular (Aristotle 1991: Metaphysics, Book I, Ch. 5, 986a20–30, 343). The two elements of each pair possess mutually exclusive qualities, he writes, and all of the elements on the same side share qualities, so Male, One, Light, and Good are closely associated (while being dissociated from Female, Many, Darkness, and Bad), in accord with the logical of dualisms identified by Plumwood.

Aristotle at times strains to place things into opposition. Actually, compared to the similarities between them, the differences between male and female humans are certainly few, for example, and forcing gender into two discrete values is itself highly problematic. Complementary, as expressed for instance in the classic Chinese notion of yin-yang, would be a more apt understanding of their relation. Aristotle endows his worldview so heavily in oppositions that two pairs of opposites, hot-cold and dry-moist, in all of their possible combinations, become the basis of the four fundamental elements that constitute the physical world (Aristotle 1991:Generation and Destruction, Bk. II, Ch. 2, 330a25, 245).[12] But to posit oppositions is to deny or discount the qualities that unite things. Like Plato's dualisms, Aristotle's opposites dissociate because each side is fully contrary to and independent of the other, rather than admitting both differences and similarities, as well as complementarities and interdependencies.

Divorce, Physics, and Power

Aristotle repeatedly de-emphasizes relationships in his physics, preferring to define the qualities and movements of objects without reference to other objects. An object is seen as heavy in an absolute sense, not just compared with other objects. Aristotle's avoidance of relation appears clearly, for example, in his theory of motion. Objects move due to their inherent qualities rather than interactions. An object floats because it has the property of lightness. Why, you might ask, do large ships float? Today, science understands floating as an interaction of an object and a medium with different densities. But for Aristotle, things move because of their own "nature," such as fire with its upward locomotion (Aristotle 1991: Physics, Book II, Ch. 1, 192b30–193a5, 181–182).

For this giant of Western philosophy, relations hardly have any ontological status at all (Aristotle 1991:Metaphysics, Book I, Ch. 9, 990b15–20, 351). Physical outcomes in the world such as motion and position must therefore be explained solely by the attributes of objects themselves. Strange explanations ensue. Consider Aristotle's understanding of a building:

> What is heavy travels down by its nature and what is light travels up by its nature, and so the stones and the foundation are down, then earth right above because it is lighter, and finally wood at the very top since it is the lightest.
>
> *(Aristotle 1991:Physics, Book II, Ch. 9, 200a1–15, 196)*

Rejecting that relations are true and real means, Aristotle must awkwardly and forcefully insert the causes of motion into the objects themselves: "A motion is in a movable [object], for it is of the movable that it [motion] is the actuality, and it [motion] is caused by that which can move [the movable]" (Aristotle 1991:Physics, Book III, Ch. 3, 202a10–20, pp. 200–201).

Aristotle goes to great lengths to omit relationships, context, and the surrounding environment of events from his science. In doing so, he helped establish the intellectual groundwork for modern people to diminish their relationship with nature, even while he set forth a metaphysics of immanence in which nature is real and relevant. None of this is to say that Aristotle was anti-nature like his teacher Plato but rather that his logic, metaphysics, and science helped establish and reinforce conceptual divisions undergirding alienation from nature.

It is important to remember that power was never far from the motivations driving Aristotle, Plato, and their colleagues. Aristotle aligns Male, Odd, Right, Light, and Straight with the Good, and Female, Even, Left, Darkness, and Curved (respectively) with the Bad (Aristotle 1991:Metaphysics, Bk. I, Ch. 5, 986a22–30, 343). Even when he recognizes that male and female must collaborate in procreation, he defines male as a capacity and female not by a complementary capacity, but by an incapacity: "The male provides the moving cause and the form in generation … while the female provides merely the matter—and that is a mark of the greater 'divinity' of the male" (Lloyd 1996:138).[13] Classical Greek women had few rights compared with citizens, who were men. Philosophies that divide, demote, and disempower reinforced the dominion of Athenian (male) citizens.

Although his theory of immanence contradicts the theory of transcendence of his teacher Plato, Aristotle's divisive conceptualizations—his taxonomies and systematizations of knowledge about the natural world—lead us to an outcome similar to the one we encounter with Plato's Forms: a turning away from lived experience (that might generate traditional ecological knowledge (TEK), for example) toward the workings of the human mind. Indeed, he wrote, "The activity of a god, then, which surpasses all other activities in blessedness, would be contemplative. Consequently, of human activities, too, that which is closest in kind to this would be the happiest."[14] Although it may bring immediate happiness for some, this shunning of the embodied, intimate knowledge described by TEK may bring environmental ruin for all. Elsewhere in this volume, Elizabeth Allison (Chapter 5) argues that TEK can ground and fund the types of partnership ethics Carolyn Merchant promotes and moreover that it is "well-suited to engaging with the 'wicked problems' of global environmental change, such as climate change" (Allison 2018, 87). TEK need not remain an esoteric and marginalized form of knowledge disconnected and alienated from modern epistemic systems. Both Allison and Laura Alice Watt, also in this volume, envision TEK making inroads into contemporary life and science. Watt has observed TEK-like knowledge—a rich and detailed landscape knowledge—arising among senior land managers in a U.S. Bureau of Land Management field office, accreted over time through many years of repeated, lived interactions with the living landscape (Watt 2018).

As elite male citizens of the polis, neither Plato nor Aristotle would have experienced the kind of direct, phenomenal interaction with complex, sensuous, productive nature that a farmer, hunter, or even a potter or carpenter must have had. These White males of the ancient world may have set the stage for the early modern privileging of White men over nature figured alternately as machine and female, two imaginaries that endorsed positions of male power and control over nature.

Enter Modernity

Rejecting Aristotle's teleology, the seventeenth-century philosopher-scientists whom Merchant discusses in *TDN* aligned themselves with Plato, even though Aristotle's philosophy dealt more extensively and explicitly with natural science. They took up Plato's Pythagorean cosmology, which suggests that mathematical structures, like Newton's equations of mechanics, represent the true nature of things. For the early modern philosophers, change was the outcome of these structures rather than simply the expression of a tendency (Collingwood 1967:93–94; Galilei 1890:Il Saggiatore, vol. 6, p. 232; Tillyard 1959:46).[15] Galileo, the "father of modern science," established the new cosmological conception by re-stating the

Pythagorean-Platonic standpoint of transcendence. The universe, he famously declared, is a book written by God in the language of mathematics. It is open before our eyes, but it cannot be read until we have learned the language of mathematics in which it is written, with letters of triangles, circles, and other geometrical figures, without which it is impossible for humans to comprehend.[16] The Pythagorean-Platonic idea that numbers and formulas underlie nature and cause all change in the physical world eased the way for nature to be thought of as a machine. Since the early modern period, mainstream modern science, with exceptions as pointed out previously—in addition to German Romantic works by Alexander von Humboldt (1769–1859) and Ernst Haeckel (1834–1919), among others—has focused (not exclusively) on the organizing principle of separation, the construct of a machine with separate parts. As the post-modern physicist David Bohm writes, "the order physics has been using is the order of separation" (Bohm 1988:65). The human mind became the master of dead, lifeless machine-like nature (Collingwood 1967:96).

Through exhaustive accounts in texts and artwork from the period, in *TDN* Merchant reveals the will to power and control that motivated philosophers and scientists such as Sir Francis Bacon, René Descartes, and Thomas Hobbes to replace the organic worldview of the cosmos with a mechanistic one. Nature became passive material awaiting and even inviting manipulation by "man" (Merchant 1990). In the excitement of their stunning cosmological discoveries, these early modern thinkers, brilliant as they were, seem to have confused the tool that they used to study nature and document change in the natural world— mathematics—with nature itself. Edward T. Hall called this phenomenon "extension transference": people confusing human creations or mental models with what they were created to represent.[17] The extension in this case is mathematics; it is being transferred onto nature as a whole. In the process, Galileo and those following suit subordinated the human body and its senses and dissociated them from nature by inserting the tools of science between the two. Today, their program moves ever closer to completion. Only infrequently are human senses used directly to know nature in ways vital to science and the economy. Microscopes, electronic sensors, and other devices instead tell us what is out there.

Gender played an important role in the re-visioning of nature. Bacon and others cast nature in female terms and used imagery of sexual conquest, perhaps forceful, to encourage the unconstrained application of science for human ends, including pleasure. They did not seek to "exert a gentle guidance over nature's course," but rather to "conquer and subdue her." Bacon urges us to "bind her to your service and make her your slave." Nature, he says, "betrays her secrets more fully when in the grip and under the pressure of art [technology] than when in enjoyment of her natural liberty" (Farrington and Bacon 1964:93, 99 in "Thoughts and Conclusions on the Interpretation of Nature or a Science Productive of Works").[18] Early modern philosophers drove an antagonistic wedge between people and nature. Nature envisioned as dead, passive object allows exploitation; nature imagined as female invites domination.

By these developments, key early-modern natural philosophers enhanced, augmented, and advanced the dissociations that had germinated in ancient Greece. Consider the primary assumptions of mechanism that Merchant identifies. The first, "matter is composed of particles," refers back to the dissociating atomism of the ancients. The second assumption, "the universe is a natural order," implies Aristotle's law of identity, which I have also discussed above. The third, "knowledge and information can be abstracted from the natural world," is an epistemological assumption of context independence that says that valid and proper knowledge can—or perhaps should—be produced by considering events and things out of the contexts in which they occur, echoing Aristotle's method. It says that we can study how things behave in a universal sense, by considering their innate qualities, not the situations they are found in, not the relations they are embedded within.

The fourth assumption, "Problems can be analyzed into parts that can be manipulated by mathematics," asserts that the analytical method—breaking complex problems down into separate parts that can be considered individually with little or no weight given to the *relations* among the parts—is a sufficient basis of knowledge. The final assumption that "sense data are discrete" implies that even at the fundamental level of perception and sensation, nature comes to us in discrete quantities. There is no continuum of color in the sky, for instance, only a series of discrete colors. This assumption models perception as a mechanistic process and thus models human biology as a machine. Descartes explicitly considered the human body, that most personal part of nature, a machine: "So, also, the human body may be considered a machine, so built and composed of bones, nerves, muscles, veins, blood, and skin that even if there were no mind in it, it would not cease to move" (Descartes 1960:80). Placing the human body in the mechanical world of nature, Descartes goes further even than Plato in dividing mind from body. He radically separates not just rationality but consciousness itself, claiming that everything besides God and the human mind is machine— even a gorilla, a sparrow, or the human body itself.

The foregoing (and, I believe, much of Merchant's synthesis in *TDN*) must not be seen as a comprehensive description of modern Western cosmological thought but rather a distillation of dominant—and thus critically important—themes arising in early modernity and persisting to today. These themes have shaped our relationships with nature, sanctioning capitalist exploitation, as Merchant argues. Yet Western thought, fomenting and churning in various cultural and geographic cauldrons over the last half millennium, has hardly been uniform and unitary. Countercurrents and exceptions include not only the Romantics, as mentioned above, but the whole history of the science of ecology, the West's first true science of interconnection with long roots in European imperialism and Calvinism (Grove 1996). Elsewhere in this volume, Mark Stoll (Chapter 10) traces a genealogy (in Calvinism) of Western thought that runs counter to the cosmology of disconnection described here and in *TDN*. Coinciding approximately with the first two centuries of the rise of mechanism in the West, Reformed Protestants, seeking to recognize God's glory and God's work in nature, sought a unity of spirit and nature. Alexander von Humboldt, William Paley, and others developed important cosmological ideas and advances in the earth sciences upon which ecology is built (Stoll 2018). They developed a holistic, interconnected, non-mechanical view of nature. The question is, how can this intellectual history and its outcome in contemporary ecological science become as influential in everyday modern thought and policy-making as the mechanical paradigm undergirding capitalism and the corresponding, virtually unlimited, devouring of nature as collection of inert, lifeless, and open-for-exploitation "resources"?

Divorce and an Ethical Quandary

The conceptual dissociations dividing up Western thought and setting humans, particularly White men, over and above all nature re-conceived as machine not only constitute a justification for exploitation of nature but also have both directed and reflected a dearth of intimate engagement with the natural world—Hughes' Great Divorce. Phenomenal dissociations in the form of our loss of sensual engagement with living, pulsating nature make real and experiential the machine conception of the cosmos. Their ramifications are not merely that we have lost contact with the realm of the natural, upon which our lives nevertheless depend. But—perhaps equally important—we have lost contact with the consequences of our own choices and actions in life, which play out somewhere "out there," beyond our perceptual (and usually even cognitive) horizon. Our ultimate dependence on nature demands that we care about nature since doing so is, in the end, caring for ourselves. Yet we cannot see how our lives touch nature as our individual choices percolate and disperse out through material and informational networks spanning the globe. The information from below—from nature and oppressed, abused, or silenced others—the critical information about life support systems, hardly reaches people as they make choices in their daily lives that affect those others.

These phenomenal dissociations between modern people and their own consequences present a haunting problem for ethics. Ethics must at some level be concerned with aligning one's choices with one's values, but how can this be done when the outcomes of our choices are remote and unseen and the choices thus correspondingly deprived of meaning? Even in a deonotological system of ethics—that is, one that judges morality based on the degree to which a person follows rules or fulfills duty, not on consequences—a nearly complete rupture between choice (or action), on the one hand, and consequences, on the other, begins to drain ethics of meaning. Imagine for a moment a person sealed within a bubble that allows in only information selected by an imperium. Within the bubble this person flips switches and pulls levers that effect change in the world outside the bubble. The imperium feeds arbitrary information into the bubble in response to the person's actions, perhaps with an eye toward controlling that person's actions. A complete decoupling of the person from the sphere where her actions play out renders the idea of ethics utterly ludicrous. The *partial* decoupling today between modern people and the consequences of their actions disturbingly renders the idea and project of ethics *partially* ludicrous. Phenomenal dissociations alienate us from physical engagement with the very thing that allows us to be ethical beings—the consequences of our own actions—and thus promote unethical, damaging choices that propagate harms to nature and human others, who then become our silent victims at a distance.[19] Therein lies the moral quandary of the divorce from nature that is amplified by the machine conception of the cosmos.

Finding the Human Place in Nature

Through these steps that include dissociating concepts and material divorce from nature, the conceptual death of nature thus ultimately leads to the material death of nature. By building on ancient divisive metaphysical assumptions to render nature dead, passive, and available without constraint for use, prominent early modern philosopher-scientists helped to establish conditions necessary for a modern advancement of the ancient urban turn from nature. Nature deadened, divorced, and alienated from everyday life nevertheless feels the impacts of our choices. An ethical crisis has emerged in which we modern people are robbed of our ethical subjectivity, finding it difficult to align our actions with our values (Worthy 2013:64–68). These conditions perpetuate the avalanche of destructive choices that one by one bring nature ever closer to material, not just conceptual, death.

Later in her career, Merchant has been advocating for her partnership ethic, which "holds that the greatest good for the human and nonhuman communities is in their mutual living interdependence" (Merchant 2003:191). A partnership ethic demands a particularist relation with human and nonhuman others, following that principle held by many ecofeminists. The needs of nonhuman "partners" in the natural world must be represented in decision-making, and to know those needs requires engaged, sensuous interaction with those others in their living state. "Trees, rivers, endangered species, tribal groups, minority coalitions, and citizen activists all find representation along with business at the negotiating table," writes Merchant (2000:7).[20] Institutions of industry, science, and technology must thus come to know nature not as an abstraction but rather as a sphere of life demanding respect—an alive realm, a living place. Contributions of chaos and complexity theory are helping to attune modern science to the agency of nature, as Merchant discusses extensively in one of the latest volumes in her prodigious output, *Autonomous Nature: Problems of Prediction and Control from Ancient Times to the Scientific Revolution* (Merchant 2016). Her work thus comes full circle, from a pivotal, deeply influential study of the loss of living nature to an ethical framework for regaining connection and involvement with—and care for—nature.

Notes

1   Portions of this chapter are excerpted or adapted from my book *Invisible Nature: Healing the Destructive Divide between People and the Environment*. Amherst, NY: Prometheus Books, 2013 (Worthy 2013). Used by permission of the publisher.
2   Merchant examines this concept extensively in *Autonomous Nature: Problems of Prediction and Control From Ancient Times to the Scientific Revolution* (Merchant 2016).
3   I discuss dissociation and its problems extensively in *Invisible Nature* (Worthy 2013).
4   Again, my concern here is with the most influential, mainstream currents of Western intellectual tradition. Countercurrents are many, such as Baruch Spinoza's seventeenth-century monistic cosmology that rejects René Descartes's dissociating mind–body dualism.
5   For example, in the Phaedo Plato writes of the perceptible world,

> Did we not say some time ago that when the soul uses the instrumentality of the body for any inquiry, whether through sight or hearing or any other sense—because using the body implies using the senses—it is drawn away by the body into the realm of the variable, and loses it way and becomes confused and dizzy, as though it were fuddled, through contact with things of a similar nature?
>
> *(Plato 1961:Phaedo, 79c, 62)*

By "similar nature" Plato means that the physical world is fuddled and dizzy.
6   On freedom from interference from the body, see, among other passages (Plato 1961: Phaedo, 79d, pp. 62, 63).
7   On the body as prison, Plato wrote,

> Every seeker after wisdom knows that up to the time when philosophy takes it over his soul is a helpless prisoner, chained hand and foot in the body, compelled to view reality not directly but only through its prison bars…Well, philosophy takes over the soul in this condition and by gentle persuasion tries to set it free. She points out that observation by means of the eyes and ears and all the other senses is entirely deceptive.
>
> *(Plato 1961:Phaedo, 82d–83b, 66)*

8   Elsewhere, Plato makes clear that bodily pleasure, along with other senses and emotions, must be expelled from the self to ensure entrance into this intellectual heaven. He writes, "There is one way, then, in which a man can be free from all anxiety about the fate of his soul—if in life he has abandoned bodily pleasures and adornments…and has devoted himself to the pleasures of acquiring knowledge" (Plato 1961:Phaedo, 114d–e, 95).
9   Plato implies that death is a healing of the "illness" of life in the *Phaedo* when he has Socrates order Crito to offer a cock to Asclepius, Greek god of medicine and healing, in a ritual marking recovery from illness. These were Socrates' last words, claims Plato (Plato 1961:Phaedo, 81a, 118a, pp. 64, 98).
10   There are many examples in the passages cited here: (Aristotle 1991:Nichomean Ethics, Book VII, Ch. 4–5, pp. 512–513).
11   Sociative logics are a family of old and new logics in which the validity of an implicational formula requires some genuine connection of reasoning or content between the antecedent and the consequent. The two cannot thus be otherwise totally unrelated.
12   Sambursky argues that the progress of Western physics was impeded by Aristotle's commitment to the fundamental status of opposites: "The history of physics has proved that all this theory of absolutely opposed qualities, even when presented with dialectical brilliance in the form of thesis and antithesis, leads nowhere" (Sambursky 1960:89–91).
13   See Aristotle's "On the Generation of Animals" (Aristotle 1941:On the Generation of Animals, 732a1ff).
14   "So since the intellect is divine relative to a man, the life according to this intellect, too, will be divine relative to human life … . Happiness, then, would be a kind of contemplation"

(Aristotle 1991:Nicomachean Ethics, Bk. X, Ch. 7–8, 1177b30, 1178b20–25, 1178b30–33, pp. 549–551).
15 Translated and quoted in Jesseph's "Galileo, Hobbes, and the Book of Nature" (Jesseph 2004:202).
16 Galileo wrote,

> Philosophy is written in this vast book, which lies continuously open before our eyes (I mean the universe). But it cannot be understood unless you have first learned to understand the language and recognize the characters in which it is written. It is written in the language of mathematics, and the characters are triangles, circles, and other geometrical figures. Without such means, it is impossible for us humans to understand a word of it, and to be without them is to wander around in vain through a dark labyrinth.
> *(Galilei 1890:Il Saggiatore, vol. 6, page 232; Translated and quoted in Jesseph's "Galileo, Hobbes, and the Book of Nature" (Jesseph 2004:202)*

See also (Galilei 2000). For an alternative translation, see (Galilei 1957:238).
17 "Extension transference…this common intellectual maneuver in which the extension is confused with or takes the place of the process extended" (Hall 1981:25). Extension transference occurs for instance when symbols are mistaken for the things symbolized (as in worshipping idols), when written language is valued above lived, spoken language (for instance when African-American school children are told that their street language is inferior to the language that they are to learn in school), when methodology takes precedence over empirical data (as when the paradigms of "hard science" are applied to the social world), and more generally when artifice is considered the "real" world, not the culturally and historically specific extensions of a particular culture. We become preoccupied with material goods, and they take the place of relationships with people and nature. Hall sees extension transference as a main source of alienation from self and heritage worldwide when modern systems supplant traditional lived cultures (Hall 1981:29–30).
    Extension transference was at work when Plato said that the Forms are more real than the tangible world. Likewise, it happened when the mechanistic view of nature, arising from early modern peoples' experience with machines (which are human extensions), became reified in modern cosmology, which re-envisioned nature as a machine. Extension transference resembles but differs from Alfred North Whitehead's concept of "The Fallacy of Misplaced Concreteness," which means the "accidental error of mistaking the abstract for the concrete" (Whitehead 2011:64).
18 Bacon wrote, "I come in very truth, leading to you Nature with all her children to bind her to your service and make her your slave." (Farrington and Bacon 1964:62 in "The Masculine Birth of Time.") The idea of sexual and rape imagery of nature is explored in (Merchant 1990:171–172)
19 I discuss this problem in depth in *Invisible Nature* (Worthy 2013).
20 Projects have long been in the works to give nature and its constituents their say, such as The Council of All Beings advanced by John Seed and Joanna Macy and the recent Bay Area Rights of Nature Tribunal, which put a major development project on trial with testimony from nature (Anon n.d.; Seed and Macy 1988).

Bibliography

Allison, Elizabeth. 2018. "Bewitching Nature." In *After the Death of Nature: Carolyn Merchant and the Future of Human–Nature Relations*, edited by K. Worthy, E. Allison, and W. Bauman. New York: Routledge.

Anon. n.d. "Bay Area Rights of Nature Tribunal April 30th in Antioch CA." Earth Law Center. Retrieved June 3, 2016 (www.earthlawcenter.org/elc-in-the-news/2016/3/bay-area-rights-of-nature-tribunal).

Aristotle. 1941. *The Basic Works of Aristotle*. New York: Random House.

Aristotle. 1991. *Selected Works*. 3rd edition. Translated by Hippocrates, G. Apostle and Lloyd P. Gerson. Grinnell, IA: Peripatetic Press.

Bohm, David. 1988. "Postmodern Science and a Postmodern World." Pp. 57–68 in *The Reenchantment of Science: Postmodern Proposals*, edited by D. R. Griffin. Albany, NY: State University of New York Press.

Burnet, John and Philip Whalen. 1957. *Early Greek Philosophy*. New York: Meridian Books.

Callicott, J. Baird. 1996. *Earth's Insights: A Multicultural Survey of Ecological Ethics from the Mediterranean Basin to the Australian Outback*. 1st edition. Berkeley: University of California Press.

Collingwood, R. G. 1967. *The Idea of Nature*. New York: Oxford University Press.

Descartes, René. 1960. *Meditations on First Philosophy*. 2nd (rev.). New York: Bobbs-Merrill.

Farrington, Benjamin and Francis Bacon. 1964. *The Philosophy of Francis Bacon; an Essay on Its Development from 1603 to 1609, with New Translations of Fundamental Texts*. Chicago, IL: University of Chicago Press.

Fuhrmann, Andre. 2003. "Sociative Logics and Their Applications: Essays (Review)." *Philosophical Quarterly* 53(210):137–141.

Galilei, Galileo. 1890. *Le Opere Di Galileo Galilei*. Firenze: Le Monnier.

Galilei, Galileo. 1957. *Discoveries and Opinions of Galileo: Including The Starry Messenger (1610), Letter to the Grand Duchess Christina (1615), and Excerpts from Letters on Sunspots (1613), The Assayer (1623)*. New York: Anchor Books.

Galilei, Galileo. 2000. "The Assayer." *History of Modern Philosophy*. Retrieved www.philosophy.leeds.ac.uk/GMR/hmp/texts/modern/galileo/assayer.html.

Gouldner, Alvin Ward. 1965. *Enter Plato: Classical Greece and the Origins of Social Theory*. New York: Basic Books.

Grove, Richard H. 1996. *Green Imperialism: Colonial Expansion, Tropical Island Edens and the Origins of Environmentalism, 1600–1860*. Cambridge: Cambridge University Press.

Hall, Edward Twitchell. 1981. *Beyond Culture*. Garden City, NY: Anchor Books.

Hughes, J. Donald. 2009. *An Environmental History of the World: Humankind's Changing Role in the Community of Life*. 2nd edition. London: Routledge.

Jesseph, Douglas M. 2004. "Galileo, Hobbes, and the Book of Nature." *Perspectives on Science* 12(2):191–211.

Lloyd, G. E. R. 1996. *Adversaries and Authorities: Investigations into Ancient Greek and Chinese Science*. Cambridge: Cambridge University Press.

Merchant, Carolyn. 1990. *The Death of Nature: Women, Ecology, and the Scientific Revolution*. 2nd edition. San Francisco, CA: Harper & Row.

Merchant, Carolyn. 2000. "Partnership Ethics: Business and the Environment." Pp. 7–18 in *Environmental Challenges to Business, 1997 Ruffin Lectures, University of Virginia Darden School of Business*, edited by P. Werhane. Bowling Green, OH: Society for Business Ethics.

Merchant, Carolyn. 2003. *Reinventing Eden: The Fate of Nature in Western Culture*. New York: Routledge.

Merchant, Carolyn. 2016. *Autonomous Nature: Problems of Prediction and Control from Ancient Times to the Scientific Revolution*. New York: Routledge.

Plato. 1961. *The Collected Dialogues of Plato: Including the Letters*. New York: Pantheon Books.

Plumwood, Val. 1993. *Feminism and the Mastery of Nature*. London: Routledge.

Sambursky, Samuel. 1960. *The Physical World of the Greeks*. London: Routledge and Paul.

Seed, John and Joanna Macy. 1988. *Thinking like a Mountain: Towards a Council of All Beings*. Philadelphia, PA: New Society Publishers.

Soper, Kate. 1995. *What Is Nature?: Culture, Politics and the Non-Human*. Oxford: Blackwell.

Stoll, Mark. 2018. "The Other Scientific Revolution: Calvinist Scientists and the Origins of Ecology." In *After the Death of Nature: Carolyn Merchant and the Future of Human–Nature Relations*, edited by K. Worthy, E. Allison, and W. Bauman. New York: Routledge.

Sylvan, Richard. 2000. *Sociative Logics and Their Applications: Essays*. Aldershot; Burlington, VT: Ashgate.

Tillyard, E. M. W. 1959. *The Elizabethan World Picture*. New York: Vintage Books.

Watt, Laura Alice. 2018. "Landscape, Science, and Social Reproduction: The Long-Reaching Influence of Carolyn Merchant's Insight." In *After the Death of Nature: Carolyn Merchant and the Future of Human–Nature Relations*, edited by K. Worthy, E. Allison, and W. Bauman. New York: Routledge.

Whitehead, A. N. 2011. *Science and the Modern World*. Cambridge: Cambridge University Press.

Worthy, Kenneth. 2013. *Invisible Nature: Healing the Destructive Divide between People and the Environment*. Amherst, NY: Prometheus Books.

3

CAROLYN MERCHANT'S *THE DEATH OF NATURE*

Launching New Trajectories in Interdisciplinary Research

Heather Eaton

Introduction

Carolyn Merchant provided an invaluable contribution with her work on *The Death of Nature: Women, Ecology and the Scientific Revolution* (Merchant 1980). The exposure of discernible historical processes in Euro-Western contexts that led to the depreciation of nature was original, insightful, and provocative. Merchant revealed that knowledge production, especially around natural sciences, was replete with biases against women and the natural world, which has led to their mutual oppression. Some responses were sceptical of, and resistant to, the evidence that eminent scientists, notably Francis Bacon, held misogynist views tied to denying the vitality of natural processes. Others found that Merchant's analysis provided explanatory power about the trajectory of Euro-Western exploitation and deterioration of the natural world.

The impact of *The Death of Nature* (hereafter *TDN*) is difficult to calculate precisely. The book galvanized efforts to recognize and critique the operative Euro-Western mechanistic worldview. It supported efforts to probe the ambiguous relationship this worldview has with cultural processes that devalue and denigrate the natural world. *TDN* was part of an impetus to dismantle this worldview, and in accord with other efforts to engender ecological worldviews.

This chapter considers *TDN* as a valuable book for its unprecedented historical investigation, and for its impact on the development of ecofeminist research. Merchant's unique research themes, feminist analyses, and historical critiques propelled many others to pursue and deepen topics found in *TDN*. The book could be envisaged as a kind of launch pad for further potent research. Three such launch pads will be suggested in this chapter: offering a new lens for understanding and critiquing formative narratives and history(ies); analyzing the interconnections of ecology, feminism, and domination; and elevating the importance of understanding worldviews. While this book was not unique in bringing forth these themes, it was foundational to new research and interpretative directions that became influential in feminist and ecological research. The metaphor of launch pad illustrates that something powerful was launched with *TDN*. Furthermore, and unlike a single rocket with one trajectory, this book became a launch pad for several powerful intellectual rockets with different trajectories.

Situating *The Death of Nature*

Before describing the new trajectories *TDN* established, it is important to situate it among other related publications. The book was initially published in 1980, and like all unique contributions to the world of ideas, there are always precursors as well as companion texts and ideas. Prior to the emergence of Merchant's book on the North American scene, books such as *New Woman, New Earth* by Rosemary Radford Ruether (1975), *Woman and Nature: The Roaring Inside Her* by Susan Griffin (1978), [1] and Mary Daly's *Gyn/Ecology: The Metaphysics of Radical Feminism* (Daly 1978), had already had an impact within many ecological and feminist contexts. Some of these books and researchers dealt explicitly with historical trajectories that connected women and nature, and with contemporary feminism and ecology. At times, these topics were associated with Christian cultural influences and theological traditions and transformations. When *TDN* appeared, it engaged with all of these topics.

Meanwhile, in different contexts, the contributions and insights of influential and radical thinkers and activists such as Murray Bookchin (1982) were gaining attention. The *Domination of Nature* by William Leiss (1972), Jean François Lyotard's *The Postmodern Condition: A Report on Knowledge* (Lyotard 1979), Gerda Lerner's *The Creation of Patriarchy* (Lerner 1987), Clive Ponting's *A Green History of the World: The Environment and the Collapse of Great Civilizations* (Ponting 1991), and Louis Dupré's *Passage to Modernity: An Essay on the Hermeneutics of Nature and Culture* (Dupré 1993), brought attention to the need for historical and social scrutiny of worldviews, domination, hierarchy, patriarchy, and ideological dualisms and polarities. They also traced how the shift from organic to mechanistic ideas about the natural world and ensuing cultural practices could have taken place.

Carolyn Merchant's unique contributions in *TDN* and subsequent books took place within this multidisciplinary groundswell of deliberations in which Euro-Western academics and activists were grappling with understanding and resisting mounting ecological ruin. This required interdisciplinary exchanges that were uncommon in academic milieus. *TDN* was a strong surge in this multi-disciplinary historical, analytic, and intellectual groundswell.

Much has been written about the book. Countless historians of science, environmental historians, feminists, and religious and secular scholars have referred to aspects of it.[2] *TDN* became one of the founding books for ecofeminism and the environmental humanities.

The following is a reflection on what I see as launch pads found in *TDN* that have subsequently been developed by others. I am not suggesting that Merchant was the sole originator of these launch pads, or that there were not predecessors to her work, although I do think that she offered unique historical assessments of science. I am suggesting that many used *TDN* to launch or strengthen their own approaches to topics covered in the book. In other words, it provided invaluable evidence that enabled others to take these arguments even further, as will be discussed in three research trajectories launched by *TDN*.

A New Lens for Understanding History(ies)

As an historian, Merchant was wading through contemporary ecological and gender quagmires that originated in the past, and that could also explain something of the present. However, this was not simply historical research. The purpose was to enable in-depth comprehension of ecological and gender interconnections established in the past and feeding into the present, in order to change cultural directions. A further goal was to expose a naiveté, if not a safeguard from reproach, surrounding the erudition, objectivity, and prestige of the fathers of modern science. They had become like the revered "church fathers" of the Modern scientific understanding of the world.

Merchant's key themes—concern for the ecological crisis and its roots, an assessment of scientific knowledge and neutrality, a probing of the ideologies hidden within the oppressions of women, and the interconnections among these three—were the basis of *TDN*. The full title reveals the line of inquiry Merchant was undertaking. The results were, in part, a revision of Enlightenment history, a piercing examination of the rise of science, and an exposure of the devaluation of women and the natural world in the production of scientific knowledge. Merchant exposed a trend of knowledge production based on oppression.

Thus one launch pad boosted new and critical interpretations of Euro-Western history. These novel interpretations are a blend of the social construction of ideas and cultural metaphors, including the social construction of women, and then of how these influence social patterns that manipulate the material realm. This is a challenging undertaking, as it requires tools and insights from several disciplines: ethics, philosophy, gender, and ecology.

It is now acceptable to blend such analyses, but not all academic realms embrace such mixtures. Some found that Merchant's approach led to inexactness and a generalist vision of historical events. Others found her interpretations biased. For example, the least receptive cluster of responses came from the historians of science, who gave *TDN* a cool reception (Soble 1995:192–215; Pesic 1999:81–84; Iddo 1998:47–61). Much of this had to do with Merchant's treatment and criticism of Francis Bacon. Some posit that exaggerated associations among women, rape, torture, and science were extracted from Bacon.[3] Others found she over-emphasized tangential themes and then manipulated them to discredit scientific methods.

However, Merchant was not alone in making such connections. Sandra Harding also made the connections between science and gender, and was also countered by others who saw these as outlandish claims stretched from a few phrases found in Bacon's corpus (Harding 1980:305–324; Vickers 2008:117–141). Katherine Park offered her interpretation as to why Merchant's book was ignored (Park 2006:487–495). Park suggested that there was resistance to examining the methodologies and biases within the development of field of the history of science. Merchant's approach was subtle and nuanced and formed a "rich, energetic and provocative argument," that was not within accepted methodological boundaries[4] (Park 2008:490).

In spite of these reproaches, Merchant later both clarified and fortified her position (Merchant 2006:513–533). She explained how the relationships between production and reproduction became a foundation for her socialist ecofeminism, which was grounded in material change. Her interest in the dialectic between society and science (influenced here by the Frankfurt School) was crucial in understanding women, nature, ecological problems, and feminist interests. The focus on power and power over were, for Merchant, a necessary addition to these analyses. Merchant defends her approach by suggesting that the book's challenge was mainly "to the pedestal on which historians had tended to place the Scientific Revolution" (Merchant 2006:517). Again, this theme of revering science in ways that religious institutions had been revered, and showing how some religious biases such as narratives of progress were smuggled in from earlier theological views of progressive narratives, would be a common thread that ran through much of her work. She was unpopular also because she questioned the grand narratives that understood the Scientific Revolution and subsequent scientific developments and discoveries as progress. To this day historians and philosophers of early modern science rarely cite the book.

One could debate whether or not Merchant got all the points right. Were her interpretations accurate, or was she using Bacon also as a rhetorical device? One could ask whether Bacon really meant this or that. Was Merchant doing a revisionist reading? While these questions are surely relevant in some contexts, Merchant's appraisal of biases toward the need to control the natural world—that became embedded in the scientific revolution—was well received by many others.

Certainly, *TDN* was favorable to environmental theorists, and can be seen as contributing to the growing field of ecological or environmental humanities (Eckersley 1998:183–185). A central question in the book and within the field is how images of the natural world develop and are accepted into the social imaginary and cultural processes. Merchant focuses on how metaphors become materially manifested and embedded in history. For example, the shift from perceiving nature as organic, active, and alive, with a spiritual vitality, to that of nature as dead, mechanistic, passive, and void of presence is crucial to understanding the contemporary environmental crisis (not to mention the differences in the ways other peoples with different worldviews understand the rest of the natural world). Understanding this shift is important for understanding and explaining how the ideological and material trajectories led to ecological ruin in the name of progress.

Within the field of environmental humanities is a recognition of the need for a bridge between science and the humanities, and in particular a bridge between the best of the earth sciences and images and ideas of an alternative, viable ecological future (Oppermann and Iovino 2017). Such a bridge requires the kind of amalgam that Merchant uses in the book. For some, it is too generalist. For others, this blend of scientific, cultural, literary, historical, and philosophical perspectives is innovative, creative, and necessary. This inter and multidisciplinary approach was inaugurated by Merchant and taken up by and endorsed by other environmental humanities scholars.

One assumption is that such multidisciplinary exchanges contribute to a new ecological imaginary, or worldview. Scientists, nature writers, religious thinkers, and many others share this quest for imagining a new or different more ecologically aware vision for earth's future. They are envisioning new metaphors and novel approaches to science. From the concept of "living matter" in Vladimir Vernadsky's *The Biosphere* (Vernadsky [1926] 1997) to *Gaia* (Lovelock 1979), *Biophilia* (Wilson 1984), *The Symbiotic Planet* (Margulis 1998), and *Vibrant Matter* (Bennett 2010), creative approaches to science continue to develop with the assumption that there is a persistent and intricate vitality within the natural world.

Since publication of *TDN*, novel insights have emerged from entanglement concepts, new materialisms, social complexity theory, and more. The project known as *The Journey of the Universe* is an important and multifaceted contribution to these efforts.[5] These multidisciplinary blends are needed to build bridges and forge new paths. While not in a direct lineage from *TDN*, the later directions can be seen as part of what Merchant was researching, critiquing, and proposing. *TDN* is in alliance with critiques of ideological and social biases in science, explorations of the relationships between scientific and cultural commitments, and examinations of the role of science in ecological decline and restoration.

Although it is true that Merchant's overall analysis and approach lends itself to both appraising and reinforcing generalist visions, she simultaneously espouses postmodernist incredulity toward metanarratives, naiveté, and certainty. The innovative cross-disciplinary blend of *TDN* became more appreciated and emulated as the years progressed. This offered new lenses on a historical past as well as providing a model for collaboration to envision a viable future. When *TDN* was written, most postmodern analyses did not yet have critical traction. Thus Merchant offered an interesting critique of cultural biases and ideologies, similar to various deconstructive postmodern approaches, while asserting the need for social directions rooted in equality and ecological stability, in the vein of constructive postmodern proposals.

Ecology, Feminism, and Domination

TDN also served as a launch pad for the scholarly coverage of connections between Euro-Western concepts of women and nature. Merchant's in-depth research traced the feminizing of nature, the naturalizing of women, and their mutual subordination. This galvanized much interest and many activities. Topics surrounding the domination of women and the subjugation of nature flowed through academic and popular cultures in fluid exchanges.[6] Tomes have subsequently been researched and written on the historical exposures of the woman/nature connection, the material intersections of women and the natural world, and the linkages between feminism and ecology. Hierarchical dualisms were studied and critiqued (Plumwood 1993). *TDN* became a foundational book for ecofeminists, because it provided not only a conceptual connection between ecology and feminism—it also provided the most comprehensive exposure to date of the historical linkages between women and nature. It was thus groundbreaking (Warren 1998:186–188).

This historical focus on women and nature, and the subsequent expansion of ecofeminisms in their myriad forms, were of immeasurable importance. These associations opened eyes, launched countless research topics, and sparked intense debates. These analyses of history were fresh, insightful, provocative, and convincing. They resonated and they stuck, to the point that today, in many activist and academic contexts, the domination of women and the natural world are understood as structurally, ideologically, and materially connected. These analyses became foundational to understanding the interlocking and mutually reinforcing dynamics of most forms of domination.

Ecofeminisms became additional supports for feminist revolutions. All this work has further launched and emboldened feminists, expanded into feminisms and gender pluralities, and can readily be interpreted as part of third-wave feminisms. It is important to note that the ecofeminist connections launched by *TDN* reinforced a scrutiny of the ideologies and mechanisms of domination, which are now seen as bound together. Most of gender studies, critical race theories, queer studies, animal studies and ecojustice scholarship engage in intersectional analyses to understand the issues. While it cannot be said that *TDN* is the origin of intersectionality, it is evident that Merchant's multidisciplinary blend was expanded and developed into what is now termed intersectionality.

There is much written on the history of domination and the myriad inquiries into various master–slave dialectics, patriarchy, hierarchies, and colonial ideologies. There has been noteworthy momentum in understanding how domination works: how it is symbolized and embedded in worldviews or social imaginaries through processes of legitimization within science, religion, institutions, ideologies, public policies, and mechanisms of enforcement. Domination(s) has (have) been dissected and recognized as operating in social patterns of relationships, personal identity structures, daily habits, and patterns of thought. It seems fair to claim that *TDN* was an important part of the efforts to expose the subtle and blatant, fluid and forceful aspects of domination. This focus is closely related to a third trajectory of research that *TDN* launched, that of worldview analyses.

The Importance of Worldviews

Discussions about worldviews are relatively frequent, especially among those who consider that aspects of systemic ecological crises are related to the operating worldview of modernity.[7] This is something that Merchant was already emphasizing in *TDN*. To tackle all of the historical and contemporary topics around worldviews is neither useful nor feasible here (Eaton 2017). Further, definitions of worldviews are abundant and nebulous.[8] As Robert Cummings Neville writes, a

> Worldview is a useful vague notion that facilitates communication in multi-disciplinary and multi-cultural contexts in many marvelous ways. (yet) … when thinkers assign precise meanings to the notion of worldview, and when these precise meanings differ, communication often breaks down.
> *(Cummings Neville 2009:233)*

Still, it may be beneficial to present some recent perspectives on worldviews related to Merchant's exposure of some aspects of the Enlightenment worldview.

It is key to realize that human societies do not live according to a worldview as a set of beliefs. Nor do societies simply employ signs, symbols, and narratives. The difference is that humans, individually and collectively, operate within them—in other words, they do not relate to worldviews in a dialectic manner. It is the case, rather, that humans live within worldviews. These are not cognitive maps: we are embedded and entangled within them. The shift from one worldview to another is neither straightforward nor well understood, especially at a societal level. Merchant's contribution in exposing the worldview that led to the "death of nature" cannot be underestimated. While she did not venture into an in-depth worldview analysis, she did expose the complex weave among ideas, scientific legitimacy, social sanction, and practices of domination that were accepted as "normal and natural," as modern. This exposure contributed to seeing the cracks within the worldview of modernity. Any contemporary study of multiple aspects of worldviews must acknowledge that Merchant's work was formative.

The most comprehensive work on worldviews has come from *The Worldviews Group*.[9] This multidisciplinary European research group is a combination of scholars from the humanities and sciences. Together they have initiated in-depth studies of the components, explanations, and functioning of worldviews. They sense the increasing ineptitude of most societies in addressing escalating social and ecological problems, due to the concepts and commitments buried within operative worldviews. They perceive multiple levels of fragmentation, which they connect to an inability to maintain a coherent worldview in the fast-paced pluriform, information saturated, hyper-mobile, and postmodern worlds in which we live. Their motivation is to resist fragmentation and to develop modes of integration (not homogenization) of the multiplicity of global worldviews. It is a sophisticated project, with detailed analyses of worldview(s), in several publications.

The Worldviews Group defines the term worldview in publications ranging from forty to four hundred pages. In general, the reflection on worldviews reveals a complex and relational tapestry of intertwining ideals, beliefs, practices, values, and influences. Simply defined, worldviews are an amalgam of the visions, ideas, ideals, and practices that interweave to produce cultural values, governance systems, and social identities. Cornelius Castoriadis and Charles Taylor use the term 'a social imaginary' to convey the same idea (Castoriadis 1987 Taylor 2004).

Rosemary Radford Ruether suggests that worldviews combine the cultural-symbolic levels—the ideological superstructures—that reflect and sanction the social, economic, political, and religious orders (Ruether 1993). They are social blueprints. Val Plumwood (1993) did a superb dissection of patriarchal worldviews in *Feminism and the Mastery of Nature*. Currently, the research into connections between worldviews and ecological issues is staggering. The journal *Worldviews: Global Religions, Culture and Ecology* continually covers a large range of such topics. Since Merchant's trailblazing work, it is apparent that ecological issues are as entangled within cultural ideologies and worldviews as within economics, technology, sciences, social organization, and ecological management.[10] Many scholars have addressed ecological issues by examining and critiquing the histories, contours, and limits of the prevailing Euro-Western worldview. Their common quest is to unearth the ideals and theories embedded in the social imaginary that has led to vast ecological ruin in the name of progress.

TDN elaborated on the colonizing nature of dominant and dominating narratives and patriarchal worldviews, with an insistence on narrative analysis. This has been a launch pad for extensive worldview analysis, cultural critique, social resistance, and imagining new narratives. But we have not gone far enough in our attempts to understand worldviews. Although work to lay bare the elements of worldviews is extensive, comprehension of the impetus to develop them, or of the need for *Homo sapiens* to live within worldviews, has not been developed. This requires entering into the multidisciplinary fields of symbolic consciousness and apprehending how humans evolved or emerged as a species living within worldviews of symbols and multiple narratives (Eaton 2011).

Not only does the lack of such studies reveal how difficult the work of worldview comprehension is, it also explains why they are so difficult to change. Worldview transformation is a massive procedure. In *TDN*, Merchant did not go this far into the topic and issues of worldviews. However, her work was a launching pad for analyses of patriarchal worldviews. From there, work has continued in other important ways.

Today we are in a post-structuralist moment of polydoxies, unsteady or suspicious narratives, many narratives, post truths, false facts, and many other epistemological challenges. Yet humans continue to be a symbolic species, forming and re-forming symbols and worldviews. The question remains: Where, after the metanarratives, can legitimacy reside? (Lyotard [1979] 1984).

Some Reflections Moving Forward

Ecological success and viability for our society will depend, at least in part, on the generation of a powerful ecological imaginary to challenge the governing utilitarian and exploitative social imaginary, or dominant worldview. The claim, as some suggest, is that decisive moments in social transformation require the development of a counter-imaginary. The counter-imaginary for our moment is an ecological imaginary.

Carolyn Merchant has offered us a great deal with *TDN*. Her methods included exposure, analysis, critique, and deconstruction. Nonetheless, her goals were constructive social transformation. She seeks a viable ecological future with social equalities. *TDN* launched trajectories of inquiry and insight that have journeyed far—and returned with newfound treasures to share.

There are no simple answers to the question: What are the drivers of social change? Some people focus on myriad historical aspects, similar to Merchant. Others address specific ideologies, colonial legacies, economics, religions, and the countless specificities, policies, and practices within each. Social theorists continue to work with notions of power and identity and underscore the cultural constructions of identity as well as their mutability. Others see social transformation bound up with views of the self: a fluid composite of hybrid-embodied identities, interwoven with somatic memories and affect, within a fusion of tactility, movement, and emotions. Identities are steadied in embodied narratives providing coherence and intelligibility. This explains why new ideas or narratives, with no sensory experiences, often *feel* foreign, unfamiliar, and wrong. It also can explain the personal and social resistance to worldview transformations.

TDN was involved in uncovering bias, ideologies, and the limits of Euro-Western science. Merchant gave licence to scathing critiques of the formulations of, and cultural adaptations to, histories. Her work supported further research into the intersecting modes of domination. I believe her main motivation and preoccupation was to extricate the present from the past, so that the present can follow new paths, which are based on learning from those critiques of the past and new insights from the present. A further goal was to advance visions that are compelling, alluring, and constructive for a way forward. Carolyn Merchant's contributions have been outstanding, beginning with *The Death of Nature*, which launched new, fresh insights, with potential and promise.

Notes

1 See also Susan Griffin's Foreword in this volume.
2 The Social Citation Index lists 360 citations of the book from 1980 to 1996, with the number of citations increasing over these years (Forbes and Jermier 1998). In the same issue of *Organization and Environment*, see a lengthy discussion about the book's positive reception and a list of reviews (Merchant 1998).
3 This is a key complaint against Merchant, and presented in some depth in Brian Vickers. "Francis Bacon, Feminist Historiography, and the Dominion of Nature." 69, (1), 2008, pp. 117–145.
4 Park explains many of the issues with the book from the perspective of historians of science and why they mistrust and rarely cite, this book. Park also defends the innovative method Merchant employs, as well as some key insights.
5 *The Journey of the Universe* project represents a film, with additional commentaries from leading scientists, a book, an educational series and an informative web site. See http://journeyoftheuniverse.com.
6 There are countless books on ecofeminism, women and environment, and/or gender and ecology. See Heather Eaton and Lois Ann Lorentzen, "Ecofeminism: An Overview," The Forum on Religion and Ecology. http://fore.yale.edu/disciplines/gender/. For a bibliography see *The Forum on Religion and Ecology*, http://fore.yale.edu/files/Gender_Bibliography_Oct2014.pdf: See entries in *Encyclopedia Britannica, Stanford Encyclopedia of Philosophy, Encyclopedia of Political Thought, International Encyclopedia of Ethics,* and other reference texts including *Wikipedia* https://en.wikipedia.org/wiki/Ecofeminism as well as many books, articles, online sites.
7 Of course, this as also launched by Lynn White in "The Historical Roots of Our Ecologic Crisis," in *Science* (White 1967).
8 For a list of publications on Worldview, see David Naugle's web page: http://www.leaderu.com/philosophy/worldviewbibliography.html. Others depict the varieties, and the current disintegration, of stable worldviews as discussed in *Worldview Flux: Perplexed Values for Postmodern Peoples* (Norwine and Smith 2000).
9 *The Worldviews Group* consists of Diederik Aerts (theoretical physics), Bart De Moor (engineering sciences), Staf Hellemans (sociology), Hubert Van Belle (engineering sciences) and Jan Van der Veken (philosophy). Their web site lists some of their publications: www.vub.ac.be/CLEA/dissemination/groups-archive/vzw_worldviews/ They also publish in other fora on aspects of worldviews.
10 The journal *Worldviews: Global Religions, Culture, and Ecology* covers most of these topics. See www.brill.com/worldviews-global-religions-culture-and-ecology

Bibliography

Aerts, Diederik. www.vub.ac.be/CLEA/dissemination/groups-archive/vzw_worldviews/ Accessed Nov. 6, 2017.

Bennett, Jane. 2010. *Vibrant Matter: A Political Ecology of Things.* Durham, NC: Duke University Press.

Boesel, Chris and Catherine Keller. 2009. *Apophatic Bodies: Theology, Incarnation, and Relationality.* New York, NY: Fordham University Press.

Bookchin, Murray. 1982. *The Ecology of Freedom: The Emergence and Dissolution of Hierarchy.* Palo Alto, CA: Cheshire Books.

Castoriadis, Cornelius. 1987. *The Imaginary Institution of Society*, translated by Kathleen Blamey. Cambridge, MA: MIT Press.

Cummings Neville, Robert. 2009. "Worldviews." *American Journal of Theology and Philosophy*, 30(3):233.

Daly, Mary. 1978. *Gyn/Ecology: The Metaphysics of Radical Feminism*. The Women's Press: London.

Dupré, Louis. 1993. *Passage to Modernity: An Essay in the Hermeneutics of Nature and Culture*. New Haven, CT: Yale University Press.

Eaton, Heather. 2011. "An Ecological Imaginary: Evolution and Religion in an Ecological Era." Pp. 7–23 in *Ecological Awareness: Exploring Religion, Ethics and Aesthetics*, edited by Sigurd Bergmann and Heather Eaton. Berlin: LIT Press.

Eaton, Heather. 2017. "The Challenges of Worldview Transformation: To Rethink and Refeel Our Origins and Destiny." Pp. 121–137 in *Religion and Ecological Crisis*, edited by Todd LeVasseur and Anna Peterson. New York: Routledge.

Eaton, Heather and Lois Ann Lorentzen. "Ecofeminism: An Overview." *The Forum on Religion and Ecology*. http://fore.yale.edu/disciplines/gender/ and http://fore.yale.edu/files/Gender_Bibliography_Oct2014.pdf. Accessed Nov. 6, 2017.

Eckersley, Robin. 1998. "The Death of Nature and the Birth of the Ecological Humanities." *Organization & Environment* 11(2):183–185.

Forbes, Linda and John Jermier. 1998. "Language, Organization, and Environment: An Introduction to the Symposium on *The Death of Nature*." *Organization & Environment* 11 (2):180–182.

Griffin, Susan. 1978. *Woman and Nature: The Roaring Inside Her*. London: The Women's Press.

Harding, Sandra. 1980. "The Norms of Social Inquiry and Masculine Experience." *Proceedings of the Biennial Meeting of the Philosophy of Science Association* 2:305–324.

Iddo, Landau. 1998. "Feminist Criticisms of Metaphors in Bacon's Philosophy of Science." *Philosophy* 73: 47–61.

Leiss, William. 1972. *The Domination of Nature*. New York: G. Braziller.

Lerner, Gerda. 1987. *The Creation of Patriarchy*. Oxford: Oxford University Press.

Lovelock, James. 1979. *Gaia: A New Look at Life on Earth*. Oxford: Oxford University Press.

Lyotard, Jean Francois. ([1979] 1984). *The Postmodern Condition: A Report on Knowledge*, translated by Geoffrey Bennington and Brian Massumi. Minnesota: The University of Minnesota Press.

Margulis, Lynn. 1998. *The Symbiotic Planet: A New Look at Evolution*. New York: Basic Books.

Merchant, Carolyn. 1980. *The Death of Nature: Women Ecology and the Scientific Revolution*. New York: Harper & Row.

Merchant, Carolyn. 1998. "*The Death of Nature*: A Retrospective." *Organization & Environment* 11(2):198–206.

Merchant, Carolyn. 2006. "The Scientific Revolution and The Death of Nature." *Isis* 97 (3):513–533.

Naugle, David. www.leaderu.com/philosophy/worldviewbibliography.html. Accessed Nov. 6, 2017.

Norwine, Jom and Jonathan M. Smith. 2000. *Worldview Flux: Perplexed Values for Postmodern Peoples*. Lanham, MD: Lexington Books.

Oppermann, Serpil and Serenella Iovino. 2017. *Environmental Humanities: Voices From the Anthropocene*. London: Rowman & Littlefield.

Park, Katharine. 2006. "Women, Gender, and Utopia: *The Death of Nature* and the Historiography of Early Modern Science." *Isis* 97(3):487–495.

Pesic, Peter. 1999. "Wrestling with Proteus: Francis Bacon and the 'Torture' of Nature." *Isis* 90(1):81–94.

Plumwood, val. 1993. *Feminism and the Mastery of Nature*. London: Routledge, 1994.

Ponting, Clive. 1991. *A Green History of the World: The Environment and the Collapse of Great Civilizations*. London: Sinclair-Stevenson.

Ruether, Rosemary Radford. 1975. *New Woman, New Earth*. Minneapolis: Seabury Press.

Ruether, Rosemary Radford. 1993. *Gaia and God: An Ecofeminist Theology of Earth Healing*. San Francisco, CA: Harper.

Soble, Alan. 1995. "In Defense of Bacon." *Philosophy of the Social Sciences* 25:192–215.

Taylor, Charles. 2004. *Modern Social Imaginaries*. Durham, NC: Duke University Press.

Vernadsky, Vladamir. [1926] 1997. *The Biosphere*. Edited by Mark McMenamin. Translated by David Langmuir. New York: Springer.

Vickers, Brian. 2008. "Francis Bacon, Feminist Historiography, and the Dominion of Nature." *Journal of the History of Ideas* 69(1):117–141.

Warren, Karen. 1998. "The Legacy of Carolyn Merchant's *The Death of Nature*." *Organization & Environment* 11(2):186–188.

White, Lynn. 1967. "The Historical Roots of Our Ecologic Crisis." *Science* 155 (3767):1203–1207.

Wilson, E.O. 1984. *Biophilia*. Cambridge, MA: Harvard University Press.

Worldviews: Global Religions, Culture, and Ecology. www.brill.com/worldviews-global-religions-culture-and-ecology. Accessed Nov. 6, 2017.

4

FROM A PARTNERSHIP TO A FIDELITY ETHIC

Framing an Old Story for a New Time

Norman Wirzba

In *Reinventing Eden: The Fate of Nature in Western Culture*, Carolyn Merchant took us on a grand tour of the roles the biblical Garden of Eden story has played in the imaginations and histories of Western culture. She shows us how the memory of Eden as the attainment of paradise has been used to underwrite the exploration and domination of nature (and women, and racial minorities, and indigenous peoples).[1] Given this story's problematic and often violent influence, and its tendency to work within oppositional polarities (like nature and culture, male and female, self and other), she suggests that we need a new story to make sense of humanity's place on earth, because without a new story it will be hard to secure the new ethic—Merchant's *partnership ethic*—we need to live responsibly with others. Put succinctly, "'mastering' nature to reclaim Eden has nearly destroyed the very nature people have tried to reclaim" (Merchant 2004:3). Though Eden has sometimes inspired people to live more harmoniously with human and nonhuman others, the dominant attempts to create paradise have resulted in communities and places that are saturated with wounds and punctuated with degradation.

It isn't simply that people are wayward or have "fallen" out of right relationship. The world itself, in its fragmentation, antagonism, and pain, bears witness to the effects of a mythic Fall. Moreover, when people have enlisted the story of Eden to recover or renew Paradise—as when in modernity they wedded a religious salvation narrative with the tools of science, technology, and capitalism to create a better world—they have often exacerbated the damage done to others and their places. This suggests that the story of Eden is itself "fallen," having outlived its usefulness. Understandably, Merchant asks, "Do not the earth and its people need a new story?" (Merchant 2004:3).

Stories matter because they help us make sense of *who we are*: are we heroes, villains, farmers, shoppers, good, bad, whole, and/or broken? They also tell us *where we are*: are we in wilderness (however that is understood), on a stage, in a store, on sacred ground, in a city (however that is configured)? And they tell us *what to do*—should we farm, shop, drop out, watch, create, receive, pray, play?—and *to what end or purpose?*—is it all for fleeting pleasures, an eternal reward, and/or simply to pass the time? Stories, in other words, give narrative expression and dramatic form to the basic dispositions and assumptions that guide our living. Stories communicate the ethos that inspires and helps us find our bearing in life. They help us determine the meaning and significance of things, and they help us perceive what matters, which is why stories play an invaluable role in moral formation and the clarification of values. Depending on the stories we tell, we will form people to strive, expect, and desire in particular sorts of ways. Which is why it makes good sense to say that a new ethic will require a change in the stories people live by. "Enacting a partnership ethic entails creating a new narrative or set of narratives about the human place in history and nature" (Merchant 2004:240).

In this chapter, I will argue that the Garden of Eden story has not outlived its usefulness. It can be retold in such a way as to give valuable insight to the partnership ethic Merchant desires. But first we need to attend to how the characters and elements of this story have come to be framed and understood. As this chapter will show, what people mean by terms like "nature" or "world," and how they think of their action and place in the world, can vary dramatically depending on the historical period and geophysical context they find themselves in. Drawing on the recent work of historians and anthropologists, especially that of Timothy Ingold, I will argue that crucial shifts in sensibility occurred in late medieval/early modern times that cast the story of Eden in a new and distorting light. We now live in a culture that is shaped decisively by a philosophical story long in the making that enshrines separation and distance and that opens up practices of domination that are new to the history of humanity. This philosophical story, along with the dualist metaphysic and epistemology it endorses, has been the dominant story for a long time, and has made it very difficult to read the Garden of Eden in ways that do not endorse dominion. When we attend to this biblical story in terms of its agrarian context, and when we appreciate its larger theological vision, we discover that Eden presents a compelling picture of human identity and vocation, a picture that can be of great help to us today as we try to develop an ethic—what I will call a *fidelity ethic*—that heals human relationships with the earth and with each other.

Narrating Places—What's Wrong With "Environment"?

Stories presuppose a place where the action happens. What a place "is," and what we think of its character are hardly obvious. Places can be named and narrated in a variety of ways. The term "environment," for instance, evokes a world that is outside of us and in which we move: it is the air, water, and land (and their many creatures) that are above, around, and beneath us. When asked, most will say environments are important because they depend on them to breathe, drink, eat, and fuel their ambition. Environments contain the stuff of life, which is why we go *into* them so that we can *draw out* what we need.

I find this to be an unhelpful way of speaking because, in and of itself, the word "environment" fails to specify the meaning and significance of the things "outside." It doesn't tell us enough about the philosophical, even religious, character of the world, and by failing to do that, it doesn't give people a moral or spiritual orientation either. If I say I live in an environment I have said very little that would help me know whether the place matters (and how) or whether I am living well or poorly where I am.

It is important to underscore that the way people act is a feature of *where* and *who* they think they are. If I believe myself to be a cook in a kitchen, then the appropriate thing for me to do is to bake and prepare food. But if I believe myself to be a teacher in a classroom, then I had better get on with the task of teaching students. How we think about a place, who we think a person to be, what we understand agency to be about—these are crucial elements that demand clarity if our goal is to have an ethic that helps us to live more cooperatively, responsibly, even beautifully, in the world and with each other.

Because the term environment does not tell us much about meaning or significance there is little within its grammar that would prevent us from characterizing the world as basically one big warehouse, store, or shopping mall that we enter to get the things we need. According to this narration there is nothing sacred about the world. The things we meet are more or less reducible to commodities that people engage via the various modes of shopping, and the actors within this narration are basically shoppers who move through the world surveying, inspecting, purchasing, and enjoying the things they freely choose. If we don't find our current place appealing we can simply move to another place much like we visit another store.

In *The Death of Nature: Women, Ecology and the Scientific Revolution* Merchant gave a powerful account of how the modern transformation of nature into a vast assemblage of mechanisms prepared the way for the commodification of the world, what the philosopher Martin Heidegger famously called the reduction of things to a "standing reserve" (Heidegger 1953). Merchant argues that, "Because nature was now viewed as a system of dead, inert particles moved by external, rather than inherent forces, the mechanical framework itself could legitimate the manipulation of nature" (Merchant 1980:193). This picture of the world as mechanism turns out to be an ideal context in which a shopping, consumerist narration of life can emerge: "as a conceptual framework, the mechanical order had associated with it a framework of values based on power, fully compatible with the directions taken by commercial capitalism" (Merchant 1980:193). This grand story that consigns nature to a stockpile or store of commodities waiting to be purchased by us was new to the history of humanity. It was hardly inevitable. It had to be argued for and promoted. Given its depleting and destructive legacy, it clearly needs supplanting. We should ask: Can the story of the Garden of Eden be properly heard in this mechanical, mercantile context?

Besides being unhelpful for determining the value of things and places, the more fundamental problem with the language of environment is that it is also a distorting way of speaking that misrepresents our being-in-the-world. The distortion I am talking about is deep. It will take some time to clarify.

Searching for a Better Story's Setting

It is telling that for some people the birth of an environmental sensibility coincided with humanity's flight into space. Views of the entire globe captured from the vantage point of barren space helped many people see something of the earth's beauty and its fragility. This new and distant global position gave them the perspective they needed to advocate for Earth's protection. What we need to appreciate, however, is that it is precisely the epistemological position of separation and distance that gets in the way of a more honest understanding of our place in the world.

In a number of essays gathered in *The Perception of the Environment* and *Being Alive* the Scottish anthropologist (and scholar of indigenous traditions) Tim Ingold has argued how distance and detachment—often carried out in the name of scientific objectivity—are the primary forms of distortion that falsify our being-in-the-world. Modern science has certainly exacerbated this tendency, but its roots go back far into our ancient past, as when philosophers like Aristotle argued that the world consists of things (proper and common nouns) that are (either primary and secondary) substances.[2] A substance is a thing that is what it is by not being something else. In other words, Aristotle gave us a metaphysical picture of the world that is comprised of things that in their most fundamental nature or essence stand apart and are self-standing. Things may enter into relationship with other things, but relationality comes after. If people want to know what something is, it needs to be classified as separate from something else. Hence the vision of knowledge as a classificatory scheme that isolates things into categories like class, species, and genus.

The fundamental error in this position is that it presumes the identity of things, indeed their essence and their life, to reside *within* things. This is a mistake. No thing lives from out of itself or in terms of itself. The proof of this is that living things breathe, drink, eat, build, recline, grow, procreate, die (to name just a few of the things they do)—all of which presuppose a tight and inextricable involvement with countless others. Things are not merely *in* relation. They *are* their relations. If this is true then the "forms" of things, that which allows us to identify them, do not pre-exist the relationships and movements that give rise to them.[3] What beings *are* is a feature of the relational becomings that involve them with others. To understand what a human being is therefore requires that we attend to what such a being *does*, what it *gives* and *receives*. Life is not a static thing, but a dynamic movement that is accomplished in the interactions we have with myriads of (seen and unseen) others.

People tend to be confused about this because they are caught within what Ingold calls a "logic of inversion." According to this logic, movement and design in the world are the outward effect of an internal intention of some sort. These internal intentions reflect mental schemata that have developed as a result of an internal mind (or soul) appropriating cultural models (think here of Clifford Geertz who once said that culture is "the imposition of an arbitrary framework of symbolic meaning upon reality" [Geertz 1964:39]). Symbolic meaning is not in the world, but is instead imposed upon a world by a meaning-giving mind. The problem with this way of characterizing things is that it assumes a being enclosed within itself. "By way of inversion beings originally open to the world are closed in upon themselves, sealed by an outer boundary or shell that protects their inner constitution from the traffic of interactions with their surroundings" (Ingold 2011:68). We have never been enclosed within ourselves. This is true before we are born (as our belly buttons bear witness), while we are alive (as our bodies play host to billions of microbes), and after we die (as we become food for others).

The confusion about identity can also be described as a basic distortion in the ways we think about life. If we return to ancient Greek philosophy again, turning especially to the two thinkers who have exercised an extraordinary influence on the development of Western culture, we see the wide assumption that life is the power of movement within things. For Plato it was the power of a soul that, like a hand in a glove, animated a body *from within* to make the various movements in the world that it does. For Aristotle, though having rejected his teacher Plato's account of a pre-existing, immaterial soul descending into and inhabiting a body, life too was understood to be a power or *entelechy* operating within a body enabling it to exercise the movements of growth, reproduction, locomotion, and thought. For both, the life that happens in the world is not really "in" the world because the power of life is first enclosed within beings that then exist alongside others in places that act as their container.[4]

The French phenomenologist Maurice Merleau-Ponty once argued that it is not possible to be a sentient, living being in an insentient, dead world. Once we take seriously that a human being does not *have* a body (that is controlled from inside) but *is* a body, and once we recognize how bodies are necessarily stitched into a world of countless other bodies, then it becomes apparent that our activity and movement—our aliveness—are also the world's activity and movement in and through us. To be sentient, says Ingold,

> is to open up to a world, to yield to its embrace, and to resonate in one's inner being to its illuminations and reverberations. Bathed in light, submerged in sound and rapt in feeling, the sentient body, at once both perceiver and producer, traces the paths of the world's becoming in the very course of contributing to its own renewal.
>
> *(Ingold 2011:12)*

Or as he put it in an earlier essay:

> life is not a principle that is separately installed inside individual organisms ... life is a name for *what is going on* in the generative field within which organic forms are located and "held in place." That generative field is constituted by the totality of organism–environment relations, and the activities of organisms are moments of its unfolding. Indeed once we think of the world in this way, as a total movement of becoming which builds itself into the forms we see, and in which each form takes shape in continuous relation to those around it, then the distinction between the animate and inanimate seems to dissolve.
>
> *(Ingold 2000:200)*

This discussion about the identity and life of beings has profound implications for the way we think about our being-in-the-world. We are not self-enclosed things that enter into a container or onto a stage that consists of other self-enclosed things that we then engage in various ways. Nor is the world a surface that consists of many movable bits. We are sometimes tempted to think of the world as apart from us, separate and more-or-less distant, because we have privileged sight as the primary sense faculty. But when we appreciate that touch is the most fundamental sensory capacity, and acknowledge how taste is crucial for the maintenance of life, then it becomes apparent that we are not first and foremost spectators looking into or onto a world, but rather participants always already within it. Indeed, without our constant, ongoing bodily participation in the movements of others, something like the observation of them would scarcely be possible.[5]

To help us understand the world and our involvement in it, Ingold proposes that we think of places as a "meshwork." He rejects the image of a "network," though recently made popular by writers like Bruno Latour, because it does not quite capture the depth and dynamism of our entanglements with others. A network still presupposes a world that consists of heterogenous bits and pieces of things that then become assembled in various ways. Ingold argues that we should move away from this imagery because it keeps us trapped in an atomistic world consisting of innumerable self-standing points. A more accurate characterization of the world is to describe it as a tangle of threads and pathways along which organisms move. To be-in-the-world is not to occupy a container or stage, nor is it simply to come alongside others from time to time. It is, rather, to be a "wayfarer," constantly receiving from and giving to others as together we move along various lines of development. Ingold summarizes his position in the following:

> My contention is that lives are not led inside places but through, around, to and from them, from and to places elsewhere. I use the term *wayfaring* to describe the embodied experience of this perambulatory movement. It is as

wayfarers, then, that humans inhabit the earth ... human existence is not fundamentally place-*bound* ... but place-*binding*. It unfolds not in places but along paths. Proceeding along a path, every inhabitant lays a trail. Where inhabitants meet, trails are entwined, as the life of each becomes bound up with the other. Every entwining is a knot, and the more that lifelines are entwined, the greater the density of the knot. Places, then, are like knots, and the threads from which they are tied are lines of wayfaring.

(Ingold 2011:148–149)

We can now see how misleading a term such as "environment" is, especially if we characterize it as the collection of things that "surround" us. The places that make our life possible are *sites of entanglement* in which each and every thing is always already interacting and exchanging with others. That means each place is forever unfinished because it is always open to further development and becoming. Indeed, it *is* this development. People do not ever enter into this becoming from outside, nor do we have the option of exiting it. We are always already within it, moving along geophysical, biochemical, social-cultural lines of development. "There are human becomings, animal becomings, plant becomings, and so on. As they move together through time and encounter one another, these paths interweave to form an immense and continually evolving tapestry" (Ingold 2011:9).

This way of thinking about the human place in the world is not new. It is very old, and widely assumed by many traditional and indigenous societies, including the agrarian societies of scripture. Numerous historians and anthropologists, for instance, have described the ways in which various indigenous peoples have understood (and still believe) themselves to move within a moral community that includes rocks, trees, streams, plants, and human and non-human animals like ravens and deer and bison. They have believed their world to be

a cosmos that is alive, sentient, empowered and moral. This animated, enchanted view of the universe as inhabited by a community of beings constantly in communication and exchange with human beings underlies processes of *interanimation* that define and enliven people in places and places in people.

(Thornton 2007:4)

The names of things in the world, rather than serving to distinguish them from other things or, as was the case with Western explorers, serving to reflect the explorer's vanity (as when rivers or mountains were named after the person who "found" them), made clear the relationships and the history of involvements that existed between people and the thing named. These are languages that are dominated by verbs rather than nouns because verb phrases have a better capacity "to define the environment in terms of its actions, motion, and processes" (Thornton 2007:81).[6]

In his magisterial account of the development of the nature/culture dichotomy in *Beyond Nature and Culture*, the French anthropologist Philippe Descola argues convincingly that the idea of a natural world apart from human beings and subject to its own autonomous laws is a distinctly modern idea. Though indigenous peoples made distinctions between kinds of creatures, these distinctions did not represent an ontological divide. Instead, distinctions rested upon differing forms of behavior. The crucial presupposition was that the world of diverse beings constituted a vast continuum of interconnectedness that is governed by complex regimes of sociability, all held together by forces of vitality, energy, nurture, and fecundity. One's place or position along the continuum depended on the nature of the relationships that bound entities to each other.

Habits of thought that developed in modernity that posit an ontological divide between humans and nature reflect a rupture in this more ancient sensibility. Following Merleau-Ponty, Descola argues that it was not modern science that facilitated the idea that nature is a separable, autonomous realm, but rather the other way around: a new way of thinking about the world made possible the new science. As one example of this changing sensibility Descola describes the 15th century development of an homogenous, linear perspective. How the world came to be perceived depended on the placing of things on axes that are established by the observer:

> a subjective impression serves as the starting point for the rationalization of a world of experience … . Such an "objectification of the subjective" produces a twofold effect: it creates a distance between man and the world by making the autonomy of things depend upon man; and it systematizes and stabilizes the external universe even as it confers upon the subject absolute mastery over the organization of this newly conquered exteriority.
>
> *(Descola 2013:59–60)*

This new linear, mathematical (and masculine?) perspective that began in the realm of painting would eventually be applied to physics and the sciences more generally. The end result? The world could now be neatly divided into things governed by natural laws *and* the thinking that does the governing. The former is the realm of nature and the latter is the realm of culture. This distinction would eventually in the 19th century be enshrined and enforced in the very structures of higher education that distinguished *Kulturwissenshaft* and *Naturwissenschaft*, and a university curriculum that separated knowledge into the social and natural sciences.

Much more can and needs to be said to nuance a story that has here been greatly simplified. For instance, the work of Bruno Latour is important to mention in this regard because the nature/culture dualism as so far described, though perhaps a philosophical ideal, and perhaps a deep human desire,[7] has *in practice* been much more difficult to sustain. The regimes of knowledge production and the practices of technology, agriculture, and medicine demonstrate that we have never really been modern. As should be expected, the moment one takes embodiment seriously, the worlds of nature and culture constantly intermingle (Latour 1993).

Even so, this more recent story needs to be understood as we attempt to address the many degraded ecosystems and communities that constitute our planet. The modern desire to separate humanity from earth (as though people are somehow exempt from geo-eco-chemical-biophysical processes), and the dream of mastery over the realms of nature and the structures of life that has followed from this separation (as though people could engineer their way to a new paradise), are bringing us to the point that many now describe as an eco-apocalypse. It is not simply that people have adopted forms of behaviour that are now clearly perceived to be destructive. The problem goes much deeper to the levels of metaphysics and epistemology, where the drive to separate and isolate finds its root. What has become plain is that scientific facts and big data are not enough to see us through. These we have in greater abundance than humanity has ever known. The problem with isolated facts is that they do not make clear our dependence upon and involvement with the things supposedly known. And without a felt sensitivity for our relationships to things it is hard to see how people will muster the love that will be necessary to care for those we depend upon.

Moving forward we are going to need to find ways to be instructed in a new sensibility that fosters a deep and detailed appreciation for the countless ways in which humanity is entangled in the movements and lives of countless others. This sensibility will be the basis for cultivating the dispositions and skills that will equip people to exercise appropriate care. This new sensibility depends on the telling of new stories, or perhaps the fresh hearing of old stories, stories that give us a different philosophical picture and narration of the world.

To summarize: in addition to the Garden of Eden story, there is a deep set of metaphysical and epistemological commitments that have fueled modern stories of technological mastery and control. These grand philosophical stories, along with the institutions they have inspired, have made it very difficult to hear the Eden story in anything but dominating ways. As philosophical commitments to separation, dissection, and recombination have taken hold in the various domains of education, urbanization, economics, labor, engineering, design, politics, and religion (to name a few), it has become much more difficult to hear, let alone appreciate, narratives that bear witness to humanity's complex and deep entanglement with others. Traditional and indigenous people who speak of land, plants, and (human and nonhuman) animals as one vast moral community are considered primitive. Individuals like St. Francis of Assisi, who speak of fellow creatures as sisters and brothers, have too often been dismissed as kooks.[8]

Retelling an Old Story

How should we move forward? We should start by making clear that technological, industrial cultures operate out of a philosophical story that presumes separation and desires mastery. This story, worked out in the many dimensions of our current life, is not "objective" or innocent. As Merchant's work so clearly shows, it has been creatively imagined, richly supported, and widely deployed. It is also deeply alienating, fragmenting, and destructive. It needs to be challenged and replaced.

For the remainder of this chapter I will argue that the Garden of Eden story, when read and retold in a new/old light, can play a powerful role in developing the ethic we need in a time of ecological degradation. To recover this story, however, means that we must reposition it in its agrarian context, and then also recognize that its modern re-tellings have often violated its meaning.[9] At its root, this is a story that binds creatures to each other and to their creator and sustainer. But to appreciate this we need to highlight some of its crucial elements.

We can begin with how the first human being is narrated. Adam is not a self-standing being who acts upon the world. Instead, this person is the ground itself animated by the divine breath of life to become the creature that it is. As the Hebrew noun *adam* communicates directly, there is no human life apart from its origin in, perpetual dependence upon, and eventual (upon death) destination into *adamah*, the Hebrew term for soil. Moreover, this human creature shares with all plants and animals this same bond with the earth. Altogether they are soil animated by the breath of God. Human life is not lived in separation from others. To live well and to live intelligently, people must learn the skills that draw them more deeply into life with others and then develop the affections that enable people to care for the creatures they live with and alongside. "The Lord God took the man and put him in the garden of Eden to till it and keep it" (Genesis 2:15). This is not a story of domination or exploitation, but rather one of service and attunement to others.

The Garden of Eden story does not underwrite the distance from and separation between human beings and their worlds. It is, instead, a story of human entanglements with the land, its diverse creaturely life, and with God. Human identity is shaped by the soil and human vocation is directed toward the care of its creatures. It is also a foundational story in the sense that it sets the stage for Israel as a nation called to live in a land according to the requirements of justice and *shalom*. As is clear, Israelites often fail in their responsibilities. But what is also clear is that their responsibilities were not restricted to human beings. Faithfulness to God required of them that they seek the flourishing of the land and its creatures. The prophet Hosea put it plainly: God indicts Israel for the faithlessness and injustice that leads to a land that mourns and creatures that languish (4:1–3).

Following Ingold, we might say the earthling named *adam* must learn to wayfare with other creatures, must move deeply into the garden meshwork, and then commit to making this place its home by knotting itself to the life-lines of other creatures. In this work, Adam's inspiration is none other than the gardening God who loves soil, comes so near to it as to kiss it and breathe into it divine, creating, nurturing, and sustaining life. The God who creates the world and all its creatures, the God in whose image human beings are made, is not ever distant from soil or rain or creatures. Instead, this is a God who constantly faces creation (Psalm 104), enters into covenant relationship with all creatures (Genesis 9), and promises to heal the life that becomes ill, befriend the creatures that become lonely, nurture the ones who are hungry, and reconcile those who are at odds with or alienated from each other (Colossians 1). This is a creating God who does not ever want to be separated from creation, which is why scripture ends not with human beings escaping Earth to enter some faraway, ethereal heaven, but with God descending to earth to live with mortal creatures forever (Revelation 21).

This brief narrative of God's desire to be with creatures rather than apart from them, a narrative that is worked out in rich and various detail throughout scripture (and then also in subsequent theological writing), shows that it is a great error to assume that scripture endorses a transcendent God who is distant from the world. Though it may well be true that Christians have at varying times spoken of God's transcendence as God's distance from the world (Merchant speaks this way when she writes: "The intellectual construction of a transcendent God is yet another point in a narrative of decline. The separation of God from nature legitimates humanity's separation from nature and sets up the possibility of human domination and control over nature" [Merchant 2004:29]), this way of speaking demonstrates the power of the philosophical story I have described to distort our thinking about God in profound ways. God is transcendent, but not in the sense of distance. God's transcendence is a feature of God's reality being of a fundamentally different kind than creaturely reality. And because God's reality is unlike finite, creaturely reality, that means God can be present to and immanent within every creature as its creating and sustaining power. God does not exist in a competitive or coercive relationship with creatures. As some theologians (like John of Damascus) argued, the best way to make sense of God's creative activity is to describe it as an act of hospitality: God "makes room" for what is not God "to be," and then commits to nurture it into the fullness of its life. When this is understood then it is also apparent that accounts of creation *ex nihilo* that describe God as dominating creatures are fundamentally confused.[10]

There is much more that can be said about the Garden of Eden story and its value for our time. But enough has been told to demonstrate that rather than licensing mastery over others, this story is more properly understood as an invitation to enter into caring and faithful life with others. The famous "fall" of humanity in Genesis 3 is not simply a fall out of life with God. It is a refusal of creatureliness and an unwillingness to accept one's responsibility for the care of each other and the whole created world.[11] When the Eden story is developed alongside other stories of scripture, it can serve as the foundation for what I call a *fidelity* ethic, an ethic that acknowledges from the beginning that human life is possible and only makes sense in terms of relations with a bewildering array of creatures and places, and that the primary question is whether or not we are *loving* toward the lives on which we depend.

I prefer the term "fidelity" over Merchant's choice of "partnership" because it is too easy for a term like partnership to operate within the dividing, separating metaphysic that I have identified as a central problem for our time. It is worth noting that a dominant arena in which the language of partnerships is used is the world of commerce, a world in which the relationships that bind business people together are, for the most part, optional and susceptible to being broken at a given time. If the characterization of life that I have given is at all correct and true to the ways embodied life moves, then our relationships with each other are never optional. They are constitutive and indispensible. We are necessarily knotted to each other, working out our lives as we travel along paths with other creatures. The question is not whether we will choose to enter into relationship with others but whether we will be *faithful* to those with whom we are always already in relationship. In other words, the term fidelity does a better job communicating that we do not ever choose to be in relationship. To "be" is to "be in relation." The only question we get to decide is *how* we will be in relation.

Speaking this way does not put me in disagreement with many of the aspirations and emphases that inform Merchant's partnership ethic. I support her precepts that there should be:

1. Equity (in some sense) between human and nonhuman communities;
2. Moral consideration for both human and other species;
3. Respect for cultural and biological diversity;
4. Inclusion of women, minorities, and nonhumans in ethical codes of accountability; and
5. Ecologically-informed management that seeks the health of human and nonhuman communities (Merchant 2004:224).

Her emphases on mutual interdependence and obligation, her desire to see all species represented at the tables of deliberation, and her hope that we will leave patterns of domination and hierarchy behind are all important goals that we must rally behind. If I have proposed that we speak in terms of a fidelity rather than a partnership ethic, it is because I think that the most fundamental task moving forward is to challenge the metaphysical picture and the epistemological stance that keeps us separate and in an oppositional frame of mind. This philosophical story has been the dominant story of our time, and it has shaped (and distorted) our hearing of other stories, even the story of the Garden of Eden, that we need to hear.

To ask if we are faithful to each other, to other creatures, and to this earth is already to have acknowledged, even if only implicitly, that we cannot live, let alone live well, without them. We only ever live because we move through a meshwork. This is something the language of partnership does not do because it presumes actors who are more or less self-standing who then choose (for whatever reason) to enter into relationship with others. To participate in the healing of the earth and its diverse communities is going to require of us a deeper, felt appreciation for the character of life as always *life together*. It is going to require of us an affective sensibility in which we understand that we have no life apart from the health and flourishing of land and other creaturely life.

Being in relation with others is not optional or occasional. It is necessary, inescapable, embodied, and far-reaching. A fidelity ethic offers us an invitation to develop the skill and sympathy, and discover the pain and the joy that a faithful life entails. Sometimes partnership, as when we come alongside and work with others, will be the appropriate response. But at other times, the better response will be to listen and learn, attend and defend, or simply get out of the way. The ways of fidelity are varied. To learn them we will need first to overcome the delusion that we could ever live alone or apart.

Notes

1 In *The Fall of Man and the Foundations of Science* (Harrison 2007) Peter Harrison gives further account of the development of modern science as an effort to recover pre-fallen Adam's knowledge of the world. Eden as paradise signaled not only as a place, but also as a way of knowing that encouraged scientific pursuits now configured in a particular sort of way. Rather than being in conflict with religion, Harrison shows how modern science built upon a theological understanding of the world.

2 Kenneth Worthy (2013) has made a similar argument in this book and in *Invisible Nature: Healing the Destructive Divide Between People and the Environment*.

3 Ingold is clear that his account calls into question the neo-Darwinian paradigm that describes evolution as the mutation, recombination, replication, and selection of transmissible genes (or memes) that are interior to things, giving them their identity. This paradigm assumes that genes are "carriers of received information" that then "order and arrange the formless, 'plasmic' material of the environment in the actualization of the phenotypic product ... the fallacy of this way of thinking lies in supposing the form miraculously precedes the processes that give rise to it ... the way to overcome the fallacy is simply to reverse the order, so as to give primacy to the process of ontogenesis—to the fluxes and flows of materials entailed in making and growing—over the forms that arise within them. Though the solution may be simple, however, the implications are profound" (Ingold 2013: 7). When it is understood that the life and identity of beings is not internal to them but is instead constantly being realized in the relationships that nurture, instruct, inspire, and receive them, then it is also clear that the transhumanist dream of personal immortality as the upload and transference of the self as a discrete information pattern is profoundly misguided.

4 It is important to note that as Christians thought about persons and the world they found this ancient Greek metaphysical account, and the substance ontology it supported, inadequate. If the world is God's creation, and God is a relational, triune being (three persons, but one being or essence), then relationality is at the heart of all reality constituting all life and movement. People are not atomistic individuals but creatures living in interdependent relation with other creatures and with God. See John Zizioulas' *Being as Communion* for an account that describes this new relational ontology (Zizioulas 1997).

5 For a multi-faceted examination of how embodied touch changes the way we interpret self, world, and God, see the recent collection of essays published in *Carnal Hermeneutics* (Kearney and Treanor 2015).

6 Ingold makes this point more philosophically when he says, "If nothing exists in and for itself, but is only the more or less ephemeral embodiment of activity-in-relation-to-others, then the whole project of classification—which groups and divides things

according to fixed attributes—becomes impossible. There can be no common nouns. Nor, moreover, can there be proper nouns in anything like the conventional sense. For persons are not beings that move, they *are* their movements. It is in their very patterns of activity that their presence lies. And places are not so much locations to be connected as formations that arise within the process of movement, like eddies in a river current. In short, in such a world names are not nouns but verbs: each one describes a going" (Ingold 2011:168).

7 I am thinking here specifically of the desire to be freed of the demands of manual, agricultural labor and the care of fellow creatures. The "progress" of civilizations and the "success" of individuals within them are often judged by the ability to have life and the world on one's own terms. The dream of mastery and control over one's own fate, and thus also the desire to take leave of the relationships and responsibilities that accompany our embodiment, runs deep. This is desire that is well captured in the Garden of Eden story when it describes the human desire to refuse creatureliness and instead pursue the life of a god.

8 Pope Francis's recent encyclical *Laudato Si* represents a commendable effort to rehabilitate Francis of Assisi for human and ecological understanding.

9 In *Scripture, Culture, and Agriculture: An Agrarian Reading of the Bible*, Ellen F. Davis (2008) does crucial work establishing the agrarian context of the Garden of Eden story and others besides. She shows how interpretations of the story that endorse mastery are foreign to an ancient Israelite sensibility. The work of the historian of science Peter Harrison is also important because he shows in his book *The Bible, Protestantism, and the Rise of Natural Science* (Harrison 1998) and in his essay "Subduing the Earth: Genesis 1, Early Modern Science, and the Exploitation of Nature" (Harrison 1999) that prior to the modern period discussions of human dominion focused on the need to bring human, carnal passions under control. Texts of Genesis did not serve to warrant mastery over or exploitation of creatures and the earth until roughly the seventeenth century.

10 The histories of Christian imperial conquest are a clear example of how Christians have been profoundly mistaken in their understanding of God and the meaning of creation. Properly understood, creation *ex nihilo* is practically synonymous with creation *ex amore*, and thus calls into question any and all subjugation of others. For an analysis of the troubled history that misunderstands this teaching, see the work of Whitney Bauman (2009) and Willie James Jennings (2010).

11 I have developed these themes in greater detail in *From Nature to Creation: A Christian Vision for Understanding and Loving Our World* (Wirzba 2015).

Bibliography

Bauman, Whitney. 2009. *Theology, Creation, and Environmental Ethics: From Creatio ex Nihilo to Terra Nullius*. New York: Routledge.

Davis, Ellen F. 2008. *Scripture, Culture, and Agriculture: An Agrarian Reading of the Bible*. New York: Cambridge University Press.

Descola, Philippe. 2013. *Beyond Nature and Culture*. Chicago: The University of Chicago Press.

Geertz, Clifford. 1964. "The Transition to Humanity." In *Horizons of Anthropology*, ed. S. Tax. Chicago: Aldine.

Harrison, Peter. 1998. *The Bible, Protestantism, and the Rise of Natural Science*. Cambridge: Cambridge University Press.

Harrison, Peter. 1999. "Subduing the Earth: Genesis 1, Early Modern Science, and the Exploitation of Nature." *Journal of Religion*, 79:86–109.

Harrison, Peter. 2007. *The Fall of Man and the Foundations of Science*. Cambridge: Cambridge University Press.

Heidegger, Martin. 1953. "The Question Concerning Technology." In *Basic Writings*, ed. David Krell. San Francisco, CA: Harper Perennial.

Ingold, Tim. 2000. *The Perception of the Environment: Essays on Livelihood, Dwelling and Skill*. London: Routledge.

Ingold, Tim. 2011. *Being Alive: Essays on Movement, Knowledge and Description*. London: Routledge.

Ingold, Tim. 2013. "Prospect." In *Biosocial Becomings: Integrating Social and Biological Anthropology*, eds. Tim Ingold and Gisli Palsson. Cambridge: Cambridge University Press.

Jennings, Willie James. 2010. *Christian Imagination: Theology and the Origins of Race*. New Haven, CT: Yale University Press.

Kearney, Richard and Brian Treanor. 2015. *Carnal Hermeneutics*. New York: Fordham University Press.

Latour, Bruno. 1993. *We Have Never Been Modern*. Cambridge, MA: Harvard University Press.

Merchant, Carolyn. 1980. *The Death of Nature: Women, Ecology and the Scientific Revolution*. San Francisco, CA: Harper & Row.

Merchant, Carolyn. 2004. *Reinventing Eden: The Fate of Nature in Western Culture*. New York: Routledge.

Thornton, Thomas. 2007. *Being and Place Among the Tlingit*. Seattle: University of Washington Press.

Wirzba, Norman. 2015. *From Nature to Creation: A Christian Vision for Understanding and Loving Our World*. Grand Rapids, MN: Baker Academic.

Worthy, Kenneth. 2013. *Invisible Nature: Healing the Destructive Divide Between People and the Environment*. Amherst, NY: Prometheus Books.

Zizioulas, John D. 1997. *Being as Communion: Studies in Personhood and the Church*. Crestwood, NY: St. Vladimir's Seminary Press.

5

BEWITCHING NATURE

Elizabeth Allison

My headed exploded when I read *The Death of Nature.*

I sat in a wood-paneled college reading room, my oversize Peruvian sweater warding off New England's winter chill. My eyes widened with shock as I discovered that large swaths of history had been excised from my high school history textbooks. As I learned of the oppressions and obscurations of patriarchy, my faced reddened with incipient feminist outrage. I was appalled that my high school Advanced Placement European History course had deemed the massacre of hundreds or thousands of women as witches to be so insignificant as to be excluded from a comprehensive year-long survey.

The year was 1990. *The Death of Nature: Women, Ecology, and the Scientific Revolution* (hereafter *TDN*, Merchant 1980) had been released with a new Preface reflecting on the intensification of ecological degradation since the 1970s, when the original thinking for the book occurred. The Preface also addressed prospects for new intellectual paradigms such as process physics, far-from-equilibrium thermodynamics, and chaos theory to challenge the mechanistic model of nature. Having immersed myself in an explication of the parallels between particle physics and Eastern religions by Fritjof Capra ([1975] 1984) during a transcontinental flight back from a college semester in Nepal, I was primed to absorb these ideas.

At this point in my journey, my professional goals were unformed. Environmental studies courses and research in Nepal had shown me the anthropogenic and androcentric threats haunting the places I loved. *TDN* revealed the roles of worldviews, ideology, and science in constructing societies that revered or vilified nature. I was deeply curious about how more life-embracing societies might arise from revisions to our atomistic, reductionistic thinking, and was committed to the role of environmental education in reshaping thought and action. These commitments led me on a foray through youth development work, environmental restoration, environmental education, and program management, before I found my way back to academia to continue research in lived environmental ethics.

More than 15 years after I first engaged with Carolyn Merchant's work on that mind-expanding day, a solid recommendation from Carolyn, delivered to the search committee from Italy where she was lecturing, helped me land my first assistant professor position. I began teaching in an interdisciplinary department, focusing on the role of religions and worldviews in shaping environmental management policies and practices. A few years later, I launched a graduate program in the emerging transdisciplinary field of Religion and Ecology. Looking back, I can see that my future professional trajectory was initiated when I picked up *TDN* on that snowy winter day.

Toward an Ethic of Flourishing

Carolyn's presence in the Department of Environmental Science, Policy, and Management at the University of California–Berkeley was one of the factors that drew me there for graduate studies after a stint of ethnographic fieldwork in the Himalayas. With the guidance she offered in understanding the history of environmental philosophies and ethics, and the expertise that the rural sociologist Louise Fortmann offered in understanding the micro-dynamics of rural communities in developing countries, I was able to construct a study that offered a descriptive account of local environmental ethics, in the service of building a normative account of flourishing that could be extended to other places and times (Allison 2009). Notably, the Society and Environment program of the Environmental Science, Policy, and Management department in the early 2000s was rich with women professors including, along with Merchant and Fortmann, Nancy Peluso, Sally Fairfax, Claudia Carr, and Kate O'Neill, and this plethora of learned and distinguished role models was crucial to creating space for women scholars and helping us find our voices in the cacophony of the public sphere.

My research and writing explore how a new, more life-giving environmental ethic, of the kind discussed in *Earthcare* (Merchant 1996), *Reinventing Eden* (Merchant 2003), and *Radical Ecology* (Merchant 2005) can arise from tracing the history of the Western material-scientific ethic, and from understanding the beliefs and practices of people who locate value, power, and spirituality in nonhuman nature. In the context of climate change and global mass extinction, I investigate how the human relationship with nonhuman nature became so one-sided and dominating, and describe alternative possibilities. In particular, traditional ecological knowledge (TEK) appears to offer alternate ontologies and epistemologies that bring more equity and relatedness to the human–nature convergence. TEK is well-suited to engaging with the "wicked problems" of global environmental change, such as climate change, which affects all aspects of lives and livelihoods.

During graduate school, first at Yale and then at UC Berkeley, study in sites where Cartesian dualism had not dominated helped loosen the hold of the mechanistic paradigm on my intellect. The focus on precision, prediction, and control, so necessary for the rise of modern science in Merchant's estimation, was less evident in the Himalayas, where religious and familial values took priority. Fieldwork in the Himalayan nations of Nepal and Bhutan helped me understand the role of Vajrayana Buddhism in shaping lived environmental ethics at the local and national levels (Allison 2004, 2007, 2009). Building on Merchant's theory that understanding worldviews can lead to a revised understanding of human–Earth relations, I continue to seek examples of contemporary lived environmental ethics among local communities that might then inspire more just and flourishing ways of life in other places. Such lived environmental ethics bear important parallels with Merchant's "partnership ethic" that seeks to build equitable partnerships, imbued with respect and moral value, between humans and nonhuman nature (Merchant 2003, 2016). While living examples of partnership ethics can be found in small-scale societies around the world, the insights from these close partnerships between humans and nonhuman nature have not yet significantly informed national and international environmental policy discourses. This chapter argues that non-Western epistemologies, such as those found within traditional ecological knowledge, are more congruent with a partnership ethic, and discusses ways in which current dominant Western epistemic practices may impede the widespread acceptance of a partnership ethic. To be practicable, and to avoid the dangers of cultural appropriation, adoption of a partnership ethic requires revisions in Western understandings of ontology, epistemology, ethology, ethics, and philosophy.

The Death of Nature: Mechanistic Foundations of Control

TDN carefully unpacks the religious, cultural, philosophical, political, economic, ecological, and technological shifts in European culture between 1500 and 1700 that changed the ways humans understand and interpret nature, in many ways creating current understandings of modernity and progress. In TDN, Merchant identifies the intellectual and ideological strands that shaped an antagonistic relationship with nature in the modern industrialized West. She shows that the mechanistic paradigm and Cartesian dualism are among the thought patterns that underwrite human domination of nature.

In the ontology of the mechanistic paradigm, matter is divisible, corpuscular, passive, inert, and insensate, and thus ripe for management and control (Merchant 1980:228–234). The mechanistic paradigm, according to Merchant, seeks power and control to create a certain, consistent, predictable world. Matter is context-independent and can be re-arranged according to mathematical rules. Matter is subject to manipulation and instrumental use. Mathematical formalism is the guide for rationality and certainty, which can be observed through linear laws of causality. Furthermore, wild, uncontrollable nature is linked with the female, to be brought under masculine control. In this view, women are seen as closer to nature, and subject to wild sexual passion. Such disorderly women were eventually accused of witchcraft in an effort to re-assert the social order. While the extent of the practice of witchcraft is unknown, we do know that such practices contained an animist view of nature, and were used by people dispossessed of power in the social order. Witchy women tread the boundary between human society and nonhuman nature.

The modern worldview permitted the indiscriminate use of nonhuman nature because nature was seen as lacking intrinsic value and thus available for human instrumental purposes. Merchant's detailed analysis of *how* we in the West came to find ourselves in a position in which the needs of nonhuman nature and wild species are afforded little consideration provides a springboard for efforts to envision new ways of thinking that assign value more equitably between human and nonhuman communities. Merchant's approach holds liberatory potential for oppressed human and nonhuman communities: in identifying the context and sources of power-imbued social constructions that shape worldviews, perceptions are destabilized and denaturalized so that they can be seen as selected possibilities among many.

The Partnership Ethic: A Path of Flourishing

At the end of *TDN*, Merchant calls for a new ethic based on holism rather than mechanism, egalitarianism rather than hierarchy, decentralization rather than concentration of power, and labor-intensive rather than capital-intensive means of production. She suggests that these principles have the potential for "reversing both the subjugation of nature and women" (Merchant 1980:294). In subsequent works such as *Reinventing Eden: The Fate of Nature in Western Culture* (2003) and *Autonomous Nature* (2016), Merchant further develops a new ethic that supports reciprocal engagement with a lively, sensate nature. Moving beyond holism, her partnership ethic offers an alternate path forward that places humans and nature as "equal, interacting, mutually responsive partners," recognizing the actions of humans and nonhumans as being in dynamic relationship, mutual support, and reciprocity with each other (Merchant 2003:26).

Merchant's articulation of a partnership ethic seeks to avoid the pitfalls of egocentric ethics—those oriented around fulfilment of the human ego that have led to widespread environmental degradation and reinforce human vices of greed and lust. Her partnership ethic also runs counter to biocentric ethics, which seem to prioritize the well-being of nonhuman nature over the well-being of impoverished and suffering human communities, a re-ordering of value that all but the most misanthropic deep ecologists would identify as immoral.

Merchant's partnership ethic is based on five precepts:

1. Equity between human and nonhuman communities;
2. Moral consideration for both humans and other species;

3.   Respect for both cultural diversity and biodiversity;
4.   Inclusion of women, minorities, and nonhuman nature in the code of ethical accountability; and
5.   An ecologically sound management that is consistent with the continued health of both the human and nonhuman communities (Merchant 2003:224).

The precepts of the partnership ethic correlate with aspects of the mechanistic ontology documented in *TDN*, serving as correctives to this insensate paradigm. Where the mechanistic paradigm posits passivity, Merchant proposes moral consideration and respect. Where the mechanistic paradigm posits division and atomism, Merchant seeks inclusion and equity.

Merchant's call for a partnership ethic arises directly from her understanding of history, in which comprehensive narratives, or worldviews, help organize our perceptions of the world. Like *The Universe Story* of Brian Swimme and Thomas Berry (Swimme and Berry 1992), or the *Journey of the Universe* of Brian Swimme and Mary Evelyn Tucker (Swimme and Tucker 2014), Merchant sees a need for a 'new story'—an overarching vision of the human place in the world—in an evolutionary ecological context. She writes, "My own view is that out of the global ecological crisis a new story or set of stories will emerge, but the new stories will arise out of new forms of production and reproduction as sustainable partnerships with nature are tested and become viable" (Merchant 2003: 38).

Traditional Ecological Knowledge as a Type of Partnership Ethic

In the present day, examples of partnership ethics can be found in small-scale societies around the world, in which local people live in close and sensitive relationships of interaction and reciprocity with their surroundings. They are contemporary animists, whose societies may include diviners, oracles, shamans, and witches. The environmental knowledge gleaned from long-term, intimate observation of a place has come to be known as "traditional ecological knowledge" (TEK): a holistic and encompassing body of knowledge permeating local lifeways, and often conveyed through story, ritual, or song. TEK transcends and dismantles the hardened Western boundaries between science and religion, conveying appropriate relations with the natural environment through narrative, cultural, and spiritual means.

Continuous history of inhabitance over time shapes a particular way of knowing about and caring for the landscape that weaves together religious, spiritual, political, and empirical ways of knowing. Passed down through the generations and conveyed through stories, TEK is "a cumulative body of knowledge, practice, and belief" about the inter-relationships of living beings and their surroundings (Berkes 2008). TEK is practical knowledge about local ecosystems applied through ethnobotany, medicinal plant and healing knowledge, weather and seasonal predictions, hunting relationships, land use, taboos, and sacred natural sites.

In my study sites in the Himalayas, I found an alternative to the Western scientific paradigm. In the Himalayan ecological paradigm, humans were not separate from nonhuman nature, but in constant contact and communion both with other species and with unseen deities that influenced both household-level and regional resource use decisions. In my fieldwork, I identified both livelihood practices and religio-ethical beliefs shaping resource use into a practicable culturally-situated environmental ethic (Allison 2004, 2007, 2009, 2017a, 2017b). As I analyzed the interweaving of Vajrayana Buddhism and ecological practice among villagers and land managers in the Himalayas, I found an alternative to the scientific reductionist paradigm that Merchant has so carefully documented.

For example, the paradigm of the Vajrayana Buddhists of eastern Bhutan, grounded in religion, emphasizes interdependence (co-arising), non-harming, non-instrumentality, value across generations, and community. This paradigm is not limited to the human community, but extends outward in time and space, encompassing multiple realms of being. The local environmental ethic promotes the flourishing of life and valuing all living beings. I was astonished during my first visit to Bhutan when a friend drinking tea in my apartment refused to swat a mosquito that was tormenting us both. The mosquito could have been the mother of either one of us in a former life, my friend explained, and for that reason, we must treat it with the honor and kindness we would extend to the one who had given birth to us. Killing the mosquito would be tantamount to matricide, and would unleash a flood of negative karma. Within the modern Western scientific epistemology, holistic ways of knowing do not appear to be knowledge at all but instead are understood as cultural practices, religious rituals, worldviews, superstitions, and the like. However, urban and internationally educated Bhutanese colleagues, inhabiting a less dualistic paradigm, were able to sit comfortably with both modern Western scientific views and the ontology of Vajrayana Buddhism.

Democratizing Knowledge Production

Before the recent upsurge in interest in everyday forms of knowledge-making over the past few decades, ordinary people were not understood to construct knowledge. Scientists were the sole possessors of authority and agency to determine what counted as science and what was mere superstition or habit. The scientific establishment controls access to its corridors of power through such gate-keeping mechanisms as elite university education and publications in top-tier journals. Armed with such credentials, the scientist is "modest witness," whose third person, passive voice prose removes the specificity and marked social location of any observer, and places the scientist in a 'neutral' omniscient position, reporting objectively on what has taken place (Haraway 1997). This voice of authority is neutral, unmarked by qualities of gender, race, socio-economic class, or other indicators of position or dependency.

Innovations in studying knowledge, via for example, citizen science, everyday religion, and grounded theory, have opened the process of knowledge construction to include the knowledge constructed in people's ordinary lives. In parallel intellectual movements that value subjective experience, religious studies scholars have adopted a 'bottom up' approach in 'lived religion' examinations of religious belief and practice, which prioritize the experience of ordinary people in understanding how religion works (McGuire 2008; Ammerman 2007). Similarly, social scientists have employed the grounded theory approach, which allows social theory to arise from observed conditions (Glaser and Strauss 1967).

In light of current challenges to expertise and scientific knowledge, it is important to distinguish between, on the one hand, disciplinary efforts to democratize knowledge production, such as through citizen science, civil science, traditional ecological knowledge, and the study of everyday religion, and, on the other, the potentially radically relativistic and ungrounded belief that "everyone lives in their own reality" and there is no single, indivisible truth but rather myriad refracted perceptions that are all valid in their own ways. Superstition, prejudice, bigotry, and habit are rife, and appeal to humanity's baser instincts. Following Donna Haraway (1988), we must insist on "better accounts of the world," valuing those accounts that are more life-promoting and guide human ingenuity toward broadening vistas of perspective. Those better accounts must be "friendly to earthwide projects of finite freedom, limited material abundance, modest meaning in suffering, and limited happiness" (Haraway 1988:579). Merchant's partnership ethic, which emphasizes the centrality of equity and respect, provides the necessary ethical foundation for a responsible and inclusive program of 'doing science,' or developing better accounts of the world. The accounts of the world that deserve attention and amplification are, therefore, those that honor the range of diversity that exists across many dimensions, and promote the flourishing of the widest spectrum of beings. Those accounts that seek to amass the fruits of the world for the benefit of a select few are justifiably marginalized.

Haraway's epistemological program is one of several that contribute to the democratization of knowledge without succumbing to unmoored relativism. Haraway's stance adopts aspects of both feminist standpoint epistemology, which focuses of the particular social location and material conditions of a social actor, and critical realism. Like some forms of traditional ecological knowledge, Haraway's theoretical work on human interactions with nonhuman animals destabilizes the centrality of the human subject, and opens space for the activity and even intentionality of nonhuman subjects. In an adjacent epistemological vein, the anthropological perspective that considers multiple ontologies suggests that differing ontologies, or understandings of what exists, inhabit and create different worlds (Ingold 2011; Descola 2013; Yeh 2016). In this approach, different worlds may co-exist or interpenetrate one another. Critical realism is the perspective that there *is* a knowable consensus reality that can be discovered through repeated, replicable observations, and that these observations are shaped by the observer's social location (Bhaskar [1975] 1997). In these epistemological perspectives, observations are repeated, both by individuals and by epistemic communities, and are grounded on *experience*. This perspective differs from the "alternative facts" perspective in that the information derived from this approach is non-dogmatic, replicable, and open to revision. Information derived through scientific means, whether Western or Indigenous, is constructed through repeated observations accreted over time, and validated through utility (Fortmann 2008:8). If and when new observations contradict the current understanding of a phenomenon, the theory is amenable to revision and adjustment through further observation and testing. While Western science often shuns anomalies that do not fit within the existing paradigm, the paradigm must eventually change to accommodate new information (Kuhn [1962] 1996). The craze for "alternative facts" is far less flexible and plastic: it cannot accommodate new information, but instead rejects as fake news all information that does not fit with pre-established views and desired political outcomes.

Epistemic Justice as Foundational for an Ethic of Flourishing

While living examples of partnership ethics can be found in small-scale societies around the world, the insights from these close partnerships between humans and the rest of the natural world have not, for the most part, made their way into national and international environmental policy discourses.[1] Global relations of power and privilege tend to marginalize and exclude insights from traditional ecological knowledge from entering the dominant strands of environmental discourse. As feminist philosopher Lorraine Code points out, knowing is a political activity (Code 2006). Definition of an object of scientific study is inherently political: the terms and approaches brought to bear on the object of study open some pathways of inquiry and foreclose others (Allison 2015). Historians and philosophers of science have shown how scientific knowledge is constructed on a hierarchy, with quantitative, physics-like disciplines at the top, and more subjective qualitative disciplines ranked lower. In the hierarchy of knowledge that pervades international understanding of environmental issues, biophysical scientific studies of the environment are seen as possessing the most value, with social sciences and the humanities further down the scale, and other ways of knowing too often discounted or excluded (Jasanoff 2004). These discursive formations reinforce the political and epistemic power of economically and politically dominant nations, while submerging other voices and perceptions.

Through constructions of difference, discursive practices establish a hierarchy in the moral order as well (Neumann 2004; Plumwood 1993) elevating the concerns, beliefs, and practices of the privileged over those of others who are hierarchically constructed as less worthy or valuable. As Merchant has shown, the objective, mechanistic, scientific paradigm developed in early modern Europe became the model not only for the pursuit of scientific knowledge in subsequent centuries, but also the standard by which the validity of many other types of inquiry were judged to have authority. The supposed objectivity and impartiality of the scientific model elevated this particular form of knowledge over others.

Power relations that control what counts as knowledge and what knowledge is valued can limit the ability of marginalized groups to introduce their ways of knowing into general discourse. Those lacking the markers of credibility and authority, such as advanced academic degrees, association with elite institutions, membership of the dominant ethnic group, or male gender, may be excluded from consideration in Western societies (Fortmann 2008:6–7). Dualistic thinking, in which men are associated with the rational, objective, and dominant intellectual faculties, while women are associated with emotional, unruly, submissive, and subjective embodiment, can exclude women from science and other scholarly endeavors (Merchant 1980, 2005; Plumwood 1993). Dualistic thinking also separates people of color and those of non-dominant ethnicity into the category of emotional, irrational "nature." At the same time, women's intimate engagement with nonhuman nature, through horticulture, collection of food, fuel, and medicinal herbs, food preparation and child-rearing afforded particular insights about the working of the natural world (Merchant 2005:197). Feminist critiques of science have suggested that a 'reconstructive knowledge' would be based on principles of interaction, change and process, complexity and contextuality (Merchant 2005:107).

Indigenous ways of knowing and TEK are often holistic lifeways that permeate the totality of individuals' and communities' perceptions and actions in daily life. That is, they are embedded and context-dependent. Thus, the knowledge contained therein cannot be easily dissected and extracted for applications to novel situations or contexts. Modern Western scientific knowledge, based on a reductionistic, atomistic view of nature, is constructed from mobile, stable, and combinable bits of knowledge (Latour 1987). As Merchant has observed, this sort of knowledge is based on the idea that nature can be broken down into its smallest independent constituent parts, and then seamlessly and endlessly recombined into new permutations.

Dominant epistemic practices may impede the adoption of a partnership ethic because the dominant society lacks the hermeneutic tools to comprehend and address communications of some of the groups that would form this partnership. Without necessary hermeneutic tools to understand communications from nonhuman nature and from marginalized and oppressed groups, their potential contributions to a partnership ethic may be overlooked. Ostensibly, this gap arises from a lack of peer-reviewed published material incorporating traditional ecological knowledge. However, the epistemic problems run deeper. In the context of Indigenous and traditional ecological knowledge, unadorned 'facts' cannot be extracted from the context in which they are generated and the spiritual and cultural values embedded in them (Martello 2004; Nadasdy 1999; Berkes 2008). This contextual, value-laden, embodied knowledge sits uneasily with the context-independent and value-free paradigm of Western scientific knowledge. In addition, a deeper set of epistemic practices that authorize and control the flow of research and information about ecological systems serves to exclude some kinds of knowledge. A devastating epistemic effect of colonialism is the "'disappearing' of knowledge, where local or provincial knowledge is dismissed due to privileging alternative, often Western, epistemic practices" (Dotson 2011:236).

The exclusion of TEK from global policy forums and larger contributions to a partnership ethic is the result of what feminist philosopher Miranda Fricker (2007:1) calls "epistemic injustice": injustice "done to someone specifically in their capacity as knower". In particular, "hermeneutic injustice"—one of Fricker's two types of epistemic injustice—occurs when society lacks the hermeneutic or explanatory resources to understand the phenomenon at hand, not realizing that the phenomenon has ontological and social reality. Hermeneutic injustice is "the injustice of having some significant area of one's social experience obscured from collective understanding owing to hermeneutic marginalization" (Fricker 2007:158). This has been the case for aspects of traditional ecological knowledge that cannot be brought into collective discourse. The dominant focus on quantitative and rational approaches in scientific studies of environmental change elides insight generated through other ways of knowing. The *uncritical* and *universal* application of scientific tools, to the exclusion of other ways of knowing, enacts epistemic injustice against Indigenous, Native, and other groups who experience their surrounding environment not just as a material fact but also as a multilayered spiritual, cultural, psychological, and emotional context in which meaning is imbued in both animate and inanimate aspects of the surroundings.

Importantly, hermeneutic injustice is structural, not perpetrated. The injustice arises from a collective gap in knowledge, not a particular malicious intent. As Fricker (2007:151) writes, "Different groups can be hermeneutically disadvantaged for all sorts of reasons, as the changing social world frequently generates new sorts of experience of which our understanding may dawn only gradually". The structural and power-laden consequences of hermeneutic injustice have largely excluded traditional ecological knowledge—the types of knowledge that embodies and embraces a partnership ethic—from global environmental policy forums. The realization of a partnership ethic requires greater epistemic justice and cultivating the epistemic virtues of listening receptively and reserving judgment to keep an open mind about credibility, validity, and reliability.

Rethinking Nature's Thinking

To develop a partnership ethic that takes seriously the needs of rivers, trees, and mountains, as well as badgers and bacteria, requires recognition that other life forms are active agents in producing and conveying information. Humans need to develop methods of acknowledging and comprehending the information that nonhumans are sharing. Many Indigenous and non-Western peoples ascribe agency, and even intention, to the activity of nonhuman nature (Nelson 1983, 1989; Scott 1996; Berkes 2008). In recent decades, environmentalists, epistemologists, and ethologists have variously explored ways to close the gap between human and nonhuman minds, increasing the possibilities for recognition and comprehension of nonhuman forms of communication (Seed et al. 1988; Bateson 1979; Leopold [1949] 1966; Bekoff and Pierce 2009; Fouts and Mills 1997; Goodall 2010; de Waal 2017; Safina 2015). In the 1980s, John Seed and Joanna Macy pioneered a creative method of helping humans imaginatively enter into the lives and emotions of nonhumans called a Council of All Beings (Seed et al. 1988; Macy and Brown 1998). In this process, human participants seek to imaginatively enter the experience of other life forms and ecological features to then convey to the assembled Council how a particular human intervention, such as a river dam or shopping mall, would affect them.

Attention to the evolutionary continuity of consciousness brings into focus nonhuman animals' use of language and tools, as well as their emotional states and morality, as the ethologists Marc Bekoff and Jane Goodall have shown (Bekoff 2013; Bekoff and Pierce 2009; Goodall 2010). Ethologists and philosophers have documented the flow of communication between humans and nonhuman animals (Bekoff and Pierce 2009; Goodall 2010; Pepperberg 2013; Rothenberg 2006). Trees communicate among themselves and with the larger world, including the human world (Haskell 2017; Wohlleben 2016). This recent work adopts the perspective that other life forms are not instinct-driven or insensate automatons—'dead' nature—but rather have significant interests and preferences, which ought to be recognized and valued (Waldau and Patton 2006). The movement toward embracing the personhood of other living beings is not dissimilar to other movements of liberation for women, Indigenous people, LGBTQ people, people of color, and other oppressed human groups.

If humans have labeled nonhuman nature as "unthinking," in what ways do we interfere with various beings' ability to understand themselves? Fricker (2007:163) writes,

> When you find yourself in a situation in which you seem to be the only one to feel the dissonance between received understanding and your own intimated sense of a given experience, it tends to knock your faith in your own ability to make sense of the world, or at least the relevant region of the world.

Can our lack of hermeneutic appreciation for Bornean orangutans' inner life affect how they collectively experience the loss of more than half their species in the past 60 years? As epistemic shifts begin, acknowledging that knowledge systems extend beyond human knowing, we will need to develop hermeneutic tools for understanding these other messages, whether they come in the form of whale songs or mycorrhizal fungi networks in tree roots that send signals between trees (Haskell 2017). Cutting-edge scientists, Indigenous societies, and religious traditions agree that "mind" is not limited to human intelligence. However, the interpretation of the semiotics of living systems is in its infancy among industrialized societies (Kohn 2013; Bateson 1979; Reichel-Dolmatoff 1976; Wallace 2005).

Conclusion: Toward Embodied Ethics and Epistemologies

New cosmological stories are necessarily polyfocal and polyvocal. Within this polyphony, attention to epistemic practices and epistemic justice is necessary to ensure that all voices can join the chorus. Communication is necessarily reciprocal, dependent on an audience "willing and capable" of receiving the communication (Dotson 2011:238). The feminist theorist Kirstie Dotson (2011:238) argues that to deny entire populations of people such communicative reciprocity amounts to "epistemic violence":

> a refusal, intentional or unintentional, of an audience to communicatively reciprocate a linguistic exchange owing to pernicious ignorance. Pernicious ignorance should be understood to refer to any reliable ignorance that, in a given context, harms another person (or set of persons).

While Dotson's analysis is limited to human persons, a broader swath of persons—animal, plant, bacterial, ecosystemic persons—must be included for the realization of a partnership ethic. In this broader consideration it is necessary to examine what epistemic practices might blind and deafen us to the communications of nonhuman partners. Fricker (2007:152) observes, "we try hardest to understand those things that it serves us to understand" and further, in some areas, the powerful have "no interest in achieving proper interpretation, perhaps indeed where they have a positive interest in sustaining the extant misinterpretations". Such attention to power structures should remind us immediately of the self-serving 'deadening' of nonhuman nature, which has allowed humans to exploit it in what the historian Lynn White, Jr. has called "a mood of indifference" (White 1967). When it does not serve human dominance or the mechanistic paradigm to understand the communications of nonhuman nature, many humans tend to discount, ignore, or reject such communications.

In an effort to allow broader perspectives on the relationship between human and nonhuman nature to flourish, I bring attention to nondominant perspectives in my teaching and writing, seeking ways to identify components of practicable environmental ethics, especially in relation to climate change, from the lived experience of people who have close associations with nonhuman nature (Allison 2015, 2017a). My articles also explore the spirituality of traditional ecological knowledge in the Himalayas, showing how TEK upends the Western dualistic view of science and religion (Allison 2004, 2007, 2017b). I endeavor to create feminist spaces for the hearing and telling of human–nature stories, similar to the feminist space I was privileged to experience as a graduate student with Louise Fortmann and Carolyn Merchant at UC Berkeley. As a graduate student at Yale, well before I met Carolyn, I founded the student interest group FERNS—The Faith Environment Religion Nature Spirituality Network, which continues to this day and has recently launched a journal. At the California Institute of Integral Studies, I established the graduate program in Ecology, Spirituality, and Religion in 2013, to provide a home for transdisciplinary research that explores the role of religions, spiritualties, worldviews, and philosophies in responding to environmental degradation.

Enacting a viable, practicable partnership ethic requires advances in ontology, epistemology, ethology, ethics, and philosophy. The powerful and succinct statement of partnership ethics that Merchant presented in 2003 and has refined in the years since offers a starting point for research and critical reflection on the philosophical and political preconditions necessary for the implementation of such an ethic. In this way, Merchant's laconic partnership ethic is not dissimilar to the "land ethic"[2] that wildlife ecologist Aldo Leopold devised in the 1940s (Leopold [1949] 1966). As Leopold did, Merchant packs a great deal of meaning and insight into a few brief lines. Like the land ethic, Merchant's partnership ethics deserves sustained discussion and interpretation to bring it into practice (Leopold, Flader, and Callicott 1991; Callicott 1987, 1989, 2014; Meine 2004; Flader 1994). The challenges to Western ontology, epistemology, ethology, and ethics are more than enough to keep a cadre of scholars busy for many years.

At the same time, the current state of Earth does not allow for leisurely perusal of epistemological intricacies, but instead requires inspired and efficacious action. Thus, as people concerned with the fate of the world, we are all charged with implementing the precepts of the partnership ethic in our lives as much as possible. We can begin practices of epistemic justice with human communities. We can listen with compassion and empathy to marginalized groups about the realities of their lives. We can begin to take down the epistemological barriers that prevent taking seriously information from dreams, intuition, and other human ways of knowing. We can value and treat as epistemologically significant the wonder, awe, and enchantment that the natural world inspires in us. We can listen as Indigenous leaders collect and share stories and testimonials about how their lifeways and landscapes are changing with climate change. And we can value the inherent animism and spirituality of small children (Gopnik 2009; Miller and Barker 2015), respecting their engagements with realms beyond the rational and material so that they can grow into moral partners with human and nonhuman nature (Dunlap and Kellert 2012; Kahn and Kellert 2002; Kellert 2012; Louv 2013).

Notes

1 Indigenous groups have asserted their right to participate in the governance of the Arctic, the Convention on Biological Diversity, and other national and regional issues (Young 2016; Martello 2004; Huntington 2011). For example, Indigenous groups are involved in the governance of the Arctic through such venues as the Inuit Circumpolar Council, which has Consultative Status II at the United Nations, and the Arctic Council, comprised of Arctic states and Arctic Indigenous organizations. However, participation of Indigenous groups and incorporation of TEK in global environmental policy and governance has not reached levels representative of either the significance of Indigenous insights, nor on par with any sort of representational equity.
2 "A thing is right when it tends to preserve the integrity, stability, and beauty of the biotic community. It is wrong when it tends otherwise."

References

Allison, Elizabeth. 2004. "Spiritually-Motivated Natural Resource Management in Eastern Bhutan." Pp. 528–561 in *The Spider and the Piglet*, edited by Karma Ura and Sonam Kinga. Thimphu: Centre for Bhutan Studies.

Allison, Elizabeth. 2007. "Religious Protected Sacred Sites of Khumbu." Pp. 12–15 in *Sacred Sites of Khumbu Region*, edited by Ang Rita Sherpa. Kathmandu, Nepal: The Mountain Institute.

Allison, Elizabeth. 2009. *Enspirited Places, Material Traces: The Sanctified and the Sacrificed in Modernizing Bhutan.* PhD diss., Environmental Science, Policy, and Management, University of California Berkeley.

Allison, Elizabeth. 2015. "The Spiritual Significance of Glaciers in an Age of Climate Change." *Wiley Interdisciplinary Reviews: Climate Change* 6(5):493–508.

Allison, Elizabeth. 2017a. "Toward a Feminist Care Ethic for Climate Change." *Journal of Feminist Studies in Religion* 33(2):152–158.

Allison, Elizabeth. 2017b. "Spirits and Nature: The Intertwining of Sacred Cosmologies and Environmental Epistemologies in Bhutan." *Journal for the Study of Religion, Nature, and Culture* 11(2):197–226. doi:10.1558/jsrnc.18805

Ammerman, Nancy Tatom. 2007. *Everyday Religion: Observing Modern Religious Lives.* Oxford: Oxford University Press.

Bateson, Gregory. 1979. *Mind and Nature: A Necessary Unity.* New York: Dutton.

Bekoff, Marc and Jessica Pierce. 2009. *Wild Justice: The Moral Lives of Animals.* Chicago: University of Chicago Press.

Bekoff, Marc. 2013. *Ignoring Nature No More: The Case for Compassionate Conservation.* Chicago: University of Chicago Press.

Berkes, Fikret. 2008. *Sacred Ecology.* New York: Routledge.

Bhaskar, Roy. [1975] 1997. *A Realist Theory of Science.* London: Verso.

Callicott, J. Baird. 1987. *Companion to "A Sand County Almanac": Interpretive & Critical Essays.* Madison, WI: University of Wisconsin Press.

Callicott, J. Baird. 1989. *In Defense of the Land Ethic: Essays in Environmental Philosophy.* Albany, NY: State University of New York Press.

Callicott, J. Baird. 2014. *Thinking Like a Planet: The Land Ethic and the Earth Ethic.* New York: Oxford University Press.

Capra, Fritjof. [1975] 1984. *The Tao of Physics: An Exploration of the Parallels Between Modern Physics and Eastern Mysticism.* Toronto: Bantam Books.

Code, Lorraine. 2006. *Ecological Thinking: The Politics of Epistemic Location*. New York: Oxford University Press.

Descola, Phillipe. 2013. "Beyond Nature and Culture." In *The Handbook of Contemporary Animism*, edited by Graham Harvey. Durham, UK: Acumen.

Dotson, Kristie. 2011. "Tracking Epistemic Violence, Tracking Practices of Silencing." *Hypatia* 26(2):236–257.

Dunlap, Julie and Stephen R. Kellert. 2012. *Companions in Wonder: Children and Adults Exploring Nature Together*. Cambridge, MA: MIT Press.

Flader, Susan. 1994. *Thinking Like a Mountain: Aldo Leopold and the Evolution of an Ecological Attitude Toward Deer, Wolves, and Forests*. Madison, WI: University of Wisconsin Press.

Fortmann, Louise. 2008. *Participatory Research in Conservation and Rural Livelihoods: Doing Science Together*. Chichester, UK: Wiley-Blackwell.

Fouts, Roger and Stephen Tukel Mills. 1997. *Next of Kin: What Chimpanzees Have Taught Me About Who We Are*. New York: William Morrow.

Fricker, Miranda. 2007. *Epistemic Injustice: Power and the Ethics of Knowing*. Oxford: Oxford University Press.

Glaser, Barney G. and Anselm L. Strauss. 1967. *The Discovery of Grounded Theory: Strategies for Qualitative Research*. Chicago: Aldine.

Goodall, Jane. 2010. *Through a Window: My Thirty Years With the Chimpanzees of Gombe*. Boston: Mariner Books/Houghton Mifflin Harcourt.

Gopnik, Alison. 2009. *The Philosophical Baby: What Children's Minds Tell Us About Truth, Love, and the Meaning of Life*. New York: Farrar, Straus and Giroux.

Haraway, Donna. 1988. "Situated Knowledges: The Science Question in Feminism and the Privilege of Partial Perspective." *Feminist Studies* 14(3):575–599.

Haraway, Donna Jeanne. 1997. *ModestWitness@SecondMillennium.FemaleManMeetsOncoMouse: Feminism and Technoscience*. New York: Routledge.

Haskell, David George. 2017. *The Songs of Trees: Stories From Nature's Great Connectors*. New York: Viking.

Huntington, Henry P. 2011. "Arctic Science: The Local Perspective." *Nature* 478 (7368):182–183.

Ingold, Tim. 2011. *The Perception of the Environment: Essays on Livelihood, Dwelling and Skill*. London: Routledge.

Jasanoff, Sheila. 2004. "Skinning Scientific Cats." Pp. 179–182 in *Green Planet Blues: Environmental Politics from Stockholm to Johannesburg*, edited by Ken Conca and Geoffrey D. Dabelko. Boulder, CO: Westview Press.

Kahn, Peter H. and Stephen R. Kellert. 2002. *Children and Nature: Psychological, Sociocultural, and Evolutionary Investigations*. Cambridge, MA: MIT Press.

Kellert, Stephen R. 2012. *Birthright: People and Nature in the Modern World*. New Haven, CT: Yale University Press.

Kohn, Eduardo. 2013. *How Forests Think: Toward an Anthropology Beyond the Human*. Berkeley: University of California Press.

Kuhn, Thomas S. [1962] 1996. *The Structure of Scientific Revolutions*. Chicago, IL: University of Chicago Press.

Latour, Bruno. 1987. *Science in Action: How to Follow Scientists and Engineers Through Society*. Cambridge, MA: Harvard University Press.

Leopold, Aldo. [1949] 1966. *A Sand County Almanac: With Essays on Conservation From Round River*. New York: Ballentine Books.

Leopold, Aldo, Susan Flader and J. Baird Callicott. 1991. *The River of the Mother of God and Other Essays*. Madison, WI: University of Wisconsin Press.

Louv, Richard. 2013. *The Nature Principle: Reconnecting With Life in a Virtual Age*. Chapel Hill, NC: Algonquin Books.

Macy, Joanna and Molly Young Brown. 1998. *Coming Back to Life: Practices to Reconnect Our Lives, Our World*. Stony Creek, CT: New Society Publishers.

Martello, M. L. 2004. "Global Change Science and the Arctic Citizen." *Science & Public Policy* 31(2):107–115.

McGuire, Meredith B. 2008. *Lived Religion: Faith and Practice in Everyday Life*. Oxford: Oxford University Press.

Meine, Curt. 2004. *Correction Lines: Essays on Land, Leopold, and Conservation*. Washington, DC: Island Press.

Merchant, Carolyn. 1980. *The Death of Nature: Women, Ecology, and the Scientific Revolution*. San Francisco, CA: Harper & Row.

Merchant, Carolyn. 1996. *Earthcare: Women and the Environment*. New York: Routledge.

Merchant, Carolyn. 2003. *Reinventing Eden: The Fate of Nature in Western Culture*. New York: Routledge.

Merchant, Carolyn. 2005. *Radical Ecology: The Search for a Livable World, Revolutionary Thought/Radical Movements*. New York: Routledge.

Merchant, Carolyn. 2016. *Autonomous Nature: Problems of Prediction and Control From Ancient Times to the Scientific Revolution*. New York: Routledge.

Miller, Lisa and Lisa Barker. 2015. *The Spiritual Child: The New Science on Parenting for Health and Lifelong Thriving*. New York: St Martin's Press.

Nadasdy, Paul. 1999. "The Politics of TEK: Power and the 'Integration' of Knowledge." *Arctic Anthropology* 36(1/2):1–18.

Nelson, Richard K. 1983. *Make Prayers to the Raven: A Koyukon View of the Northern Forest*. Chicago: University of Chicago Press.

Nelson, Richard K. 1989. *The Island Within*. San Francisco, CA: North Point Press.

Neumann, Roderick P. 2004. "Moral and Discursive Geographies in the War for Biodiversity in Africa." *Political Geography* 23(7):813–837.

Pepperberg, Irene M. 2013. *Alex & Me: How a Scientist and a Parrot Discovered a Hidden World of Animal Intelligence—And Formed a Deep Bond in the Process*. New York: HarperCollins.

Plumwood, Val. 1993. *Feminism and the Mastery of Nature*. London: Routledge.

Reichel-Dolmatoff, Gerardo. 1976. "Cosmology as Ecological Analysis: View From the Rain-Forest." *Man* 11(3):307–318.

Rothenberg, David. 2006. *Why Birds Sing a Journey Through the Mystery of Bird Song*. New York: Basic Books.

Safina, Carl. 2015. *Beyond Words: What Animals Think and Feel*. New York: Henry Holt.

Scott, Colin. 1996. "Science for the West, Myth for the Rest? The Case of James Bay Cree Knowledge Construction." In *Naked Science: Anthropological Inquiry into Boundaries, Power, and Knowledge*, edited by Laura Nader. New York: Routledge.

Seed, John, Johanna Macy, Pat Fleimg, and Dailan Pugh. 1988. *Thinking Like a Mountain: Towards a Council of All Beings*. Philadelphia: New Society Publishers.

Swimme, Brian and Thomas Berry. 1992. *The Universe Story: From the Primordial Flaring Forth to the Ecozoic Era*. San Francisco, CA: Harper San Francisco.

Swimme, Brian and Mary Evelyn Tucker. 2014. *Journey of the Universe*. New Haven, CT: Yale University Press.

de Waal, Frans. 2017. *Are We Smart Enough to Know How Smart Animals Are?* New York: W.W. Norton.

Waldau, Paul and Kimberley Patton. 2006. *A Communion of Subjects: Animals in Religion, Science, and Ethics.* New York: Columbia University Press.

Wallace, Mark I. 2005. *Finding God in the Singing River: Christianity, Spirit, Nature.* Minneapolis: Fortress Press.

White, Lynn. 1967. "Historical Roots of our Ecologic Crisis." *Science* 155(3767):1203–1207.

Wohlleben, Peter. 2016. *The Hidden Life of Trees: What They Feel, How They Communicate: Discoveries From a Secret World.* Carlton, Vic.: Black Inc.

Yeh, Emily T. 2016. "How Can Experience of Local Residents Be Knowledge? Challenges in Interdisciplinary Climate Change Research." *Area* 48(1):34–40.

Young, Oran R. 2016. "Governing the Antipodes: International Cooperation in Antarctica and the Arctic." *Polar Record* 52(02):230–238.

6

LEADING AND MISLEADING METAPHORS

From Organism to Anthropocene

Holmes Rolston III

We need Carolyn Merchant today, more than ever. Her showing of the power of dominant metaphors, of paradigm shifts reshaping, misshaping our history is happening all over again on the contemporary scene. She can make us much the wiser if we see that the twenty-first century is in even more danger than the sixteenth or seventeenth of being misled by high powered and arrogant ideals. Facing an Anthropocene Epoch, we need her insights into how limited metaphors get elevated into commanding worldviews, how the strictures of an ideology control us with controlling images of nature.

Organisms and Machines

Merchant laments the loss of the organic category, which she couples with the feminine category.

> The world we have lost was organic …Central to the organic theory was the identification of nature, especially the earth, with a nurturing mother: a kindly beneficent female who provided for the needs of mankind … . The metaphor of the earth as a nurturing mother was gradually to vanish as a dominant image as the Scientific Revolution proceeded to mechanize and to rationalize the world view … . The female earth and virgin earth spirit were subdued by the machine.
>
> *(Merchant [1980] 1990:1–2)*

The contemporary worldview is more complex than either organism or machine.

For the pre-scientific ancients, earth, soil, was female perhaps. But they did not know they were on a planet—that comes thanks to the Scientific Revolution. Earth, upper case, our home planet, is dominant in our thinking, expanded from earth, lower case, the soil. Taken to the planetary level, that projection requires some analysis. We are specifying the fertility and creativity, not the gender.

We do not really think that ecosystems are feminine, much less that Earth is a feminine planet—despite the Lovelock Gaia metaphor. Those are category mistakes, rather like thinking of God as being male. One ought not to sex type planets—the feminine Venus, or the male, war-like Mars.

The origin of sexuality in evolutionary natural history is a puzzle. Many species propagate by cloning, but this is a disadvantage for most species because it does not permit sufficient interchange of genetic information. Sexuality provides more adept generativity, and that does characterize planet Earth. We may speak of the whole genesis rhetorically or symbolically as feminine, Mother Earth; we also need to translate this into claims that are more philosophically and scientifically exact. We mean that there are generative forces that have produced the biota that surrounds us. Nature is the primal and programmatic fountain of being and value.

The Scientific Revolution was characterized by the transition from the organism to the machine as the dominant metaphor. "Between the sixteenth and seventeenth centuries the image of an organic cosmos with a living female earth at its center gave way to a mechanistic world view" (Merchant, 1990 [1980]:xvi). "The new mechanical order and its associated values of power and control would mandate the death of nature." "The removal of animistic, organic assumptions about the cosmos constituted the death of nature–the most far-reaching effect of the Scientific Revolution ... . Nature was now viewed as a system of dead, inert particles, moved by external forces" (Merchant 1990 [1980]:190, 193).

The first successes of that Scientific Revolution were astronomical, in physics, and we still do think of physics and astronomy as mechanical and non-organic. Isaac Newton's celestial mechanics was perhaps the greatest breakthrough in this revolution. This interprets mathematically the motions of solar system bodies as resulting from forces operating on them, largely gravitation. This has since expanded to dynamic astronomy, including celestial body rotation, tidal evolution, mass and mass distribution determinations for stars and galaxies, fluid motions in nebulas, and so on. But this is all covered rather well by the machine metaphor. We can predict eclipses of the Moon to the exact minute a hundred years hence.

Robert Boyle argued that the transforming image of the seventeenth century was the famous astronomical clock in the tower at Strasbourg. The clock kept time, had astronomical features, and every hour human actors came out, originally the Virgin Mary with child and the Three Kings, who praised the child.

> According to us, it [the world contrivance] is like a rare clock, such as may be that at Strasbourg, where all things are so skillfully contrived that the engine being once set a-moving, all things proceed according to the artificer's first design, and the motions of the little statues that at such hours perform these or those things do not require (like those of puppets) the peculiar interposing of the artificer or any intelligent agent employed by him, but

perform their functions on particular occasions by virtue of the general and primitive contrivance of the whole engine.

(Boyle [1686] 1996:13)

The first artificer was soon pushed out by the mechanistic paradigm. Despite the fact that machines commonly have their intended functions, their uses, scientists concluded that this contrivance was a purposeless machine.

Used as metaphor, this fed into the model that all events were clockwork, from the astronomical heavens to human behaviors. That is far too reductionist for human behaviors, but for the clockwork heavens and earth physics it is still not a bad image. Whatever moves—stars, planets, mountains, rivers, particles of dirt—moves as and only as physical forces push it so. Used appropriately and within its limitations, I accept a mechanical concept of astronomical and physical events, and I suspect Merchant does too.

The problem is that, pushed to a worldview: the nothing-but clockwork, purposeless machine view takes us where it took Steven Weinberg, a Nobel laureate: "The more the universe seems comprehensible, the more it seems pointless" (Weinberg [1977] 1993:154).

But one doesn't have to go there. One can find wonder and beauty in the mathematical nature of physics and astronomy, as did both Newton and Einstein. Einstein concluded, famously, that "the eternal mystery of the world is its comprehensibility" (Einstein 1970:61). Eugene P. Wigner, a physicist and mathematician, contends that

> the enormous usefulness of mathematics in the natural sciences is something bordering on the mysterious and that there is no rational explanation for it … . The miracle of the appropriateness of the language of mathematics for the formulation of the laws of physics is a wonderful gift which we neither understand nor deserve.
>
> *(Wigner 1960:2, 14)*

As far as our capacities for thought reach, whether in word or in mathematics, the universe seems unreasonably "reasonable," intelligible, despite the fact that we can no longer visually represent, verbally model, or perceptively sense it. The math still works even in realms where sense and intuition do not easily serve.

Rather curiously, it is with high level abstract mathematics that the human mind is so adept at probing micronature and cosmology. Thinking of nature as a great clock, it was easy to forget that all but a few of the "natural" numbers going into the equations were in fact artifacts, gained with ingenious theories that constructed the looking units, schemes composed in the attending mind. Nature, unobserved, contains no ergs, seconds, or meters, and no wavelengths. These were really not objective units, only intersubjective ones, shared by those educated into an agreement about their appropriateness. This seeming objectivity came with conceptual overlays that in their very success had become invisible.

We need to stay alert to the paradox that these universal physical sciences, which seem so powerful in interpreting what results from the primordial explosion, also drastically oversimplify. Neither mathematics nor other forms of physics anywhere know the categories of life and death, nor mind and conscious experience, which become the phenomena that most cry out to be explained. Even within physical cosmology, the factual claims (as with those involving the anthropic principle) may be mathematical, based on values in equations, but the cosmological interpretation of these facts is not. The interpretation is historical, metaphysical, theological.

The clockwork world, if a machine, turns out to be a sophisticated one. The electron, and all other atomic entities, are really what are called superpositions of quantum states, nested sets of possibilities as regards their forthcoming world lines, partly indeterminate matrices, partly coagulated this way and not that way by, among other things, the demands of observation or interactions with other particles. We make the glasses through which we darkly see, but also partly make the events we see. The electrons, as charge clouds and waves, have increasingly complex interactions with each other and with a nucleus that also becomes more complex as it is built larger.

The nucleus itself, in fact, proves even more complex than the electron shell, and here too the particles, mostly protons and neutrons, are simultaneously to be thought of as waves, with protons charged although neutrons are not. Like the electrons, the protons and neutrons too have probability locations. They are bound together by dramatic new forces, the nuclear forces, which are so short-range as never to be manifest macroscopically. Analogously to the electrons in their shells, the nucleus too emits and absorbs radiation and is subject to excitation. If it is interconnectedness we wish, there is plenty of that in physics.

A challenge to the hard world of determinism has come in chaos theory (as Merchant notices in the preface she added to the 1990 edition of *The Death of Nature: Women, Ecology, and the Scientific Revolution*) (Merchant [1980] 1990). Physical systems, although largely determinate or statically determinate, can contain elements of chaos. These include both determinate chaos, such as the intersection of two or more previously unrelated causal lines, and indeterminate chaos, such as events linked to random radioactive decay, or trigger events where systemic outcomes originate in small-scale threshold events that are genuinely open and might have been otherwise. This has been observed in weather patterns, with the memorable image of a butterfly's wings in China affecting the weather in California. There is still mathematics here, but it also turns out that in complex systems, this involves solving equations that become so complex that their solution is impossible with any computer either on hand or on the horizon.

Returning to what Merchant laments as a lost worldview, nothing in contemporary astrophysics or microphysics would regularly be interpreted as "organic" or in any "nurturing mother" image. There is no "death of nature" because the astronomical worlds and the microphysical worlds were never alive—*pace* the Whiteheadians with their panpsychism, or whatever the Medievals and their predecessors thought. Still, elements in this enlarged scientific description are of a wonder full, awe inspiring, and "user-friendly" universe. Discoveries commonly gathered under the name "the anthropic principle" find that astronomical phenomena such as the formation of galaxies, stars, and planets depend critically on the microphysical phenomena. In turn, those mid-range scales where the known complexity mostly lies depend on the interacting microscopic and astronomical ranges.

This, we now say, is a "fine-tuned" universe. The astrophysical start up begins to look something like a set-up. That can put this cosmic machine on a course that results, rarely but in parts of it at least, in organic creativity, as proved by events on Earth. Martin Rees, British astronomer, even refers to the heavens as "our cosmic habitat" (Rees 2001). So Merchant can get back into the conversation.

Merchant, as a feminist, is always concerned to link the exploitation of nature with the exploitation of women. Merchant cites, and laments, Francis Bacon: "She [nature] is put in constraint, molded, and made as it were new by art and the hand of man; as in things artificial.... Nature takes orders from man and works under his authority" (Bacon, cited in Merchant [1980] 1990:170–171). "I am come in very truth leading to you nature with all her children to bind her to your service and make her your slave" (p. 170). Nature is a disorderly female who needs to be shaped into a better servant of her man.

A machine is not a woman; a woman is not a machine, and this juxtaposition needs to be analyzed. It is true that those prone to exploit will exploit whatever they can, nature and women alike, or poor, or minorities, the needy, the sick, or markets. Bacon's language, as Merchant observes, is revealingly sexist, as he links dominion of women and dominion of nature. Meanwhile, it strikes me that, on the whole, women are as pleased to enjoy the benefits of the scientific revolution as men—glad to have wealthy husbands, if not wealth of their own, amply enjoying consumption and the technologically-gained comforts in life. Given opportunity, they pursue power in business and politics with all the assertive enthusiasm of men (*vide* Margaret Thatcher, Indira Gandhi). There is more to the feminine psyche than the desire to be a nurturing mother.

Merchant finds that what is distinctive about males, especially those educated into the Scientific Revolution, is their capacity to reason, compared to the caring, nurturing capacities of women. She hopes that there is place for emotions, for tender-minded thinking. So far as she thinks that men demonstrate tough-minded thinking better than women, she can undermine her own argument, because she so amply demonstrates herself exactly those powers of reason in her historical analysis.

Survival of the Better Informed

The astronomical picture is of a paradoxically vast, simple, mechanical, but user-friendly universe. The biological picture is undoubtedly organic, which Merchant will welcome, and yet this too has proved challenging. To use a metaphor, it has proved difficult to "flesh out" organisms as machines. Biology is radically different from physics because of the struggle. Survival is the name of the game; nature is red in tooth and claw.

There is a feminine dimension that connects with the past. The evolutionary picture is of nature laboring in travail. The root idea in the English word "nature," going back to Latin and Greek origins, is that of "giving birth." Birthing is creative genesis, which certainly characterizes evolutionary nature. Birthing (as every mother knows) involves struggle. Earth slays her children, a seeming evil, but bears an annual crop in their stead. This pro-life, generative impulse is the most startling and valuable miracle of all. The "birthing" is nature's orderly self-assembling of new creatures amidst this perpetual perishing.

Merchant knows that this historical coupling of organism and the feminine is well founded. The original meaning of "nature" is "to give birth," Latin: *(g)nasci, natus*, a root in such words as native, nation, natal, navel. The root goes back to the Greek for giving birth, *ginomai*, surviving in such words as genesis, gene, progeny, pregnant, genius, gentile, generate. Such origins have given nature a feminine cast, which is not surprising, since females give birth. Generalizing, the whole system is Mother Nature. Mother Nature is a symbolic term, like Uncle Sam or Santa Claus, that does stand for something real: the prolific creative system to which we give the more mundane name Earth (like Uncle Sam stands for a real nation, and: "Yes, Virginia, there is a Santa Claus"). They remain mythical terms even while they stand for something real. Meanwhile we do not think that Earth is a mythical term, though it can be a symbolic term, because it is a real place.

But now the problem is not the *death of nature*, but *death in nature*. Nature is nothing but death. The evolutionary slaughter seems so uncaring. Again, there is a more inclusive perspective. The very idea of adapted fit also requires a niche, a place to be, and includes a life support system. The organism is selected to "fit in" as much as to control. An ecology is a home. That takes Merchant to her focus on ecosystems, toward which we are headed.

As dominant a metaphor as any in contemporary biology is *information*. Those who took physics a century back were taught that there are two fundamental things in the world: matter and energy. Einstein found that matter and energy are different forms of the same thing. Recently the biologists have been insisting on another metaphysical level: information. That is what is coded in the DNA, a "cybernetic" molecule. Indeed this "coding" and "information" can seem as literal as metaphorical. They seem pretty much fact of the matter.

Events on Earth stand in marked contrast with events on other planets, such as the gases that swirl around Jupiter. The life story is different, because in biology, unlike physics, chemistry, geomorphology, or astronomy, something can be learned. An organism is "informed" about how to make a way through the world, how to cope in its niche. Past achievements are recapitulated in the present, with variations; these results get tested today and then folded into the future.

Random mutation figures into a larger generative process; species generate and test new possibilities. The challenge is to get as much versatility coupled with as much stability as is possible. This requires optimizing twin maxima, keeping past knowledge while exploring the nearby search space for better adaptation. The genes function to conserve life; they also make possible a creative up-flow of life struggling through turnover of species and resulting in more diverse and complex forms of life, producing more out of less over millennia. The molecular processes are quite sophisticated; organisms regularly result that, engineers may say, are quite well built—as with dragonfly wings.

There is, we might notice, nothing feminine about this—although the natural history does result in more elaborated caring. This caring is by both female and male organisms; often, however, natural selection results in more caring for the young in females. Merchant with her feminism anticipates this "ethic of caring" (Merchant [1989] 2010:272) as characteristic of her webworked partnership ethic.

This evolution of more caring results not simply in caring for mates and the offspring, but in increasing webworked interdependence—equally for males and females. Life at such a boundary needs, above all, information, for it is such information by which it can form, or inform, matter and energy into the living molecules by which life is generated, regenerated, and maintained. If we are using metaphors, such as coding and information, to describe historical facts, is this leading or misleading?

Do we dare to say that the system is "headed" toward discovering more and more information? Some events do happen repeatedly. Consider forests. The phenomenon of forests is so widespread, persistent, and diverse, appearing almost wherever moisture and climatic conditions permit it, that forests cannot be accidents or anomalies in the Earth processes but rather must be a characteristic expression of the creative process. Likewise with grasslands. Consider species. One does not go from zero to five or ten million species, over several billion years, setbacks notwithstanding, by accident. Photoreceptors and eyes have evolved multiple times, discovering and reusing some basic light sensitive molecules. Flight has evolved on several occasions.

Something is at work additionally to life aimlessly tracking changing environments. The Earth has potential unfolding, and, whatever the accidental elements, we need to put an arrow on evolutionary time, at least on the up-building parts of it. Science discovers fertility in the system. Speaking of Mother Earth is the rhetorical, popular, classical way of doing this. Further, since nature is not particularly self-explanatory, this has often also been coupled with a Father God, who authorizes and undergirds this earthen creativity. But neither the female nor the male gender is the issue; the issue is parenting, come to focus on Earth, the only place where we know that this birthing has taken place. We need a historical account first, and then an ethic adequate for this creativity by which more comes out of less.

There is a systemic process, profoundly but partially described by evolutionary theory, a historical saga during which spectacular results are achieved. This value, commonly termed "survival value," is better interpreted as valuable information, coded genetically, that is apt for "living on and on" (*sur-vival*), for life's persisting in the midst of its perpetual perishing. This fecundity was classically termed "Mother Earth" or "Divine Creation." The fact of the matter is literally true, whatever we may think of the mythology used to explain it. Earth is a fertile planet, and in one sense that fertility is the deepest value category of all. Dismissing the mythology does not dissolve the valuable facts. Has evolutionary nature any *telos*? Does the genetic information produce more capacity for caring? Have we then moved to misleading metaphor? We might need Merchant's insights to find out.

Ecosystems and Partnerships

> The machine image that has dominated Western culture for the past three hundred years seems to be giving way to something new. Some call the transformation a 'new paradigm'; others call it 'deep ecology'; still others call for a postmodern ecological world view.
>
> *(Merchant [1980] 1990:xvii)*

Merchant knows science; she is after all a professor of the history of science; she majored in chemistry and once did graduate work in physics. She appeals to ecology, and analyzes "ecological revolutions." She can be anti-mechanism, anti-control, anti-capitalism, anti-technology, anti-reductionism, anti-instrumentalism, anti-maps and measurements, but she is pro-organism, pro-ecology and human ecology, pro-process, pro-webworks, pro-holism, pro-community (citing Leopold). "Ecological thinking, however, offers the possibility of a new relationship between humans and nonhuman nature that could lead to the sustainability of the biosphere in the future." "Ecology also offers a new ethic for grounding human relations with nature" (Merchant [1989] 2010:263).

Merchant seeks a partnership ethic, men partner with women, humans partner with nature. "Ecological thinking constructs nature as an active partner." "Nonhuman nature is an actor; human and nonhuman interactions constitute the drama" (Merchant [1989] 2010:23). This is well enough as a general principle, although it is rather hard to think of our relationship with wolves, or butterflies, crocodiles, snakes, whooping cranes, as partners. Mostly they just want to be left alone. We do have relationships with them. Are we partners with the wilderness areas we have set aside? Or with the giant sequoia trees? There is considerable drama in Americans setting aside 758 wilderness areas, or in international efforts to save over 5,000 endangered or threatened species. Humans are certainly related to their ecosystems; the "webwork" metaphor gets at this. Are we "partners" with anything, at least anything important to us in our webwork?

Are we partners with nonhuman nature? That depends on how you want to spin this metaphor—or, Merchant would say, what "social construction" we choose. Yes, if one wishes to consider as "partner" a dynamic Earth where the biota is inextricably linked to atmospheric, oceanic, and terrestrial processes. It is remarkable how, once the life forces are underway, they remold the environment out of which they first came further in a prolife direction. Life is not passive before geological and meteorological vicissitudes, but is interactive with these forces. The soil with its humus results from what otherwise would be only mineralogical earth. The atmosphere with its oxygen, carbon dioxide, and ozone shielding layer is a product of plant and animal life. The rivers and springs flow moderated by runoff which is controlled by vegetative cover, plant respiration, and evaporation rates. Life to some extent modifies its climate. There are feedback loops set up between the organic and the nonliving world, and these sometimes become feed forward loops. The phenomenon of organism on the planet does not simply accept a random physico-chemical nature, but rebuilds it with results that are more favorable to life. If one wishes to be feminine about it, the Earth is the womb from whence we come and which we really never leave. When we really do understand all this storied achievement taking place on our home planet, an *ought* arises from an *is* that is of *value, valuable*, able to generate momentous value.

Entering the Anthropocene Epoch?

"Ecological revolutions," Merchant argues, "are processes through which different societies change their relationships with nature" (Merchant [1989] 2010:23). *The Economist* announces: "Welcome to the Anthropocene"—the newest revolutionary relationship with nature (Economist, The 2011). Erle Ellis, celebrating what he calls the "Planet of No Return: Human Resilience on an Artificial Earth," concludes,

> We must shoulder the mantle of planetary stewardship … . Creating that future will mean going beyond fears of transgressing natural limits … . Most of all, we must not see the Anthropocene as a crisis, but as the beginning of a new geological epoch ripe with human-directed opportunity.
>
> *(Ellis 2011:44)*

He joins colleagues in the *New York Times*: "The new name is well deserved … The Anthropocene does not represent the failure of environmentalism. It is the stage on which a new, more positive and forward-looking environmentalism can be built" (Marris et al. 2011).

This high profile discourse showcases the expanding human genius. Is there any way to conceive of humans and nature in mutual partnership in this forthcoming Anthropocene? Or does there come with this ecological revolution a fear of human domination of nature returning with a vengeance?

We need to re-figure conservation in this novel future in which we celebrate a new epoch, named after ourselves. The way forward for conservationists is to embrace an ever-increasing human management of the landscape, perpetual enlargement of the bounds of the human empire. Humans are in the driver's seat. The Anthropocene is "humanity's defining moment" (Seielstad 2012). We are "the God species" (Lynas 2011). The editors of a *Scientific American* special issue, "Managing Planet Earth," ask "What kind of planet do we want? What kind of planet can we get?" (Clark 1989).

With such calls for controlling Earth, and mindful of Merchant's warnings about controlling metaphors, we worry that those who forget history are condemned to repeat it. Perhaps she can help us use history as a corrective for better focus on our controlling assumptions.

A more considered if still Anthropocene future is celebrated in *An Ecomodernist Manifesto*, advocated by a dozen and a half international environmental leaders. We "describe our vision for putting humankind's extraordinary powers in the service of creating a good Anthropocene" (Asafu-Adjaye et al. 2015:7). Their dominant metaphor (social, material, natural) is "freedom," which appeals to us all. But the question, combining "eco" and "modernism," is: Are we seeking freedom from nature, control over it, or freedom within nature, harmony with it? "Modernism is the long-term evolution of social, economic, political, and technological arrangements in human societies toward vastly improved material well-being, public health, resource productivity, economic integration, shared infrastructure, and personal freedom" (Asafu-Adjaye et al. 2015:28). This is extraordinary humanism, but what are the human relations with nature?

The ecomodernists hope for "an ecologically vibrant planet" (Asafu-Adjaye et al. 2015:31). Surely this modern humanism will treasure ecosystem services. But no. These ecomodernists anticipate what they call "decoupling." "Human technologies ... have made humans less reliant upon the many ecosystems that once provided their only sustenance" (p. 9). Yes, technology can be "double-edged" (p. 17); there is serious threat of environmental deterioration, such as with climate change, or pollution, but future humans can fix these human-caused problems. With increasing industrial agriculture and rising harvest yields, there are no foreseeable limits to producing food. People now are free to and prefer to live in cities, and they will prefer fewer children. This frees up landscapes no longer needed. So the freer humans are, the more they can let selected natural areas go free, wildlands, restored forests. Humans will, of course, often want to recreate in such areas, they are even freer if they have such opportunity. Humans encountering original nature can be "important for their psychological and spiritual well-being" (p. 25).

> Taken together, these trends mean that the total human impact on the environment, including land-use change, overexploitation, and pollution, can peak and decline this century. By understanding and promoting these emergent processes, humans have the opportunity to re-wild and re-green the Earth—even as developing countries achieve modern living standards, and material poverty ends.
>
> *(p. 15)*

Such decoupling results in more freedom for humans and more freedom for nature. "Decoupling raises the possibility that societies might achieve peak human impact without intruding much further on relatively untouched areas. Nature unused is nature spared" (p. 19).

But none of this sounds like partnership. "We affirm one long-standing environmental ideal, that humanity must shrink its impacts on the environment to make more room for nature, while we reject another, that human societies must harmonize with nature to avoid economic and ecological collapse" (p. 6). The dominant hope is, that "the trajectory of the Anthropocene" is "The Great Acceleration"—to use the title of Will Steffen (Steffen et al. 2015). When human progress is progressively upscaled, peaked out, managing an engineered planet, the importance of ecosystem services is downscaled.

There is nothing here of nature as an active partner, nothing of a drama of interdependence. Entering the Anthropocene denatures us—even if this is, as the ecomodernists themselves worry, "not a world we want" (Asafu-Adjaye et al. 2015:26). Merchant was involved in a seminar entitled "The Fate of Nature in the Anthropocene" during the academic year 2015–2016. Perhaps we will hear from her more directly analyzing, unmasking the framework of justifications in the Anthropocene. She now says she prefers an Epoch of Sustainability, and dislikes any thinking of an Anthropocene Epoch.

Earth: Planet with Promise

Merchant laments the death of nature and claims that long-standing senses of community and participation were lost in the Scientific Revolution. Can any of those ancient worldviews still offer insight for modernists entering the Anthropocene Epoch?

Prominent among those classic worldviews, going back three millennia was Jewish monotheism, continued in the Christian faith, still vital in the Medieval period. This tradition does have a father God, patriarchs, and limited the role of women. Nonetheless, both Judaism and Christianity were convinced that the earth was divine creation. The ancient Hebrews had their promised land, a land flowing with milk and honey, their corner of landscape which they envisioned, in ideal if not in real, as a garden earth, a sacred gift, provisioned for life. The Hebrews discovered *who* they were as they discovered *where* they were.

Jesus saw the presence of God clearly in the natural world in which he resided, the birds of the air, the flowers of the field. Not even the grandeur of the courts of Solomon exceeded the glories of the lilies. Divinely given, earthen nature is the original act of grace. Made in the image of God, humans did have dominion over nature, yet humans were put in their place, stewards, trustees of a creation found to be very good.

Today and for the century hence, a powerful and increasingly attractive wordview is to see Earth as a planet with promise, destined for abundant life. When Earth's most complex product, *Homo sapiens*, becomes intelligent enough to reflect over this earthy wonderland, nobody has much doubt that this is a precious place. Rocket scientists, loving their marvelous, high-tech machines, are still concerned to celebrate our organic, vital planet. Viewing Earthrise from the Moon, the astronaut Edgar Mitchell, was entranced:

> Suddenly from behind the rim of the moon, in long, slow-motion moments of immense majesty, there emerges a sparkling blue and white jewel, a light, delicate sky-blue sphere laced with slowly swirling veils of white, rising gradually like a small pearl in a thick sea of black mystery. It takes more than a moment to fully realize this is Earth … home.
>
> *(Mitchell, quoted in Kelley 1988, at photographs:42–45)*

The astronaut Michael Collins recalled being earthstruck: "Earth is to be treasured and nurtured, something precious that must endure" (Collins 1980:6). Even Edward O. Wilson, scientist and secular humanist, still exclaims, "The biospheric membrane that covers the Earth, and you and me, … is the miracle we have been given" (Wilson 2002:21).

We love our home country, cherished often as a divine gift. The American landscape with its purple mountains' majesties, fruited plains, its fauna and flora from sea to shining sea is divinely created, no less than Canaan from the Negev to Mount Hermon. John Muir, recalling the Psalmist, sings, "The forests of America, however slighted by man, must have been a great delight to God; for they were the best he ever planted" (Muir [1911] 1988:331; Psalm 104.16). And landscapes around the globe, east and west, north and south, on six continents (though not the seventh) have proved homelands that peoples can come to cherish and on which they can flourish. We are increasingly concerned to be ecologists who know the logic of our home, "*oikos*"; or, to reach for a religious word, ecumenists, those whose vision is the "*oikumene,*" the whole inhabited Earth. That promises an ecologically-based partnership ethic of global dimensions.

The challenge of the last millennium has been to pass from the medieval to the modern world, building modern cultures and nations, an explosion of cultural development, made possible by science and technology. Merchant contends that this aggressive vision has led us astray. She is right to challenge us that, in the next millennium, we must learn to contain those cultures within the carrying capacity of the larger community of life on our home planet. We are natives of nations and we are Earth natives too.

The ancient Hebrews insisted that they were given a blessing with a mandate.

> You shall walk in all the way which the Lord your God has commanded you, that you may live, and that it may go well with you, and that you may live long in the land which you shall possess … . Hear therefore, O Israel, and be careful to do [these commandments] that it may go well with you,

and that you may multiply greatly, as the Lord, the God of your fathers, has promised you, in a land flowing with milk and honey.

(Deuteronomy 6)

That the land flows with milk and honey (assuming good land husbandry) has to be coupled with divine law, if there is to be a sustainable society. Again, Merchant is not so interested in divine law, nor are many of our contemporaries today.

But before dismissing this as archaic patriarchy, consider what that law urged. The Hebrew prophets insisted that their promised land does not flow with milk and honey for all unless and until justice rolls down like waters. There can be no intelligent human ecology except as people learn to use land justly and charitably. Nor is this only an ethic for dripping honey into human mouths. Fauna and flora are included within their covenant. "Behold I establish my covenant with you and your descendants after you, and with every living creature that is with you, the birds, the cattle, and every beast of the earth with you" (Genesis 9.5). This is "the covenant which I make between me and you and every living creature that is with you, for all future generations" (Genesis 9.12–13). "Keep them alive with you" (Genesis 6.19). There is no "death of nature" in the Bible.

Spelled in the lower case, earth is the ground under our feet; we can own it and manage it to our liking, or live in a penthouse and hardly ever touch it. Spelled in the upper case, Earth is not something we outgrow or rebuild and manage to our liking; it is the ground of our being. We humans too belong on the planet; it is our home, as much as it is for all the others. But the glistening pearl in space may not be something we want to possess, so much as a sacred biosphere we ought to inhabit with love. "Welcome to the Anthropocene!"—seen as an epoch in which the dominant species—humans—increasingly treasure their planet with promise. With that conviction, we can bring Merchant forward to the cutting edge of the world agenda today.

References

Asafu-Adjaye, John, Linus Blomqvist, Stewart Brand, Barry Brook, Ruth de Fries, Erle Ellis, Christopher Foreman, David Keith, Martin Lewis, Mark Lynas, Ted Nordhaus, RogerPielkeJr., Rachel Pritzker, Joyashree Roy, Mark Sagoff, Michael Shellenberger, Robert Stone, and Peter Teague. 2015. "An Ecomodernist Manifesto." www.ecom odernism.org/manifesto

Boyle, Robert. [1686] 1996. *A Free Enquiry into the Vulgarly Received Notion of Nature*, ed. E. S. Davis and M. Hunter. Cambridge: Cambridge University Press.

Clark, William C. 1989. "Managing Planet Earth." *Scientific American* 261 (3, September): 46–54.

Collins, Michael. 1980. "Foreword." In Roy A. Gallant, *Our Universe*. Washington, DC: National Geographic Society.

Economist, The. 2011. "Welcome to the Anthropocene," May 28, 2011, Vol. 399, Issue 8735.

Einstein, Albert. 1970. *Out of My Later Years*, revised reprint edition. Westport, CT: Greenwood Press.

Ellis, Erle. 2011. "The Planet of No Return." *Breakthrough Journal*, 2(Fall):39–44. http://breakthroughjournal.org/content/authors/erle-ellis/the-planet-of-no-return.shtml

Kelley, Kevin W., ed. 1988. *The Home Planet*. Reading, MA: Addison-Wesley.

Lynas, Mark. 2011. *The God Species: Saving the Planet in the Age of Humans*. Washington, DC: National Geographic.

Marris, Emma, P. Kareiva, J. Mascaro, and Erle C. Ellis. 2011. "Hope in the Age of Man." *New York Times*, December 8, p. A-39.

Merchant, Carolyn. [1980] 1990. *The Death of Nature: Women, Ecology, and the Scientific Revolution*. San Francisco, CA: Harper SanFrancisco.

Merchant, Carolyn. [1989] 2010. *Ecological Revolutions*. Chapel Hill, NC: The University of North Carolina Press.

Muir, John. [1911] 1988. *My First Summer in the Sierra*. San Francisco, CA: Sierra Club Books.

Rees, Martin. 2001. *Our Cosmic Habitat*. Princeton, NJ: Princeton University Press.

Seielstad, George A. 2012. *Dawn of the Anthropocene: Humanity's Defining Moment*. Alexandria, VA: American Geosciences Institute. (ebook)

Steffen, Will, et al. 2015. "The Trajectory of the Anthropocene: The Great Acceleration." *The Anthropocene Review* 2(1):81–89.

Weinberg, Steven. [1977] 1993. *The First Three Minutes*. New York: Basic Books.

Wigner, Eugene P. 1960. "The Unreasonable Effectiveness of Mathematics in the Natural Sciences." *Communications on Pure and Applied Mathematics* 13(1):1–14.

Wilson, Edward O. 2002. *The Future of Life*. New York: Alfred A. Knopf.

PART II

Environmental History

7

PERSONAL, POLITICAL, AND PROFESSIONAL

The Impact of Carolyn Merchant's Life and Leadership

Nancy C. Unger

As I began to think about composing this chapter, I was shocked by the realization that while Carolyn Merchant and I have exchanged various emails, we have only met twice, and one of those times was a brief encounter at a conference. Yet Carolyn looms large in my life—she is in many ways responsible for my career. Like other contributors to this volume, I have predicated much of my own research on her work. A large part of this chapter focuses on her intellectual influence. Early in my career I authored a number of environmentally-themed essays, but struggled to fulfill my desire to make a coherent, major contribution. While my career took a somewhat winding and nontraditional path, Carolyn's scholarship helped me to find my niche as an environmental historian. Once I found my book project, *Beyond Nature's Housekeepers*, I finally hit my stride. As Carolyn had done before me, I combined interest in women's history with the environmental past. In view of the ways in which gender and place have constantly shaped my own life, I focused on how popular notions of what it meant to be a man or a woman changed over time, while also being continuously impacted differently by factors as seemingly gender-neutral as the environment and environmental issues. I start this chapter, however, on a more personal note by discussing Carolyn's impact on my teaching. I also explore how she helped to shape both my feminist consciousness and my sense of myself as an academic, both leading ultimately to my position as a full professor and department chair.

Becoming an Environmental Historian

In 1994 I was laid off from my position as a lecturer at San Francisco State University. My grading assistant had earned his undergraduate degree at Santa Clara University and suggested that I give its history department a call. Rather to my surprise, I learned that they were looking for a lecturer to replace a professor about to embark on a year's sabbatical. During the interview I lied my head off about all the things I felt prepared to teach. Although my training is in the politics of the Progressive Era, I confidently agreed to all the courses they named. Colonies and Constitution? Sure! History of the American West? Of course! A seminar in Historical Writing? Why not? American Women's History? California History? I actually had some experience teaching those two. But as accustomed as I was to saying "yes" first and scrambling to put the course together later, when asked if I could design the university's first environmental history class, I paused. The interview team explained that the coming academic year would feature a campus-wide Institute on Environment, and such a course would be a key component. This sounded like a challenge even for a "how hard can it be?" adjunct like myself, who always believed that any teaching schedule, no matter how daunting, beat unemployment.

It wasn't until the next day that I called to confirm that Environmental History would be one of the six courses I was committed to teaching. The minute I hung up, I hit the panic button. What had I done? Environmental History? I wasn't entirely sure I knew what it was. However, as an undergraduate I had loved Roderick Nash's *Wilderness and the American Mind* (Nash 1973), and, as a scholar of the Progressive Era, I was well versed in Theodore Roosevelt's conservation leadership. So I began casting about for books to assign, thinking that with any luck, I might be able to stay a page or two ahead of my students. I settled pretty quickly on William Cronon's *Changes in the Land: Indians, Colonists, and the Ecology of New England* (Cronon 1983), and Donald Worster's *Rivers of Empire: Water, Aridity, and the Growth of the American West* (Worster 1992). What I needed now was a core text. In view of the bonanza of texts available today, pickings were then relatively thin, particularly because I didn't want to assign a narrative. I considered the third edition of Rod Nash's *American Environmentalism: Readings in Conservation History* (Nash 1989), but then found Carolyn Merchant's *Major Problems in American Environmental History* (Merchant 1993). I wanted my students (and me) to grapple with exactly what Carolyn's book provided: key documents and provocative essays that would invite us to draw our own conclusions, to think critically and creatively.

Reading Carolyn's textbook in preparation for my class was a marvelous introduction to the field. I quit feeling overwhelmed and intimidated because I was too busy being fascinated and challenged. Once the quarter began, the biology professor who was in charge of the Institute on Environment asked how my class was going. I raved about Carolyn's book and about how much my students and I were enjoying debating the meaning of the various documents, and arguing over the different viewpoints presented in the scholarly articles. I noted that Carolyn was just up the road at Berkeley and said wistfully that I wished she could talk to my class. The biology professor listened thoughtfully and said, "Why don't you invite her to come? The Institute has a budget. We'll pay for her hotel and a modest honorarium, and put on a breakfast for you and your students, and invite the larger campus community."

I had taught more than eight years within the California State University system, driving back and forth between my home in Mountain View, to San Francisco State, and what was then Cal State Hayward. In all those years as a "Road Scholar," I had never had a request for additional funding approved, let alone had one offered to me. After I came out of my faint, I quickly accepted.

Enter Carolyn Merchant

And so it was that I met Carolyn. I was thrilled that such an eminent scholar was willing to come to our campus, and so pleased that my students were going to have the chance to interact with the author of the book that had spurred so much learning and critical thinking. I expected her to be brilliant, which of course she was. But she was also funny and charming. And I know that my impression isn't merely due to a memory burnished by time, because the university taped her session and for years I showed it on the last day of my environmental history courses.

Not only did Carolyn captivate my students, but after her presentation she took the time to talk to me about my career path. My children were young at that time. I was struggling to combine career and family, and worried that I was going to be a career lecturer. Carolyn offered some thoughtful reflection born out of her own experience. It was reassuring to know that Carolyn too had faced similar challenges, yet managed to enjoy raising her children without sacrificing her career. Even more important, she was enormously supportive and encouraging. When a scholar of Carolyn's reputation treats you not as a charlatan but as a colleague and a peer, you can't help but stand a little taller and think a bit more highly of yourself. It was a vote of confidence I sorely needed.

As my one-year contract at Santa Clara was repeatedly renewed, Environmental History became one of my regular offerings. When Carolyn asked me if I'd review *Major Problems in American Environmental History* for the press as they prepared to create the second edition, I was flattered. And because I wanted to impress her, I put a lot into the review. Doing so meant I had to think long and hard about all that I had been learning about environmental history, what was working in my classroom, what wasn't, and how to go about teaching the course in the best way possible. That course continued to evolve and became a staple, contributing to the university's decision to approve a three-pronged tenure track position: 50% History, 25% Environmental Studies, and 25% Women and Gender Studies.

Undoubtedly due in large part to the letter of recommendation that Carolyn took the time to write on my behalf, I began that assistant professorship in the fall of 2000, just as my first book, *Fighting Bob La Follette: The Righteous Reformer*, was published (Unger [2000] 2008). That monograph earned favorable reviews in scholarly journals and in the *New York Times*, and won the Wisconsin Historical

Society Book of Merit Award. Nevertheless, I learned that to earn tenure I was expected not only to teach in all three areas that made up my position, but to publish in them as well. And so it came to pass that Carolyn not only contributed significantly to my success in the classroom through her scholarship and personal encouragement, and helped me to gain a tenure track position after more than fourteen years as a lecturer, but also paved the way for the research that would ultimately broaden my scholarly reputation and cement my career.

Merchant Inspires New Directions in Research

Wondering what project I could undertake to satisfy all three prongs of my position, I found inspiration in Carolyn's groundbreaking article, "Women of the Progressive Conservation Movement: 1900–1916," which included a sentence that resounded deeply: "Man the moneymaker had left it to woman the moneysaver to preserve resources" (Merchant 1984:65). It helped me think from a different perspective about a period I thought I knew very well. And it encouraged me, as I continued to develop both my environmental history and women's history courses, to pursue the fascinating overlap between the two fields that increasingly intrigued both me and my students.

My decision to focus my research at the intersection of environment and gender was strongly reinforced when both Richard White and Vera Norwood noted in their essays for the *Pacific Historical Review* forum, "Environmental History, Retrospect and Prospect," the need for broader and more thoughtful and analytic investigations into the powerful relationship between gender and the environment throughout history. "Environmental history," Norwood noted, "is just beginning to integrate gender analyses into mainstream work" (Norwood 2001:84). That assessment was particularly striking coming, as it did, after Norwood described the kind of ongoing and damaging misperceptions about nature and gender that are perpetuated by ignorance concerning the role of diversity, including gender, within environmental history. White concurred with Norwood, but he also issued a clear warning about the current trends in including the role of gender: "The danger ... is not that gendering will be ignored in environmental history but that it will become predictable—an endless rediscovery that humans have often made nature female. Gender has more work to do than that" (White 2001:109). Indeed, it did—and still does.

Yet as prescient as White and Norwood appear, their essays came four years after Melissa Leach and Cathy Green had made a similar call in the British journal *Environment and History* (Leach and Green 1997), and more than a decade after Carolyn proposed in the *Journal of American History* that gender perspective be added to conceptual frameworks in environmental history (Merchant 1990). And Carolyn hadn't just been calling for this work; she'd been pioneering it, most significantly with her paradigm-changing *The Death of Nature: Women, Ecology and the Scientific Revolution* (hereafter *TDN*). In this profound work she sought "to examine the values associated with the images of women and nature as they relate to the formation of our modern world and their implications for our lives today" (Merchant 1980:xxi). Her nuanced examination of the Scientific Revolution showed how the mechanistic worldview of modern science sanctioned the exploitation of nature, unrestrained commercial expansion, and a new socioeconomic order that subordinates women.

Carolyn's recognition of the link between the exploitation of nature and the subordination of women deepened my thinking as both a scholar of American women's history and as an environmental historian, and challenged me to explore the intersections of those two fields. In combination with "Women of the Progressive Conservation Movement," Carolyn's *Ecological Revolutions: Nature, Gender, and Science in New England* (Merchant 1989), demonstrated how the broad philosophical ideas and theories about gender and environment explored in *TDN* could be applied to American history. It was exciting stuff, especially her vision of New England as a "mirror of the world," in which, as evolutionary ecological changes were dramatically sped up, relations between men and women were also radically altered. Her *Earthcare: Women and the Environment* (Merchant 1996) raised issues about the problematic assumptions of women as caregivers that further deepened my thinking about history. It also helped to shape my feminist consciousness. Those views were reinforced by Carolyn's *Reinventing Eden: The Fate of Nature in Western Culture* (Merchant 2003). As my university's environmental studies program drafted its mission statement, I remember arguing forcefully during a meeting to a skeptical senior colleague that the language promoting stewardship over nonhuman nature should be abandoned in favor of recognizing nature as an equal partner. It was the first time my fears about making enemies and jeopardizing my tenure bid were trumped by my philosophical convictions.

Building on Merchant's Foundations

It was time for me to start exploring some of the important intersections that Carolyn had identified. The sophistication of Carolyn's intellect makes her work especially appealing to scholars not only in this country, but throughout the world, as evidenced by the number of her works translated into multiple languages. I saw as my mission to apply her theories and philosophies to American history in layperson's terms using practical examples. It's the kind of "meat and potatoes" history that I do best. Much of my work is dedicated to revealing the powerful role that gender has played in the ways Americans have viewed the environment, and environmental issues, based largely on how social norms defined a "natural" or "true" man or woman. Although these qualities were routinely described as the result of one's biological sex and were therefore supposedly essential and eternal, in fact they stemmed from gender prescriptions and therefore changed dramatically over time, especially when compounded by additional factors including economic class, race, ethnicity, age, and reproductive abilities.

Several of my early environmental history efforts were co-authored by Marie Bolton, an American historian working in France who is deeply interested in environmental history, especially concerning California. Carolyn's collection of documents and essays *Green Versus Gold: Sources in California's Environmental History* (Merchant 1998), had demonstrated to us that there was an audience for histories focused on the environmental aspects of this single state. We produced a number of essays and articles (Bolton and Unger 2002, 2004, 2010a, 2010b, 2012). All but one of these works focuses on California, and in every one we followed Merchant's lead in tracing various aspects of the history of ecological and human interactions in the development of place.

Writing with Marie is always a delightful experience, and our early works in particular added to my confidence as an environmental scholar, but our publications were read primarily in France. Moreover, despite our shared emphasis on California's environmental history, the articles and essays we wrote together did not seem to be moving toward a cohesive body of work. My first chance to really build on what I had learned from Carolyn and reach an American audience came with an opportunity to contribute to Rachel Stein's edited collection, *New Perspectives on Environmental Justice: Gender, Sexuality, and Activism* (Unger 2004). In the book's introduction Rachel describes my essay "Women, Sexuality, and Environmental Justice in American History," as providing

> examples of individual North American women of various races whom we might view as contemporary environmental justice activists. Surveying pre-Columbian Native American women, enslaved African American women, early urban reformers and birth-control advocates, environmentalist Rachel Carson, lesbian back-to-the-land movements, and Women of all Red Nations, Unger argues that such women approached environmental issues and sexuality/reproductivity as interlocking in varied ways, and pursued those intersections as a means of resisting oppression and struggling for greater self-determination and social and environmental justice.
>
> *(Stein 2004:9)*

The Pieces Fall into Place

I had found my niche. I would continue to use my skills as an American historian to demonstrate, as vividly as possible, some of the core truths and ideas set out in Carolyn's groundbreaking philosophies that were generating exciting new thinking all around the world. My essay "Gendered Approaches to Environmental Justice: An Historical Sampling" appeared in the edited collection *Echoes from the Poisoned Well: Global Memories of Environmental Injustice* (Unger 2006a). Two years later I published "The Role of Gender in Environmental History" in *Environmental Justice* (Unger 2008).

Carolyn's insistence that gender has always had a major impact on how Americans think about the environment and how they treat it and react to it revealed an important truth that I was determined be recognized and appreciated beyond the academy. My first serious effort to engage a non-scholarly audience in meaningful thought about gender, environmental justice, and ecofeminism was to write an article that eschewed those terms in favor of more user-friendly language less likely to intimidate or alienate the general reader. The result was "The 'We Say What We Think' Club: Rural Wisconsin Women and the Development of Environmental Ethics," published in the glossy, highly illustrated *Wisconsin Magazine of History* (Unger 2006b). Despite its non-scholarly venue, the article received an honorable mention for the 2007 Alice Hamilton Article Prize of the American Society for Environmental History. I was so pleased with the article, and the enthusiastic readers' responses it generated, that I followed it up with two more in that magazine: "Women for a Peaceful Christmas: Wisconsin Homemakers Seek to Remake American Culture," and "Wisconsin's League against Nuclear Dangers: The Power of Informed Citizenship" (Unger 2009–2010, 2012–2013). In all these works I explore both the strengths and weaknesses of the assumptions Carolyn identified in *Earthcare* about women as caregivers for the environment. I reveal as well the healing possibilities that can emerge when, as she urges, nonhuman nature is treated as a partner, rather than an entity to be either exploited or stewarded. I began to augment the presentations I was giving at academic conferences with illustrated talks to whatever more general audiences would have me, becoming a regular at the Humanist Community of Silicon Valley.

In 2002 I began teaching lesbian and gay American history at my Jesuit university, an experience I detailed in "Teaching 'Straight' Lesbian and Gay History," for the *Journal of American History* (Unger 2007). Becoming immersed in that subject matter led me to build further on the foundation established by Carolyn. I explored new connections within gender and environment in "The Role of Nature in Lesbian Alternative Environments in the United States: From Jook Joints to Sisterspace" for the edited collection *Queer Ecologies: Sex, Nature, Biopolitics, and Desire* (Unger 2010).

Continued Inspiration

Despite my various publications, it was the opportunity to write a blind review for *Environmental History* of (unbeknown to me) one of Carolyn's works that gave me the feeling that I had arrived as an environmental historian. In 2009, editor Mark Cioc invited me to evaluate a submission by an undisclosed author, the routine among peer-reviewed journals. It was an original and thought-provoking manuscript, and Mark termed the suggestions I offered to further hone its thesis and strengthen its arguments "a great review." When the revised article appeared in the journal as "George Bird Grinnell's Audubon Society: Bridging the Gender Divide in Conservation" (Merchant 2010), I felt pride that it incorporated my recommendations, and chagrin that I hadn't recognized the manuscript as Carolyn's. Even in draft form, it was pure Merchant—a deft weaving of gender and environmental theory firmly grounded in compelling evidence. It is among my favorites of all her many works.

Carolyn's work inspired me to continue to bring to the historical record concrete examples of the interactions between gender and environment in the United States. But, like many an environmental historian before me, I was faced with students and a general public that seemed convinced that "environmental history" really meant "history of the environmental movement." A subset of that belief was that when such histories were devoted to women, they would consist solely of biographies or vignettes of women environmentalists, women nature writers, or ecofeminists. It became increasingly clear to me that what was needed was a monograph that revealed how prescribed gender roles led American women to react differently from men to the environment and environmental issues, from the pre-Columbian period to the present, not just since the first Earth Day in 1970. Carolyn's many works, which range across time periods to engagingly demonstrate human and environmental relationships, served as an inspiration and model. The result was my book *Beyond Nature's Housekeepers: American Women in Environmental History* (Unger 2012), which I summarized as:

> From pre-Columbian times to the environmental justice movements of the present, women and men frequently responded to the environment and environmental issues in profoundly different ways. Although both environmental history and women's history are flourishing, explorations of the synergy produced by the interplay between environment and sex, sexuality, and gender are just beginning. Offering more than "great women in environmental history," this book examines the intersections that shaped women's unique environmental concerns and activism, and that framed the way the larger culture responded. Women discussed include Native Americans, colonists, enslaved field workers, pioneers, homemakers, municipal housekeepers, immigrants, hunters, nature writers, soil conservationists, scientists, migrant laborers, lesbians, nuclear protestors, and environmental justice activists. As women, they fared, thought, and acted in ways complicated by social, political, and economic norms, as well as issues of sexuality and childbearing.
>
> The housekeeping role assigned to women has long been recognized as important in environmental history. But that emphasis ignores the vast range of their influence and experiences. Enslaved women, left to do the fieldwork in disproportionate numbers, used their environmental knowledge to subtly undermine their masters, hastening the coming of the Civil War. Many pregnant women, faced with childbirth on the western trails, eyed frontier environments with considerable apprehension. In more recent times, lesbians have created alternative environments to resist homophobia and, in many economically disadvantaged communities, women have been at the forefront of the fight against environmental racism.
>
> Women are not always the heroes in this story, as when the popularity of hats lavishly decorated with feathers brought some bird species to near

extinction. For better, and sometimes for worse, women have played a unique role in the shaping of the American environment. Their stories feature vibrant characters and shine a light on an underappreciated, often inspiring, and always complex history.

Beyond Nature's Housekeepers was a finalist for the California Book Award. It was also gratifying to see the connection between my work and Carolyn's recognized in one review: "Unger builds on previous studies of the environment by scholars such as Carolyn Merchant" (Maudlin 2014:87).

Embracing Different Forms of Scholarship

Carolyn has also been my role model (and unsuspecting mentor) with respect to the types of scholarship she does. Her willingness to produce top-quality reference works (handbooks, encyclopedias, and the like, including *The Columbian Guide to American Environmental History* (Merchant 2005) and *American Environmental History: An Introduction* (Merchant 2007)), made me re-think my resistance to such work. When I saw how user-friendly and stimulating her reference volumes were, I began to appreciate their importance to the field. So when I was working on *Beyond Nature's Housekeepers*, I accepted an invitation to write the essay on gender for the *Oxford Handbook of Environmental History*. Writing that essay, ultimately titled "Women and Gender: Useful Categories of Analysis in Environmental History" (Unger 2014b), renewed my veneration of Carolyn. Pressed to make the piece less Americentric, I became even more acutely aware of my woeful ignorance of the environmental histories beyond the borders of the United States, and marveled once again at the depth, but especially the breadth, of Carolyn's expertise. The fact that she produced the region-specific *Green Versus Gold: Sources in California's Environmental History* (Merchant 1998) as well as the sweeping coedited three-volume *The Encyclopedia of World Environmental History* (Merchant, Krech, and McNeill 2004), is testament to her ability to create comprehensive studies at both the macro and micro level. Having conquered my resistance to reference works, I recently co-produced *A Companion to the Gilded Age and Progressive Era* (Nichols and Unger 2017) with Christopher McKnight Nichols. We solicited and edited essays by leading scholars on a wide array of subjects in the various subfields within the period. Pulling together and polishing the work of others seemed like a Herculean task, and my admiration increased for Carolyn's expertise and productivity in editing diverse works into a coherent whole.

In the last few years my focus has returned to my first love in history, the Progressive Era, resulting in the prize-winning *Belle La Follette: Progressive Era Reformer* (Unger 2016a). But Carolyn's imprint on my professional life remains indelible. I felt compelled, for example, to include a section on La Follette's environmental activism. And once again I teamed up with my friend and colleague Marie Bolton, this time to produce the essay "'Mother Nature is Getting Angrier': Turning Sacred Navajo Land into a Toxic Environment" (Bolton and Unger 2015), with yet another co-authored environmental essay currently in the works. Perhaps most significantly, in my role as a public intellectual I continue to bring broad recognition some of the key concepts first revealed by Carolyn. Venues for my talks on gender in environmental history include the Commonwealth Club in San Francisco (Unger 2014a), Town Hall Seattle (available on C-SPAN) (Unger 2013), and regional offices of the Environmental Protection Agency. CNN.com featured my op-ed on women's environmental leadership on its homepage in celebration of Earth Day (Unger 2013); I've spoken about women in environmental history on National Public Radio (Gardner 2014, 2015); was featured on KQED (Public Radio for Northern California) on the fiftieth anniversary of the Wilderness Preservation Act (Krasny 2014); and gave the keynote at the "Out for Sustainability" conference in San Francisco (Unger 2016b), the same year that *Time* ran my op-ed on the role of place in LGBTQ history (Unger 2016c). It's rewarding and exciting work that brings the importance of environmental history to wider audiences, and keeps me ever grateful for Carolyn's sustained leadership.

Merchant's Ongoing Influence

All who have contributed to this volume, of course, engage with various aspects of the myriad contributions of Carolyn Merchant. For me that impact has been personal and professional, affecting multiple aspects of my life: my teaching, my scholarship, and my efforts to balance career and family. Her work has inspired some of my best thinking, and empowered me to foster creative and critical thinking in others. Carolyn's disciples are legion and we all are profoundly grateful for the breadth and depth of her work. It is a thrill to watch the ongoing ripple effect of her thinking on the field she has been so central in creating—to watch her important legacy unfold in my own life and in the lives of so many others.

References

Bolton, Marie and Nancy C. Unger. 2002. "Pollution, Refineries, and People: Environmental Justice in Contra Costa County, California, 1980." Pp. 425–437 in *The Modern Demon: Pollution in Urban and Industrial European Societies*. Christoph Bernhardt and Genvieive Massard-Guilbaud, eds. France: University of Clermont Press.

Bolton, Marie and Nancy C. Unger. 2004. "The Case for Cautious Optimism: California Environmental Propositions in the Late Twentieth Century." Pp. 81–102 in *La Californie: Périphérie ou laboratoire?* Annick Foucrier and Antoine Coppolani, eds. Paris: L'Harmattan.

Bolton, Marie and Nancy C. Unger. 2010a. "Housing Reconstruction After the Catastrophe: The Failed Promise of San Francisco's 1906 'Earthquake Cottages'." *Annales de Demographie Historique* 2:217–240.

Bolton, Marie and Nancy C. Unger. 2010b. "Rivers of Republic, Rivers of Empire: The Transformation of a Young Soldier, 1892–1893." Pp. 340–350 in *Waterways and Colonies: France and Its Empires (17th–20th centuries)*. Mickaél Augeron and Robert DuPlessis eds. Paris: Les Indes Savantes.

Bolton, Marie and Nancy C. Unger. 2012. "Hope and Disappointment: San Francisco Housing Reconstruction after the 1906 Earthquake and Fire." Pp. 57–68 in *San Francisco: Á L'ouest D'Éden*. Sophie Vallas, ed. France: Presses Universitaires de Provence.

Bolton, Marie and Nancy C. Unger. 2015. "'Mother Nature is Getting Angrier': Turning Sacred Navajo Land into a Toxic Environment." Pp. 31–45 in *Environmental Crisis and Human Costs*. Ufuk Özdağ and François Gavillon, eds. Madrid: Universidad de Alcalá.

Cronon, William. 1983. *Changes in the Land: Indians, Colonists, and the Ecology of New England*. New York: Hill & Wang.

Gardner, Sarah. 2014. "Women Led Air Pollution Protests from the Start." Marketplace program, National Public Radio, July 14. Recording online. www.marketplace.org/topics/sustainability/we-used-be-china/women-led-air-pollution-protests-start

Gardner, Sarah. 2015. "An Environmental Movement is Awakening in China." Marketplace program, National Public Radio, March 16. Recording online. www.marketplace.org/2015/03/16/sustainability/environmental-movement-awakening-china

Krasny, Michael. 2014. "Celebrating 50 Years of the Wilderness Act." KQED Radio, September. Recording online. www.kqed.org/a/forum/R201409030930

Leach, Melissa and Cathy Green. 1997. "Gender and Environmental History: From Representation of Women and Nature to Gender Analysis of Ecology and Politics." *Environment and History* 3:343–370.

Maudlin, Erin Stewart. 2014. "Review of Beyond Natures Housekeepers." *History: Reviews of New Books* 42 (3, May):87–88.

Merchant, Carolyn. 1980. *The Death of Nature: Women, Ecology and the Scientific Revolution*. New York: HarperCollins.

Merchant, Carolyn. 1984. "Women of the Progressive Conservation Movement, 1900–1916." *Environmental Review* 8(1):57–85.

Merchant, Carolyn. 1989. *Ecological Revolutions: Nature, Gender, and Science in New England*. Chapel Hill: University of North Carolina Press.

Merchant, Carolyn. 1990. "Gender and Environmental History." *Journal of American History* 76(March):1117–1121.

Merchant, Carolyn, ed. 1993. *Major Problems in American Environmental History*. Boston: DC Heath.

Merchant, Carolyn. 1996. *Earthcare: Women and the Environment*. New York: Routledge.

Merchant, Carolyn. 1998. *Green Versus Gold: Sources in California's Environmental History*. Washington, DC: Island Press.

Merchant, Carolyn. 2003. *Reinventing Eden: The Fate of Nature in Western Culture*. New York: Routledge.

Merchant, Carolyn and Shepard Krech III and J. R. McNeill. 2004. *The Encyclopedia of World Environmental History*. New York: Routledge.

Merchant, Carolyn. 2005. *The Columbian Guide to American Environmental History*. New York: Columbia University Press.

Merchant, Carolyn. 2007. *American Environmental History: An Introduction*. New York: Columbia University Press.

Merchant, Carolyn. 2010. "George Bird Grinnell's Audubon Society: Bridging the Gender Divide in Conservation." *Environmental History* 16 (January):3–30.

Nash, Roderick. 1973. *Wilderness and the American Mind*. New Haven, CT: Yale University Press.

Nash, Roderick. 1989. *American Environmentalism: Readings in Conservation History*. New York: McGraw-Hill.

Nichols, Christopher McKnight, and Nancy C. Unger, eds. 2017. *A Companion to the Gilded Age and Progressive Era*. New York: Wiley-Blackwell.

Norwood, Vera. 2001. "Disturbed Landscape/Disturbing Process: Environmental History for the Twenty-First Century." *Pacific Historical Review* 70(1):77–90.

Stein, Rachel, ed. 2004. *New Perspectives on Environmental Justice: Gender, Sexuality and Activism*. New Brunswick, NJ: Rutgers University Press.

Unger, Nancy C. 2004. "Women, Sexuality, and Environmental Justice in American History." Pp. 45–60 in *New Perspectives on Environmental Justice: Gender, Sexuality, and Activism*. Rachel Stein, ed. New Brunswick, NJ: Rutgers University Press.

Unger, Nancy C. 2006a. "Gendered Approaches to Environmental Justice: An Historical Sampling." Pp. 17–34 in *Echoes from the Poisoned Well: Global Memories of Environmental Injustice*, Sylvia Washington, ed. New York: Rowman & Littlefield/Lexington Books.

Unger, Nancy C. 2006b. "The 'We Say What We Think' Club: Rural Wisconsin Women and the Development of Environmental Ethics." *Wisconsin Magazine of History* (Autumn):16–27.

Unger, Nancy C. 2007. "Teaching 'Straight' Gay and Lesbian History." *Journal of American History* 93(March):1192–1199.

Unger, Nancy C. [2000] 2008. *Fighting Bob La Follette: The Righteous Reformer*, 2nd ed. Chapel Hill: University of North Carolina Press. Madison: Wisconsin Historical Society Press.

Unger, Nancy C. 2008. "The Role of Gender in Environmental History." *Environmental Justice* 1(3, September):115–120.

Unger, Nancy C. 2009–2010. "Women for a Peaceful Christmas: Wisconsin Homemakers Seek to Remake American Culture." *Wisconsin Magazine of History* 93 (2, Winter):2–15.

Unger, Nancy C. 2010. "The Role of Nature in Lesbian Alternative Environments in the United States: From Jook Joints to Sisterspace." Pp. 173–198 in *Queer Ecologies: Sex, Nature, Biopolitics, and Desire*, Catriona Mortimer-Sandilands and Bruce Erickson, eds. Bloomington: University of Indiana Press.

Unger, Nancy C. 2012. *Beyond Nature's Housekeepers: American Women in Environmental History*. New York: Oxford University Press.

Unger, Nancy C. 2012–2013. "Wisconsin's League Against Nuclear Dangers: The Power of Informed Citizenship." *Wisconsin Magazine of History* 96 (2, Winter):42–53.

Unger, Nancy C. 2013. "American Women in Environmental History." Talk on January 16 at Town Hall Seattle. C-SPAN broadcast online. www.c-span.org/video/?310544-1/american-women-environmental-history

Unger, Nancy C. 2014a. "Beyond Nature's Housekeepers: American Women in Environmental History." Commonwealth Club, San Francisco, CA, March 4. Podcast. www.commonwealthclub.org/events/archive/podcast/beyond-natures-housekeepers-american-women-environmental-history

Unger, Nancy C. 2014b. "Women and Gender: Useful Categories of Analysis in Environmental History." Pp. 600–643 in *Oxford Handbook of Environmental History*. Andrew Isenberg, ed. New York: Oxford University Press.

Unger, Nancy C. 2016a. *Belle La Follette: Progressive Era Reformer*. New York: Routledge.

Unger, Nancy C. 2016b. "From Fire Island to Fab Summit: An LGBTQ Environmental History." Fab Planet Summit, 4 June, San Francisco, CA. Audio recording. https://

soundcloud.com/out4s/from-fire-island-to-fab-planet?in=out4s/sets/fab-planet-summ
it-2016

Unger, Nancy C. 2016c. "The Revolutionary Role of the Gay Bar in American History."
Time, 13 June. http://time.com/4367475/gay-bar-history-pulse-orlando/

White, Richard. 2001. "Environmental History: Watching a Historical Field Mature."
Pacific Historical Review 70(1):103–111.

Worster, Donald. 1992 reprint. Rivers of Empire: Water, Aridity, and the Growth of the
American West. New York: Oxford University Press.

8

CAROLYN MERCHANT AND *THE ECOLOGICAL INDIAN*

Shepard Krech III

When it was published in 1999, *The Ecological Indian: Myth and History* (Krech 1999) received praise from three scholars on the dust jacket. Two—the anthropologist William C. Sturtevant and the historian James Axtell—were distinguished for their research and publications on North American Indians, on which *The Ecological Indian*, which subsequently elicited both strong approval and intense debate, was tightly focused (e.g. Harkin and Lewis 2007).[1] At the time, the third scholar, Carolyn Merchant, was of undisputed reputation, best known not for research on North American Indians but for widely acknowledged strengths in intellectual history, gender studies, and the analysis of environmental and cultural transformations in early modern Europe.

The praise on the dust jacket of *The Ecological Indian* was strong, warm, and generous. Merchant herself remarked that the work was "a stunning, provocative reassessment of the image of the noble Indian living harmoniously within nature," providing "a new picture of Indians as sophisticated humans who both changed the land and responded to its changing ecology," and that anyone "who cares about the past human role in transforming nature and its implications for today will find the book stimulating, indispensable, and timely."

Needless to say, the words of all were gratefully received by me and by the publishers. However, given the focus of *The Ecological Indian*, while the selection of Axtell and Sturtevant could be readily understood, few people outside our scholarly circles, perhaps, could have predicted Merchant's involvement. It was not that the disciplines in which she and I had gained advanced degrees were so different—as mentioned, Axtell, like Merchant, is a historian (and I was trained as an anthropologist), but this difference hardly disqualified him to comment authoritatively. Rather, it was because the link between my work and Merchant's (or between the two of us personally) was not, at least not at first glance, obvious.

For one thing, Merchant did not participate in the meetings of the major academic society dedicated to the history of indigenous people, in particular those of North America, the American Society for Ethnohistory, or in its journal, *Ethnohistory*—whereas in both the society and the journal Axtell, Sturtevant, and I were all active presences. Yet, as will become apparent, the links were there, and what I wish to do here is speak to the connections, both intellectual and personal, between us, to the influence on me of Merchant's research and teaching, and to what I see as reasons for her advance praise.

The Disciplines

First, as for the different training—me as anthropologist, Merchant as historian—it is important to remember that at the time of the publication of *The Ecological Indian*—on the cusp of the millennium—the long-standing separation between history and anthropology in theory, methodology, and subject matter had evaporated in many areas of the two disciplines, especially in the hands of those who identified themselves as anthropological historians, historical anthropologists, ethnohistorians, historians of indigenous people, environmental historians, and the like. In an important sense the cracks, or interstices, between the disciplines as traditionally constituted were loci of new and productive action. The growing closeness and convergence of history and anthropology could be seen clearly in the content of endnotes or bibliography that made clear the convergence of the two mother disciplines, as well as the next generation's hyphenated ones. The commonalities emerged in assumptions about theory and time as well as about how to make sense of human culture, behavior, and history. Even if differences over narrative and in certain disciplinary conventions, such as the form of citations, lingered, the convergence between the two disciplines, while under way for a long time, had been nothing short of remarkable in the two decades preceding the millennium (Krech 1991).

Carolyn Merchant's Research and *The Ecological Indian*

In the 1990s, when I was framing, researching, and writing *The Ecological Indian*, Carolyn Merchant had already published several works germane to my research. She was surely best known for *The Death of Nature: Women, Ecology, and the Scientific Revolution* (hereafter *TDN*) (Merchant 1983), a groundbreaking work in the cultural and intellectual history (not to mention the history of gender) in the early modern era. She had also published a work on ecological change in North America. Titled *Ecological Revolutions: Nature, Gender, and Science in New England* (Merchant 1989), this work takes the reader through successive structures of relationships with the environment in the northeastern part of North America, from Native American to ones embedded first within colonial agriculture and then rooted in capitalist and mechanistic structures.

I referred to both *TDN* and *Ecological Revolutions* in *The Ecological Indian*. In the endnotes the close reader can find citations to three of Merchant's works: those two plus an essay, "The Realm of Social Relations: Production, Reproduction, and Gender in Environmental Transformations" (Merchant 1990), published in a 1990 collection titled *The Earth as Transformed by Human Action* and edited by B. L. Turner and others.

My references to Merchant occurred in a chapter titled "Eden," which although wide-ranging, principally concerned demographic change in Native America and estimates of the size of the aboriginal population on the eve of the arrival of newcomers from Europe, as well as of the extent of depopulations (mainly from epidemic disease) after Europeans arrived. The citations occurred specifically in several densely compressed paragraphs on the thickly populated, urbanized, resource-depleted, environmentally changed continent of Europe that emigrants and travelers left behind when they traveled to North America, where they encountered a New World, initially perceived to be paradisiacal, and that they subsequently and unhesitatingly altered greatly (Krech 1999:95–96, 265–266 n. 42, 44, 46).

The contribution of Merchant's work cited in these paragraphs was outsized compared to the brevity of the referencing text and citations. *The Ecological Indian* was a controlled work. It was brief: only 225 pages of main text—albeit with 40-plus pages of endnotes. Its intent was not to rehash the well-known role of people of European descent in environmental change in North America—which did not preclude the charge that it ignored such role. The charge, I have argued elsewhere, was unfounded. Not only was mention made on several occasions in this book of the unquestioned role of newcomers in ecological havoc in the New World, but the background—the history of environmental change in Europe—lays bare the assumptions about the relationship between humans and the environment brought by newcomers to America. It is fair to say that Merchant's work in the places cited was among the most important that informed my understanding of that background and that, alongside other works, alerted me anew to the potential of similar change unleashed by people of European descent after they arrived in the New World (Krech 2007).

"Nature Transformed": The Summer Institutes

These citations did not spell the end of the relationship between *The Ecological Indian* and Carolyn Merchant's work. Far more was going on in the 1990s. The hint is in the Preface, where one can read the following among the acknowledgements:

> For three weeks in the summers of 1996 and 1998, Carolyn Merchant, Timothy Silver, and I ran … a National Endowment for the Humanities Institute at the National Humanities Center. Each summer, twenty selected

> high-school teachers came to the table ... to discuss and debate 'Nature
> Transformed: Imagination and the North American Landscape,' and I am
> grateful to all for considering and critiquing ... the ideas forming in several
> chapters of *The Ecological Indian.*
>
> *(Krech 1999:11)*

In other words, the major years of conceptualizing and writing *The Ecological
Indian* coincided with what would be the first two of three iterations of an NEH
Institute for high school teachers co-taught with Merchant and the environmental historian Tim Silver. The goal of each Institute was to teach environmental history to 20 high school teachers so that on their return to their schools
around the country they might adapt what they learned from us and each other
for existing courses or new electives—and basically spread the idea of the need for
comprehension of the history and analysis of the relationship between people and
the environment in America. We led this Institute three times—in the summers
of 1996, 1998, and 2000, and in this and the following section I'd like to focus in
some detail on it, for it also played an important role in establishing a link
between Merchant and *The Ecological Indian.*

These Institutes were a remarkable experience for us all, from the education
staff to the teachers who were our students, to us, the three leaders. The education staff at the National Humanities Center, Research Triangle Park, North
Carolina, led by Richard Schramm, saw the Center's applications through to
success at the National Endowment for the Humanities in a time of tight budgets
and sharply declining support for the summer seminar/institute category, and
cared for the teachers who made the cut and came to the Center for the three-
week course. The participants were mainly high school history teachers. They
competed for 20 spaces at the seminar table each year; this Institute was timely
and places in it were highly sought after—requests for applications numbered
500–600 in 1996 and again in 1998.[2]

A poster that advertised Nature Transformed in 1996 stated that the Institute
would "explore the relationship between the ways men and women have
thought about their surroundings and the ways they have acted toward them. It
will ask," the text continued,

> how Native Americans conceptualized nature and saw themselves in it and
> how they lived and are now living upon the land. It will study the shifts in
> perception that transformed nature from wilderness to ecosystem, and it will
> consider how these transformations affected the forests, plains, and deserts of
> North America.

It stated further that through a case study focused on the landscape of central North
Carolina, participants would be able both to "read" this landscape and to apply
what they learned to the areas where they teach. The course would "demonstrate

how the participants' own locales can serve as texts for the teaching of environmental history," and would enable teachers to show their own students "how the forces that shaped the American landscape also shaped the American past."[3]

It would be difficult to teach with another person and not reflect deeply on how he or she makes sense of the world—in particular worlds distant in time or space, each therefore, as has been remarked, a "foreign country" (Lowenthal 1985). Whereas the work of both of my colleagues was important to the developing thesis of *The Ecological Indian*—Tim Silver's *New Face on the Countryside* comes immediately to mind—I focus here on the links with Carolyn Merchant.

Even though the syllabus changed with each iteration of the course, primarily in the amount of reading, the structure remained basically the same. Merchant, Silver, and I taught as a team on the first day, but the structure and readings were Merchant's: participants read essays on (and arrived at the seminar table prepared to talk about) ecological history, ecological prophecy, ecological imperialism, and ecological revolution, by Donald Worster, William Cronon, Alfred Crosby, and Merchant, respectively. All were reprinted in Merchant's collection of sources—documents and essays in a book assigned to the class titled *Major Problems in American Environmental History* (Merchant 1993).

In the days that followed, each of us took a 4–5-day section of the 3-week course. After that initial day I took charge of the first week, for the simple reason that my topic was the experience of American Indians, who were the first to arrive in North America. I helped guide us through essays crucial as background for the analysis that was taking shape in *The Ecological Indian*; through ideas gaining in coherence as chapters or parts of chapters—on, for example, the image of the Ecological Indian, Pleistocene extinctions, the prevalence and uses of fire, demography (population size, density, and decline), the hunt for buffaloes, deer, and beaver, not only because they represented important sources of food and useful products, but because on one level the behavior of American Indians toward their prey, including what can be measured as conservationist or not, must be understood in terms of culturally-based ethno-ethological and ethno-ecological premises.

In his week—the third week of the 3-week institute—Silver spoke of thinking and teaching about environmental history in a particular place, from a particular local perspective, as we marched about the North Carolina Piedmont, either in the woods surrounding the National Humanities Center or in field trips to nearby Stagville, an eighteenth-century plantation, and the Duke Homestead, a nineteenth-century tobacco farm, where we learned about trees, succession, ecology, soil, tobacco, cotton, kudzu, and slavery; the Mason-Dixon, Smith and Wesson, and Air Conditioner lines; and southern manhood, southern burdens, southern culture, and other matters.[4]

Merchant's was the second week, between mine and Silver's. It was pithy, analytical, and demanding; both abstract and document laden, theory interrupted by concrete detail and personal stories, including reflections on the extent of changes through time of personal knowledge of and travel in the world by one's ancestors and oneself, and Merchant's anecdotes about her own experiences, including burning a prairie (to restore health and growth) with unintended consequences on her own personal life.[5]

Merchant prefaced and began her week with definitions of key words, including conservation, ecology, nature, resources, wild, and wilderness, drawing on the *OED*, Vandana Shiva (1992), Raymond Williams's *Keywords* (Williams 1983), Gary Snyder's *The Practice of the Wild* (Snyder 1990), and other works. The first day she had asked participants to identify and then compare and contrast the assumptions about nature and human nature, the approaches to environmental history, and prophecies about the course of environmental change of the four aforementioned scholars (Worster, Cronon, Crosby, and Merchant). All four essays were influential, as the students—the high school teachers—quickly began to talk about different narratives and different courses of environmental change, up (ascensionist) or down (declensionist), good or bad. In the course of the week for which Merchant bore responsibility, the participants read and discussed the documents and essays in eight of fifteen chapters in *Major Problems* (Merchant 1993), six in their entirety and two partially, supplemented by several key works that had not appeared in that edited volume—importantly, Merchant's essay on "Reinventing Eden: Western Culture as a Recovery Narrative." During his week, Silver assigned a ninth chapter to *Major Problems*—on soil exhaustion in the tobacco South. I chose to substitute materials for a tenth chapter in *Major Problems* titled "Native American Ecology and Culture Contact," about which I shall have more to say. In many ways, Merchant's week provided a comprehensive primer, a crash course, on American environmental history.[6]

There was little doubt about the enthusiasm displayed by the teachers for Nature Transformed. At the final dinner at the end of each session of the Institute, when we all said things intended to be clever but were perhaps above all silly, the teachers who were our students made clear what they wanted to lampoon and remember. And in my memory a lot had to do with Merchant, especially her burning prairie (alluded to previously), which left an impression on every class. One group of students remarked, "Imagine prairies burning,/ Restoring mother earth./ But is it really female?/ Depends on what it's worth." Another, to the tune of "This land is your land, this land is my land..." sang, "As I was walking, I saw a wildfire/ Most likely set by Merchant's righteous ire/ Seeing capitalist development, she torches the establishment/ This land, transformed for you and me." And in another skit modeled on "Jeopardy," the first question concerning Carolyn was "What is a typical response to a date with Carolyn?" The answer: "Fire trucks on the prairie."

As for us (Merchant, Silver, Krech), in our inevitable response, which in the end we called "The Tragedy of the RJR Commons [the commons being our dining area in the National Humanities Center]," our refrain at the end of each verse was "Ascensionist? Declensionist? Don't sit on the fencionist"—the clarion call, at least in Nature Transformed, with a nod to Merchant (and others), for narrative and identifying the course, past, present, or future, of environmental change.[7]

There also seemed little doubt about the value placed by the participants on what they learned during Nature Transformed and how they thought they might apply it to the curricula of the secondary schools in the different parts of the country where they taught. They designed strategies to implement and incorporate environmental history in projects, such as the investigation of local mining operations (for a school in northern California), discussion of the impact of water usage in southern California or the impact of Los Angeles freeways on Watts (California), research on historical changes in the Mississippi River (Illinois), a focus on ideological diversity and personal narratives of place and movement (Montana), the study of the impact of oil and sugar on local ecosystems and people (Louisiana), and scrutiny of ways that dams have altered environments (Oregon).[8]

In their evaluations (collected by the Center for NEH), which no doubt affected our success in the ever more challenging funding sweepstakes, they wrote comments such as "enriched and enthusiastic with ... a different view of the environment"; "an opportunity to see things in a less provincial light"; faculty who "questioned, pushed, and helped us probe, but we were never expected to believe the 'party line'"; "I now see the complexity and interrelationship of historical events"; "our discussions were engaging, active, and ever informative"; "stimulating, inspiring experience ... engaging and thought-provoking"; "the most demanding and difficult [institute of a dozen that this person had attended over 23 years] ... made me more reflective, aware ... and a better teacher"; "one of the best academic experiences I have ever had"; "my third NEH summer seminar and the *best* summer experience I have had".[9]

Nature Transformed and *The Ecological Indian*

Given that two of the three NEH Institutes took place in the mid-to-late 1990s, at the very moment I was writing *The Ecological Indian*, I too read (and in my case, re-read), along with our students, *Major Problems*, which presented not one but two opportunities to think about Merchant's take on environmental history. This proved to be *my* crash course in a very current iteration of American environmental history.

The impact was significant. Most importantly, it helped cement in place a narrative that was taking shape in what became the Introduction to *The Ecological Indian*—not the basic idea of scrutinizing the fit between the longstanding and persistent idea of what was called the Ecological Indian and actual American Indian behavior through time; that notion was ancient (in the history of the birth of my project) and was funded by the Woodrow Wilson International Center and the National Humanities Center during fellowship years in 1992–93 and 1993–94. Instead, engaging in depth with Merchant's text *Major Problems* reinforced for me what would become some of the underpinnings of *Ecological Indian*:

the importance of defining one's terms clearly at the outset; identifying and then making operational the major aspects of the idea, that is, ecology and conservation; understanding the implications of changes in our understanding of succession, stasis, and chaotic dynamics in ecosystems, for the indigenous people who lived in and helped create those ecosystems both prior to and after the arrival in the New World of newcomers from Europe. Equally important was the link between what I called the Image of the Ecological Indian and what is widely known (and reported) as the invention of tradition. In *The Ecological Indian*, the most recent version of the Image was the iconic (and ironic) representation of Iron Eyes Cody as the Crying Indian in the 1970s campaign for Keep America Beautiful. My awareness of the crucial nature of these ideas would not have come together as readily as it did without Merchant's crash course in environmental history presented during her week of Nature Transformed.

There was more. Throughout her work Merchant has displayed an appreciation of the importance of exploring the links between infrastructure and superstructure—while keeping one's feet firmly planted. She makes this clear, especially in "Ecological Revolutions," an essay in the first chapter of *Major Problems*, extracted from a previously published analysis in the journal *Environmental Review* (Merchant 1987). I agree with her on the importance of investigating not merely the major systems of human production but the connections between these systems on the one hand and attitudes and behavior toward the natural world on the other. Not surprisingly, they are complex due to the tensions and contradictions inherent in complex systems of knowledge, meaning, and behavior.

None of this means that Merchant and I are in perfect lockstep—Are any two scholars?—which returns us to my earlier allusion that during the week for which I was responsible, I substituted my own readings for the chapter in Merchant's *Major Problems* titled "Native American Ecology and Cultural Contact," which dealt exclusively with American Indians. I did this for two reasons, one of which was limited time and the other was due to the fact that her focus in the selections in *Major Problems* did not entirely fit with what I wished to accomplish. With hindsight, a third reason was the increasing realization that, as the analysis in *The Ecological Indian* sharpened, it was becoming clear that there would be differences in our reading of the history of ecology and conservation in Native North America.

One example of the problem was the essay by the historian Calvin Martin called "Micmacs and French in the Northeast" included in *Major Problems*. One could perhaps understand why this had been reproduced. Martin's best-known work appeared four years after this essay was originally published. Titled *Keepers of the Game*, the book won the Albert J. Beveridge Award from the American Historical Association. Clever and well written, it also however attracted attention in the form of an edited volume titled *Indians, Animals, and the Fur Trade*, which, as the subtitle declared, was billed as a critique of Martin's new book (Martin 1978; Krech 1981). The critics were anthropologists at ease with ethnohistorical methodology, which included working sensibly with documentary as well as ethnographic evidence.

Collectively, the authors fundamentally undermined Martin's thesis not just in *Keepers of the Game*, but also in earlier analyses incorporated in that book such as the one in *Major Problems*. There were not only problems with data and temporal sequences, which rendered impossible an extension of Martin's thesis beyond the cases he discussed, but also problems with basic assumptions in the specific case that came under his lens. The most devastating analysis for the latter surely was William Sturtevant's foray into Indian thought about disease causation and fundamental concepts such as "other-than-human" or "supernatural," an analysis that exposed Martin's argument as seriously wanting (Sturtevant 1981).

Not only was there little desire on my part to rebut anew in Nature Transformed what had already been broached in considerable detail years before (in *Indians, Animals, and the Fur Trade*); it also became apparent that *The Ecological Indian* would complicate and perhaps even disrupt the story that Merchant was crafting in her sweepingly ambitious theorization of what she called "revolutions" in the connections between production, reproduction, and consciousness, and the implications of such for on-the-ground relationships between humans and nature—or, to be more precise, for the relationship between American Indians and the animals that they hunted.

Merchant's excerpt in *Major Problems* (titled "Ecological Revolutions") of the aforementioned previously published essay demonstrates some of the difficulties of sweeping generalization. In that essay she contrasts three societal structures: Native American, Preindustrial, and Industrial, with the second, the result of a so-called Colonial Revolution, and the third, the outcome of a Capitalist Revolution. Among the many differences in these three structures were so-called "symbols of nature": the Native American society was said to be marked by "animism" and "reciprocity between humans and nature," the Preindustrial by "organicism, religious retribution, [and] fatalistic acceptance of nature," and the Industrial by "mechanism, domination, and mastery of nature." Other differences were in "Nonhuman nature": for Native Americans animals, rocks, and trees were "active subjects"; in preindustrial society these were passive objects and commodities; and in industrial society, objects had become scientific objects and natural resources. Finally, human production also varied, from hunting-gathering-fishing and nonintensive cultivation for Native Americans, subsistence agriculture for preindustrial society, and intensive market agriculture for industrial society (Merchant 1989:24–25; Merchant 1993:22–31).

In my view, there are numerous attractions in seeking generalization, in model-building; and there is much utility in what Merchant has said. But the models can also close one's mind to alternatives; for example, they can preclude the possibility that people whose societies do not qualify for preindustrial status can have a serious impact on nature through their productive activity. Or they can deny that such impacts exist among people who are animists. But how can this be squared with the belief, held by animists in Native North America or elsewhere, that prey properly approached, thought about, considered, and treated will reanimate or reincarnate? How can one kill too many given such belief? Or that prey that do not appear because they have gone to spaces such as underground prairies? How can one conserve an animal population, if conservation is defined as intentional, agential behavior to prevent waste, depletion, despoliation, environmental destruction, extirpation, extinction, and the like—all common to the meaning of conservation since the fifteenth century—given such beliefs (for broader implications, see Krech 2005:78–86). It was becoming apparent, at least to me, that the indigenous people emerging in *The Ecological Indian* were quite different from those who peopled Merchant's *Ecological Revolutions*—for which reasons I constructed my own narrative in the week for which I was responsible.

Coda

Until I retired from Brown University, I stayed in close touch with Carolyn Merchant ever since we shared the seminar table at the summer institutes at the National Humanities Center. We collaborated with others on the development of the website Nature Transformed, which was based on the institute of the same name. We were regular dinner partners at the banquet of the annual meeting of the American Society for Environmental History. Together, she and I held fellowships in the ecological humanities at the NHC, funded by the John D. and Catherine T. MacArthur Foundation. Together, we edited, with John McNeill, the three-volume *Encyclopedia of World Environmental History* (Krech, Merchant, and McNeil 2004). Together, we spoke in the same session on George Bird Grinnell at an annual meeting of the ASEH. Her talk was released in book form in 2016 with Yale University Press (Merchant 2016). For a long time, Carolyn and I birded annually at the annual meeting of the ASEH, and on other occasions, including in the San Francisco Bay Area when I gave a talk at Berkeley on *The Ecological Indian*, and in Maine, where I have a camp on the coast, and she and Charlie Sellers, her long-time partner and spouse, visited.

Charlie was at least one source—I have always suspected the most important—of Carolyn's theoretical inspiration. He has a way of summing up what others were (or ought to have been) thinking, and expressing it offhand, a quip clothed in the vernacular. For example, in response to a question about landscape change in his lifetime in North Carolina, which he had known from his youth, I remember him saying simply, "Greened up." Reforestation and a different aesthetic for sure, ascension perhaps, from the early twentieth century deforested landscape. In Maine, on August 19, 2012, Carolyn and Charlie and I ran two hours offshore into the Gulf of Maine in my lobster boat. Our destination was Mt. Desert Rock, from which the bald outline of Acadia was visible far in the distance, and there, offshore but an area of shoaling and upwelling, we saw hundreds of birds including greater shearwaters, gannets, Wilson's storm-petrels, red phalaropes, red-necked phalaropes, and at least three other species of shorebirds. Charlie captured many with his camera. Birds have long been one of our shared interests—an obsession, perhaps, for Charlie and me. But those who have read Carolyn's *Ecological Revolutions* will know that it is full of birds, and that birds represent a connection with her long-standing interest in conservation organizations in the nineteenth century, including Audubon, and the role of women therein. That association continues in her recent book on Grinnell (Merchant 2016), for which (to come full circle) Yale asked me to comment for the dust jacket.

Notes

1 *The Ecological Indian* is in its thirteenth printing.
2 The Author's Files: Nature Transformed Archive. Letter, D. Arnold to R. Schramm, September 10, 1998.
3 The Author's Files: Nature Transformed Archive. Poster for Nature Transformed: Imagination and the North American Landscape. An Institute for High School Teachers, Grades 9–12. June 24–July 12, 1996, National Humanities Center, Research Triangle Park, North Carolina.
4 The Author's Files: Nature Transformed Archive. Syllabus, June 22–July 10, 1998 (also for June 26–July 14, 2000).
5 The Author's Files: Nature Transformed Archive. Class Notes.
6 The Author's Files: Nature Transformed Archive, Class Notes
7 The Author's Files: Nature Transformed Archive. Notes, final dinners, 1996, 1998, 2000.
8 The Author's Files: Nature Transformed Archive. "Implementing the Teaching of Environmental History, July 10, 1998."
9 The Author's Files: Nature Transformed Archive. Participant Evaluations.

Bibliography

Harkin, Michael E. and David Rich Lewis, eds. 2007. *Native Americans and the Environment: Perspectives on the Ecological Indian*. Lincoln: University of Nebraska Press.
Krech, Shepard, III, ed. 1981. *Indians, Animals, and the Fur Trade: A Critique of "Keepers of the Game"*. Athens: University of Georgia Press.
Krech, Shepard, III. 1991. "The State of Ethnohistory." *Annual Review of Anthropology* 20:345–375.
Krech, Shepard, III. 1999. *The Ecological Indian: Myth and History*. New York: Norton.
Krech, Shepard, III, Carolyn Merchant, and John McNeil, eds. 2004. *The Encyclopedia of World Environmental History*, 3 vols. New York: Routledge.
Krech, Shepard, III. 2005. "Reflections on Conservation, Sustainability, and Environmentalism in Indigenous North America." *American Anthropologist* 107:78–86.
Krech, Shepard, III. 2007. "Beyond *The Ecological Indian*." Pp. 3–31 in *Native Americans and the Environment: Perspectives on the Ecological Indian*, eds. Michael E. Harkin and David Rich Lewis. Lincoln, NE; Laramie, WY: University of Nebraska Press/American Heritage Center.
Lowenthal, David. 1985. *The Past is a Foreign Country*. Cambridge: Cambridge University Press.
Martin, Calvin. 1978. *Keepers of the Game: Indian–Animal Relationships and the Fur Trade*. Berkeley: University of California Press.
Merchant, Carolyn. 1983. *The Death of Nature: Women, Ecology, and the Scientific Revolution*. New York: Harper & Row.

Merchant, Carolyn. 1987. "The Theoretical Structure of Ecological Revolutions." *Environmental Review* 11:265–274.

Merchant, Carolyn. 1989. *Ecological Revolutions: Nature, Gender, and Science in New England.* Chapel Hill: University of North Carolina Press.

Merchant, Carolyn. 1990. "The Realm of Social Relations: Production, Reproduction, and Gender in Environmental Transformations." Pp. 673–684 in *The Earth as Transformed by Human Action: Global and Regional Changes in the Biosphere over the Past 300 Years*, eds. B. L. Turner *et al.* Cambridge: Cambridge University Press.

Merchant, Carolyn, ed., 1993. *Major Problems in American Environmental History: Documents and Essays.* Lexington, MA: D.C. Heath.

Merchant, Carolyn. 2016. *Spare the Birds! George Bird Grinnell and the First Audubon Society.* New Haven, CT: Yale University Press.

Shiva, Vandana. 1992. "Resources." Pp. 206–207 in *The Development Dictionary: A Guide to Knowledge as Power*, ed. Wolfgang Sachs. London: Zed Books.

Snyder, Gary. 1990. *The Practice of the Wild.* New York: North Point Press.

Sturtevant, William C. 1981. "Animals and Disease in Indian Belief." Pp. 177–188 in *Indians, Animals, and the Fur Trade: A Critique of "Keepers of the Game"*, ed. Shepard Krech III. Athens: University of Georgia Press.

Williams, Raymond. 1983. "Nature." Pp. 219–224 in *Keywords*. New York: Oxford.

9

ALL OUR RELATIONS

Reflections on Women, Nature, and Science

Debora Hammond

> Our kind vandalize the earth, And yet you give me hope
> *(Wendell Berry,* A Country of Marriage, *Berkeley, 1971)*

Introduction

Confronted with the insanity of nuclear proliferation and the parallel dilemmas of social injustice and environmental degradation, I enrolled on a doctoral program in the History of Science at the University of California at Berkeley in 1989 to explore alternative paradigms in science. I had spent the previous 15 years teaching in various capacities, becoming actively involved in the nuclear freeze and bioregional movements in the early 1980s. Seeking to understand the rationale informing the policies and practices of the reigning power structure, I chose to interrogate science as the foundation of humanity's perception of reality in the modern world, believing that the solutions to the myriad challenges confronting the planet required a re-orientation in our thinking, and a transformation of the dominant worldview.

Ultimately focusing on the evolution of systems thinking as a promising alternative perspective, I spent eight years at UC Berkeley, with Carolyn Merchant as my primary mentor. I am profoundly grateful for her inspiration and guidance, and for the concrete support she offered throughout my graduate career and beyond, from her advocacy of my admission to the History of Science Program to her role as chair of my dissertation committee from 1993 to 1997. In addition to enrolling in her graduate seminar on Environmental History, Philosophy and Ethics, I served during several semesters as a graduate student instructor (GSI) in both her Environmental History and her Environmental Philosophy and Ethics undergraduate courses. This exposure to Carolyn's work in the general field of environmental studies, in particular her groundbreaking contributions to ecofeminist theory, provided an enormously valuable complement to my primary field in the history of science, creating an ideal context for the development of my own work on the history of systems thinking and its relevance as a framework for social change.

In recounting the evolution of my understanding of systems thinking as an alternative paradigm, with significant implications for social and environmental policy and practice, I document here the ways in which Carolyn's work has provided a critical foundation for my own research and teaching, as a Professor of Interdisciplinary Studies in the Hutchins School of Liberal Studies at Sonoma State University (SSU) in northern California. My dissertation, *Toward a Science of Synthesis: Evaluating the Heritage of General Systems Theory* (Hammond 1997), later published as *The Science of Synthesis: Exploring the Social Implications of General Systems Theory* (Hammond 2003), drew considerable inspiration from the philosophical and ethical orientation articulated in Carolyn's work, and nurtured an active and rewarding membership in the International Society for the Systems Science. The interweaving of these two threads—environmental philosophy and systems thinking—has continued to inform my work over the past 20 years. Serving as Director of SSU's Master's Program in Organization Development, beginning in 2009, has inspired my current interest in how to operationalize these theoretical insights and ethical commitments.

Transcending the Mechanistic Paradigm: An Ecofeminist Orientation

My impulse to pursue graduate studies in the History of Science was inspired by several books published in the late 1970s and early 1980s on two key themes: (1) the limitations of mechanistic science, its inadequacy for addressing the complex challenges facing humanity, and the need for a new more holistic paradigm; and (2) the re-emergence of the feminine, as a challenge to patriarchy, reflected in perspectives on feminist spirituality and ecofeminist theory. The parallel emergence of these two strands of thinking struck me at the time, and seemed to me to be integrally interconnected. Beginning with *The Death of Nature* (hereafter *TDN*) (Merchant 1980), Merchant's collected writings eloquently address many facets of this interconnection. Although other authors launched me on my initial inquiry, they ultimately led me to Carolyn's work.

With regard to critiques of mechanistic science, the most significant influence in the early evolution of my own thinking was Fritjof Capra's *The Turning Point* (Capra 1982). In his Preface he describes how new concepts in 20th century physics "have brought about a profound change in our world view; from the mechanistic conception of Descartes and Newton to a holistic and ecological view" (p. 15). He notes that the multifaceted crises facing the modern world are systemic and interrelated, and, further, that they are rooted in what he describes as "a crisis of perception." He then goes on to suggest:

> We live in a globally interconnected world, in which biological, social, and environmental phenomena are all interdependent. To describe this world appropriately we need an ecological perspective, which the Cartesian world-view does not offer. What we need, then, is a new "paradigm"—a new vision of reality; a fundamental change in our thoughts, perceptions, and values.
>
> *(p. 16)*

It was the concept of this "new paradigm" that provided the initial motivation for my interest in studying the history of science and exploring alternatives to the mechanistic orientation dominant in Western science.

My inquiry was further inspired by the parallel emergence of feminist spirituality and ecofeminism, as relatively new orientations within the broad field of feminist theory. One of the most influential texts that furthered my interest in the interface between the rise of feminist consciousness and critiques of mechanistic science was Susan Griffin's *Women and Nature: The Roaring Inside Her* (Griffin 1978). The first section of "Book One: Matter" is subtitled "How Man Regards and Makes Use of Woman and Nature." Griffin[1] provides an evocative contrast between the authoritative voice of science as it was evolving in the sixteenth and seventeenth centuries, and the concurrent declarations that fed the persecution of thousands of "witches." In consideration of the nature of matter, she writes, "It is decided that matter is passive and inert, and that all motion originates from outside matter." Matter, of course, is associated with the feminine and the body, while the masculine provides the source of motion, the soul (p. 5). Further, "the demon resides in the earth, it is decided, in Hell, under our feet. It is observed that women are closer to the earth" (p. 7).

Given this background, it was with great delight that I discovered Merchant's *The Death of Nature*. Here was a book that resonated with the full spectrum of my own inquiry. Her exploration of the "connections between social change and changing constructions of nature" mirrored my own questions about the ways in which the dominant frameworks of scientific thought determine the structures of our human institutions (Merchant 1980:xvi). In her Preface to the 1990 edition, she summarizes the key theme:

> Between the sixteenth and seventeenth centuries the image of an organic cosmos with a living female earth at its center gave way to a mechanistic world view in which nature was reconstructed as dead and passive, to be dominated and controlled by humans.
>
> *(Merchant 1980:xvi)*

Capra (1982) quotes her work in support of his own thesis:

> In investigating the roots of our current environmental dilemma and its connections to science, technology, and the economy, we must re-examine the formation of a world-view and a science which, by reconceptualizing reality as a machine rather than a living organism, sanctioned the domination of both nature and women.
>
> *(Merchant 1980:xvii; cited in Capra 1982:41)*

In documenting the dramatic changes in science during this period, Merchant locates them within a larger cultural, political, and economic landscape, tracing the parallel transformations taking place in the social order. Acknowledging the problem with essentializing the connection between women and nature, Merchant nevertheless makes an important case for the significance of cultural beliefs and norms in relation to both nature and gender. The concept of the earth as a living being, generally conceived as female, was central to the organic worldview prior to the emergence of modern science. Merchant argues that the conception of nature as dead, inert matter, allowed for greater exploitation of the earth's resources, ushering in the industrial revolution and the triumph of modern capitalism.

UC Berkeley History of Science: An Environmental Perspective

My primary goal in enrolling in the History of Science program was to explore the connection between new paradigms in science and what I saw as a re-emergence of the feminine, reflected in an emphasis on relationship and an appreciation of the interconnectedness of all phenomena. In my application I had specifically noted my interest in working with Carolyn; although her academic home was in the Conservation and Resource Studies (CRS) Program in the College of Natural Resources, she could serve as chair of my dissertation committee and played a key role throughout my eight years at Berkeley.

Through my association with Carolyn, I was employed for most semesters as a Graduate Student Instructor (GSI) in the CRS Program (currently part of the Department of Environmental Science, Policy and Management), most frequently with Carolyn and occasionally with other members of the CRS faculty, including Alan Miller and Arnold Schultz. These courses offered a broad range of perspectives on humanity's relationship with the environment that informed and broadened the direction and scope of my doctoral research.

Alan Miller's introductory course on Environmental Issues, along with his text, *Gaia Connections: An Introduction to Ecology, Eco-ethics and Economics* (Miller 1991), provided an excellent overview of a broad range of environmental issues embedded in an explicit economic and political critique, which served me well in my own teaching in the Hutchins School of Liberal Studies, beginning in the spring of 1996. An unpublished manuscript Alan co-authored with Paul Gersper, entitled "Conservation and Resource Studies Major: University of California, Berkeley," (Gersper and Miller n.d.) describes the mission of the CRS program, articulating a critical concern for the future of education, more relevant today than ever. Key themes include the importance of cultivating a social and political consciousness, embodying a democratic pedagogy, and "develop[ing] a concern for transformation within the personal life and the social order" (pp. 5, 7). Carolyn's teaching and writing clearly embody this transformative approach. Her courses, both graduate and undergraduate, integrated broadly interdisciplinary content, interactive inquiry, creative projects to engage the imagination, exploration of personal values, and an explicitly activist orientation. Upon completion of my doctorate, I was fortunate to join the faculty of the Hutchins School of Liberal Studies, which embodies a pedagogy very much aligned with that of the CRS Program. The opportunity to work so closely with Carolyn during my years at UC Berkeley not only informed and enriched my own teaching and research over the past 20 years, but also played a critical role in my appointment in the Hutchins School.

Environmental History

Merchant's work in environmental history has contributed substantially to my teaching in the integrated general education program that is the hallmark of the Hutchins School, as well as providing a broad theoretical framework for my work in the history of science. In contrast to the dominant trend in historical studies, which tends to limit its concern to the role of human actors, as an environmental historian, Merchant highlights the role of nature as a central player in the drama of history.

Her first major contribution to U.S. environmental history, *Ecological Revolutions: Nature, Gender and Science in New England* (Merchant 1989), lays out the case for a consideration of nature in history, expanding Karl Marx's emphasis on the relations of production as the foundation for the social order, by including nature as an essential factor in production, and introducing the concept of reproduction—both biological/ecological and social—as a critical interface between the factors of production and the cultural constructs evolving out of and shaping those relations. Not only does her consideration of reproduction highlight the significant contributions of women and nature, Merchant's articulation of these factors underscores the interactive dynamics of these relationships as co-creative and mutually determined. This insight is fundamental in my conception of the significance of systems thinking as an alternative paradigm, in its emphasis on interrelationship and mutual dependency.

Two of her later texts, *Major Problems in American Environmental History* (Merchant 1993) and *Green Versus Gold: Sources in California's Environmental History* (Merchant 1998), provide extensive collections of primary documents informing an analysis of ecological transformations in the United States as a whole and California in particular. They are excellent resources for making this history come alive through first-person accounts and other commentary from the period. In her undergraduate course on Environmental History, I appreciated the way she encouraged students to arrive at their own interpretations of primary sources, working in small discussion groups. Instilling an appreciation for the role of nature in history, one of the more original and creative assignments in the course was to write an environmental history from the perspective of a nonhuman actor. This interactive pedagogy, with its emphasis on student inquiry, echoes the values of partnership and inclusion that she articulates throughout her work. One of the qualities I most admire and respect about Carolyn is the integrity reflected in the alignment between her philosophical orientation and her actual practice as an educator. This reflects another important dimension of systems thinking, which seeks to transcend the artificial divide between theory and practice, and between the values and commitments of different disciplinary perspectives.

Carolyn's graduate seminar in environmental history, philosophy, and ethics was among the most inspirational of my graduate education. Through this course I was introduced to major scholars in the field; the most influential in relation to my own research were Donald Worster, *Nature's Economy: A History of Ecological Ideas* (Worster [1978] 1994), Greg Mitman, *The State of Nature: Ecology, Community, and American Social Thought, 1900–1950* (Mitman 1992), and William Cronon, ed., *Uncommon Ground: Rethinking the Human Place in Nature* (Cronon 1995). These three texts echoed my ongoing inquiry into the relationship between humanity's conception of nature, particularly as articulated in scientific frameworks, and the structure of the social order.

Significantly, in relation to the subtitle of Cronon's text, "Rethinking the Human Place in Nature," at Carolyn's recommendation I was invited in the spring of 2000 to participate in a working group sponsored by the National Science Foundation and hosted by the National Center for Ecological Analysis and Synthesis in Santa Barbara, CA on the topic: "Rethinking the 'and' in Humans and Nature: Ecology at the Boundary of the Human Dimension." Building on the weeklong conversation, the participants presented a symposium on the topic at the annual meeting of the Ecological Society of America that summer (Hammond 2001). The symposium was lively and well-attended; what emerged from the discussion following the presentations was an overwhelming sense of frustration among graduate students with the limitations of the emerging field of ecology as currently taught in the university, specifically in terms of the narrow focus on quantifiable data and the lack of consideration of social and cultural factors in relation to the environment.

Environmental Philosophy and Ethics

The sense of frustration expressed in the symposium provides an excellent segue into a discussion of the significance of Merchant's work on environmental philosophy and ethics in the evolution of my own thinking. The sentiments expressed by these ecology graduate students clearly demonstrate the reduction-ism still prevalent in the scientific community, even in a field that professes to study relationships among interacting elements in a complex system.

The course on environmental philosophy and ethics was most closely aligned with my own research interests, and I was fortunate to be hired during four semesters, once with Carolyn, twice with other instructors, and once on my own, as the primary instructor. In her 1992 syllabus, Carolyn describes the course as "A cross-cultural comparison of human environments as physical, socio-economic, and technocultural ecosystems with special emphasis on the role of beliefs, atti-tudes, ideologies and behavior." The basic content of the course formed the fra-mework of her book *Radical Ecology: The Search for a Livable World* (Merchant 1992, 2nd ed. 2005), which had been published just prior to that semester. Most compelling to me was the scope of topics addressed and the introduction to the broad array of orientations in the field. Among the more enduring insights, and central to in my articulation of the implications of systems thinking, was her dis-cussion of egocentric, homocentric, and ecocentric ethics. Further, given my concern with the limitations of mechanistic science, I was inspired by her analysis of the transformation, in the sixteenth and seventeenth centuries, from an organic to a mechanistic worldview, which she identified as the foundation of the ego-centric orientation, justifying the domination of nature and fueling the rise of laissez-faire capitalism, as well as the prevailing neoliberal ideology in the global political economy of the twenty-first century.

One of the characteristics that most impressed me about Carolyn's teaching was the way she introduced such a wide range of perspectives without privileging any particular orientation. Prior to entering graduate school, I had tended to see the environmental movement as a more or less unified phenomenon, and this course helped me to appreciate the complex nuances underlying often fraught divides. I especially admired Carolyn's inclusion of topics that tended to be dis-missed in the academic community, such as spiritual ecology, spiritual ecofemin-ism, and alternative paradigms in science. One text in particular, Riane Eisler's *The Chalice and the Blade* (Eisler 1987), is controversial in building on the idea of essentially peaceful and egalitarian prehistoric goddess-worshipping cultures, which she argues were destroyed by invasions from more violent, hierarchical and patriarchal cultures. Nevertheless, Eisler offers a provocative insight in her dis-cussion of the contrast between dominator and partnership cultures, which Mer-chant integrates in her later work (*Earthcare: Women and the Environment*, [Merchant 1996:217] and *Reinventing Eden: The Fate of Nature in Western Culture* [Merchant 2004:224]), where she introduces the concept of partnership ethics, encompassing the following five precepts:

1.   Equity between the human and nonhuman communities;
2.   Moral considerations for humans and nonhuman nature;
3.   Respect for cultural diversity and biodiversity;

4.   Inclusion of women, minorities, and nonhuman nature in the code of ethical accountability.
5.   An ecologically-informed management that is consistent with the continued health of both the human and the nonhuman communities.

Although her work has had significant influence in the evolution of ecofeminist thinking, Merchant encouraged consideration of arguments critical of that orientation. One reference in particular that highlighted contrasting viewpoints was Janet Biehl's *Rethinking Ecofeminist Politics* (Biehl 1991), which promotes the radical political orientation of social ecology as a more liberating framework for both men and women. Biehl characterizes ecofeminism as spreading "theism, irrationalism, and mystification in both the ecology and the feminist movements," which she sees as undermining the Enlightenment project and divorcing ecological concerns from political engagement.

Biehl's reference to the Enlightenment raises a theme that was central to my work on the history and significance of systems thinking. Inspired by the insights of the Frankfurt School of Critical Theory, particularly in the work of Max Horkheimer and Theodor Adorno (*Dialectic of Enlightenment* [Horkheimer and Adorno 1972]), I wrote the following in the Prologue to my book *The Science of Synthesis: Exploring the Social Implications of General Systems Theory*:

> Although the rise of mechanistic science in the seventeenth century is often associated with the emergence of political democracies in the West, this dual heritage from the Enlightenment contains an inherent dialectical tension. As critical theorists in the Frankfurt School have argued, the promise of progress through the control of nature ultimately entails the control of human nature, undermining the liberal impulse of democracy and the ideals of social justice that are also part of the Enlightenment tradition.
>
> *(Hammond 2003:2)*

Just as Biehl appeals to the liberal ideals of the Enlightenment in her critique of ecofeminism, emphasizing political engagement and a narrowly positivistic rationality, she fails to appreciate the potential for domination and control inherent in the underlying ethos.

The same kind of tension can be seen in perspectives on mechanistic science. In contrast to arguments about the limitations of the mechanistic paradigm that I had found compelling, I was surprised to discover that appeals to more holistic, organic conceptions of nature and science tended in most academic circles to be dismissed as retrograde and reactionary, if not delusional, and often associated with authoritarian and fascist implications. (See especially Martin Lewis (1995), "Radical Environmental Philosophy and the Assault on Reason") I was truly mystified by this perspective, and it became a central theme in my dissertation research, which drew a great deal of inspiration from the rich tapestry of philosophical and ethical frameworks to which I was introduced in Carolyn's Environmental Philosophy and Ethics course.

Further insights gained in teaching the course in 1989 with Yaakov Garb, a graduate student in the School of Education, and in 1994 with Patsy Hallen, a visiting professor from Murdoch University, enriched my own teaching of the course in the fall of 1996, as I was finishing up my dissertation. In the intervening years, Carolyn had published *Key Concepts in Critical Theory: Ecology* (Merchant 1994, 2nd ed. 2006), a collection of essays aligned with the topics of *Radical Ecology*, which I used in my course. It is a comprehensive collection of essays, which has also been integrated into our curriculum in Hutchins. In addition to topics mentioned above, it begins with a section on "Critical Theory and the Domination of Nature," which served as my initial introduction to the work of the Frankfurt School. Another chapter that informed my inquiry into the relationship between environmental philosophy and systems thinking was Vandana Shiva's "Development, Ecology, and Women," particularly with regard to the contemporary political climate (Shiva 1988).

The passage of the North American Free Trade Agreement (NAFTA) in 1994 accelerated concerns with the widening impact of economic globalization, on both human society and the environment. Shiva's article illuminated the consequences for women and ecology in the so-called developing world, arguing that development on the model of the West is dependent upon the continued subjugation and marginalization of reproductive labor. In this context, the readings for my course also included a chapter from David Korten's *When Corporations Rule the World* (Korten 1995), appropriately entitled "The Ecological Revolution," which further outlined the consequences of globalization:

> In the name of modernity we are creating dysfunctional societies that are breeding pathological behavior—violence, extreme competitiveness, suicide, drug abuse, greed, environmental degradation at every hand … . The threefold crisis of deepening poverty, environmental destruction, and social disintegration manifests this dysfunction.
>
> *(p. 261)*

These perspectives from Shiva and Korten reinforce a central theme throughout Carolyn's work, articulating the poverty of modernity in devaluing and ignoring the essential contributions of nature and women in the reproduction of the conditions of life on the planet.

Highlighting many of the same themes, Arnold Schulz's course on Ecosystemology, provided a perfect complement to the rich tapestry of topics addressed in Carolyn's courses, inspiring and informing the eventual focus of my dissertation research. This course, which I joined as teaching assistant for four semesters, introduced many of the concepts central to the evolution of the field of systems thinking. Given my research interests, Arnold introduced me to C. West

Churchman, who was then teaching a course on ethics in the Peace and Conflict Studies program at UC Berkeley, after his retirement from the School of Business. When West heard about my interest in systems theory, clearly enthused by the topic, he suggested that it all began with four men who met at the Center for Advanced Study in the Behavioral Studies at Stanford in 1954: Ludwig von Bertalanffy, Kenneth Boulding, Ralph Gerard, and Anatol Rapoport. Building on their mutual interests, they founded the Society for General Systems Research (SGSR), currently the International Society for the Systems Sciences (ISSS). Both Arnold and West had been active members in the Society, and West served as its President in 1989–1990. Beginning in 1994, I became actively involved in the ISSS, serving as President in 2006 and hosting the 50th annual meeting at Sonoma State. The history of this particular organization and its founders became the topic of my dissertation, with Arnold serving as the fourth reader on my committee.

In Search of an Alternative Paradigm

To contextualize my interest in the history of systems theory it is necessary to review the evolution of my inquiry in relation to my graduate study in the History of Science. As noted above, I started out intending to examine the significance of new "paradigms" in physics, growing out of developments in relativity theory and quantum mechanics. However, as I began to explore further, it became increasingly clear that the biological sciences provided a much more fertile ground for interrogating the meaning and significance of mechanistic science. Jack Lesch, Professor of History of Biology, nurtured an appreciation for late nineteenth and early twentieth century developments in the field of theoretical biology, while David Hollinger, Professor of American Intellectual History, introduced me to the parallel evolution of social theory, providing a solid foundation for my inquiry; both served as additional readers on my dissertation committee. In my second year in the program, I began to explore the debates between the vitalists and the mechanists during this period, focusing specifically on the work of Hans Driesch (1867–1941) and Jacques Loeb (1854–1924).

The critical distinction between the two views has to do with the nature and source of organization in living systems. For vitalists, physical and chemical laws alone are not adequate to explain the complex organization of living organisms and their seemingly purposive behavior. As one of the dominant spokesmen for this view, Driesch argued that some kind of organizing intelligence was necessary, appealing to the Aristotelian concept of *entelechy*, as a kind of "form-giving agency or force that regulates and directs the development and functioning of organisms" (Hammond 2003:34). In contrast, Loeb was an outspoken advocate for the materialistic reductionism of the mechanistic perspective, arguing that consciousness and life are merely "epiphenomena" of physical and chemical interactions. Significantly, his orientation was integrally bound up with his emphasis on the manipulation and control of living organisms.

A third perspective can be seen in the work of Ernst Haeckel (1834–1919), a German biologist credited with coining the term 'ecology,' whose work I had explored in depth in Carolyn's graduate seminar. A seminar on European Intellectual History with Martin Jay provided an opportunity to integrate his work into my own ongoing inquiry. Both Driesch and Loeb begin with a dualistic orientation, conceiving of matter in purely passive terms, incapable of acting on its own behalf. For Driesch it is acted upon by an organizing intelligence; for Loeb, by the forces of natural law (and of course humankind, under the guiding hand of science). For Haeckel, on the other hand, matter itself possesses a kind of innate intelligence and is capable of self-organization. In the process of exploring the significance of these various theoretical commitments, I discovered the work of Ludwig von Bertalanffy (1901–1972), a theoretical biologist who introduced the concept of organismic biology. Influenced by the earlier arguments of Hans Driesch, Bertalanffy suggested that there were laws of organization, unique to living systems and irreducible to physics and chemistry, that could be studied scientifically.

The Society for General Systems Research

Having thus been familiarized with the basic orientation of Bertalanffy's thought, I was particularly intrigued to learn that he was one of the founders of the Society for General Systems Research that West Churchman had mentioned. In fact, Bertalanffy was the one who initially proposed the idea of "general systems theory," in a seminar at the University of Chicago in 1937, to refer to the study of laws of organization that apply to all kinds of complex systems. I was also somewhat familiar with Kenneth Boulding, through his groundbreaking work in the field of ecological economics, as well as his active role in the anti-war movement during the Vietnam era. That they were both involved in the development of a society for the study of systems theory piqued my interest in learning more about their respective contributions to that newly emerging field. For a project in the history of science, the institutional framework of the society provided an ideal focus, and thus the topic of my dissertation was born.

From the beginning, I was intrigued to discover the generally negative connotation of systems theory in the literature on social theory. Much of this derived from the association of systems theory with the fields of systems engineering and systems analysis, which later became known as the "hard" systems approaches. These tended to be seen as supporting technocratic and hierarchical approaches to social organization. In contrast, many of the presentations that I observed at the annual meetings of the Society (at that point having become the International Society for the Systems Sciences/ISSS) documented and reinforced efforts to facilitate more inclusive and collaborative approaches to decision-making in human systems. As a result, the overarching thesis of my dissertation was that systems theory could, and often did, nurture more democratic forms of social organization.

I outlined the tension between divergent views on the social implications of systems theory in terms of the following polarities, between potentially liberating orientations and those that reinforce tendencies toward domination. These two perspectives might be described in relation to the concepts of partnership and domination, so central to Merchant's own work.

Partnership	*Domination*
Self-organization	Externally imposed order and control
Free will, creativity, spontaneity	Determinism
Participatory decision-making	Hierarchical decision-making
Democracy	Technocracy

In *TDN*, Merchant observes similar contrasts in the implications of the organic worldview in the sixteenth century, identifying three variations in organic theories of society:

1. hierarchical, based on a conservative view of the social order rooted in the feudal system;
2. communal, based on the model of village communities with a leveling of hierarchies; and
3. revolutionary, advocating a complete overthrow of hierarchies and a return to a Golden Age of harmony with nature (Merchant 1980: 69–70).

These varying interpretations of organic or systemic worldviews illustrate the difficulty inherent in any attempt to draw conclusions about their respective social implications. Nonetheless, it is instructive to examine what the systems theorists themselves thought about the social significance of their work. Not surprisingly, even among the founders of the SGSR there were highly divergent views. Ralph Gerard represented one end of the spectrum of orientations. Influenced by the work of Herbert Spencer, and his organismic conception of society, Gerard favored a more repressive brand of holism, promoting a benevolent form of social control with scientists as the brain of the social organism. Jim Miller was also inspired by organismic approaches, particularly as reflected in the work of Lawrence Henderson and Walter Cannon, both of whom advocated centralized social control as analogous to the regulatory processes in living organisms.

Encouraged in this pursuit by Alfred North Whitehead, Miller was passionate about integrating biological, social and psychological dimensions into a comprehensive theoretical framework for the study of human behavior. Working with Gerard and Anatol Rapoport as the core of the group, he initiated the Behavioral Science

Committee at the University of Chicago in 1949, which moved to the University of Michigan in 1955 and continued to meet through the 1960s. One result of this collaborative inquiry was the publication of Miller's immense tome, *Living Systems* (Miller 1978), which addressed the dynamics of interactions between matter, energy and information across seven levels of living systems, from the cell to society and what he called the "supranational system" (Hammond 2003:181–182).

In contrast to the organismic orientation of Gerard and Miller, Kenneth Boulding proposed what he called an ecological model for understanding social systems, rejecting their emphasis on centralized regulation and control. One of the 20 subsystems that Miller describes in his book is the "decider," the nature of which is critical in evaluating the social consequences of these models. Among Boulding's many contributions, one of the most significant with regard to the evolution of applied systems thinking is his emphasis on the importance of dialogue in the decision-making process, embodying a commitment to meaningful inclusion of all members of the social system in question. Although he worked closely with Gerard and Miller, Rapoport's perspective was more closely aligned with that of Boulding. In contrast to the dominant trend in game theory and other approaches to modeling interactions among institutional actors, Rapoport was best known for his work on non-zero-sum games. Significantly, both he and Boulding were very active in the anti-war movement and contributed substantially to the field of Peace and Conflict Studies.

Bertalanffy brings yet another perspective to the mix; most significant for my purposes was his profound animosity toward the behaviorist orientation in psychology, which he referred to as the "robot model" of man. He was particularly critical of the mechanistic and reductionist assumptions at the root of contemporary science and worldviews. Foreshadowing Capra and Merchant, he blamed the mechanistic approach for much of the dysfunction in the modern world. Despite the disparate commitment of the five founders, however, they were united in their critique of the reductionism inherent in the dominant trends in contemporary research. The primary aim of the SGSR was to overcome the disciplinary divides that hindered the ability of humankind to understand and address the complex challenges confronting humanity in the wake of the Second World War. They sought to nurture an appreciation for the complex interplay of environmental, technological, socio-political, economic, psychological, and ideological dynamics underlying these challenges.

Further Inquiry

The SGSR was only one of the many organizations that constellated around the concept of system. In recent years, one focus of my research has been on tracing the lineages of the various schools of thought and communities of practice in the systems field. My interest in this line of inquiry has been further stimulated by my role as the academic coordinator of the Organization Development (OD)

Master's Program at Sonoma State beginning in the fall of 2009. When I was initially approached by Saul Eisen to take over the role, he described the field as a synthesis of systems theory and humanistic psychology. OD practitioners are trained to facilitate collaborative decision-making and planning in organizations, from nonprofits and public agencies to corporations and community alliances. They embody what I sought to portray in my dissertation as the potentially liberating aspect of a systems approach.

In learning more about the field of OD, I became increasingly interested in exploring what scholars from various fields mean by the term "systems theory." Although there are similarities in orientation between OD and the general systems community, the genealogies of these and other systems-oriented traditions vary widely, with corresponding differences in their respective ideological commitments and practical applications. My attempt to articulate these strands of intellectual history is published as "Systems Theory and Practice in Organizational Change and Development," in Darrell Arnold's *Traditions of Systems Theory: Major Figures and Contemporary Developments* (Hammond 2014). It examines the historical trajectories and theoretical perspectives of a broad spectrum of systems-oriented traditions, including systems engineering, systems analysis, operations research, management science, general systems theory, cybernetics, system dynamics, sociotechnical systems, organization development, soft systems methodology, and organizational learning.

A central current in my ongoing inquiry has been an articulation of the philosophical and ethical implications of a systems approach, inspired by Merchant's parallel perspectives on *environmental* philosophy and ethics. My thinking along these lines was first developed in a paper on "Evaluating the Ethical Implications of Systems Thinking" (Hammond 1994), which I wrote in the early stages of my dissertation research. It was further elaborated in "Philosophical and Ethical Foundations of Systems Thinking" (Hammond 2005). Most recently, I have drawn on the essential points from that article for an introductory chapter on the "Philosophical Foundations for Systems Research," for the edited volume *A Guide to Systems Research: Philosophy, Processes and Practice* (Hammond 2016).

The two later essays articulate my interpretation of ontological, epistemological, and ethical commitments of a systems orientation. At the most basic level, a systems ontology encompasses a shift from a mechanistic to a more holistic and organic conception of nature; a parallel shift from an atomistic and dualistic orientation to a concern with networks, patterns, and processes; and an emphasis on organization, interaction, interdependence and relationship. A systems epistemology highlights the dynamic and dialectical nature of knowledge; the role of perception, interpretation, and creation of meaning; the involvement of the observer in the process of observation; and the importance of considering multiple perspectives. An ethics informed by these ontological and epistemological principles would reflect a shift in emphasis from control to collaboration, from competition to interdependence, from hierarchical to participatory decision-making processes, and from an exclusive emphasis on objectivity to an inclusion of subjectivity and reflexive self-awareness. This orientation embodies Merchant's ethic of partnership between humans and the natural world.

Conclusion

My intellectual journey has followed a meandering and circuitous path over the past three and a half decades, from a critique of mechanistic science, to an exploration of the meaning and significance of systems thinking, and finally into the practical implementation of ecologically sustainable and socially just organizational change. Throughout the quest certain themes have remained, most significantly in terms of the need for a transformation in our collective modes of being in the world, from domination and control to partnership and collaboration.

Merchant's identification of the mechanistic worldview as the foundation for the egocentric ethic that underlies much of the current dysfunction in the modern world serves as a guiding insight throughout my own work. In conceiving of nature, and by extension the social order, in atomistic and dualistic terms, a mechanistic orientation ultimately reinforces an ethos of competition and greed. Even a homocentric orientation, in its failure to acknowledge the interdependence between humans and nature, reinforces the exploitation of the natural world and ultimately undermines the social fabric.

In contrast, an ecocentric orientation acknowledges our interdependence, nurturing an ethic of partnership and shared agency, as Merchant has so eloquently articulated. This orientation echoes Bertalanffy's conception of general systems theory, particularly his emphasis on the potential for creativity and self-organization in living systems. Building on these insights, my 1999 article, "From Dominion to Co-creation: A New Vision of Reality beyond the Boundaries of the Mechanistic Universe" (Hammond 1999) explores the potential implications of a "post-mechanistic" science, in which "we are placed back in the context of our own experience ... [as] active participants in the creative processes of the universe" (p. 11). Understanding our interdependence with all our relations, we embody a commitment to working for the good of all.

Note

1 See also Susan Griffin's Foreword to this volume.

References

Biehl, Janet. 1991. *Rethinking Ecofeminist Politics*. Boston: South End Press.
Capra, Fritjof. 1982. *The Turning Point: Science, Society, and the Rising Culture*. New York: Simon & Schuster.
Cronon, William, ed. 1995. *Uncommon Ground: Rethinking the Human Place in Nature*. New York: W.W. Norton.

Eisler, Riane. 1987. *The Chalice and the Blade: Our History, Our Future.* San Francisco, CA: Harper & Row.

Gersper, Paul L. and Alan S. Miller. n.d. *Conservation and Resources Studies Major: University of California—Berkeley.* Unpublished manuscript.

Griffin, Susan. 1978. *Woman and Nature: The Roaring Inside Her.* New York: Harper & Row.

Hammond, Debora. 1994. "Evaluating the Ethical Implications of Systems Thinking," Conference on Science, Technology, and Religious Ideas, Institute for Liberal Studies, Kentucky State University, Frankfort, Kentucky, April 7–9. Unpublished paper.

Hammond, Debora. 1997. *Toward a Science of Synthesis: The Heritage of General Systems Theory.* Dissertation. University of California, Berkeley.

Hammond, Debora. 1999. "From Dominion to Co-creation: A New Vision of Reality beyond the Boundaries of the Mechanistic Universe." *ReVision: A Journal of Consciousness and Transformation* 21(4):4–11.

Hammond, Debora. 2001. "Re-thinking the 'and' in Humans and Nature: Ecology at the Boundary of the Human Dimension" (primary author, with G. A.Bradshaw, Ph.D), Review of Symposium, *Bulletin of the Ecological Society of America* (January).

Hammond, Debora. 2003. *The Science of Synthesis: Exploring the Social Implications of General Systems Theory.* Boulder, CO: University of Colorado Press.

Hammond, Debora. 2005. "Philosophical and Ethical Foundations of Systems Thinking." *tripleC—Cognition, Communication, Co-operation* 3(2). www.triple-c.at/index.php/trip leC/article/view/20/19

Hammond, Debora. 2014. "Systems Theory and Practice in Organizational Change and Development." Pp. 326–344 in *Traditions of Systems Theory: Major Figures and Contemporary Developments,* ed. D. Arnold. New York: Routledge.

Hammond, Debora. 2016. "Philosophical Foundations for Systems Research." Pp. 1–20 in *A Guide to Systems Research: Philosophy, Processes and Practice,* eds. M. Edson et al. Singapore: Springer.

Horkheimer, Max, and Theodor Adorno. 1972. *Dialectic of Enlightenment.* John Cumming, trans. New York: Herder and Herder.

Korten, David. 1995. *When Corporations Rule the World.* 3rd ed. 2015. Oakland, CA: Berrett-Koehler.

Lewis, Martin. 1995. "Radical Environmental Philosophy and the Assault on Reason." Annals of the New York Academy of Science. Volume 775: *The Flight from Science and Reason:* 209–230.

Merchant, Carolyn. 1980. *The Death of Nature: Women, Ecology and the Scientific Revolution.* San Francisco, CA: Harper & Row. [1990 Preface]

Merchant, Carolyn. 1989. *Ecological Revolutions: Nature, Gender, and Science in New England.* Chapel Hill: University of North Carolina Press.

Merchant, Carolyn. 1992. *Radical Ecology: The Search for a Livable World.* 2nd ed. 2005. New York: Routledge.

Merchant, Carolyn. 1993. *Major Problems in American Environmental History: Documents and Essays,* Ed. C. Merchant. Lexington, MA: D.C. Heath.

Merchant, Carolyn. 1994. *Key Concepts in Critical Theory: Ecology,* Ed. C. Merchant. 2nd ed. 2006. Atlantic Highlands, NJ: Humanities Press.

Merchant, Carolyn. 1996. *Earthcare: Women and the Environment.* New York: Routledge.

Merchant, Carolyn. 1998. *Green Versus Gold: Sources in California's Environmental History,* Ed. C. Merchant. Washington, DC: Island Press.

Merchant, Carolyn. 2004. *Reinventing Eden: The Fate of Nature in Western Culture*. New York: Routledge.

Miller, Alan S. 1991. *Gaia Connections: An Introduction to Ecology, Eco-ethics and Economics*. Lanham, MD: Rowman & Littlefield.

Miller, James Grier. 1978. *Living Systems*. New York: McGraw Hill.

Mitman, Greg. 1992. *The State of Nature: Ecology, Community, and American Social Thought, 1900–1950*. Chicago: University of Chicago Press.

Shiva, Vandana. 1988. "Development, Ecology, and Women." Pp. 1–9, 13 in *Staying Alive: Women, Ecology, and Development*. London: Zed Books; cited in Merchant, 1994.

Worster, Donald. [1978] 1994. *Nature's Economy: A History of Ecological Ideas*. 2nd ed. New York: Cambridge University Press.

10

THE OTHER SCIENTIFIC REVOLUTION

Calvinist Scientists and the Origins of Ecology

Mark Stoll

"Is the earth dead or alive?" asked Carolyn Merchant in 1992. She continued,

> The ancient cultures of east and west and the native peoples of America saw
> the earth as a mother, alive, active, and responsive to human action. Greeks
> and Renaissance Europeans conceptualized the cosmos as a living organism,
> with a body, soul, and spirit, and the earth as a nurturing mother with
> respiratory, circulatory, reproductive, and elimination systems. The relation-
> ship between most peoples and the earth was an I-thou ethic of propitiation
> to be made before damming a brook, cutting a tree, or sinking a mine shaft.
> Yet for the past three hundred years, Western mechanistic science and
> capitalism have viewed the earth as dead and inert, manipulable from out-
> side, and exploitable for profits. The death of nature legitimated its domina-
> tion. Colonial extractions of resources combined with industrial pollution
> and depletion have today pushed the whole earth to the brink of ecological
> destruction.
>
> *(Merchant 1992:41)*

Merchant had first formulated this narrative of loss of a living earth in the rise of
science and capitalist exploitation of nature a dozen years earlier, in *The Death of
Nature: Women, Ecology, and the Scientific Revolution* (hereafter *TDN*) (Merchant
1980). In that work, she discovered Western oppression of women and nature
embedded deep in the West's intellectual and religious traditions, especially their
expression in the Scientific Revolution and the Enlightenment. But Merchant
overlooked how currents of the Scientific Revolution streamed in different
channels carved by Europe's cultural and religious diversity. From one of these
"other," less mechanistic, and more organic Scientific Revolutions, flowed

modern ecological science. Moreover, the surprising fountainhead from which it flowed was the theology of John Calvin.

Merchant's narrative was part of a scholarly endeavor – amid the postwar upheaval and tumultuous movements to end war, racism, sexism, and pollution – to unearth the historical roots of terrible problems that plagued Western civilization. One of the earliest and most influential of these efforts was a brief 1967 essay by medieval historian Lynn White, Jr., "The Historical Roots of Our Ecologic Crisis." White blamed Christian disenchantment of the pagan world for the environmental crisis. Christians had banished pagan gods and spirits from the natural world and, having rendered nature a soulless thing, put it under human dominion. Ecologically-sensitive spirituality survived in non-Western religious traditions, White thought, but he saw little in the Christian tradition, aside from the teachings of St. Francis of Assisi.

Many variations on White's theme appeared in following years, as historians searched in the mindset of the West for causes for the environmental crisis. Historian Donald Worster (1994), for example, argued in *Nature's Economy: A History of Ecological Ideas* in 1977 that Western ecological thinking had been historically divided between proto-environmentalist "Arcadian" and exploitative "imperial" ways of thinking. Frederick W. Turner's popular (if less scholarly) 1980 book *Beyond Geography: The Western Spirit Against the Wilderness* (Turner 1983) turned American history into a morality tale of conflict between exploitative European Christianity and more ecological Native American spirituality. Influenced by the flourishing of feminist theory in the early 1970s, Turner used metaphors of sexual violence to describe an aggressively male Christianity destroying Indian religion's ideals of a feminine earth. Annette Kolodny (1975) had already explored the importance of gendered metaphors of the land in her literary study *The Lay of the Land: Metaphor as Experience and History in American Life and Letters*. J. Donald Hughes (1983) would take up the theme of Indian harmony with nature in his 1983 *American Indian Ecology*. Stephen R. Fox (1981), author of *John Muir and His Legacy: The American Conservation Movement*, also regarded Christianity and environmentalism as incompatible.

Although Merchant placed the moment of the disenchantment of nature in a later period, *TDN* clearly echoed White's argument. *TDN* described a contest between two worldviews, the older organismic and newer mechanistic views of nature of the Scientific Revolution. According to her interpretation, by 1700 the mechanistic view had won out and capitalistic exploitation of nature was on the rise. Merchant elaborated on this thesis in later works such as *Ecological Revolutions: Nature, Gender, and Science in New England* (with its similar subtitle) (Merchant 2010); *Radical Ecology: The Search for a Livable World* (Merchant 1992); *Earthcare: Women and the Environment* (Merchant 1996); and *Reinventing Eden: The Fate of Nature in Western Culture* (Merchant 2003). The West had made a wrong turn. As she concluded in *TDN*, "The sick earth … can probably in the long run be restored to health only by a reversal of mainstream values and a revolution in economic priorities" (Merchant 1980:295).

Despite its undeniable insight, Merchant's narrative overlooked those scientists who diverged from the path to Cartesian–Newtonian mechanism. The earth sciences of biology and geology relied more on observation of the living, changing world around us than on the scientific method or mathematical determinism. Moreover, scientific interests reflected the fracturing of Christendom after the Reformation. Out of Calvinism and its understanding of God's presence in nature, rather than out of a pre-modern view of nature as female, arose the ecological sciences of America and Britain. From the seventeenth to the nineteenth centuries, Reformed Protestants in the Calvinist tradition (which includes Puritans, Congregationalists, Presbyterians, Huguenots, Swiss Reformed, Dutch Reformed, and not a few Anglicans) produced most of the major advances in the earth sciences. Calvinists were by far the most enthusiastic writers of the genre of natural theology, in which the author examines the evidence in nature of the existence and attributes of God. In the United States, Reformed Protestants would lay the foundations for the science of ecology.

From Calvin to Science

Nature's outsized role in Calvinist theology led many scientists from the Reformed tradition to study nature for evidences of God's existence, presence, and providence. John Calvin had advanced a radical notion of providence in which God directed the motion of even the smallest particle. Rejecting the First Mover of Thomas Aquinas, or any possible clockwork universe for that matter, he insisted that the Creator

> is also a Governor and Preserver, and that, not by producing a kind of general motion in the machine of the globe as well as in each of its parts, but by a special providence sustaining, cherishing, superintending, all the things which he has made, to the very minutest, even to a sparrow.
>
> *(Calvin 1845:1.16.1)*

Everywhere Calvin looked in nature, he saw the glory of God shining. "Wherever you turn your eyes," he wrote,

> there is no portion of the world, however minute, that does not exhibit at least some sparks of beauty; while it is impossible to contemplate the vast and beautiful fabric as it extends around, without being overwhelmed by the immense weight of glory.
>
> *(Calvin 1845:1.5.1)*

Because Calvinists believed Adam's Fall had clouded human reason, they mistrusted logical proofs of God's existence and instead turned to nature to find God in his works. By the middle of the seventeenth century, Reformed clergy had grown interested in natural science. Puritan minister John Ray (1627–1705) was author of numerous important scientific books. His three religious books, especially *The Wisdom of God Manifested in the Works of Creation* of 1691, presaged a popular new genre, physico-theology, an updated form of natural theology. In 1713, Anglican vicar William Derham (1657–1735) penned a long-popular work, *Physico-Theology, or a Demonstration of the Being and Attributes of God from His Works of Creation*. Derham's purpose was typical of the genre:

> for the Proof of the Christian Religion against Atheists and other Infidels, to improve this occasion in the Demonstration of the *Being* and *Attributes* of an infinitely wise and powerful Creator, from a Cursory Survey of the Works of Creation.
>
> *(Derham 1747:3)*

Anglican priest William Paley (1743–1805) drew from Ray and others to produce the classic *Natural Theology; Or, Evidence of the Existence and Attributes of the Deity, Collected from the Appearances of Nature* of 1802, which went into innumerable editions on both sides of the Atlantic to become required college reading for generations of students, including Ralph Waldo Emerson and Charles Darwin. Scottish Presbyterian minister and amateur scientist Thomas Dick (1774–1857) followed in 1823 with one of the last of these bestselling reconciliations of religion and science, *The Christian Philosopher, or the Connection of Science with Religion*, the popularity of which in both Britain and America sent it into new editions for decades, and which found its way into the hands of teenaged John Muir.

English America's first native-born scientists were New England ministers, whose college education fitted them for intellectual inquiry of all kinds. Two of the most important were Increase Mather (1639–1723) and his son Cotton (1663–1728). Increase "highly valued my Lord *Verulam's* [Francis Bacon] Writings, and *Gassendus's* [Pierre Gassendi] Works; but above all others, he most esteem'd the Philosophical Works of the honourable *Robert Boyle*" (Mather, Mather, and Calamy 1725:66). When Increase was in England, he visited Boyle, a prominent author in both science and theology, who gave him copies of his books (Winship 1996:64). In 1684, Increase co-founded the (short-lived) Boston Philosophical Society on the model of the Royal Society, the world's first scientific society, founded two decades earlier. That year he published a book on comets, *Kometographia*, and in 1685 published two other books on scientific subjects, *An Essay for the Recording of Illustrious Providences* and *The Doctrine of Divine Providence* (Hall 1988:165–173). Near the end to his Preface to *An Essay for the Recording of Illustrious Providences*, Mather lamented his inability to contribute more to science: "I have often wished, that the *Natural History of New-England*, might be written and published to the World; the Rules and method described by that Learned and excellent person *Robert Boyle* Esq. being duely observed therein" (Mather 1684:n.p.).

The most important American Puritan-scientist, however, was Cotton Mather, whose work enlisted science for Calvinist orthodoxy against the skeptical Enlightenment. Mather evinced an early interest in science and in college considered a career in medicine before choosing the ministry, as had his father, three uncles, and grandfather. He had a lifelong fascination with medicine and science and read Boyle's *The Christian Virtuoso*, Ray's *The Wisdom of God Manifested in the Works of the Creation*, and Derham's *Physico-Theology*. In 1701 Mather received the first honorary Doctor of Divinity awarded an American by the University of Glasgow. Between 1712 and 1724 he sent a string of dispatches he called "Curiosa Americana" to the Royal Society, which elected him Fellow in 1713. He wrote the only comprehensive medical book in colonial America, the extensive but unpublished *Angel of Bethesda*, in which he defended his controversial advocacy of inoculation during the smallpox epidemic of 1721 (Middlekauff 1971:279–304; Silverman 1984:41–42, 167–168, 243–254, 406–410). Boyle, Ray, and Derham inspired one of Mather's best-known books, *The Christian Philosopher* of 1721, the first general book on science written in America. In it he developed the idea of "the Twofold Book of GOD"—nature and revelation—to make the case that scientific knowledge of creation led to "a PHILOSOPHICAL RELIGION; And yet how *Evangelical!*" As the priest of the temple of God that is creation, man could well answer the end of his existence: "To glorify GOD." To Cotton Mather, every creature was a preacher, and even the smallest blade of grass proof of the existence, power, and glory of God. Science would evangelize for Reformed Protestantism (Mather 1721:1–2, 3, 8, 13).

Calvinists Establish Natural Science in North America

Wherever Reformed Protestants settled in America, natural history was pursued with greatest enthusiasm. Puritan Congregationalists and Scottish Presbyterians led the way, whether in New England, New York, Philadelphia, or Charleston. Charleston, Philadelphia, and Boston formed early centers of the study of natural history, which mainly amateurs pursued until the middle of the nineteenth century (Smallwood and Smallwood 1941:42–49, 57–100; Freemon 1985).

Reformed universities played an important role in spreading love of natural history. At Puritan Harvard College, established 1636, botany ("the nature of plants") numbered among topics of instruction from its earliest days. Harvard professor Charles Morton wrote a superior natural science curriculum in 1686 that informed and inspired students for over 40 years. (Science blossomed at Yale College, founded by Puritan Congregationalists in 1701, only in the nineteenth century.) Since non-Anglicans were barred from attending either Oxford or Cambridge, colonial Congregationalists and Presbyterians who sought the best medical training studied at the universities of Leiden and especially Edinburgh, both of which offered an innovative course of study with heavy emphasis on natural history. Scientists of the Royal Society and the Continent, like Linnaeus, eager to learn about and acquire specimens of flora and fauna of the colonies, carried on correspondence with a number of Americans and British immigrants, especially from Presbyterian Scotland (among them Cadwallader and Jane Colden of New York; Alexander Garden and John Lining of Charleston, South Carolina; and William Smith, first provost of the College of Philadelphia, now the University of Pennsylvania).

In Charleston, where the leisured, cosmopolitan, slave-owning elite gathered, a vital natural science tradition arose from the work of Reformed immigrants like Garden and Lining and New York-born Lutheran pastor John Bachman. Beaufort-born Stephen Elliott, tutored by Connecticut Congregational clergyman Abiel Holmes, graduated from Yale and published *A Sketch of the Botany of South-Carolina and Georgia* (1816–1824). John Edwards Holbrook was born in Beaufort of New England parentage, grew up in Massachusetts, trained at Brown University and in Europe, and returned to Charleston in 1812 to set up a medical practice. Holbrook produced the landmark five-volume *North American Herpetology* in 1842 (see Stephens 2000). Unfortunately, after about 1830 obsession with the defense of slavery distracted from natural history. The war put an end to it for many decades (Smallwood and Smallwood 1941:102–129; Rowland, Moore, and Rogers 1996:398–400; Taylor 1998:126).

Philadelphia far surpassed Charleston in quality and prominence of its institutions, its libraries and publications—and its popular interest in natural history. Founded by Quakers, Philadelphia was English America's largest colonial city and its cultural, scientific, and sometime political capital. Anti-Calvinists, Quakers on both sides of the Atlantic produced a flurry of important work in botany in the eighteenth century. English Quaker Peter Collinson occupied the center of a vast network of scientific and botanic correspondents from America to Britain and the Continent, from Benjamin Franklin to Linnaeus. American Quaker interest in the natural world began with the work of Pennsylvania's founder, William Penn, whose interest in botany led to his election in 1681 to the Royal Society. He explained his interest in natural science in a letter of 1683 that tied the experiential religion of the Quakers to the experiential nature of the scientific method. Both he and the Fellows of the Royal Society "are votaries to the prosperity of their harmless and useful inquiries," he wrote. "It is even one step to heaven to return to nature, and ... a natural knowledge or the science of things from sense and a careful observation and argumentation thereon, reinstates men and gives them some possession of themselves again" (Penn to John Aubrey, 1683, quoted in Underwood 1976:143). These ideas of the presence of God in nature and natural history's innocuous and useful character inspired Quakers as much as Puritans (Cantor 1997). Quaker botanists in America included James Logan and three generations of Bartrams: William Bartram, his son John, and his grandson Thomas Say.

However, non-Quaker immigrants flooded into Pennsylvania and Reformed Protestants made up the greater proportion of Philadelphia's naturalists. Benjamin Franklin, born Presbyterian in Boston, formed the American Philosophical Society there in 1742 on the model of the Royal Society. Pennsylvania botanist Benjamin Smith Barton, descendant of an Irish Anglican minister on his father's side and a Dutch Mennonite bishop and Quakers on his mother's, studied at the Universities of Edinburgh and Göttingen before taking a position as professor of natural history at the University of Pennsylvania and serving as an officer in the American Philosophical Society (Ewan et al. 2007). Dutch-born Gerard Troost, graduate of the University of Leiden, was a co-founder in 1812 of the Philadelphia Academy of Natural Sciences and its first president until 1817 (Glenn 1905). Scottish-born merchant and pioneering geologist William Maclure succeeded him (Baatz 1988). Another Scot, Alexander Wilson (christened in Paisley, Scotland, by the future president of Princeton College, John Witherspoon), produced the landmark nine-volume *American Ornithology* between 1808 and 1814, which inspired John James Audubon's work (Wilson 1983; see also Merchant 2016:116–146).

While the best natural science in British America came out of Charleston and Philadelphia, these cities could not compare with Boston's enthusiasm for natural history, which extended far deeper and wider in the general population. In New England, even farmers began to record the day that the first spring flowers opened or the first birds returned for the summer and to take walks in the woods. This broad interest in the natural world later fostered the work of Ralph Waldo Emerson and Henry David Thoreau (Judd 1997). Bostonians founded a short-lived Linnaean Society in 1814 and the much more successful Boston Society of Natural History in 1830. Devout Congregationalist science professor Benjamin Silliman's rise to prominence in the natural sciences at Yale, where he taught from 1804 to 1864, was emblematic of this interest, as was the simultaneous rise of science at Harvard. The visit in 1846 of Swiss Reformed Protestant Louis Agassiz to deliver a series of lectures instigated the establishment at Harvard of the Lawrence Scientific School in 1847 and an offer of a professorship.

In the nineteenth century, a stream of books by British and American Anglican and Reformed authors promoted the idea that study of the works of God in nature constituted an easily available, innocent, and morally profitable activity. Congregational minister Edward Hitchcock exemplified the American pastor-naturalist. An avid amateur scientist since his teens, Hitchcock attended Yale and came under Silliman's spell. The two became lifelong friends and colleagues. After he assumed the pulpit of the Congregational Church in Conway in 1821, he wrote to Silliman of his worries regarding whether his pastoral duties and scientific avocation were compatible: "Must these pursuits be altogether abandoned? Or is there such a thing as pursuing them with a supreme reference to the glory of God?" (Hitchcock to Silliman, December 1, 1822, quoted in Lawrence 1972:22). Silliman assured him they were indeed proper for a minister. In 1825, Hitchcock accepted an invitation to be the first professor of chemistry and natural history at newly organized Amherst College. Publishing in both geology and natural theology, he became America's foremost Christian geologist and a powerful defender of natural theology until his death in 1864. Hitchcock published his magnum opus, *The Religion of Geology*, in 1851. Lake Hitchcock, the glacial lake that once covered the Connecticut River Valley, is named for him (Lawrence 1972; Hitchcock 1863:281–297).

Providence, Cosmos, Ecology

If Calvinists wandered in the woods to commune with the spirit of God while they studied his works, their theology also promoted ecological holism. They looked out on an organismic world, not a mechanistic or clockwork universe. Calvin was certainly no scientist, but his doctrine of an active God in an active creation of mutually interacting parts had profound implications for the work of Reformed scientists. As Calvinists abhorred idleness, Calvin's God was not "sitting idly in heaven" but "vigilant, efficacious, energetic, and ever active" (Calvin 1845:1.16.4, 1.16.3). Calvin's was no idle universe, either; it was a world of development and change. As sixteenth-century Huguenot Bernard Palissy declared,

> I know well that it is written in the Book of Genesis, that God created all things in six days, and that he rested on the seventh, but for all that, God did not create these things to leave them idle, therefore each performs its duty according to the commandment it received from God. The stars and planets are not idle; the sea wanders from one place to another, and labours to bring forth profitable things; the earth likewise is never idle; that which decays naturally in her she renews, she forms over again—if not in one shape, she will reproduce it in another.
>
> *(Palissy, quoted in Morley 1852:319)*

Reinforced by currents of Neoplatonism in the Protestant world of the late eighteenth and early nineteenth century, Calvinist ways of thinking about nature promoted biological holism and acceptance of change and process in natural history, the foundational concepts of the work of the nineteenth century's greatest biological scientists, Alexander von Humboldt and Charles Darwin.

In 1851, Silliman made a pilgrimage from Yale to the Berlin home of the great hero of American natural science, Alexander von Humboldt. His trek symbolized the natural sympathy that Reformed science held for the holistic science that Humboldt championed. No Reformed scientist before Darwin would have greater influence than the early nineteenth-century explorer-scientist Alexander von Humboldt, who was lionized in Reformed nations, nowhere more so than in the United States. Particularly influential in the English-speaking world was the publication, beginning in 1814, of his multi-volume *Personal Narrative*. In vivid prose, these books described the adventures and discoveries of the first half of his unprecedented scientific journey of exploration between 1799 and 1804 into the interior of South America, although the last volume ended before the last segments of his travels in Cuba, Mexico, and the United States. His series of lectures published in English as

Aspects (or *Views*) *of Nature* was also widely read. The five volumes of his great masterwork, *Cosmos*, were released serially in the 1840s and 1850s to huge anticipation and acclaim in America, and Humboldt's popularity entered a second phase lasting into the 1870s. Present, as Humboldt was, at the youth of American science, he represented both authority and inspiration to multitudes of young naturalists and scientists (Rupke 2008; Walls 2009; Sachs 2006; Cittadino 1999).

Humboldt grew up in a pious household dominated by his dour mother, descendant of Huguenot, Scottish, and Reformed-German businessmen, professors, doctors, and theologians (Borsche 1990:20). His travels of scientific discovery derived major inspiration from the friendship and example of Georg Forster. Forster and his father, Johann Reinhold Forster, a Prussian naturalist and Reformed pastor, had accompanied Captain James Cook on his voyage of discovery and written a famous account of it. Forster argued for a holistic approach to the sciences. Only by overcoming the petty divisions of the sciences may the observer attain a unified understanding of the diversity of nature, the immediate revelation of God, he felt, and thereby draw nearer to the Creator (Forster 1894:1–25).

The characteristically Reformed style of science that Humboldt founded, and which the Anglophone world embraced with enthusiasm, combined detailed measurement of natural phenomena with observation of their interrelations, an insistent focus on the unity in the diversity of the world. Despite their overall secular tone (without any gushing over God's presence in nature), Humboldt's works contained in varying degrees noticeable Calvinistic moralism and hints of spiritual wonder at the unity in diversity of the cosmos. He decried the sins of man while he betrayed a true love of the natural world. Humboldt noted the vanity of human works, much as Calvin had when he called "all the works of men … nothing but vileness and pollution" (Calvin 1845:3.12.4) compared with God's works, and nature's ceaseless activity, much like Palissy:

> Thus does man, everywhere alike, on the lowest scale of brutish debasement, and in the false glitter of his higher culture, perpetually create for himself a life of care. And thus, too, the traveler … [is] everywhere met by the unvarying and melancholy spectacle of man opposed to man … .
>
> Thus pass away the generations of men!—thus perish the records of the glory of nations! Yet when every emanation of the human mind has faded—when in the storms of time the monuments of man's creative art are scattered to the dust—an ever new life springs from the bosom of the earth. Unceasingly prolific nature unfolds her germs,—regardless though sinful man, ever at war with himself, tramples beneath his foot the ripening fruit!
>
> *(Humboldt 1850b:21, 173)*

Like Calvin, Humboldt brought out the moral influence of active nature upon humans who know to see and to listen.

For the physical world is reflected with truth and animation on the inner susceptible world of the mind. Whatever marks the character of a landscape: the profile of mountains, which in the far and hazy distance bound the horizon; the deep gloom of pine forests; the mountain torrent, which rushes headlong to its fall through overhanging cliffs: all stand alike in an ancient and mysterious communion with the spiritual life of man.

(Humboldt 1850b: 154)

Everything proclaims a world of active organic forces. In every shrub, in the cracked bark of trees, in the perforated ground inhabited by hymenopterous insects, life is everywhere audibly manifest. It is one of the many voices of nature revealed to the pious and susceptible spirit of man ... .

(Humboldt 1850b: 201)

Like Calvin, to whom nature was the theater of God's glory and humans were but the degraded image of their Creator, Humboldt's praise of nature contrasted with his impression of humanity, which in most of his work took second place behind the natural world. His grand final opus, the five-volume *Cosmos*, contained no anthropological volume. Its focus was on the natural world and on its moral, spiritual, and intellectual effect on humanity. The ringing declarations of the opening chapter pointed the way forward to a Reformed ecological science of nature that would arise in the next century:

Nature considered *rationally*, that is to say, submitted to the process of thought, is a unity in diversity of phenomena; a harmony, blending together all created things, however dissimilar in form and attributes; one great whole (Τὸ πᾶν [*tò pan*]) animated by the breath of life. The most important result of a rational inquiry into nature is, therefore, to establish the unity and harmony of this stupendous mass of force and matter, to determine with impartial justice what is due to the discoveries of the past and to those of the present, and to analyze the individual parts of natural phenomena without succumbing beneath the weight of the whole. Thus, and thus alone, is it permitted to man, while mindful of the high destiny of his race, to comprehend nature, to lift the vail [*sic*] that shrouds her phenomena, and, as it were, submit the results of observation to the test of reason and of intellect.

(Humboldt 1850a:24–25)

As the very title *Cosmos* indicated, the central concept underlying all Humboldt's work was nature's unity in diversity. Here his work was foundational to Protestant natural science.

Humboldt's *Personal Narrative* was one of many Reformed influences on Charles Darwin. He attended the University of Edinburgh to study medicine but was captivated by the natural science courses instead. Giving up medicine, he went to Cambridge with the intent of taking holy orders. He read Paley and later recalled, "I hardly ever admired a book more than Paley's *Natural Theology*" (Darwin 1859a). Humboldt's *Personal Narrative* inspired Darwin's first thoughts about traveling the world as a naturalist, which soon became reality when he joined the momentous voyage of the HMS *Beagle*. Darwin took the *Personal Narrative* with him on the voyage of the *Beagle* and used it as a model for *Voyage of the Beagle*, the book that first made him famous. A year into the five-year voyage, he wrote a friend, "I formerly admired Humboldt, I now almost adore him" (Darwin 1887:210). Later, he commented, "I never forget that my whole course of life is due to having read and re-read as a youth his 'Personal Narrative'" (Darwin 1887:305). Darwin's "chief favourite," however, was Puritan poet John Milton's *Paradise Lost*, with its poetic descriptions of Eden and the Fall of Adam and Eve, which he always took with him on shore excursions (Darwin 1887:57). The Reformed vision of a complex, interconnected universe—with disregard for the supernatural and consideration for the element of time—led to Darwin's vision of an interconnected universe that evolved, not by direction of the divine spirit, but under guidance of natural law. He famously concluded *Origin of Species*,

> It is interesting to contemplate an entangled bank, clothed with many plants of many kinds, with birds singing in the bushes, with various insects flitting about, and with worms crawling through the damp earth, and to reflect that these elaborately constructed forms, so different from each other, and dependent on each other in so complex a manner, have all been produced by laws acting around us.
>
> *(Darwin 1859b:489)*

In one sense, Darwin's theory of natural selection also resembles Calvin's doctrine of eternal election, or predestination. Selection by nature for survival and election by God for salvation both take place for reasons over which the individual has no control. Nature's "damned" go extinct, while Calvin's damned go to hell (Rupke 2008:24–25, 169–173, 185–192; Worster 1994:133–137).

Birth of Ecology

In Germany, too, Reformed natural theology and Neoplatonism came together to give birth to ecology as a new branch of biology. As Lutheranism recovered from the terrible shocks of the bloody religious wars of the seventeenth century, Germans turned with interest to English developments in theology and natural science. Philosophical idealism appeared in the nineteenth century in the influential form of the *Naturphilosophie* of Fichte, Goethe, Shelling, and Hegel. Humboldt's works reinforced *Naturphilosophie*'s unity of spirit and nature and extended its influence.

Scientist and philosopher Ernst Haeckel, raised in a pious Prussian Lutheran family to emerge as Darwin's German champion, re-interpreted scientific holism both with and without its spiritual component into the twentieth century. Humboldt's *Aspects of Nature* and *Kosmos* deeply impressed him. Haeckel credited Humboldt's *Kosmos* in his *Generelle Morphologie der Organismen* of 1866, a thoroughly Darwinian work in which he coined "*Oecologie*" (ecology) as a science of the interaction of individual organisms (Haeckel 1866:441–442).

Humboldt's vision of the phenomena of nature interconnected in a cosmic unity also deeply affected German Protestant Karl Möbius. Möbius first formulated the ecological concept of a community of biota in his study of the biological "community" of an oyster bank. To describe this community, in 1877 he coined the term "biocoenosis," from the Greek roots for "life-sharing" (König 1981; Kölmel 1981). Building on Humboldt's pioneering insights into plant geography, German Oscar Drude focused on the geographical distribution of plants in his "phytogeography." *Naturphilosophie* influenced Drude's *Die Ökologie der Pflanzen* ("Plant Ecology") in 1913, among many other fundamental works. This line of study later culminated in the taxonomy of plant societies of Swiss Reformed botanist Josias Braun-Blanquet, especially in his important *Plant Sociology* of 1931 (Matagne 1999; Cooper 2003:37; Tobey 1981). The son of a Danish Lutheran minister and closely related to four others, Eugenius Warming spoke of the coastal landscape of his youth with deep feeling and rather mystical reverence. His investigation of plant communities built on Humboldt's ideas and led to the publication in 1895 of the foundational and oft-translated *Plantesamfund: Grundträk af den Ökologiska Plantegeografi* ("Plant Community: Introduction to Ecological Plant Geography"), the first textbook with the term "ecological" in the title (Prytz 1984:10, 12, 102–3, 188; Lekan 2004:53–56).

The works of these European scientists provided models and inspiration for early American ecologists, almost all of whom were Reformed Protestants. A Congregationalist and admirer of Puritan theologian Jonathan Edwards as a youth, Illinois professor Stephen Forbes introduced Möbius's idea of the biological community to America (Croker 2001:15, 64, 105, 126). Forbes's holistic study of the biota of a lake was a founding paper in the new science of ecology. Warming inspired another Congregationalist, Henry Chandler Cowles, to study the plant communities in sand dunes near Chicago. Cowles developed a theory of plant succession that used organic analogies and terminology to describe the development of a dune plant community from an embryo to maturity to death (Hagen 1992:16–20; Cittadino 1999). One of Cowles's students, Presbyterian Victor Shelford, influentially developed the concept of animal communities (Croker 2001:50, 103). Drude inspired "devoutly religious" but unchurched Frederic Clements[1], student of Congregationalist Charles Bessey, chair of botany of the University of Nebraska (Sears 1974). Working with his wife Edith, granddaughter of Presbyterian minister John Robert Young and an accomplished biologist in her own right, and applying Drude's methods to Nebraska, Clements devised a Humboldt-influenced theory of ecology that the plant community was itself an organism. As he wrote in his 1916 landmark *Plant Succession*:

> The developmental study of vegetation necessarily rests upon the assumption that the unit or climax formation is an organic entity. As an organism the formation arises, grows, matures, and dies … . The life-history of a formation is a complex but definitive process, comparable in its chief features with the life-history of an individual plant.
>
> *(Clements 1916:3)*

With its suspicion of man in the landscape, American ecology betrayed greater Calvinist influence than did German ecology. Ever since Adam was driven from the Garden after the Fall, wherever sinful humans went, "the harmonies of nature are turned to discords," in the words of Congregationalist conservationist George Perkins Marsh (Marsh 1864:36). To Forbes, if the environment was an organism, ecology was the equivalent to physiology, and his own practical role as a biologist was like a physician's in healing his "patient." "Human interference with the natural order of plant and animal life gives rise to reactions which correspond closely to those of bodily disease," he wrote (quoted in Croker 2001:112). Forbes remarked that "primeval nature … presents a settled harmony of interaction among organic groups which is in strong contrast with the many serious mal-adjustments of plants and animals found in countries occupied by man" (Forbes 1880:5). Clements even more sternly excluded man from any healthy climax plant community (Hagen 1992: 21, 23, 37–38, 47–48; Tobey 1981:79–80). For a Reformed Protestant, human presence on the land upsets ecological balance.

As Carolyn Merchant has described, a woman first used the word "ecology" in the United States (Merchant 1981:6–7). While Reformed Protestant men were running around in the woods and fields seeking nature's unity in diversity, Reformed Protestant women were bringing science to the running of the household. Born in 1842, Congregationalist Ellen Swallow Richards founded the public health movement in the United States. Swallow used the word "oekol-ogy" (ecology) in its root sense of "science of the household," which she defined as the scientific study of the home environment to improve health and nutrition. The first woman admitted to the Massachusetts Institute of Technology and its first female instructor, she was recognized for eminence in industrial and envir-onmental chemistry. Deeply religious, with an "extra dash of puritanism," as a friend put it, her goal was to ensure that everyone had the health and energy to be industrious and fully useful to society. She founded the field of home eco-nomics to promote those old Puritan virtues—efficiency and good stewardship—in the household. "In the strenuous life of a modern community, distractions crowd so closely upon every hand that unless a woman has method in the use of her time, it is frittered away and nothing useful is accomplished. One of the most disheartening things of the day is to see the waste of time and energy in the occupation of nine-tenths of American women" (Hunt 1912:24, 290; see also Clarke 1973). The word "ecology," of course, soon took on a different meaning than Richards had hoped, as the science of the natural and not the human household. Perhaps ironically, in true Reformed fashion, Richards nevertheless felt a deep love for nature. Her work, wrote biographer and friend Carolyn L. Hunt,

> had its beginning in a place of marvelous natural beauty, for during her whole life a Puritan sense of duty and a Spartan self-control had kept her in study, in office, and in laboratory when a passion for natural beauty would have led her into the open country.
>
> *(Hunt 1912:262)*

Many strands of modern environmentalism have origins in the Reformed Protestant tradition, contrary to what Lynn White would have one believe. Despite the mathematical clockwork universe of Enlightenment physics and chemistry that Carolyn Merchant highlights, Calvinist-inflected earth science promoted the organismic world of biology and geology. The pious Reformed imperative to study God's works yielded surprisingly diverse results, from science in universities and schools to ecological holism. They included a moral element that often elevated the natural world as it was (or seemed to be) and regarded presence of fallen man as an unwanted invasion. The science of ecology owes its origins not to reaction to the mechanistic universe of the Scientific Revolution but to the Calvinist fascination with the divine unity in a diverse creation. Darwin's "tangled bank" owed far more to Calvin's idea of providence than to Bacon's scientific method or Newton's laws of motion. Thus does modern ecological thought have sources in sixteenth-century theology.

Note

1 Genealogical evidence suggests Clements was raised Methodist, a non-Calvinist denomination, but documentation is lacking. Hence the professional relationship with his Presbyterian wife is interesting; she seems to have been the dominant partner intellectually, while Frederic took most of the credit for their work.

References

Baatz, Simon. 1988. "Philadelphia Patronage: The Institutional Structure of Natural History in the New Republic, 1800–1833." *Journal of the Early Republic* 8(2):111–138.

Borsche, Tilman. 1990. *Wilhelm von Humboldt*. Munich: Beck.

Calvin, John. 1845. *Institutes of the Christian Religion: A New Translation*. Tr. by Henry Beveridge. Edinburgh: Calvin Translation Society.

Cantor, Geoffrey. 1997. "Quakers in the Royal Society, 1660–1750." *Notes and Records of the Royal Society of London* 51(2):175–193.

Cittadino, Eugene. 1999. "A 'Marvelous Cosmopolitan Preserve': The Dunes, Chicago, and the Dynamic Ecology of Henry Cowles." *Perspectives on Science* 1:520–559.

Clarke, Robert. 1973. *Ellen Swallow: The Woman Who Founded Ecology.* Chicago: Follett.

Clements, Frederic E. 1916. *Plant Succession: An Analysis of the Development of Vegetation.* Washington, DC: Carnegie Institute of Washington.

Cooper, Gregory John. 2003. *The Science of the Struggle for Existence: On the Foundations of Ecology.* Cambridge: Cambridge University Press.

Croker, Robert A. 2001. *Stephen Forbes and the Rise of American Ecology.* Washington, DC: Smithsonian Institution Press.

Darwin, Charles. 1859a. Letter to John Lubbock, November 22. *Darwin Correspondence Project.* "Letter no. 2532." Accessed on 14 August 2017. www.darwinproject.ac.uk/DCP-LETT-2532

Darwin, Charles. 1859b. *On the Origin of Species by Natural Selection.* London: Murray.

Darwin, Charles. 1887. *The Life and Letters of Charles Darwin,* v1. Ed. by Francis Darwin. New York: Appleton.

Derham, William. 1747. *Physico-Theology, or, a Demonstration of the Being and Attributes of God from this Works of Creation.* 2e. London: Innys.

Ewan, Joseph, Nesta Ewan, Victoria C. Hollowell, Eileen P. Duggan, and Marshall R. Crosby. 2007. *Benjamin Smith Barton: Naturalist and Physician in Jeffersonian America.* St. Louis: Missouri Botanical Garden Press.

Forbes, Stephen A. 1880. "On Some Interactions of Organisms." *Illinois Laboratory of Natural History, Bulletin* 1: 3–17.

Forster, Georg. 1894. "Ein Blick in das Ganze der Natur." Pp. 1–25 in *Ausgewählte kleine Schriften von Georg Forster.* Ed. by Albert Leitzmann. Stuttgart: G. J. Göschen'sche Verlagshandlung.

Fox, Stephen R. 1981. *John Muir and His Legacy: The American Conservation Movement.* Boston: Little, Brown.

Freemon, Frank R. 1985. "American Colonial Scientists Who Published in the Philosophical Transactions of the Royal Society." *Notes and Records of the Royal Society of London* 39(2):191–206.

Glenn, L. C. 1905. "Gerard Troost." *The American Geologist* 35:72–94.

Haeckel, Ernst. 1866. *Generelle Morphologie der Organismen: Allgemeine Grundzüge der Organischen Formen-Wissenschaft, Mechanisch Begründet durch die von Charles Darwin Reformirte Descendenz-Theorie.* v2. Berlin: Reimer.

Hagen, Joel B. 1992. *An Entangled Bank: The Origins of Ecosystem Ecology.* New Brunswick, NJ: Rutgers University Press.

Hall, Michael G. 1988. *The Last American Puritan: The Life of Increase Mather, 1639–1723.* Middletown, CT: Wesleyan University Press.

Hitchcock, Edward. 1863. *Reminiscences of Amherst College, Historical, Scientific, Biographical and Autobiographical.* Northampton, MA: Bridgman & Childs.

Hughes, J. Donald. 1983. *American Indian Ecology.* El Paso: Texas Western Press.

Humboldt, Alexander von. 1850a. *Cosmos: A Sketch of a Physical Description of the Universe.* v1. Tr. by E. C. Otté. New York: Harper & Brothers.

Humboldt, Alexander von. 1850b. *Views of Nature: Or Contemplations on the Sublime Phenomena of Creation.* Tr. by E. C. Otté and Henry G. Bohn. London: Bohn.

Hunt, Caroline L. 1912. *The Life of Ellen H. Richards.* Boston: Whitcomb & Barrows.

Judd, Richard W. 1997. *Common Lands, Common People: The Origins of Conservation in Northern New England.* Cambridge, MA: Harvard University Press.

Kölmel, Reinhard. 1981. "Zwischen Universalismus und Empirie—die Begründung der modernen Ökologie- und Biozönose-Konzeption durch Karl Möbius." Pp. 17–34 in *Karl Möbius: Beiträge zu leben und werk*. Ed. by Peter Ohm and Gerd Schriever. Krefeld, Germany: Kommissionsverlag Goecke & Evers.

Kolodny, Annette. 1975. *The Lay of the Land: Metaphor as Experience and History in American Life and Letters*. Chapel Hill: University of North Carolina Press.

König, Rudolf. 1981. "Karl Möbius, eine kurze biographie." Pp. 5–15 in *Karl Möbius: Beiträge zu leben und werk*. Ed. by Peter Ohm and Gerd Schriever. Krefeld, Germany: Kommissionsverlag Goecke & Evers.

Lawrence, Philip J. 1972. "Edward Hitchcock: The Christian Geologist." *Proceedings of the American Philosophical Society* 116(Feb. 15):21–34.

Lekan, Thomas M. 2004. *Imagining the Nation in Nature: Landscape Preservation and Germany Identity, 1885–1945*. Cambridge, MA: Harvard University Press.

Marsh, George Perkins. 1864. *Man and Nature; or, Physical Geography as Modified by Human Action*. New York: Scribner.

Matagne, Patrick. 1999. *Aux origines de l'écologie: Les naturalists en France de 1800 à 1914*. Paris: Éditions du CTHS.

Mather, Cotton. 1721. *The Christian Philosopher*. London.

Mather, Cotton, Samuel Mather, and Edmund Calamy. 1725. *Memoirs of the Life of the Late Reverend Increase Mather, D.D.* London: Clark and Hett.

Mather, Increase. 1684. *An Essay for the Recording of Illustrious Providences*. Boston: S. Green.

Merchant, Carolyn. 1980. *The Death of Nature: Women, Ecology, and the Scientific Revolution*. San Francisco, CA: Harper & Row.

Merchant, Carolyn. 1981. "Earthcare: Women and the Environmental Movement." *Environment* 22 (June):6–13, 38–40.

Merchant, Carolyn. 1992. *Radical Ecology: The Search for a Livable World*. New York: Routledge.

Merchant, Carolyn. 1996. *Earthcare: Women and the Environment*. New York: Routledge.

Merchant, Carolyn. 2003. *Reinventing Eden: The Fate of Nature in Western Culture*. New York: Routledge.

Merchant, Carolyn. 2010. *Ecological Revolutions: Nature, Gender, and Science in New England*. 2e. Chapel Hill: University of North Carolina Press.

Merchant, Carolyn. 2016. *Spare the Birds! George Bird Grinnell and the First Audubon Society*. New Haven, CT: Yale University Press.

Middlekauff, Robert. 1971. *Mathers: Three Generations of Puritan Intellectuals, 1597–1728*. New York: Oxford University Press.

Morley, Henry. 1852. *Palissy the Potter: The Life of Bernard Palissy, of Saintes*. v2. London: Chapman & Hall.

Prytz, Signe. 1984. *Warming: Botaniker og reisende*. Lynge, Denmark: Bogan.

Rowland, Lawrence Sanders, Alexander Moore, and George C. Rogers. 1996. *The History of Beaufort County, South Carolina*. v1. Columbia: University of South Carolina Press.

Rupke, Nicolaas A. 2008. *Alexander von Humboldt: A Metabiography*. Corrected ed. Chicago: University of Chicago Press.

Sachs, Aaron. 2006. *The Humboldt Current: Nineteenth-Century Exploration and the Roots of American Environmentalism*. New York: Viking.

Sears, Paul B. 1974. "Frederic Edward Clements." In *Dictionary of American Biography*. *Supplement 3: 1941–1945*. New York: Scribner.

Silverman, Kenneth. 1984. *The Life and Times of Cotton Mather.* New York: Harper & Row.

Smallwood, William Martin and Mabel Sarah Coon Smallwood. 1941. *Natural History and the American Mind.* New York: Columbia University Press.

Stephens, Lester D. 2000. *Science, Race, and Religion in the American South: John Bachman and the Charleston Circle of Naturalists, 1815–1895.* Chapel Hill: University of North Carolina Press.

Taylor, David. 1998. *South Carolina Naturalists: An Anthology, 1700–1860.* Columbia: University of South Carolina Press.

Tobey, Ronald C. 1981. *Saving the Prairies: The Life Cycle of the Founding School of American Plant Ecology, 1895–1955.* Berkeley: University of California Press.

Turner, Frederick W. 1983. *Beyond Geography: The Western Spirit against the Wilderness.* New Brunswick, NJ: Rutgers University Press.

Underwood, T. L. 1976. "Quakers and the Royal Society of London in the Seventeenth Century." *Notes and Records of the Royal Society of London* 31(1): 133–150.

Walls, Laura Dassow. 2009. *The Passage to Cosmos: Alexander Von Humboldt and the Shaping of America.* Chicago: University of Chicago Press.

Wilson, Alexander. 1983. *The Life and Letters of Alexander Wilson.* Ed. by Clark Hunter. Philadelphia: American Philosophical Society.

Winship, Michael. 1996. *Seers of God: Puritan Providentialism in the Restoration and Early Enlightenment.* Baltimore, MD: Johns Hopkins University Press.

Worster, Donald. 1994. *Nature's Economy: A History of Ecological Ideas.* 2e. Cambridge: Cambridge University Press.

11

CAROLYN MERCHANT AND THE ENVIRONMENTAL HUMANITIES IN SCANDINAVIA

Sverker Sörlin

Carolyn Merchant has experienced an exceptional reception in Scandinavia. It started early with her breakthrough book *The Death of Nature: Women, Ecology, and the Scientific Revolution* (Merchant 1980)—hereafter *TDN*, and it has continued since then. I have previously summarized the early reception of her work in a brief study limited to Sweden, the largest of the three Scandinavian countries, with a population about the same as the combined figures for her neighbors to the west, Denmark and Norway (Sörlin 1998).[1] However, twenty years later we can discern new patterns of the reception of the strand of humanities that Carolyn Merchant's work represents. If the early reception took place mainly within fields and disciplines such as Women Studies, Environmental History, and the History of Science—and, based on Google Scholar data, *TDN* is arguably the most influential book ever published in these combined fields—more recent waves of influence encompass transformations of the humanities, primarily in what is now commonly known as the interdisciplinary field of environmental humanities. Needless to say, the further we move from *TDN*—in cognitive space and in time passed—the less immediate and direct are the influences and the harder they are to detect. Still, through the intellectual developments of institutions and individuals, we can trace the roots and the lineage well enough to discern a lasting legacy of *TDN* and Merchant's assembled oeuvre, forty years after the book's gestation and original publication.

In this chapter I first revisit some of the basic elements of the first wave of reception, up to the end of the previous century, then take a closer look at the bibliographic- and metrics-based evidence for the influence of Merchant's work in Scandinavia. Finally, I take the analysis forward up to the present, focusing in particular on the integrative turn of the humanities for which her work stands out as an early, inspiring template. The chapter attempts to provide evidence and experience from all three countries—Denmark, Norway, and Sweden—but with a particular emphasis on the latter given its size and, admittedly, because of my own background.[2]

A science-gender-environment sensation

The future fame of Carolyn Merchant's *TDN* could not be known when, in 1981, it was introduced in Sweden. The first to comment on it publicly was the late Tore Frängsmyr, who then held a chair at Linköping University but was soon to become professor of history of science in Uppsala, Sweden's oldest (founded in 1477) and second-largest university. Frängsmyr introduced the book in the spring of 1981, at a seminar in the (then) Department of History of Science and Ideas at Umeå University (one of the youngest universities, starting courses in 1956), where I was an incoming graduate student. At about the same time, Frängsmyr published a favorable review of the book in the Stockholm daily *Svenska Dagbladet* (Frängsmyr 1981).

TDN touched on a problem concerning the environment, feminism, and science that was already emerging in Sweden. Both the feminist and the environmental movement had grown into significant political factors in the previous decade. The book became instantly known among faculty and students, and its views quickly filtered down to undergraduate courses and public lectures. In the Umeå department, professor Ronny Ambjörnsson reviewed *TDN* equally favorably in the other major Stockholm daily *Dagens Nyheter* (Ambjörnsson 1981). I recall a department symposium in the fall of 1981 at which I had the task of presenting and discussing the book. As an ambitious young scholar, I tried zealously to find objections to Merchant's argument, but the only thing I could really come up with was the fact that not everything in the book was new—hardly a sensational statement. In fact, I could demonstrate that it might be the case that an equally relativistic view of the scientific revolution, and also a quite realistic picture of the role of alchemy for Early Modern science, had been present in Swedish historiography for quite some time, for example, in the work of Sten Lindroth in Uppsala, especially his 1943 dissertation on the Swedish repercussions of Paracelsus (Lindroth 1943). In some small way that older scholarly resonance may have helped pave the way for Merchant in Sweden.

Such was the impact that *TDN* made that the Umeå department extended an invitation to Merchant to come and visit as a Fulbright scholar. She accepted, and during the spring semester of 1984, Merchant taught a graduate course in the department with an unusually broad range of topics, from Marvin Harris's materialist anthropology to the most recent subtleties in the philosophy of science. During her visit she co-authored a paper with sociologist Abby Peterson on pioneers in the Swedish ecofeminist movement. She went back to biodynamic and pacifist author-thinker Elin Wägner—a member of the literary Nobel Prize-conferring Swedish Academy—and other women in the early and middle parts of the twentieth century, when the term ecofeminism did not exist. From there, she took the reader well up to contemporary female eco-activists, among them authors, thinkers, and politicians. Subsequently, she has taken a continuous interest in ecological issues in Sweden, and Swedish examples surface here and there in her writings: for example, in the 1990 Foreword to the soft cover edition of *TDN*, and, more prominently, in *Earthcare: Women and the Environment* (Merchant 1995a), in which the 1984 essay was reprinted in an updated version. Merchant was invited to Sweden on several occasions, and in 1995 she was awarded an honorary doctorate by Umeå University.[3]

Nordic Nature, Nordic Model

One may wonder why it was that Merchant's work resonated so deeply with Sweden—and the Umeå intellectual milieu in particular. In the Swedish case, history goes a long way to explain the politics since the 1980s of what we may call realist sustainability. The instrumentalist paradigm that sustainability sought to redress, maybe even challenge, had had a long time to grow and become established. A tradition of political arithmetic gained ground already in the late seventeenth and early eighteenth centuries, well before the tradition of sustained yield that came to Sweden from the German states in the nineteenth century (Frängsmyr, Heilbron, and Rider 1990; Johannisson 1988). The political arithmetic portrayed nature in this powerful Baltic nation as well-endowed and a divinely privileged repository of people (labor power), plants, and animals, presented in an unusually articulated form in the patriotic economic botany of Linnaeus (Koerner 1999; Sörlin 1989). Industrialism in the nineteenth and twentieth centuries reinforced that tradition, placing particular pride in the fact that Sweden was rich in natural resources on which to build a new and glorious future (Sörlin 1988).

The oft-proclaimed sensitivity for Nordic nature and its mythological dimensions displayed in the arts was built alongside, or rather on top of, industrialized nature. It was the growth of the industrial economy, of professional elites and an urban middle class with deepening nationalist aesthetics and values, that formed the sociological basis of the esteem for wilderness and, thus, for preservationist and conservationist policies in the first decades of the twentieth century. However, these groups were also quite sensitive to the demands of industry, and responsibility for the productive capacity of the nation was sometimes used as an argument to sacrifice precious forests, waterfalls, or marshes, even among avid members of the Swedish Association for the Conservation of Nature, founded in 1909. Nature was the national common ground and the essential backbone of wealth, in particular on Sweden's northern periphery, where the aboriginal Sami population was affected by continuous territorial and judicial setbacks as the expanding resources industries rolled north to exploit its forests, iron ore, peat bogs and waterfalls for energy, and land for agriculture (Lantto and Mörkenstam 2008; Sundin 1989).

In Norway a similar resource patriotism grew based on mineral and maritime resources, and there too with fraught relations to the Sami in certain northern communities. Norwegian nationalism certainly had many elements but just as in Sweden, natural resources, especially from the north and the Arctic, were always an essential part, holding the promise of future wealth. This was reinforced when the country took the bold step of secession from the union with Sweden in 1905, reaching full independence for the first time, after having been part of Denmark since the Middle Ages and linked to Sweden for almost a century. The leading figure of Norwegian nationalism, and secessionism, Fridtjof Nansen was tellingly also a quintessential resource nationalist, as a scientist researching the nation's wealth of minerals and marine life, and as an author, artist, politician, humanitarian (winner of the Nobel Peace Prize in 1922), and an avid skier and outdoorsman, articulating and embodying in particular the masculine aspects of the emerging Norwegian persona in the world (Aasbø 2014; Huntford 1997; Jølle 2011; Nasgaard 1984).

Norwegian environmentalism, rising strongly in the 1960s and 1970s, took a more philosophical turn than it had in Sweden, due to the influence of Arne Naess and his ecosophy (Brennan, Witoszek, and Naess 1999; Naess 1989; Rothenberg 1992).[4] From a well-to-do family, Naess had been an activist in the Norwegian resistance movement during the German occupation and in the postwar decades he became both a policy advisor who helped design the future social sciences in Norway and an academic household name as a media celebrity and mountaineer. With Naess as a timid, but sharp if needed, Gandhi- and Spinoza-inspired poster boy, Norway also became the home of a pronounced academic environmentalism. His broader background can be found in a strong field studies tradition and a vernacular out-of-doors nationalism, with underpinnings in Lutheran puritanism, that was arguably even stronger than its counterpart in Sweden. Norwegian environmentalism was also stepping out on the international scene in the 1980s as *TDN* became known (Anker 2011). Just like in Sweden, Norway had early female forerunners. Hanna Resvoll-Holmsen (1873–1943) might have been Norway's "first female environmental activist" with an interest in biological diversity that has been rediscovered in the wake of modern ecofeminism after *TDN* (Aarsand 2014). Still, the initial reception was weaker than in Sweden. Reviews were fewer, but the book made some impact in women's studies circles; for instance, Norwegian educationist and gender scholar Birgit Brock-Utne (1995) mentioned it in her book *Educating for Peace*.

Denmark presents a special case. Its mainland natural resources were limited to the small assembly of sandy, limestone islands on the southeastern rim of the North Sea that made agriculture the mainstay of the economy. Industrialism was small in scale and based on food products, design, and handicraft rather than resources and energy—until in recent years, when the country has become a significant producer of wind power turbines. To some extent Denmark's relative resource paucity was countered by the resources available in its North Atlantic empire. Around the Faroe Islands, Iceland, and Greenland fishing, sealing, and whaling were major trades, with energy and minerals becoming increasingly important after World War II (Eichberg and Jespersen 1986). Denmark's first review of *TDN* was published by Kis Bonde in 1984 (Bonde 1984).

The Agenda for Global Environmental Governance

In all three Scandinavian countries, the environmental agenda was established fairly early. Remarkably focused political activity in the 1960s and 1970s included the Swedish state putting forth comprehensive environmental legislation in 1969 and hosting the first United Nations Conference on the Environment in Stockholm in 1972. This activity can be partly explained by the strong social position of scientists, who advocated environmental concerns through the nature protection committee at the Royal Swedish Academy of Sciences and through the Association for the Conservation of Nature, where scientists were prominent. The conference was the product of the political entrepreneurship by Prime Minister Olof Palme, whose internationalism paired with a sense that a whole new set of "environmental" issues were about to enter politics and that his Social Democratic party, and his country, should rather lead than trail behind in this development (Åström 1992; Engfeldt 2009; McCormick 1989).

The UN conference in 1972 resulted in several significant achievements and tangible outcomes, including the establishment of the United Nations Environment Program, UNEP. Its concluding Declaration on the Human Environment is widely recognized as a critical turning point in the emergence and institutionalization of international environmental politics and global governance (Biermann 2004; Jasanoff and Long Martello 2001; O'Neill et al. 2013). The legacy of Stockholm included the environmental summits in Rio de Janeiro in 1992 and 2012, and Johannesburg in 2002. Some developments can be directly traced back to the Stockholm Conference. Swedish diplomats in New York, and Stockholm-based scientists such as Hans Palmstierna and Bert Bolin, later co-founder and first president of IPCC, had generated a comprehensive body of scientific knowledge that convinced other countries of the need to convene a major international gathering.[5]

Nordic Environmentalism Meets Vitalism

In 1980, when *TDN* appeared, it was less than a decade after the United Nations conference on the environment in Stockholm. In the small country of Sweden, the environmental issue loomed large from the 1960s and 1970s. Compared to other countries, Sweden was early and comprehensive in its attempts to deal legally with issues such as vehicle pollution, work environments, acidification, and many other issues around environment and health. The most significant characteristic of Sweden in this respect may, however, be the relatively peaceful co-existence of the state with a comprehensive environmental movement, parts of which had strong public support and even caught the attention of the government. Furthermore, Sweden was one of the earliest European countries to establish a Green party, in 1982. The party entered parliament in 1988 and has remained there for three decades.[6]

Although the Scandinavian countries' role as early environmentalists and vanguard ecofeminists has faded somewhat into the background, it is an important feature to keep in mind if we wish to understand the reception of *TDN* in the 1980s. The women´s movement experienced a similar early flourishing in all Scandinavian countries. Women's rights and family policies (for example generous parental leave) were politically already more established in Sweden than possibly anywhere else in the world around 1980. At that time, the Swedish—and indeed Scandinavian—position as an environmental leader remained still largely unquestioned, as was the nation's reputation as a cauldron of official feminism. Both environmentalism and feminism were disproportionately represented as ideologies in the academic community, and Umeå as a modern, northern university town was fresh and fertile ground for the *TDN* seed to take root.

Despite its originality and its refreshing novelty, *TDN* in many respects is also orthodox. It deals with the great names of the scientific revolution, it visits the central scientific environments and circles, and it quotes the commonly cited sources and literature of the period. Merchant has done her homework. But she sees the whole development with new eyes, and she draws a number of hitherto lesser known figures, women in particular, into center field: Elizabeth Carter, who translated Francesco Algarotti's *Newtonianismo per le dame* (1739) to English; midwives Jane Sharp and Elizabeth Cellier; and, most important, Anne Conway, Jan Baptist van Helmont's mentor and proponent of a subtle vitalist philosophy, a personality formerly almost forgotten in the history of Western thought and marginalized in the usual chronicles of the scientific revolution. Among the names Merchant draws into her picture is also Jan Smuts, the remarkable South African holist thinker, biologist, statesman, and apartheid ideologist (Anker 2001), although late in life somewhat revising his racial politics. As an almost contemporary figure, he also serves as evidence of the wide-ranging scope of the book and the comprehensive outlook of its author: from the fertility goddesses of antiquity to non-mainstream thinkers of the twentieth century.

Precisely this maintenance of focus, across centuries and epochs, but always in fidelity to an original overarching perspective—namely, that nature and the female had served as moral institutions dethroned by scientific rationalism—may also be the core explanation to the broad appeal of the book, far beyond those groups that would normally be interested in a four hundred-page scholarly treatise on seventeenth century science. Also helpful in this respect was that the book declared right at the outset that this was its purpose: to connect history with contemporary concerns, such as the position of women in society, the environment, and the use and abuse of science in the modern world. It was the first comprehensive work of its kind, amalgamating, to use Sandra Harding's question, the "science question in feminism" with the emerging interest in the environment and its history (Harding 1986).

It was ahead of its time and was, precisely therefore, also a sign of its time. In the future, it will stand out as one of the seminal books to raise these issues, as had been done before by William Vogt, Lewis Mumford, and Rachel Carson for the environment, and by Simone de Beauvoir for feminism and Susan Griffin and Françoise d'Eaubonne for feminism related to nature (the latter coined the term *écoféminisme* in 1974) (d'Eaubonne 1974; Griffin 1978; Merchant 1990). The abuse of science had similarly been discussed by science critics such as Robert Oppenheimer and C. F. Schumacher. In contrast to these, *TDN* forms an integrated nexus of interrelated issues with mutual relations. It was really the first time that a single volume presented the contemporary interconnectedness of gender, environment, and science and linked it to a formative period of modern history that had shaped our understanding of the world. In other parts of the world, the book sometimes met resistance and provoked debate; Margaret J. Osler's skeptical review in *Isis* set the tone for its reception in some of the Anglo-American professional journals (Osler 1981).[7] Doubts diminished only after some time. In Scandinavia, it was received early and warmly. It was the same book everywhere, but the cultural, political, and intellectual climates where it was received differed wildly. Scandinavia suited it well. How well? It is time to look at the evidence.

TDN's Reception in Numbers

How can we know that *TDN* fared well in the Scandinavian countries? Some indications I have already provided: seminars, invitations, reviews, and an award. Is there more—and more tangible—evidence?

Yes, there is. A general search on the Internet reveals, first of all, that Carolyn Merchant and Scandinavia make a fairly good fit. The names of Scandinavian countries are connected to her name in relation to publications where they are mentioned. They are also mentioned when they appear in publications by herself or when these publications are cited for their Scandinavian content, which is fairly often. A topic to which Merchant turned her efforts was the role of ecofeminist movements and women's rights in Scandinavia, where she often returned to the starkly different conditions that prevailed in the United States. She had studied these issues herself, for example in the above-mentioned piece with sociologist Abby Peterson (of U.S. origin) at Umeå, first published in Sweden in 1986 and later included in her own edited volume *Earthcare* (Merchant 1995a; Merchant and Peterson 1996). Her Fulbright scholarship is noted above. This may perhaps not seem a very strong Scandinavian presence, but it is certainly far more than most American historians have achieved.

Using bibliometric data, it is possible to pinpoint more accurately the particular role played by the Scandinavian countries in the reception of Merchant's work. The overall picture is that the Scandinavian region scores well above what might be expected. That is true for Merchant's influence in general, and for all of her books for which I have been able to find data, *TDN* in particular. The data have been retrieved from the Web of Science (WoS) database, which includes publications in and citations from some thirty-three thousand journals across all scientific fields.[8]

Five books by Carolyn Merchant have been included in the survey.[9] They are (year of first publication indicated):

The Death of Nature (1980)
Ecological Revolutions: Nature, Gender, and
Science in New England (1989)
Radical Ecology: The Search for a Livable World (1992)
Earthcare: Women and the Environment (1995)
Reinventing Eden: The Fate of Nature in Western Culture (2003)

Before addressing the five books and their Scandinavian reception, let us first turn to the global usage of Merchant's work which falls largely in the humanities.[10] *TDN*, her most cited book, has a total of 1,213 citations in WoS—an impressive number by any standard for a research monograph (articles in general have a much wider circulation). In Google Scholar, by comparison, its citation number is 5,751. These citations are for the English-language version only. Translations are not counted; if they were, the figure would increase. The German *Der Tod der Natur* (1987) has 215 citations, the Italian *La morte della natura* (1986) 35, and the Swedish *Naturens död* (1994) 36, to just mention a few. The total number for *TDN* citations in all languages and editions is somewhere between six and seven thousand.

The impact of *TDN* can be fully understood only when it is compared with what are generally considered the strongest contenders among scholarly works in environmental history and feminism. William Cronon's astoundingly successful *Nature's Metropolis: Chicago and the Great West* (Cronon 1991) has received under 4,000 citations in Google Scholar. Roderick Nash's *Wilderness and the American Mind* (Nash 1967; last reissued in 2014) stands at 5,022. In feminist studies a classic such as Simone de Beauvoir's *The Second Sex* (Beauvoir 2011, originally published in French in 1949, available in English since 1952) has been cited (in its English translations, more rarely in French) around 12,000 times, according to Google Scholar —hardly a surprise given the much longer time since publication and its much wider reach across disciplines compared with a work in the history of science and ecofeminism. By comparison, a feminist classic such as Germaine Greer's *The Female Eunuch* (Greer 1970) stands at 2,700 citations. In comparison, *TDN* scores high. In addition, Merchant's *Radical Ecology* (Merchant 1992) has more than 1,500 Google Scholar citations, and several of her other titles stand between 500 and 1,000. The total for all five books listed above, in all editions, is well over 10,000 citations. She also contributed a long and in itself very influential essay to William Cronon's edited volume *Uncommon Ground* (Merchant 1995b). This was a book with a decisive social constructivist perspective, published at the peak of that tendency, and currently stands at 1,300 citations.

The WoS survey of five Merchant books published between 1980 and 2003 (translations not included) covers 1980 to 2016. The total number of citations in the (far more exclusive) Web of Science is 1,798, divided across the individual works as follows:[11]

TDN (1980) 1,213
Ecological Revolutions (1989) 219
Radical Ecology (1992) 258
Earthcare (1995) 98
Reinventing Eden (2003) 73

Distributed across 49 nations, the citations for all five works are topped by the United States with 1,087, followed by the United Kingdom with 229, and Canada with 161: these are all English-speaking nations with a cultural and cognitive closeness to the subject matter. At the very bottom of the list is a long tail with one or a handful of citations per country: Poland, Romania, Singapore, Tanzania, and many others have only one, others have two or three—over an almost 40-year long period. In these countries, Carolyn Merchant is hardly a household name in scholarly circles, although she may be better known among her closest peers who publish mostly in non-WoS outlets.

The Scandinavian countries are conspicuously high on these lists. All three rank among the 15 countries with 11 or more citations (with Nordic neighbor Finland in 17th place with 10 citations), way ahead of large countries such as Brazil, China, India, and Russia/USSR. Sweden with 33 citations ranks fifth globally, immediately after Australia in fourth place, but ahead of Germany, France, and Spain—countries five to eight times the size of Sweden in terms of population and with a far larger scholarly community in all fields, including, and perhaps especially the humanities, which are relatively under-represented in Sweden. Denmark and Norway (12 and 11 citations, respectively) have populations less than one tenth of the major European countries but their scholars cite Carolyn Merchant's work approximately on a par with them.

The data above is for all five works combined. The *citation pattern* for *TDN* is by and large congruent with the above, with the same nations—the United States, the United Kingdom, Canada, Australia, and Sweden—in the top five. Denmark and Norway are slightly more strongly represented in citations of *TDN* than in Merchant's other books. *Radical Ecology* is heavily cited in Sweden, and *Reinventing Eden* is heavily cited in Finland. The *citation trend* of all works has been increasing since the 1980s, with the growing reputation of *TDN* and other works starting to climb in the late 1980s. Peak citation frequency was reached in the 1990s with a moderate decline in the first two decades of the present century. The two top years, 1994 and 1995, have 64 and 65 citations, respectively. The average since 2010 is 34.

The absolute value of these numbers is less important for our purpose here. They matter to us more because they give a rough indication of the *relative significance* of Carolyn Merchant's work in relation to other works in the history of science, feminist studies, and environmental history. As the brief discussion above indicates, *TDN* ranks among the most influential in all three fields, albeit to varying degrees. In the history of science, the book was the subject of a special "Focus" section of the leading journal *Isis* in 2006 to which Merchant also contributed (Merchant 2006).[12] Still, most of her own fame and success from the book seems to have been harvested in the field of environmental history, where her presence has been felt more strongly than in any other field. From the perspective of the three fields combined, *TDN* may be the most influential of all works of all time, at least as judged from Google Scholar data.[13]

How Can the Scandinavian Reception Be Explained?

How can we use these quantitative data to shed light on the favorable reception of Merchant's work in Scandinavia and Sweden? Does it have something to do with these countries being unusually strong in the subject areas in question? That is hard to tell but both strands of history involved had a fairly strong development, primarily in Sweden. History of science has had a designated chair at Uppsala University since 1932 and has proliferated into the 1960s and 1970s with new positions and departments set up in several universities, including the young and new one at Umeå in the north, where Merchant was also offered her Fulbright. For a period, this was an unusual feat in a small country, to boast a half-dozen chaired positions and a growing number of Ph.D. students and mid-career faculty (Frängsmyr 1984). The Uppsala department was also part of forming an international Summer School in the History of Science with the corresponding departments in Bologna, Paris, and Berkeley (between 1988 and 2006).

Environmental history, with a strong following in the United States since the 1970s, had limited success in Europe, where disciplines such as geography and strands of history (history of science, economic history) catered to some of the needs of environmental research without the formation of a designated sub-field until the 1990s. Sweden, however, was an early adopter, with growing interest from the 1970s accelerating in the 1980s, not least among the historians of science, whom, as we remember, were among the first to introduce *TDN* to a Swedish audience. In Norway, a similar role was played by academic philosophy, which formed the backbone of core curriculum study in Norwegian universities, and through the leading position of ecosopher Arne Naess became fertile soil for ecological readings of history and Western thought (Anker 2007, 2013).[14] To that can be added that the discipline of history was nationally leaning, institutionally powerful, and flexible enough to accommodate new sub-fields, which meant that environmental history never got much of an independent foothold. In Denmark, where the history of science did not proliferate and remained a more orthodox field than in Sweden, and where environmental history had a slow start, *TDN* was engaged with mostly in gender studies circles and in Science and Technology Studies (STS).

Scandinavian countries have long embraced feminist or women's studies, with special journals having been founded since the 1970s, manifesting a wide impact on research agendas and curricula in humanities and social sciences.[15] Feminist agendas reached far outside of the academic sphere as well and affected politics—where women cabinet ministers were a common feature from the 1980s. In Norway and Sweden women held the post of Minister of the Environment; Norway was among the first countries to have such a designated position in a cabinet from 1972. Gro Harlem Brundtland, who held the post 1974 to 1979, advanced to become Prime Minister in three periods over twelve of the years between 1981 and 1996. She also led the United Nations World Commission on Environment and Development, whose report, *Our Common Future* (often called the Brundtland report) launched the concept sustainable development in 1987 (Brundtland 1987).

Perhaps most importantly for the reception of *TDN*, all three Scandinavian nations had a strong international orientation, in society in general and in academia in particular. Denmark and Norway were members of NATO, and Sweden had a well-established *de facto* collaboration with the Western defense alliance. All three countries adopted an Americanized popular culture with strong Anglo-Saxon influences in areas such as music, film, media, and design. This made Scandinavian scholars prone to develop a general Western and U.S.-centered orientation, and although this was most pronounced in the sciences and medicine, it was distinct in the human sciences as well.[16] Ultimately, the Scandinavian countries had powerful integrative forces and individuals that could foster a strong reception for a work such as *TDN*, despite its retrospective orientation toward the early modern period in Europe, which may not in and of itself be the main focus of the academic communities alerted to the book. It was rather its perspective and its wider implications for the understanding of science, gender, power, and the environment that led to its strong Scandinavian reception.

The Legacy Lives On: The Integrative Environmental Humanities

Despite the major interest showed in Merchant's work in Scandinavia, it is not possible for a single book, however important and debated, to cause major academic perturbations or the growth of entire scientific fields. Nonetheless, I will venture to suggest here that *TDN* in recent years has provided essential input into the formation of the environmentally-oriented humanities as they have taken shape in Sweden and to some extent Norway (I make fewer claims about Denmark).

The environmental humanities is challenge oriented—sometimes even challenge driven. This is especially true for issues and policies that deal with environment and climate, but they could as well be about justice, welfare, migration, poverty, or health. It is also experimental, boundary crossing, and collaborative, with a friendly attitude to so-called grand challenges, the search for solutions, and various forms of co-production of knowledge. It engages with artistic research and wields an open mind towards traditional, alternative, and untraditional ways of knowing, although it remains classically "scholarly" in almost every sense of that, admittedly wide, concept.

Among the sources of this field, we cannot ignore the feminist and postcolonial turns, including those advanced by Carolyn Merchant, Donna Haraway, Joni Adamson, Ramachandra Guha, and Deepak Kumar. Juan Martínez-Aliers' "environmentalism of the poor" was influential, along with the concept of environmental racism and research in the humanities on any number of subjects, from energy, consumption, landscapes, and biological diversity to biotechnology, urban studies, and climate change. There have been a number of attempts around the world to organize academics in the humanities to address environmental issues. Australia was home to one early initiative in the 1990s, and the term "ecological humanities" was already in use there.[17] Of course, Carolyn Merchant had been visiting and provided inspiration through invitation by Val Plumwood in the early 1990s (Eckersley 1998; Rose and Robin 2004; Sörlin 2016).[18]

Theoretical perspectives came from the so-called new materialism, *the affective turn*, science and technology studies, "queer ecologies" (Erickson and Sandilands 2010), visual and esthetic turns, and media studies. Perhaps the greatest contribution made by the environmental humanities has been to offer a forum (or several) for an eclectic gathering of a formidable number of perspectives—theoretical, empirical, chronological, and conceptual—under a single valid designation. Sources of inspiration also include the post-human turn and the "Anthropocene debates," which engage researchers in both the natural sciences and the humanities in critical discussions of a proposed new geological epoch—a proposed new name for the current time period so forcefully dominated by humanity's planetary footprint (Braidotti 2013; Waters, Zalasiewicz, and Summerhayes 2016).

That said, it is hard to find explicit organizational attempts to establish the field of environmental humanities before 2010, or even later. The first journal bearing the title *Environmental Humanities* (actually an outgrowth of the "Ecological Humanities" section that had been part of the *Australian Humanities Review* since 2004) launched in November 2012. At the time, the journal was edited at the University of New South Wales in Australia. (Currently, it is published by a multinational editorial staff that includes the KTH Environmental Humanities Laboratory in Stockholm, the University of California Los Angeles, the University of New South Wales, Sydney University, and Concordia University (Canada) as its five nodes.) Another publication, *Resilience: A Journal of the Environmental Humanities*, published by the University of Nebraska Press, appeared in January 2014. Since 2014, there has also been a special journal for interdisciplinary research on the Anthropocene, *The Anthropocene Review*, embracing the humanities as much as the sciences.

It is worth noting the early adoption of the new integrative ideas for the humanities in Scandinavian academic life. Despite the relative international insignificance of the humanities in Sweden, quite expected given the small volume of humanities research, environmental humanities (and a few other integrative humanities areas as well)[19] have become quite visible, with a designated presence in a half dozen of Sweden's less than forty universities and colleges. The KTH Environmental Humanities Laboratory (EHL) started operations in early 2012 following a 2011 donation from industrialist Carl Bennet. The EHL drew on an active and integrative Division of History of Science, Technology, and Environment, already including some of the elements that Carolyn Merchant had brought together in *TDN*. Other environmental humanities trajectories were subsequently started at the universities of Gothenburg and Linköping and in the small humanities faculty of Mid-Sweden University. In universities around the country—Uppsala, Umeå, Lund, and elsewhere—were individuals and small groups of scholars who participated in the emerging collaborations.

Funding agencies have taken on catalytic roles in promoting these structural changes. The environmental research foundation Mistra had been considering this need for more than a decade and moved from thought to action during this period by issuing a call for a national effort together with a public research agency, Formas. Under the heading Mistra Environmental Humanities, the organization was catalyzed by a report by an international group of analysts. According to the report, Sweden was already among the forerunners in the field (Nye et al. 2013). Among the Nordic countries, Denmark had led the way in the 1990s, with major centers for environmental research in the humanities, such as Menneske og natur ("Humans and nature") in Odense, led by the prominent linguist Svend Erik Larsen, whose book *Naturen er ligeglad* [*Nature Doesn't Care*] received a large audience (Larsen 1996).

Much of this development in the environmental humanities—here briefly sketched—bears the hallmark of the integrative vision, with history in a central role, as it has been in Carolyn Merchant's project and *TDN*. In the Swedish context her contribution can be traced quite literally through a series of trajectories. The link to Umeå, where Merchant was a Fulbright scholar and received an honorary doctorate, is undeniable. As I worked with colleagues and Ph.D. students in the 1990s to build a research program in environmental history (my Umeå professorship in 1993 was the first ever in the field in Scandinavia), I opted deliberately not to form a Ph.D. training program along the conventional disciplinary lines but instead wished to see enrolments from across all historical fields. When I left Umeå in the early 2000s, the university had already formed an integrative history department, and it moved on in the following decade to start a wider department for the study of "ideas and society," which included history (of several strands), religion, and philosophy.

We extended these developments in my own new environment at KTH. As director of the EHL, we hired Marco Armiero, with a Ph.D. from Naples but with the bulk of his career in the United States, where he had engaged with Carolyn Merchant's work during a period as a fellow of environmental history at Stanford and UC Berkeley, and also published an interview with her, primarily on *TDN*, in an Italian journal (Armiero 2007). In Linköping, scholars working on the feminist side of STS embraced the post-humanities. In early 2015, the thematic research units of Gender and Technological Change, respectively, were asked to lead the national Mistra/Formas Environmental Humanities Programme in collaboration with units at Uppsala, KTH, Stockholm University, and others. Uppsala University has recently moved to install a new humanities research center called CIRKUS, which signals that the integrative trend is not isolated to environment and climate but has repercussions across the humanities.[20]

This is scattered evidence, and far from exhaustive. It is presented only to suggest that some of the core builders of the environmental humanities in Sweden have, if not in any formal sense at least in some direct or derived spirit, carried the legacy of Carolyn Merchant's integrative mission to unite a value-driven, progressive ecofeminism with a critical science studies approach to the history of science, technology, and environment.

However, much remains to be done, and the future, while bright, is wide open. A sense of experimentation still characterizes the development of the field. Environmental humanities in Sweden, funded by foundations and research councils for the most part, has only barely reached this stage. Maybe this development would be easier if more components of the new integrative humanities—medical, digital, medial, and others—managed to establish themselves simultaneously. This could lead to deeper and more durable change in academic departments and faculties. Such growth in integrative knowledge environments can already be detected and can in many ways be understood as both desirable and necessary.

Of course, this does not mean that this change will automatically become reality. The past two hundred years have been characterized by a massive and, with time, accelerating, growth in the number of disciplines. In the past decade or two, this expansion has seldom given rise to new departments of the traditional sort. Instead, their numbers are decreasing. Renewal and specialization are instead being brought into more general departments or schools that have a greater internal flexibility and responsiveness to the demands of the surrounding world.

Carolyn Merchant was among the scholars who started very early to explore the connections between different strands of the humanities. Her own career, with beginnings in the sciences and her significant *TDN* book on the history of science—which would impact other fields even more profoundly—and her move to the interdisciplinary College of Natural Resources at UC Berkeley and her role in co-founding the in-itself broad field of environmental history—all this is evidence of a *de facto* emerging environmental humanities *avant la lettre*. Her work has helped spur the growth of the integrative humanities,[21] and the environmental humanities in particular, not through any programmatic statements but through what we might call her example. She always practiced it, and over the years the fields that she has taken an interest in, history in its many sub-incarnations, women's and gender studies, ecofeminism, ecocriticism, strands of philosophy and religion, have all started to come together based on the tenet that there is something to gain from taking a broad view.

Notes

1 The Scandinavian countries should be distinguished from the Nordic region, or Nordic countries, that also include Finland and Iceland.

2 I am Swedish and claim firsthand knowledge that arises primarily from my own home country. I was also a visiting professor at the University of Oslo in the spring semester of 2006, have had many commissions in Norway and have followed Norwegian cultural and intellectual affairs fairly closely since the 1990s. In Denmark, I led two international public enquiries in 2005–2006 and 2009–2010, respectively, but have had a more limited engagement with the general public and academic spheres.

3 Almost a quarter of a century down the road I may be allowed to disclose that I was the main proponent of the honorary doctorate and that I also, according to tradition, served as Carolyn's host during the days of academic celebrations in Umeå in October 1995.

4 Naess had several philosophical colleagues in Norway that were equally nature oriented, from Petter Wessel Zapffe to Sigmund Kvaløy. Naess also had considerable international influence, not least in the United States, but not much of a following in Denmark, or in Sweden, where academic philosophy never become very ecologically oriented. To some extent philosophy exerted a role in Norway that in Sweden was taken by history and geography.

5 In the few broader histories that exist of global environmental governance and sustainability politics, there are usually chapters or sections devoted to the Stockholm Conference and its crucial preparatory phase (e.g. Borowy 2013; Conca 2015; Macekura 2015; McCormick 1989).

6 Except a three-year period in the 1990s when they had failed to get the required 4 percent of the national vote.

7 See also Glick (1981) and Pagel (1981).

8 The data has been handled according to conventional principles for usage and organization. Web of Science data is tagged with many useful criteria and dimensions. In this case it is of particular importance that author affiliation (institution, department/discipline/field, country, city, address) is available. A weakness is that the database provides good coverage only in the sciences, technology, and medicine, and is weaker in the social sciences and, in particular, in the humanities. This means that Merchant's main readers, and most of those who engage professionally and deeply with her work, including critics, only show up insofar as they cite her in journals covered in the database (monographs and books are generally excluded from WoS). Broader coverage is offered by Google Scholar, which includes publications and citations in a much wider range of academic journals, culture and policy magazines, research monographs, academic books, trade books, other reports, and a hard-to-define range of general printed and online media. Google Scholar is particularly useful for getting a sense of the range, reach, and impact of publications and their authors in the humanities and social sciences—fields typically under-represented in WoS. In many cases, humanities and social science scholars make their impact to a large extent through publications and media outside of mainstream scientific circuits.

9 The data concerning these five books has been retrieved and organized by bibliometric expert Tobias Jeppsson at the bibliometric analysis unit of the Library School at the KTH Royal Institute of Technology, Stockholm. I thank Tobias deeply for his efforts and for taking time to assist me with this unusual exercise beyond his normal call of duty.

10 WoS data has low coverage of publications in the humanities and social sciences, which means that just getting cited there in any significant number is a sign that a publication reaches out. If a work in the humanities is widely cited there, it is a safe sign it is also widely cited—and much more widely—in Google Scholar.

11 The data were retrieved in August and September 2017.

12 The 50-page special section, entitled "Getting back to The Death of Nature: Rereading Carolyn Merchant" had an introduction by Joan Cadden and apart from Merchant's own piece three further contributions, by Katharine Park, Gregg Mitman, and Charis Thompson.

13 The only work of similar stature, significance, and potentially wide academic audience I can think of, with relevance for both History of Science and Environmental History, and also for, for example, Religion and Philosophy, is Arthur O. Lovejoy's seminal classic "The Great Chain of Being: A Study of the History of an Idea" (Lovejoy 1936), which despite its long citation career nonetheless stands only at 5,176 Google Scholar citations. The book was, like TDN, bestowed with a forty-year appraisal, by William F. Bynum (1975), "The Great Chain of Being After Forty Years: An Appraisal." At fifty, it was time for yet another, Daniel J. Wilson (1987), "Lovejoy's The Great Chain of Being After Fifty Years."

14 Incidentally, Merchant and Naess met on at least one occasion; I know since I hosted their encounter in my own apartment in the late spring of 1984 during her Fulbright in Umeå when I had also invited Naess to come and lecture. They had an evening of conversation over tea and biscuits and talked at length about UC Berkeley, where Naess was a visiting scholar, studying the behavior of rats, and scientists, in E. C. Tolman's psychology laboratory in 1938–39. Harold Glasser (2005), "Series editor's introduction," in Selected Works of Arne Ness.

15 The Swedish women's studies journal Kvinnovetenskaplig tidskrift started in 1980.

16 On Norwegian social science research after World War II, see Fredrik Thue (1997), Empirisme og demokrati: Norsk samfunnsforskning som etterkrigsprosjekt; idem (Thue 2009), "Americanised Social Science as Anti-Communist Containment?: The Case of the Oslo Institute for Social Research, 1945–1965"; and idem (2010), "Empiricism, Pragmatism, Behaviorism: Arne Næss and the Growth of American-styled Social Research in Norway after World War II." See also, Vidar Enebakk (2005), Mellom de to kulturer: Oppkomsten av vitenskapsstudier og etableringen av Edinburgh-skolen 1966–76; Sverker Sörlin (1992), "Introduction: The International Contexts of Swedish Science: A Network Approach to the Internationalization of Science"; Thomas Schott (1992), "Scientific Research in Sweden: Orientation Toward the American Centre and Embeddedness in Nordic and European Environments."

17 See also Chapter 16 by Patsy Hallen in this volume.

18 Ibid.

19 Medical humanities have received some support, for example in the universities of Lund and Uppsala. There are activities in the digital humanities in research units at the Royal Library in Stockholm, Umeå University (HumLab), Gothenburg University (language technologies), to mention a few. Theoretical and other justifications for infrastructures for integrative humanities are in Christine Borgman (2015), Big Data, Little Data, No Data: Scholarship in the Networked World; Joanna Drucker and Svensson (2016), "The Why and How of Middleware"; Patrik Svensson (2015), "The Humanistiscope: Exploring the Situatedness of Humanities Infrastructure."

20 Decided by the Uppsala University Board, November 15, 2017. www.teolfak.uu.se/ nyheter/artikel/?id=9698&area=2,6,16,22,23,25,26,27,28&typ=artikel&lang=sv (retrieved 16 December 2017). Preparatory work exploring the potential of integrative humanities along these lines has been ongoing for some time; see for example Anders Ekström and Sörlin (2016), Integrativa kunskapsmiljöer: Rapport från två seminarier våren 2016 [Integrative knowledge environments: Report from two seminars, spring 2016]. Further background can be found in Anders Ekström and Sörlin (2012), Alltings mått: Humanistisk kunskap i framtidens samhälle. An international agenda for broader collaboration across the Environmental Human and Social Sciences (ESSH) has also been laid out in Castree et al. (2014), "Changing the Intellectual Climate."

21 The term integrative humanities as a collective term for the growing range of prefix (medical, digital, techno-, geo-, environmental etc.) humanities is presented in Sverker Sörlin and Graeme Wynn, "Fire and Ice in The Academy: The Rise of the Integrative Humanities" (Sörlin and Wynn 2016).

References

Aarsand, Ingeborg Husbyn. 2014. "Green Fingers, Red Stockings." *New Compass: Navigation Towards Communication*. Retrieved January 26, 2018 http://new-compass.net/arti cles/green-fingers-red-stockings

Aasbø, Audun Renolen. 2014. *Skiløperkunstens litterære kraftsentrum: Fridtjof Nansen og den moderne skiidrettens framvekst [The Literary Power Center of the Art of Cross Country Skiing: Nansen and the Emergence of Modern Skiing] (printed dissertation)*. Oslo: Institute of Literature, Area Studies and European Languages, University of Oslo.

Ambjörnsson, Ronny. 1981. "Metallerna växer som i en livmoder [Metals grow as in a womb]." *Dagens Nyheter*, 14 December.

Anker, Peder. 2001. *Imperial Ecology: Environmental Order in the British Empire, 1895–1945*. Cambridge, MA: Harvard University Press.

Anker, Peder. 2007. "Science as a Vacation: A History of Ecology in Norway." *History of Science* 45:455–479.

Anker, Peder. 2011. "A Pioneer Country? A History of Norwegian Climate Politics." *Climatic Change* 1–13.

Anker, Peder. 2013. "The Call for a New EcoTheology in Norway." *Journal for the Study of Religion, Nature, and Culture* 7(2):187–207.

Armiero, Marco. 2007. "Natura: Femminile, plurale: Intervista a Carolyn Merchant." *I frutti de Demetra: Bollettino di storia e ambiente* 14:81–90.

Åström, Sverker. 1992. *Ögonblick: Från ett halvsekel i UD-tjänst [Moments: From Half a Century of Service in the Foreign Office]*. Stockholm: Bonnier Alba.

Beauvoir, Simone de. 2011. *The Second Sex*. 1st edition. New York: Vintage.

Biermann, F. 2004. "Global Environmental Governance: Conceptualization and Examples." in *Global Governance Working Paper No 12*. Amsterdam, Berlin, Oldenburg, Potsdam: The Global Governance Project. Retrieved August 20, 2017 www.glogov.org

Bonde, Kis. 1984. "Det nysgerrige menneske [The curious human]." *Naturkampen* 31:19–21.

Borgman, Christine. 2015. *Big Data, Little Data, No Data: Scholarship in the Networked World*. Cambridge, MA: MIT Press.

Borowy, Iris. 2013. *Defining Sustainable Development for Our Common Future: A History of the World Commission on Environment and Development (Brundtl and Commission)*. London: Routledge.

Braidotti, Rosi. 2013. *The Posthuman*. Cambridge: Polity.

Brennan, Andrew, Nina Witoszek, and Arne Naess, eds. 1999. *Philosophical Dialogues: Arne Naess and the Progress of Ecophilosophy*. Lanham, MD: Rowman & Littlefield.

Brock-Utne, Birgit. 1995. *Educating for Peace: A Feminist Reappraisal*. New York: Pergamon Press.

Brundtland, Gro Harlem. 1987. *Our Common Future*. Oxford: Oxford University Press.

Bynum, William F. 1975. "The Great Chain of Being After Forty Years: An Appraisal." *History of Science* 13:1–28.

Castree, N., W. M. Adams, J. Barry, S. Sörlin, et al.2014. "Changing the Intellectual Climate." *Nature Climate Change* 4(9):763–768.

Conca, Ken. 2015. *An Unfinished Foundation: The United Nations and Global Environmental Governance*. New York: Oxford University Press.

Cronon, William. 1991. *Nature's Metropolis: Chicago and the Great West*. New York: W.W. Norton.

Drucker, Joanna and Patrik Svensson. 2016. "The Why and How of Middleware." *Digital Humanities Quarterly* 10(2).

d'Eaubonne, Françoise, ed. 1974. *Le féminisme ou la mort*. Paris: Pierre Horay.

Eckersley, Robyn. 1998. "The Death of Nature and the Birth of Ecological Humanities." *Organization and Environment* 11(2):183–185.

Eichberg, Henning and Ejgil Jespersen. 1986. *De grønne bølger: Træk af natur- og friluftslivets historie* [*The Green Waves: Traces of the History of Nature and Outdoors*]. Copenhagen: Bavnebanke.

Ekström, Anders and Sverker Sörlin, eds. 2012. *Alltings mått: Humanistisk kunskap i framtidens samhälle* [*The Measure of Everything: Humanities Knowledge in Future Society*]. Stockholm: Norstedts.

Ekström, Anders and Sverker Sörlin. 2016. *Integrativa kunskapsmiljöer: Rapport från två seminarier våren 2016* [*Integrative Knowledge Environments: Report from Two Seminars, Spring 2016*]. Retrieved https://publikationer.vr.se/produkt/integrativa-kunskapsmiljoer-rapport-fran-tva-seminarier-varen-2016/

Enebakk, Vidar. 2005. *Mellom de to kulturer: Oppkomsten av vitenskapsstudier og etableringen av Edinburgh-skolen 1966–76* [*The Two Cultures: The Emergence of Science Studies and the Establishment of the Edinburgh School 1966–1976*]. Oslo: University of Oslo, diss.

Engfeldt, Lars-Göran. 2009. *From Stockholm to Johannesburg and beyond: The Evolution of the International System for Sustainable Development Governance and Its Implications*. Stockholm: Foreign Office.

Erickson, Bruce and Catriona Sandilands, eds. 2010. *Queer Ecologies: Sex, Nature, Politics, Desire*. Bloomington, IN: Indiana University Press.

Frängsmyr, Tore 1981. "Kvinnan, vetenskapen och naturens död [Women, Science and the Death of Nature]." *Svenska Dagbladet*, 24 February.

Frängsmyr, Tore. 1984. *History of Science in Sweden: The Growth of a Discipline, 1932–1982*. Uppsala, Sweden: Office for History of Science, Uppsala University.

Frängsmyr, Tore, J. L. Heilbron, and R. E. Rider, eds. 1990. *The Quantifying Spirit in the 18th Century*. Berkeley: University of California Press.

Glasser, Harold. 2005. "Arne Naess — A Wandering Wonderer: Bringing the Search for Wisdom Back to Life." Series Editor's Introduction. Pp. xii-lviii in. *Selected Works of Arne Ness 1–10*, vol. 10, edited by H. Glasser and A. Drengson in collaboration with Arne Naess and with assistance from Bill Devall, and George Sessions. Dordrecht: Springer.

Glick, Thomas. 1981. "Review of *The Death of Nature*." *Journal of the History of Biology* 14 (2):356–357.

Greer, Germaine. 1970. *The Female Eunuch*. Melbourne: Paladin.

Griffin, Susan. 1978. *Women and Nature: The Roaring Inside Her*. New York: Harper & Row.

Harding, Sandra G. 1986. *The Science Question in Feminism*. Ithaca, NY: Cornell University Press.

Huntford, Roland. 1997. *Nansen: The Explorer as Hero*. New York: Barnes & Noble.

Jasanoff, S. and M. Long Martello. 2001. *Earthly Politics: Local and Global in Environmental Governance*. Cambridge, MA: MIT Press.

Johannisson, Karin. 1988. *Det mätbara samhället: Statistik och samhällsdröm i 1700-talets Europa* [*With a Summary in English: Society in Numbers: Statistics and Utopias in the Eighteenth Century Europe*]. Stockholm: Norstedts.

Jølle, Harald Dag. 2011. *Nansen: Oppdageren* [*Nansen: The Discoverer*]. Oslo: Gyldendal.

Koerner, Lisbet. 1999. *Linnaeus: Nature and Nation*. Cambridge, MA: Harvard University Press.

Lantto, Patrik and Ulf Mörkenstam. 2008. "Sami Rights and Sami Challenges: The Modernization Process and the Swedish Sami Movement, 1886–2006." *Scandinavian Journal of History* 33(1):26–51.

Larsen, Svend Erik. 1996. *Naturen er ligeglad: Naturopfattelser i kulturel sammenhæng* [*Nature is Indifferent: Views of Nature in a Cultural Context*]. Köbenhavn: Munksgaard/Rosinante.

Lindroth, Sten. 1943. *Paracelsismen i Sverige till 1600-talets mitt* [*Paracelsism in Sweden until the middle of the seventeenth century*]. Uppsala: Almqvist & Wiksell.

Lovejoy, Arthur O. 1936. *The Great Chain of Being: A Study of the History of an Idea*. Cambridge, MA: Harvard University Press.

Macekura, Stephen. 2015. *The Rise of Global Sustainable Development in the Twentieth Century*. New York: Cambridge University Press.

McCormick, John. 1989. *Reclaiming Paradise: The Global Environmental Movement*. Bloomington, IN: Indiana University Press.

Merchant, Carolyn. 1980. *The Death of Nature: Women, Ecology, and the Scientific Revolution. A Feminist Reappraisal of the Scientific Revolution*. 1st edition. San Francisco, CA: Harper & Row.

Merchant, Carolyn. 1989. *Ecological Revolutions: Nature, Gender, and Science in New England*. Chapel Hill: University of North Carolina Press.

Merchant, Carolyn. 1990. "Ecofeminism and Feminist Theory." P. 100 in *Reweaving the World: The Emergence of Ecofeminism*, edited by I. Diamond and G. F. Orenstein. San Francisco, CA: Sierra Club Books.

Merchant, Carolyn. 1992. *Radical Ecology: The Search for a Livable World*. New York: Routledge.

Merchant, Carolyn. 1995a. *Earthcare: Women and the Environment*. New York: Routledge.

Merchant, Carolyn. 1995b. "Reinventing Eden: Western Culture as a Recovery Narrative." Pp. 132–170 in *Uncommon Ground: Toward Reinventing Nature*, edited by W. Cronon. New York: W.W. Norton.

Merchant, Carolyn. 2003. *Reinventing Eden: The Fate of Nature in Western Culture*. New York: Routledge.

Merchant, Carolyn. 2006. "The Scientific Revolution and the Death of Nature." *Isis* 97 (3):513–533.

Naess, Arne. 1989. *Ecology, Community and Lifestyle: Outline of an Ecosophy (1972), Engl. Transl.* Cambridge: Cambridge: University Press.

Nasgaard, Roald. 1984. *The Mystic North: Symbolist Landscape Painting in Northern Europe and North America, 1890–1940*. Toronto: Art Gallery of Ontario & University of Toronto Press.

Nash, Roderick Frazier. 1967. *Wilderness and the American Mind*. 1st edition. New Haven, CT: Yale University Press.

Nye, David E., Linda Rugg, James Fleming, and Robert Emmett. 2013. *The Emergence of the Environmental Humanities*. Stockholm: Mistra.

O'Neill, K. *et al.*2013. "Methods and Global Environmental Governance." *Annual Review of Environment and Resources* 38:441–471.

Osler, Margaret J. 1981. "Review of *The Death of Nature*." *Isis* 72(262):287–288.

Pagel, Walter. 1981. "Review of *The Death of Nature*." *History of Science* 19(44, part 2):148–153.

Rose, Deborah and Libby Robin. 2004. "The Ecological Humanities in Action: An Invitation." *Australian Humanities Review* 31–32.

Rothenberg, David. 1992. *Is It Painful to Think? Conversations with Arne Naess.* Minnesota: Minnesota University Press.

Schott, Thomas. 1992. "Scientific Research in Sweden: Orientation Toward the American Centre and Embeddedness in Nordic and European Environments." *Science Studies* 5:13–25.

Sörlin, Sverker. 1988. *Framtidslandet: Debatten om Norrland och naturresurserna under det industriella genombrottet* [*With a Summary in English: Land of the Future: The Debate on Norrland and Its Natural Resources at the Time of the Industrial Breakthrough*]. Stockholm: Carlsson Bokförlag.

Sörlin, Sverker. 1989. "Scientific Travel, the Linnaean Tradition." Pp. 96–123 in *Science in Sweden: The Royal Swedish Academy of Sciences 1739–1918*, edited by T. Frängsmyr. Canton, MA: Science History Publications.

Sörlin, Sverker, ed. 1992. "Introduction: The International Contexts of Swedish Science: A Network Approach to the Internationalization of Science." *Science Studies* 5:5–12.

Sörlin, Sverker. 1998. "Carolyn Merchant and The Death of Nature in Sweden." *Organization and Environment* 11(2):193–197.

Sörlin, Sverker. 2016. "Grön humaniora—vad, när, varför och varthän? [Environmental Humanities—What, When, Why, and Wither?]." *Kulturella Perspektiv* 25(1):8–19.

Sörlin, Sverker and Graeme Wynn. 2016. "Fire and Ice in The Academy: The Rise of the Integrative Humanities." *Literary Review of Canada* 24(6):14–15.

Sundin, Bo. 1989. "Environmental Protection and the National Parks." Pp. 199–226 in *Science in Sweden: The Royal Swedish Academy of Sciences 1739–1918*, edited by T. Frängsmyr. Canton, MA: Science History Publications.

Svensson, Patrik. 2015. "The Humanistiscope: Exploring the Situatedness of Humanities Infrastructure." Pp. 337–353 in *Between Humanities and the Digital*, edited by P. Svensson and D. T. Goldberg. Cambridge, MA: MIT Press.

Thue, Fredrik, ed. 1997. *Empirisme og demokrati: Norsk samfunnsforskning som etterkrigsprosjekt* [*Empiricism and Democracy: Norwegian Social Science as a Postwar Project*]. Oslo: Universitetsforlaget.

Thue, Fredrik, 2009. "Americanised Social Science as Anti-Communist Containment? The Case of the Oslo Institute for Social Research, 1945–1965." *Ideas in History* 4.

Thue, Fredrik, ed. 2010. "Empiricism, Pragmatism, Behaviorism: Arne Næss and the Growth of American-Styled Social Research in Norway after World War II." Pp. 219–229 in *The Vienna Circle in the Nordic Countries: Networks and Transformations of Logical Empiricism*, edited by J. Manninen and F. Stadler. Springer Science & Business Media BV.

Waters, Colin N., Jan Zalasiewicz, Colin Summerhayes, *et al.* 2016. "The Anthropocene Is Functionally and Stratigraphically Distinct from the Holocene." *Science* 351:6269.

Wilson, Daniel J. 1987. "Lovejoy's *The Great Chain of Being* After Fifty Years." *Journal of the History of Ideas* 48(2):187–206.

PART III

The Politics of Landscapes, Embodiment, and Epistemologies

12

LANDSCAPE, SCIENCE, AND SOCIAL REPRODUCTION

The Long-Reaching Influence of Carolyn Merchant's Insight

Laura Alice Watt

A few years ago, in the end-of-semester evaluations for my Environmental History class, one student observed, "Wow, this class really ties a lot of the information from other environmental studies classes together—everything makes so much more sense now!" This sentiment mirrors my own introduction to the field of environmental history, in the form of a graduate seminar with Carolyn Merchant the first semester of my doctoral program at UC Berkeley in 1993. I'd started my academic life as a biology undergraduate, focusing on vertebrate ecology, and also completed a master's degree in environmental management with pragmatic, applied coursework focused on the skills I'd need as an environmental professional in government agencies or non-profits. After a year interning for the Nature Conservancy, while I liked my career direction, I hadn't quite *fallen in love* with my work yet. But Carolyn's grad seminar—reading a book a week, every week, all semester, immersing ourselves in the latest publications in a young but rapidly growing field—brought together all my education up to that point in a way that I had not experienced before.

And what books, what writers! Cronon's *Nature's Metropolis* (Cronon 1991), Worster's *Wealth of Nature* (Worster 1993), White's *The Middle Ground* (White 1991)—and of course Merchant herself. I had already read Merchant's *The Death of Nature: Women, Ecology, and the Scientific Revolution* (hereafter *TDN*) (Merchant 1980) before starting graduate school, but now we dug into *Ecological Revolutions* (Merchant 1989); her unique synthesis of history, feminism, and Thomas Kuhn's theory of scientific revolutions struck me as powerful, opening up new ways of thinking about humans' relationships with the world around them. While McEvoy (1987:300–301) identified ecology, production, and cognition as key analytic levels of environmental history, Merchant further elaborated on the importance of a fourth level, that of both social and biological *reproduction*—the ways that ideas or assumptions about our relationship with the natural world keep getting re-made and reinforced, and often reinvented, through time. By adding this facet of change and dynamism, Merchant not only contributed essential insights into women's roles in environmental transformations, but helped to better articulate the *processes* of interaction between ecological systems, which I had been studying for so long, and human systems, which had only just come under the microscope for me.

A light bulb, or perhaps an entire box full of them, lit up in my head. From my earlier education, I understood a great deal about ecological dynamics, but little about how people and their cultures affect and respond to those dynamics. Natural and cultural resources were too often treated as entirely separate areas of inquiry, speaking separate languages and unaware of the other's points of view. But here was a field explicitly focused on bringing both perspectives together in unique ways, examining their interactions as a way of both explaining the past and understanding the present, and ideally contributing to an improved future as well. Environmental history seemed to open up a whole new realm of inquiry— one that has shaped my own career in varying and long-lasting ways, through my dissertation in 2001 to its adaptation and publication as a book in 2017, and now carrying me into a new research direction. This chapter discusses this arc of Merchant's direct and indirect influences on my work, particularly now forming a bridge between my completed landscape history of Point Reyes National Seashore here in northern California, and developing a new focus on the history of the Rocky Mountain Biological Laboratory in Colorado.

Landscapes as Social Reproduction

After that first semester working with Carolyn, I dug more deeply into the concept of *landscape* as a unit of study, adopted from cultural and historical geography—how people write their ideas and values into the landscape, and when later people or generations experience that landscape, how those ideas and values get re-created (Groth 1997). To me, landscape adds a more explicitly *spatial* element to Merchant's discussion of ecological revolutions, extending her analysis as a powerful tool for investigating complex interactions between communities and their environments by tracking historical changes in landscape as indicators of shifting social dynamics and structures—in other words, a crucial aspect of her concept of social reproduction. Landscapes, both out in physical reality and as portrayed through various sorts of imagery, are amalgams of "not only of what lies before our eyes but what lies within our heads" (Meinig 1979:34). People with different values or interests in a given landscape will see it through very different "lenses," resulting in contrasting perceptions of what is actually there, how it might best be used, and what significance it holds. Over time, the visual and material details of landscapes reflect the ideas and values of those who live and work in them, as the landscape is socially produced and reproduced by those people's activities, gradually becoming their "unwitting autobiographies" (Lewis 1979:12). Sometimes this re-creation serves to strengthen and maintain a community's connection with place, layer upon layer over time; in other circumstances, it continually reproduces a problematic relationship with place, such as presumptions about who "belongs" or has rights to its use.

This combination of disciplinary approaches—environmental history, landscape theory, and public lands policy and management—came together in my research exploring what happens to a working agricultural landscape following its formal protection by the National Park Service (NPS). National parks are considered national treasures, enjoy far more public support than many other federal programs, and are often touted as one of America's "best ideas" (Stegner 1983).[1] The founding legislation that created the NPS in 1916 directs the agency to preserve the parks' resources for use by the public and to manage them "unimpaired for the enjoyment of future generations."[2] But preservation is not a neutral act, and the NPS is not a neutral actor. In much the same way that a beetle stuck in amber is "preserved" but no longer living, preserving landscapes aims to prevent change, to maintain places "unimpaired" indefinitely into the future. Yet the process of protecting and managing land as parks exerts its own influence on the area's landscape, gradually changing its form and appearance to reflect and reproduce the preservation agency's own values and preferences. These changes often remain invisible to visitors, who take for granted that what they see in a preserved landscape is "how it has always been." Changes also frequently remain invisible to park staff, whose management decisions further re-shape the place to meet our expectations of what a park "should be." And if the place being preserved is a lived-in or working landscape, this process can disconnect the residents from their own homes, bringing their presence into question, and sacrificing their needs to the illusion of untouched nature and pristine wilderness—in the cases of many Native American peoples, to the point of completely dispossessing them from their homelands (Spence 1999).

My recent book, *The Paradox of Preservation: Wilderness and Working Landscapes at Point Reyes National Seashore* (2017), aims to make the effects of preservation on the land more visible through a case study of Point Reyes National Seashore, an area set aside in 1962 to provide public recreation space (see Figure 12.1). Point Reyes is unusual in that it still contains working dairy and beef cattle ranches, as well as extensive areas of federally-designated wilderness. More broadly, my book also documents how our national ideas about what a park "ought to be" have developed and changed over time, and what happens once the NPS and its particular approaches to management and national heritage become involved with preserving a lived-in, still-working agricultural landscape. The particular historical development of the agency has resulted in national standards and policies—what "counts" as heritage, for whom parks are protected, and how best to manage park resources—that do not necessarily match how local residents live and work on the landscape, nor what they value about that place (Watt 2017).

FIGURE 12.1 Drakes Beach at Point Reyes National Seashore, 2001.
Source: Photo by author.

Merchant's emphasis on social reproduction, combined with the spatial sense of landscape theory, allows the changes associated with preservation to come more clearly into view. The resulting landscapes produced by the NPS represent a series of compromises between use and protection—the terms of which are constantly being re-negotiated and re-imagined. In the fifty-five years since the Seashore's establishment, park management has contributed to a decrease of working ranches on the Point, from twenty-five in 1962 to only eleven now, many of which are now potentially threatened by a pending lawsuit regarding the Seashore's planning processes. Over the past decade, park staff forced an 80-year-old oyster operation to close, despite enormous local controversy, alternately claiming environmental harms, which were never substantiated, and alleging policy requirements, which my research shows were based in a misinterpretation of wilderness law. By making effects of management, both intended and not, more visible, my work aims to help make conservation efforts more inclusive of people in protected landscapes—arguing there is no need for a zero-sum game of sustainable agriculture versus wilderness in parks; there is room, and an essential role, for both (Watt 2017).

Science and the Power of Place

So it seems somewhat fitting that now, with the Point Reyes project described above mostly finished, I am turning toward the environmental history of science—once again following in Carolyn's footsteps! In my case, specifically delving into the history of field ecology and field stations, and the ways in which the landscape itself, and our ideas about its meaning, can shape the *kind* of science done in a given place. This new work is emerging out of my experience teaching about the practices of ecological restoration as representing a particular kind of intersection of science, history, and human desires in the landscape. Too often environmental restoration and remediation treats landscape like a *tabula rasa*, aiming to fix the past errors of human use, as if to turn back the clock, and in the process cuts off all connection to the area's previous history—denying that element of social reproduction that Merchant's work has emphasized. Restoration also implies that the resulting landscapes are purely "natural," when in reality they continue to be shaped and manipulated by humans to meet their own cultural goals and values. Partly this is a form of what Franz Vera calls "shifting baselines," the ways in which the meaning of specific words—like "park," like "wilderness"—shift over time to obscure past relationships (both ecological and cultural) and impose new meaning on the landscape (Vera 2010).

These paradoxes reflect a larger debate within the field of conservation biology, an on-going collision of an older wilderness-based conception of resource preservation with a newer view that aims to re-think resource management in the era of the Anthropocene, with its increasing recognition that all environments around the globe are now being deeply influenced by human activity in one form or another—that no natural landscapes are truly "pristine" (Marris 2011). My students puzzle through complexities of what is meant by labeling a place or an animal as "wild" or "native," or even possible implications of categorizing something as a species—after reading Darwin, with his emphasis on the ever-changing nature of nature, students begin to question the boundaries of species definitions that evolutionary adaptation seems to be constantly shifting, often faster than we realize (Losos 2014).

Looking back through Merchant's body of work, I am particularly intrigued by her translation of scientific ideas into her own articulation of an environmental ethic. From her deep reading of Enlightenment history, she identified science and technology as intersecting with the classic Edenic narrative about our relationship with the natural world, forming "the way to control nature and hence recover the right to the garden given to the first parents" (Merchant 1995:136). Yet her exploration of chaos theory, which "fundamentally destabilizes the very concept of nature as a standard or referent," makes more space for the possibility of creativity in our relationship with nature, rather than a simplistic control/domestication dynamic (p. 156). Building on chaos theory's variety of unpredictable outcomes, she insists that because ecology as a science is non-linear and non-deterministic, as well as historical, it opens up more opportunity for partnership—ecological outcomes are not predictable in the same way that a chemical reaction must always follow the same path, and Merchant argues that there's hope in that unpredictability, as it gives the natural world more agency of its own, beyond the grasp of human dominance, and moves toward a more mutually interactive paradigm of understanding complexity (Merchant 2016). This insight has led to Merchant's partnership ethic, particularly as "a viable relationship between a human community and a non-human community in a particular place, a place in which connections to the larger world are recognized through economic and ecological exchanges" (p. 162). She suggests that we use ecological perception, seeing the world as inherently connected and interdependent, to improve and heal our connection with the natural world around us.

Merchant's insights merge well with the concept of landscape, and revisiting them has shed new light on my understanding of my own work so far, and where it seems to be going. I have focused mostly on federal land managers in one way or another since starting graduate school, and find that the application of generic ideas—those developed in other places, or for other purposes—to a landscape does not always make for terribly effective management of either natural or cultural resources. At Point Reyes, park managers have cycled through differing paradigms for landscape management almost every decade since the Seashore was established—first centering on providing opportunities for developed or motorized recreation in the 1960s, then wilderness in the '70s, to ecosystem management in the '90s. And similar to what Nancy Langston documented in her research on both national forests and wildlife refuges, the best of managerial intentions can lead to "a dizzying series of unexpected effects and unintended consequences"; for instance, actions aimed at encouraging ponderosa pines in Oregon forests resulted in fewer and fewer trees, due to the misapplication of forest science developed in one place to another (Langston 1995:296). At Point Reyes, wilderness designation of over 25,000 acres has resulted in increasingly fire-prone vegetation developing across the southern portion of the Seashore, and bureaucratic definitions of which kinds of buildings "counted" (or, more to the point, did not count) as historic led to the demolition of roughly half the Peninsula's built landscape in the Seashore's first few decades of existence—so many that park staff referred to the then-Superintendent's historic preservation policy as the "D-8 policy," named for the model of bulldozer used to knock buildings down (Watt 2017:chapter 5).

In contrast, the land's history of resident peoples—indigenous natives and, sometimes, later settlers who then stuck around long enough to begin to understand the place more deeply—often offers something that needs to be considered in concert with the more intellectualized sciences. As Barry Lopez wrote so lyrically in *Arctic Dreams* of the Eskimos' relationship with their environment, "The land is like a kind of knowledge traveling in time through them" (Lopez 1986:264). The connections that form with long residence in and engagement with a given place, relying on the landscape and working within its limits, are an oft-overlooked form of knowing—one that is complementary to, rather than opposing, a more science-based approach. Sometimes labeled as traditional ecological knowledge (or TEK), it is based in being able to read stories in the land, to understand the ways in which the land itself has been produced and reproduced through human and nonhuman interactions accumulating over time, and also in accepting a level of complexity that often goes beyond the reach of science (Ruiz-Mallén and Corbera 2013).

These insights have practical implications for federal land managers. During my brief career as an environmental consultant (before returning to academia in 2006), I helped write several resource management plans for the Bureau of Land Management here in northern California. Our aim was in large part to get down on paper the "institutional knowledge" that resided in the heads of the field offices' long-time employees on the cusp of retirement. Their on-the-ground understanding of the places they worked—not really "institutional knowledge" per se, but land knowledge, or landscape knowledge—accreted over time and through many repeated interactions with those particular places, becoming something like an agency-based form of TEK. Perhaps as a result, those plans— written for the King Range National Conservation Area and the Bureau of Land Management's (BLM) Ukiah Field Office—have stood well over time, according to the agency staff, with very few amendments needed. This success is based in an approach that did not impose some outside, generic cookbook of management approaches onto the landscape; instead, we worked to express what people—both agency personnel and members of nearby communities—knew about it *through* their lived experiences, learned sometimes through simple trial and error, as well as through science and ecology. An intertwining of science and more place-based or indigenous forms of knowing is leading to new approaches for land management across the West, increasingly centered in community-based collaboration between agencies, scientists, non-profit organizations, and citizens (Charnley, Sheridan, and Nabhan 2014).

Ecologists themselves are coming to similar conclusions. In the introduction to their anthology *The Ecology of Place*, editors Ian Billick and Mary Price suggest that "the process of scientific inquiry in ecology and evolutionary biology and the way in which ecological knowledge is used to solve applied problems may differ in fundamental ways from the heretofore dominant paradigms that have been drawn from the physical sciences" (Billick and Price 2010:3). More specifically, they argue that it is the power of place that often motivates ecologists in the field, and that citizens and scientists could work more collaboratively to solve environmental problems if built upon "a sense of place that sees humans as part of the ecological system, not separate from it" (p. 437). Nearly four decades ago, Merchant's *TDN* investigated Scientific Revolution-era shifts from organic, intimate understandings of the natural world toward a more mechanistic, rational, scientific approach—I find it fascinating to now see rational science, as practiced by academics and land managers alike, arcing at least somewhat back toward the organic and place-based, seeing the landscape as a whole not a just collection of parts.

A Case Study of Science in Place: The Rocky Mountain Biological Laboratory

Now I'm turning toward a new project that will explicitly investigate this more place-based scientific inquiry developing over time—in a place where perennially returning scientists themselves are becoming nearly "indigenous," spending entire careers (occasionally extending into multigenerational careers) of summer field work attempting to understand the dynamics of a single place—to see how that kind of science might differ from that of an occasional visiting researcher. Located high (approximately 9,500 feet) on the western slope of Colorado in Gunnison County (see Figure 12.2), the Rocky Mountain Biological Laboratory (RMBL) considers its surrounding landscape to be the laboratory itself—yet it is located on

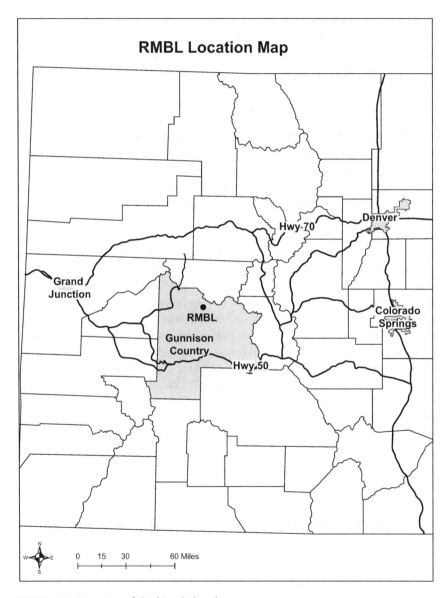

FIGURE 12.2 Location of Gothic, Colorado.
Source: Image courtesy of the Rocky Mountain Biological Laboratory Spatial Modeling Platform, S. Sprott, 2017.

the site of a former 1880s-era silver mining town, perched just below the continental divide, reflecting a past history of extractive uses in the area. Faced with a recent influx of both winter and summer recreational demands, wilderness designation, and future unknowns associated with climate change, the Lab is navigating an interesting set of challenges with regard to land management—both land that RMBL owns directly and the surrounding federal and privately owned landscapes—and scientific certainty.

It is also the place where my parents first met in 1962, where my father and stepmother still conduct biological research every year, and where I spent all of my childhood summers; it is thus a landscape that has deep personal meaning to me, representing a sense of absolute freedom, a place where I forged my closest connections to the natural world—and in some ways also to my own imagination and sense of self. Now returning as an adult after a long period of absence, I see subtle changes in the area's character, slight shifts away from my idyllic childhood vision, that have prompted me to inquire about the history of the other changes this particular landscape has undergone over the last 150 years.

The landscape of RMBL reveals a continuing, ongoing evolution in how the surrounding mountains and ecosystems have been viewed by people living in or using the area over time. The native Uncompahgre (Tabeguache) Ute peoples hunted in the high mountain valley seasonally, leaving behind arrowheads as evidence of their presence, but no indications have been found of year-round use—not surprising, given the heavy snowfall for most of the year.[3] Since the first Euro-American explorers and settlers arrived, the resources considered valuable or desirable have changed, from minerals to ecological purity, from considering the landscape as a source of wealth to a source of information and knowledge. With this shift, *how* or *where* those resources are considered valuable has also shifted. The minerals of interest in the 1870s and '80s—mostly silver, copper, lead, and coal—had to be extracted and moved to have any value; the difficulty of that process led to the demise of many small boom towns, including Gothic, first incorporated in 1879 and with a peak population of several thousand, but declared dead by a local newspaper in 1883 after a decline in silver prices. Cattle ranching has been a relative constant in the area since the 1880s, transforming summer pastures into grown animals to be shipped off to market. In contrast, the resources sought by the scientists who came later—wild, relatively undisturbed ecosystems—were valued *in situ*, and enhanced by their isolation high in the Rockies.

These different lenses through which this region has been viewed also represent changing relationships of resource control in the area. In general, the Intermountain West has been characterized as a region in which many of its landscapes and much of its economic and political geography have been created from a distance (Wyckoff and Dilsaver 1995). The early history of the region shows the importance of decisions made from afar in shaping or directing resource management decisions. Mining and railroad companies based in Denver or further east had profound effects on how and where development occurred across the Rockies' western slope through the late 1880s. At roughly the same time, the federal government, which owns over three-quarters of the land in Gunnison County, as both Forest Service and BLM land, began to influence the kinds of resource management activities that take place in the area.

In the 1920s, Dr. John C. Johnson, a biology professor and Dean at Western State College in Gunnison, decided that the abandoned townsite at Gothic would be an ideal location for an independent, high-altitude biological field laboratory. The same mountains that had made life so difficult and isolated for the hard-rock miners of the 1880s had kept others out, too, and the region north of the coal-mining town of Crested Butte remained more or less empty of human settlement. Dr. Johnson noticed that it was also one of the wettest regions in the Rockies, which contributed to its having a diverse array of different ecological habitats, all within fairly close proximity to the old townsite. Many of the dilapidated build-ings from the silver mining days remained on the site, providing a natural location to house both students and researchers.

Johnson purchased the land in 1928 and, with several co-founders, organized the new Lab as an independent non-profit organization rather than an entity affiliated with any single university.[4] They expressly followed the model of rural agrarian cooperative settlements; Johnson stressed that researchers could come and build a house on the site, bring their families for the summer, and become per-sonally involved with the development of the Lab as an entity. He envisioned RMBL as becoming a close-knit community of biologists, all with long-term interests in the work done. Johnson welcomed scientists of any discipline, both field and experimental scientists, to participate, creating "an atmosphere of informality and cross-disciplinary interest."[5] Researchers and students alike helped to build and maintain the facilities, cooked meals in the communal Dining Hall, and were encouraged to give both formal and informal seminars to the Lab community throughout the summer session; these lectures became important weekly social events, besides an occasion to share knowledge and ideas.

Facilities at RMBL were, and for the most part remain, fairly primitive; many of the early cabins did not have electricity or running water and all were heated only by wood-burning stoves. None were painted, nor did they have any dec-orative or stylistic flourishes. Larger cabins often had sinks but no bathrooms, and most of the residents relied on the combination of outhouses and a central wash house, which supplied showers and a hand-cranked washing machine (now replaced by coin-operated washers and dryers). The laboratory buildings them-selves did not have electricity or water until the 1950s, and even after that, research projects generally had to be designed to be do-able with a minimum of equipment (often shared among the scientists) or technological requirements. Up until the late 1980s there was no telephone (and until the mid-1990s no Internet) access, other than an answering machine in Crested Butte. The environmental conditions that limited the 1880s miners similarly limited the biologists; as Gothic can receive over 400 inches of snow annually, the dirt road from Crested Butte is rarely plowed before mid-late May, and the Lab's water system is turned off in early-mid September. A few caretakers stay at RMBL through the winter, but otherwise all activity is compressed into a four-month period over summer.

In adapting a mining landscape to a science-oriented one, the Lab has maintained much of its historic design and appearance (see Figure 12.3), yet leaves a subtle imprint on its surroundings, particularly through its attempts to preserve the isolation that originally caused mining to fail in the area. In the Lab's early days, Dr. Johnson made annual requests before the Gunnison County Board of Commissioners to keep the road between Crested Butte and Gothic in poor condition, so as to keep the area about the Lab "as natural as possible." He later described the landscape as "paradise for the biologist who wants to study the hundreds of species … in a very beautiful and primitive area, almost exactly as the Indians had left it only 40 years earlier." Despite slight improvements to the road over the years, he and other Lab personnel continued to do their best to "discourage the careless tourist who picks flowers and leaves picnic debris."[6]

Furthermore, the new corporation was specifically called a "laboratory," rather than a field station.[7] The word "station" suggests a stopping place on a route, but

FIGURE 12.3 Gothic, Colorado in the early 1930s.
Source: Photo by William H. Dudley; image courtesy of the Rocky Mountain Biological Laboratory.

doesn't offer any information as to the role of the place itself; it seems passive, a place to be moved through. My dictionary defines "laboratory" as "a place devoted to experimental study in any science"; in addition, it seems to imply a *pure* or *pristine* place in which to conduct said experimental studies.[8] This word choice suggests that the founders believed the area surrounding the Lab to be biologically undisturbed and intact, that it was a unique opportunity to step into "real nature" without the interfering hands of humans muddying their experimental results—despite its early history as a mining camp, and a brief resurgence of mineral interest in the early 1910s. The Lab was not just a place to shelter oneself while doing field work; it was a place in which researchers could immerse themselves and work to reveal truths about the surrounding ecological systems.

That said, the type of research work usually carried out, and what is considered "good" science at RMBL, has evolved over the years, reflecting transitions in the overall field of ecology at the national and international level. The Lab's early focus on teaching science, and primarily pursuing projects in natural history and ecological description, began to shift after World War II, particularly after the National Science Foundation was established in 1950. Greater availability of funding for field-based experimental research brought a new generation of scientists to RMBL who formed a loose consortium specifically looking for an intellectual retreat in the Western mountains where they could not only conduct field studies but also foster a newer, more conceptual and experimental approach to biology. This caused friction among some members of the Lab, resulting in a period now known as "the Gothic Wars" in the early 1960s. The founder's son, John C. "Chris" Johnson, Jr., took over the Lab's directorship, and managed to hold it together by working with the various members to ease disagreements.

RMBL continued to grow slowly until the mid-1970s, when a noticeable and steady increase in scientific productivity of lab researchers encouraged others to become involved. By the late 1980s, the Board of Trustees became concerned that the Lab was growing too much, and put a population cap in place to prevent outgrowing the facilities and the carrying capacity of the valley. Around the same time, RMBL shifted from having a summers-only director to someone employed year-round; this more-constant presence in Gunnison County strengthened ties with the local community, particularly in regard to surrounding land management. Two new lab buildings, one constructed in the early 1980s and the other in 2011, expanded the range of science that can be conducted on-site (a third new building added additional work space). With increasing attention on climate change, and elevation becoming a proxy for other forms of spatial and temporal change, the Lab's high altitude and ecological heterogeneity makes it increasingly valuable for field experiments.[9]

Yet a unique aspect of the scientific studies taking place at RMBL is how many researchers have developed life-long relationships with the area—such as my father, Ward Watt, who has returned to conduct field work on *Colias* butterflies almost every summer for over fifty years.[10] Ian Billick, the Lab's Executive

Director since 2000, is working to bring together long-term data generated at RMBL into a place-based database management system, to facilitate integration of diverse types of contextual information about the area's ecosystems, so that data collected from one study—even unpublished data, generated from researchers' observations and specimen collections over time—can be used to inform or enrich others in sometimes unexpected ways (Billick 2010). For example, maps of changes to the Lab's buildings and facilities over time can reveal previous events of soil disturbance that may be relevant to on-going ecological study—another form of the Lab and its inhabitants producing and reproducing the landscape around them, as Merchant would observe. Another example getting a lot of recent media attention is that of RMBL's accountant and long-time year-round resident billy barr (he prefers to spell his name all lower case), who kept meticulous records of snowfall and other climate data for over forty years; he began his data collection efforts primarily to alleviate boredom during the long winter months in his Gothic cabin.[11] These records are now being used to inform ecologists studying changes in migration or emergence patterns, responding to climatic changes, of a variety of organisms, such as fireweed plants, American robins, and yellow-bellied marmots (Inouye et al. 2000).[12] The distinct value of such long-term studies, offering unique insights that could not be learned without

FIGURE 12.4 Gothic Mountain and the RMBL townsite, June 2017.
Source: Photo by author.

continued intimacy with the landscape, returning year after year, is a direct outgrowth of Johnson's original design of RMBL to be a *community* of scientists.

To the casual visitor, Gothic still looks much like an old ghost town, preserved in a rustic-yet-intact state. Tiny cabins dot the townsite, following the 1880s-era street grid to some degree. The primary land management concern of the Lab is maintaining its ecological integrity as a space for experimental research, requiring that the landscape be protected from human disturbance as much as possible—yet occasionally the Lab itself requires new developments, such as additional laboratory space or residences, or updated infrastructure. Interest in the region's resources has changed markedly from the 1970s to the present and beyond. The marketing of Colorado as a tourist destination that began in places like Aspen and Vail after World War II began to catch up to these more remote mountains (Philpott 2013). The nearby Mount Crested Butte Ski Area first brought large numbers of winter tourists in the 1970s and '80s, and in recent decades there has been an explosion of summer recreational use as well, with increasing pressure from hikers, campers, and particularly mountain bikers. Wilderness designation in large portions of the surrounding Grand Mesa, Uncompahgre, and Gunnison National Forests and the Black Canyon of the Gunnison National Park have increasingly bureaucratized the landscape, requiring permits for research projects where the ecologists once had fairly free rein.

In researching the environmental history of RMBL and its surrounding landscapes, I plan to situate it within the overall history of twentieth-century science, particularly the emergence of ecology and later conservation biology as distinct sub-fields, and the role of field stations in developing those new lines of scientific inquiry. There is a growing literature in this history of science that focuses specifically on field stations (see Kohler 2002 and Vetter 2012, for instance), taking interdisciplinary approaches to investigating how the implementation of scientifically informed values on the landscape shift over time, and either coordinate or conflict with other land use patterns, such as outdoor recreation and wilderness protections. To me, conceiving of landscape as laboratory is something of an ideal, which can be hard to maintain in the face of competing interpretations of the landscape—particularly wilderness-as-playground, which is also an ideal of sorts (Watt 2017:chapter 4). Both ideals may need to be modulated by a greater acknowledgement of humans in landscape, a more pragmatic view that, in keeping with Merchant's partnership ethic, admits that human impacts can (to a point) be part of the stochastic variability of an ecosystem, instead of always being considered an unwelcome intrusion and disruption of what is natural and worth studying. Perhaps applying Merchant's recognition of the important insights from chaos theory could help to broaden the scope of "acceptable" variability to include (some) human presence.

In my investigation of this history, I plan to keep my eyes open for the evolving relationship between the science of ecology, the kinds of studies conducted at RMBL, and the evolving relationship between the returning scientists and the landscape; how the place influenced the work produced there, and how the science has affected—or reproduced, as Merchant would describe it—the landscape over time. Similarly, the landscape has produced and reproduced generations of ecological and environmental scholars, as quite a few of us "Gothic kids" have become biologists or environmental historians and continue returning to RMBL, often with our own kids as the next generation to come. I am particularly interested to see how the knowledge gained through long-term research at RMBL may at times reach beyond the realm of science, to incorporate a more personal and perhaps holistic understanding of place. In addition, I will be on the look-out for ways in which increasing recreational use of surrounding landscapes may be affecting research design: do the RMBL scientists strive to restrict access by the public, or might some of them attempt to anticipate and work around this new reality, or perhaps even re-orient their research questions to fit within a more populated environment? I hope that this work will contribute to extending Merchant's work on the history of science, perhaps documenting that arc back toward a new (or renewed) valuing of the stories and richness of place-based landscape knowledge.

The Making of an Environmental Historian

Those early days of studying with Carolyn made a deep impression on me; both the literature that we devoured and her own articulation of the importance of reproduction (both biological and social) to an understanding of both ecosystems and human systems have shaped my academic career ever since. Her seminar, and indeed the overall field of environmental history, encouraged taking a broad perspective on the interactions between humans and their natural worlds, and has informed my research in numerous ways. From studying how ideas of preservation become inscribed on working landscapes, to investigating the ways in which field science shapes and is shaped by the landscape around it, I continue to find inspiration and insight from Merchant's scholarship.

This influence extends to my personal sense of academic identity as well. Working across several disciplinary fields—I borrow heavily from two distinct academic disciplines, history and geography, but have a degree in neither, and apply their ideas and methods to public lands policy, but again without degrees in either political science or law—I've long puzzled over what to call myself as a scholar. Certainly when I was first looking for jobs out of graduate school, with my Ph.D. in environmental studies, I was not historian enough to apply for jobs in most history departments, nor geographer enough for the geography departments. It was not until I co-chaired the annual conference of the American Society for Environmental History (ASEH) in 2014 with Carolyn—we had worked together before in the context of teaching, and the conference's location that year in San Francisco made both UC Berkeley and Sonoma State logical partners for setting up local arrangements—that I finally felt comfortable calling myself an environmental historian, full stop. It was truly an honor to work side by side with her again, with enormous assistance from ASEH director Lisa Mighetto. Their combined eagerness to include a multitude of voices and disciplinary perspectives in the conference made me realize that my hesitation in self-labeling was unfounded. While my teaching and research extend out in numerous disciplinary directions, ASEH has long been my intellectual home, and so I am proud to add my name to its ranks. In many ways, that first graduate seminar with Carolyn long ago set the stage.

Notes

1 The full quote is, "National parks are the best idea we ever had. Absolutely American, absolutely democratic, they reflect us at our best rather than our worst."

2 National Park Service Act of 1916, 39 Stat. 535.

3 Ian Billick, Executive Director of RMBL, personal communication, June 2017. The many bands of Utes across western Colorado were forced onto reservations by the U. S. government in the 1870s and '80s (Simmons 2000).

4 Racial politics had a perhaps unexpected influence here; during the 1920s, Colorado politics were dominated by the Ku Klux Klan, including Denver's mayor Ben Stapleton, mostly encouraging sentiment against immigrants. Through their influence, a number of academics were fired, including the president of Western State College and Johnson as his "right hand man." Johnson successfully sued to be reinstated, based on his status as tenured faculty, and then promptly quit. Johnson had already established a campus-controlled field station in nearby Taylor Canyon called the Rocky Mountain Biological Station, but after his firing, was adamant that he would re-create the field facility as an independent organization so as not to be under the Klan's thumb. See "Former Dean Tells It Like It Was," in *Recollections of Western State College and Rocky Mountain Biological Laboratory*, John C. Johnson Jr. and Dorothy G. Johnson, eds., pp. 17–20.

5 *Prospects: The Rocky Mountain Biological Laboratory at Gothic*, published by the Board of Trustees of RMBL, 1977, p. 1.

6 John C. Johnson, "First Sight of Gothic," written August 24, 1963, reprinted in *Recollections of Western State College and Rocky Mountain Biological Laboratory*, John C. Johnson Jr. and Dorothy G. Johnson, eds., pp. 18 and 29, RMBL Archives.

7 It was originally called the Rocky Mountain Biological Station, re-using the same name as an earlier facility that Johnson established on Forest Service land in the Taylor Canyon and operated through Western State College. Officials at the college did not want Johnson to use the same name for his independent enterprise, and so within a year of its establishment, it was renamed as a Laboratory.

8 *Webster's New Collegiate Dictionary*, G. & C. Merriam Co., Publishers, Springfield, MA, 1956, p. 468.

9 Interview with RMBL Executive Director Ian Billick, June 24, 2014.

10 Dad's first summer of research was in 1962, when he met my mother. They were not at RMBL in the summer of 1964 when my sister was born, and he missed 1967 and '68 due to active duty in the Army; otherwise, he has spent at least part of every summer since then at Gothic.

11 billy's story has been made into a short film, titled "The Snow Guardian," featured on *The Atlantic*'s website: https://www.theatlantic.com/video/index/513374/snow-guardian-billy-barr/.

12 This particular study also represents the inter-generational aspect of research at RMBL, as co-authors David W. Inouye and Brian D. Inouye are father and son.

References

Billick, Ian. 2010. "Place-Based Database Management." Pp. 382–402 in Ian Billick and Mary Price, eds., *The Ecology of Place: Contributions of Place-Based Research to Ecological Understanding*. Chicago: University of Chicago Press.

Billick, Ian and Mary Price, eds. 2010. *The Ecology of Place: Contributions of Place-Based Research to Ecological Understanding*. Chicago: University of Chicago Press.

Charnley, Susan, Thomas E. Sheridan, and Gary P. Nabhan, eds. 2014. *Stitching the West Back Together: Conservation of Working Landscapes*. Chicago: University of Chicago Press.

Cronon, William. 1991. *Nature's Metropolis: Chicago and the Great West*. New York: W.W. Norton & Co.

Groth, Paul. 1997. "Frameworks for Cultural Landscape Study." Pp. 1–21 in Paul Groth and Todd Bressi, eds, *Understanding Ordinary Landscapes*. New Haven, CT: Yale University Pres.

Inouye, David W., billy barr, Kenneth B. Armitage, and Brian D. Inouye. 2000. "Climate Change is Affecting Altitudinal Migrants and Hibernating Species." *Proceedings of the National Academy of Sciences (USA)* 97:1630–1633.

Kohler, Robert E. 2002. *Landscapes and Labscapes: Exploring the Lab–Field Border in Biology*. Chicago: University of Chicago Press.

Langston, Nancy. 1995. *Forest Dreams, Forest Nightmares: The Paradox of Old Growth in the Inland West*. Seattle: University of Washington Press.

Lewis, Pierce. 1979. "Axioms for Reading the Landscape: Some Guides to the American Scene." Pp. 11–32 in D. W. Meinig, ed., *The Interpretation of Ordinary Landscapes*. New York: Oxford University Press.

Lopez, Barry. 1986. *Arctic Dreams: Imagination and Desire in a Northern Landscape*. New York: Charles Scribner's Sons.

Losos, Jonathan B. 2014. "What Darwin Got Wrong." *Chronicle of Higher Education*, January 20.

Marris, Emma. 2011. *Rambunctious Garden: Saving Nature in a Post-Wild World*. New York: Bloomsbury.

McEvoy, Arthur. 1987. "Toward an Interactive Theory of Nature and Culture: Ecology, Production, and Cognition in the California Fishing Industry." *Environmental Review* 11 (4, Winter):289–305.

Meinig, Donald. 1979. "The Beholding Eye: Ten Versions of the Same Scene." Pp. 33–48 in D. W. Meinig, ed., *The Interpretation of Ordinary Landscapes*. New York: Oxford University Press.

Merchant, Carolyn. 1980. *The Death of Nature: Women, Ecology, and the Scientific Revolution*. San Francisco, CA: HarperCollins.

Merchant, Carolyn. 1989. *Ecological Revolutions: Nature, Gender, and Science in New England*. Chapel Hill: The University of North Carolina Press.

Merchant, Carolyn. 1995. "Reinventing Eden: Western Culture as a Recovery Narrative." Pp. 132–159 in William Cronon, ed., *Uncommon Ground: Toward Reinventing Nature*. New York: W.W. Norton & Co.

Merchant, Carolyn. 2016. *Autonomous Nature: Problems of Prediction and Control from Ancient Times to the Scientific Revolution*. New York: Routledge.

McConnell Simmons, Virginia. 2000. *The Ute Indians of Utah, Colorado, and New Mexico*. Boulder: University of Colorado Press.

Philpott, William. 2013. *Vacationland: Tourism and Environment in the Colorado High Country*. Seattle: University of Washington Press.

Ruiz-Mallén, Isabel and Esteve Corbera. 2013. "Community-Based Conservation and Traditional Ecological Knowledge: Implications for Social-Ecological Resilience." *Ecology and Society* 18(4):12. Available on-line at www.ecologyandsociety.org/vol18/iss4/art12/

Spence, Mark David. 1999. *Dispossessing the Wilderness: Indian Removal and the Making of the National Parks*. New York: Oxford University Press.

Stegner, Wallace. 1983. "The Best Idea We Ever Had." *Wilderness* 46:4–13.

Vera, Franz. 2010. "The Shifting Baseline Syndrome in Restoration Ecology." Pp. 98–110 in Marcus Hall, ed., *Restoration and History: The Search for a Usable Environmental Past*. New York: Routledge.

Vetter, Jeremy. 2012. "Labs in the Field? Rocky Mountain Biological Stations in the Early Twentieth Century." *Journal of the History of Biology* 45(4, Winter):587–611.

Watt, Laura Alice. 2017. *The Paradox of Preservation: Wilderness and Working Landscapes at Point Reyes National Seashore*. Berkeley: University of California Press.

White, Richard. 1991. *The Middle Ground: Indians, Empires, and Republics in the Great Lakes Region, 1650–1815*. Cambridge University Press.

Worster, Donald. 1993. *The Wealth of Nature: Environmental History and the Ecological Imagination*. New York: Oxford University Press.

Wyckoff, William and Lary M. Dilsaver. 1995. "Defining the Mountainous West." Pp. 1–59 in William Wyckoff and Lary M. Dilsaver, eds, *The Mountainous West: Explorations in Historical Geography*. Lincoln: University of Nebraska Press.

13

THE SPIRITUAL POLITICS OF THE KENDENG MOUNTAINS VERSUS THE GLOBAL CEMENT INDUSTRY[1]

Dewi Candraningrum

Introduction: The Consequences of Cement Production in Indonesia and Beyond

The production of cement is potentially harmful to the environment. Mining has the potential to change the landscape, hydrologic cycles, and ecosystems more broadly. This threat is multiplied in heavily populated areas, because mines, factories, and the methods of producing cement require an enormous amount of energy and water, resulting in the seizure of resources by miners and corporations. Greenhouse gas emissions from cement production, through sintering limestone—the process of heating limestone and clay to 1,450 degrees centigrade with sand and iron ore—make up at least 5 percent of total global emissions, four times greater than the total global emissions produced by airplanes. Grinding sintered limestone with other materials (sand, limestone, ash, and gypsum) to produce cement results in additional side effects such as dust, smoke, air pollution around the cement factory, and toxic fumes, including nitrogen oxide and sulphur dioxide. These effects can cause major health problems if occurring in highly populated areas.

In regard to global warming and climate change triggered by human activity and the resulting natural disasters, the Kendeng Mountains Community Care Network (in Indonesian Jaringan Masyarakat Peduli Pegunugan Kedeng, or JMPPK), the public, and other stakeholders are asking the state, *"Pabrik Semen Kanggo Sopo?"* ("Cement factories for whom?"). Who will actually benefit from the construction of cement factories in the Kendeng Mountains? Is it for the health and well-being of the earth and ordinary people, for a handful of rich people, or may be even for overseas markets? Women from Kendang have been especially active in raising these questions and challenging the development narrative's valorization of progress. In 2016 several women cemented their feet into wooden boxes outside the presidential palace in Jakarta to protest mining and cement production. Their actions reverberate with Merchant's ecofeminist perspectives, which call upon women to lead an ecological revolution to restore planetary ecologies to health (Merchant 1980:xv).

The story of the protection of the Kendeng Mountains and the resistance against mining for cement, developed through ethnographic observation and interviews conducted between 2014 and 2017, tells how women have demonstrated subjectivity and agency, learned from their socio-cultural context, and developed ecological wisdom. They operate within what Merchant identifies as the organic worldview, compatible with an ecological perspective (Merchant 1980:95). These protesters' articulation of ecological language is intended to challenge isolated assumptions based in formal rational knowledge, which is sometimes dry and loses all ethical consideration of social and ecological justice. The practice of perceiving women's bodies as the manifestation of nature has given rise to social, communal, and situational conditions which have grown and evolved to this day and are intrinsically connected with the environment. An epistemic responsibility for the ecology of the Kendeng Mountains is passed down across generations of women; across the different geographical environments; and from the village to the city and the city to the village in a circular process. Not only are women concerned about the protection of the Kendeng

FIGURE 13.1 A view of the Kendeng Mountains.
Source: Image taken by the author on November 1, 2015.

Mountains, but so are men and other groups seeking social and environmental justice. As an ecofeminist scholar in Indonesia, I have found Merchant's work to be an invaluable lens through which to understand the effects of the spread of neo-liberalism and "modernity" through the complex processes of globalization. In this way, this ethnographic work in Indonesia provides further evidence of the veracity of Merchant's claims, while at the same time arguing for the continued relevance of her work.

Cement Production in Indonesia

Between 2009 and 2013, cement production increased approximately 50 percent in Indonesia due to large infrastructure projects and economic development. Economic analyses have stated that, in the near future, Indonesia is projected to be capable of fulfilling its own infrastructure needs. Since 2009, a number of cement factories have been built, with others still in the stages of planning. A few cement producers monopolize the market, including large international cement producers such as Heidelberg Cement and its offshoot company Indocement. The expansion of seaports is included in President Joko Widodo's strategy to strengthen Indonesia's capacity as a maritime state and to make Indonesia a global maritime hub. This strategy includes 24 strategic harbour projects and the expansion of 1,500 small ports, especially in Eastern Indonesia. Better connections with the east will also mean easier access to natural resources from the country's tropical rainforests. Forests throughout the Indonesian archipelago are threatened by this project if its purpose is to exploit the country's wealth of nature.

Statements released regarding cement production have been contradictory, suggesting that the cement will be utilized domestically, while in reality it is planned for export. Reports from the news outlet *Berita Satu* (online media) and press releases from Global Cement state that cement produced in Rembang is to be exported. Official statements that the production of cement will be utilized for domestic needs are contradicted by statements from the PT Semen Indonesia website, various national media reports, and Bloomberg. According to one *Berita Satu* report, "through the operation of six new factories, in 2016 the national cement industry has undergone an increase in production capacity of almost 30 percent. The total production capacity is 92 million tons, while domestic demand for cement is estimated to be around 65 million tons for this year" (Fitriani 2016). The Chairman of the Indonesian Cement Association (ASI), Widodo Santoso, stated that "The total capacity of cement factories ready to be operational this year is around 92 million tons, while demand is still far from the capacity," (Fitriani 2016). Despite this, he added that internal demand is still not able to offset the additional production capacity of the industry. Internal demand for cement within Indonesia is predicted to reach only 65 million tons, with a growth of 7.54 percent compared to the 60.44 million tons in the previous year. "For that reason, producers hope that the development of infrastructure will run smoothly, both in terms of the state budget as well as from the financial perspective of BUMN investors,"

FIGURE 13.2 PT Semen Indonesia.
Source: Photo taken by the author.

Santoso stated. "We are planning to arrange exports to Africa, Sri Lanka, Bangladesh, the Middle East, Australia, the Philippines, Papua New Guinea and East Timor," he explained. Based on data from ASI, the state's total cement exports in 2015 reached 100 million tons, up 280 percent from the previous year's 265.16 thousand tons. As many as 561.76 thousand tons of exports were in the form of cement, with the remaining 445.74 thousand consisting of clinker. A press release from Global Cement on February 25, 2016 stated that cement exported from Indonesia was to be taken from Rembang (Global Cement Staff 2016). This data states that the production of cement in Rembang is not planned to be utilized domestically but is instead for export. The international news agency Bloomberg also wrote that the overcapacity of cement production will be exported overseas, stating that PT Semen Indonesia is even interested in targeting markets in Australia (Dahrul and Suhartono 2016).

The Feminist Case of Cement Resistance in the Kendeng Mountains

The women from Kendeng sing *kidung* (a Javanese prayer song) each time they protest, in defiance of cement mines and factories throughout the Kendeng Mountains. *Kidung* is a chant of worship and prayer. The *kidung* sung during protests is dedicated to the giver of life, the creator of the universe, and is an appreciation of nature, the source of food and clean air, and the home of all humans, animals, and plants. *Kidung* is part of life for the women of Kendeng and is a reflection of their hopes and dreams. It is sung by these women during their daily activities, when working in the rice fields and terraces, while cooking or helping their children to study and when fighting for justice. In every ritual, the entire community joins in the singing of *kidung* to pray that Mother Earth will be everlasting. As a song of prayer, *kidung* usually follows the same form, referred to as *macapat* in the Javanese language. Each *macapat* has eight syllables and ends in either o, i, or u. *Macapat* represents the cycle and nature of human life, starting from birth and moving through childhood, adolescence, marriage, family life, and death (Luwih 2016). These *kidung* are also religiously sung to initiate protests in the North Kendeng Mountains.

On June 16, 2014, a number of women from Rembang, led by Sukinah (many Indonesians go by a single name), set up tents in front of the PT Semen Indonesia factory in Watu Putih, Kendeng Mountains, Rembang. Sukinah represents the phenomena of women's leadership that is often present in movements to challenge mining in Indonesia. Another powerful woman leader before her was Aleta Baun, who led the resistance against the marble mine in Mollo, NTT. Including Sukinah, nine other women rose from the movement to preserve the karst topography and biodiversity of the Kendeng Mountains: Sukinah, Sutini, Karsupi, Ambarwati, Surani, Deni, Murtini, Ngadinah, and Giyem. Each one cemented her feet into a wooden box outside the presidential palace in Jakarta. These nine women are referred to as the "Kartini Kendeng" because the grave of Kartini, an Indonesian feminist hero (who fought against girls' illiteracy and established schools for the peasants of Rembang), is less than three kilometres from the site of the cement plant in the Kendeng Mountains. Other influential women from Kabupaten [administrative district] Pati in Kendeng are Gunarti and Paini. Gunarti, from Sukolilo in Kabupaten Pati is relentless in caring for the community and teaching local residents how to protect and preserve the earth. Paini, from Kecamatan Tambakromo in Kabupaten Pati, is the only woman to have opposed through the process of litigation the establishment of the cement industry and mines and is the only woman mentioned in the lawsuit involving the cement factory, whose biggest investor comes from Germany.

The organic karst, water, and the biodiversity of Kendeng are all threatened by large-scale mining projects. The karst mountains in Kendeng stretch across Kabupaten [administrative districts] Blora, Rembang, Grobogan, Pati, and Kudus (Central Java) as well as Tuban (East Java). Their presence is crucial to the life of the local community. The excavation of the karst not only effects the ecology but also deprives farmers of their land and destroys their livelihood. The karst in Kabupaten Tuban has already been damaged from large-scale mining by the cement industry, and residents are forced to pay dearly for this with long droughts, which destroy agricultural production and produce widespread poverty resulting from the destruction of the ecology and ecosystems of the Kendeng Mountains (Vaessen 2017).

"The Kendeng karst gives us life," said one citizen (interview on August 6, 2016). "Not only for farmers and children who can play in nature, but also for the plants and birds," explained Gunarti. The Kendeng Karst is part of Mother Earth and the forests on top of the karst in Kendeng have important significance in the densely populated region because the forest functions as a buffer and water catchment area. The karst region also functions as a carbon sink against global warming, meaning that limestone mines in the karst region are at risk of increasing the rate of carbon emissions in the surrounding regions. If the karst is used up, Central Java will continue to heat up as the absorption rate of carbon declines. There are more than 200,000 people in South Pati whose livelihoods depend on the Kendeng Mountains. There are 112 relatively stable water springs in the regions of Grobogan and Sukolilo, Pati, which serve as a water source for thousands of families and fields in Sukolilo. The actual number of springs is estimated to be far greater, including those yet to be discovered, as explained by Gunretno (leader of Samin Sedulur Sikep indigenous community).

The Kendeng Mountains are of global importance to bats, birds, and butterflies. An endemic species of bat, instrumental in protecting the ecological balance, lives here, as do many species of birds, for example the beautiful green peacock, butterflies, and dragonflies. Migratory birds from North Asia come to this region to avoid the cold winters in their homelands or to use Kendeng as a corridor for further migration. Because of the importance of the Kendeng Mountains as a migration route for birds, the karst must be protected. Accordingly, Karyadi Baskoro from the University of Diponegoro has written that, "Indonesia is an important region for migratory birds, where birds from around the world come in search of the suitable climate of countries along the equator. For this purpose, only a few countries are a consideration, so if an area is a migration corridor for birds it must be protected" (interview with Baskoro 2016).

Apart from its ecological richness, the Kendeng Mountains hold immeasurable cultural riches scattered throughout the limestone mountains. The archaeological site Dampo Awang in Kecamatan Tambakromo is an ancient temple and the tomb of Sunan, and a cultural site for puppetry in Kecamatan Sukolilo and Kecamatan North Kayen, Kendeng. The karst and caves are sites for prehistoric research, with the Kendeng region containing an abundance of fossils, which are useful in the search for knowledge about the evolution of humans and the ancient history of human migration.

Considering the abundance of wealth in the Kendeng Mountains, academics have lobbied to raise awareness about Kendeng directly to President Jokowi's government. On December 29, 2015, Soeryo Abdiwibowo from IPB led the Forum for Teachers, Researchers, and Observers of Agriculture, the Environment, and Culture to submit a petition to the President of the Republic of Indonesia concerning the Ecological and Social Crisis in Java, focusing on the protection of the Kendeng Mountains. The petition was signed by more than 258 academics, cultural specialists, activists, feminists, and sympathizers for the plight of the Kendeng Mountains, all of whom are influential in Indonesia and come from almost all of the leading universities in Indonesia. However, the major activist story here comes from a group of female activists in the region.

The JMPPK sued PT SMS in the administrative court of Semarang, with PT SMS losing the court case, which was ended on November 17, 2015. The court case followed the 2015 allegations made by the plaintiff Paini concerning the ecological, cultural, and economic impacts arising from disregard for the karst system and a proper analysis of the environmental impacts of the mine.

It is impossible to maintain productive farmland without the support of the hundreds of water sources that flow from the Kendeng Mountains, which, according to local people, contain a magic that flows all the way to the east. The strong influence of this water in providing life in Rembang drove hundreds of women from the village of Tegaldowo to raise tents in opposition to PT Semen Indonesia. One woman describes the protest scene well:

> There were 85 women in the forest protesting, the men were only the brothers, and six people documenting. I didn't understand when the police or Intel asked, "Who is the field coordinator here?" I didn't understand and I wasn't the field coordinator, but I said "yes" anyway. Actually, when they said field coordinator they meant the leader. The night before we held a meeting. I told my family, "rather than suffer in the future, it is better for us to suffer now if we are the ones to bear it. The important thing is for our grandchildren to prosper." And the women were prepared. We left at six in the morning on Legi, Monday, July 16 and set up tents with all the women. After that we went to the tents. It had to be women so there would be no causalities, because we anticipated that the army would come, so it was just women (who protested). I was the one who taught them, and asked to speak to Pati. It was scary because there were lots of military for about a week. For a week, we didn't wash at all. Just our faces, and food was brought from home. We got water from home too, but it wasn't much. We didn't leave the tent at all, because as soon as we left we were chased by the police. Yeah, all women. Some of the husbands came, at night (to the tent). On top of the 85 women, there could be hundreds in the tent. I couldn't count them, but I guess there were hundreds, because they kept coming. But when the protest began there were only the 85 of us. Friends of Pati (who were working behind the scenes) warned us against inciting violence, so there were always women. Mbak Esti, Pak Jum, and Mbak Mimin were actively in charge of the tents.
>
> *(Interview with Sukinah on October 28, 2016 in Randublatung, Blora)*

The water sources that she talks about were carried in Javanese jugs (*kendi-kendi*), which were stored and managed in *Simbar Wareh* in Omah Kendeng in the North Kendeng Mountains (Kabupaten Pati, Kabupaten Grobogan and Kabupaten Blora).

The name of each water source was written on the side of each jug, but there are still many which have not been documented from Rembang, Lasem, and Tuban. Each spring has its own history: folktales, myths, beliefs, and convictions that are handed down from generation to generation. The traditional community, SAMIN Sedulur Sikep, have protected this local knowledge since before the modern Indonesian state was born. Samin Surosentika is recorded as the oldest farmer resistance movement in Southeast Asia, which resisted Dutch colonial powers. It later evolved into a spiritual movement, which, through members' identities as farmers, placed the earth and the water at the centre of the universe (Widodo 1997).

However, on August 2, 2016, the mayor of Pati and Indocement won back their claim in the administrative court of Surabaya. The judge of the administrative court of Surabaya granted the appeal of the regional government of Pati and PT SMS on July 14, 2016 (Lismanto 2016). In addition to requiring 22,025 hectares of karst land to mine limestone, PT SMS will also sacrifice 663 hectares of productive farmland for the mining of clay as a raw material for cement, and another 180 hectares of farmland for the construction of the factory.

In response to a question from Marianne Klute from "Save the Rainforest, Berlin," a spokesperson from Heidelberg Cement stated that the Pati project had already been agreed upon by all relevant parties. However, in reality the residents were not included in the planning. The traditional rights of Sedulur Sikep Samin and other local residents, who are majority Muslim, were not acknowledged or

FIGURE 13.3 Javanese water jugs.
Source: Photo taken by the Author.

respected. Heidelberg Cement simply responded to local concerns about shortages of water and drought—which will destroy their livelihood—by proposing to provide residents with jerry-cans of water. The organic karst, water, and biodiversity of Kendeng are all threatened by large-scale mining projects.

From Resource to Partnership

The earth and the soil which we are discussing are not dead entities. This argument is based on an understanding of other-than-human creatures and their own narratives as valid and legitimate. Anthropology, as the collision of human-centred symbols, reinforces acknowledging the diversity of worldviews other than our own, which have until now been considered foreign. Our semiotic systems need to adopt a form and modality that truly acknowledges the aliveness of nature and takes a critical approach to human-only centered anthropology (Kohn 2013). Thinking from a point of view other than that of humankind also indicates what we are capable of sharing with creatures other than ourselves through symbols. Animals and biodiversity of the earth, water, and air are all part of a web of life; all are constitutively and symbolically aware and interdependent. Thus, humans will be able to discard the notion of complete otherness towards things other than ourselves, which is a notion detrimental to our own livelihoods. *Ibu Bhumi wes maringi, ibu Bhumi dilarani, ibu Bhumi kang ngadili* in Javanese means that the earth has already given much, the earth has been hurt, the earth will condemn. As one informant stated,

> This is also happening in my hometown, because they underestimate the earth, and in the end make it hard for themselves, when the profits start shrinking. Better yields come to those who value the earth. Is it like that here?
> *(Interview with Gunretno on June 29, 2016, Rembang Tent)*

For Gunarti (a woman who leads the Samin Sedulur Sikep indigenous community), the earth has its own self, independent of human intervention. The ethics of partnership and equality between the earth and humans are strongly upheld in Gunarti's sense of spirituality. This view, which Merchant expresses with the idea of nature as autonomous, is real and legitimate. This idea is what gave rise to the socio-cultural environmental ethic that colors the preservation movement of the Kendeng Mountains.

> The depictions of natures-cultures, nonhuman nature, and posthuman nature all contain insights into a new relationship between humanity and nature based on the idea of autonomous nature. Autonomous nature stems from *natura creans/naturans* as the self-acting, self-creating nature of past philosophies in which nature is both creating and rebellious, predictable and unpredictable, lawful and unlawful. Autonomous nature is the nature at the root of chaos theory. And it is the nature at the edge of order and chaos in

complexity theory. ... Order and chaos, linear and nonlinear, natures-cultures, and human/nonhuman all exist and interact in the everyday world of the twenty-first century. Autonomous nature is the nature at the root of the new chaos and complexity paradigm in which humans and nonhuman nature must exist together and thrive.

(Merchant 2016:161)

The protesters raise important questions such as: Are we humans allowed to cut into mountains, trees, water reservoirs, predominantly for our own needs? Are humans allowed to divorce themselves and leave the earth trodden on? (See Kenneth Worthy's Chapter 2 in this volume) Does the earth truly live and grow? How do the farmers throughout the Kendeng Mountains perceive the earth and the water? How does Gunarti view the earth?

I see it like this. If it is bought up by other people and then just thrown aside, it will be excavated by people who don't care about the environment. It is different with people who care for the environment. They let it be (without changing it), because they feel that other living things also have rights. There was the belief when I went to Sukolilo; the landowners there who were selling their land, they believed: this is my land, my right. Even for land which is just clay, I also think that; with the excuse of rights, excuse of selling. They feel like they have an abundance of resources, so they sell it. It shouldn't be like that: "I was here first, I also look after you, it has to be protected". ... Modern education is Western, but we are living beings, that is the difference. Maybe people these days don't want to do it anymore, or only think of the short-term benefits.

(Interview with Gunarti, June 30, 2016)

This critique from Gunarti (and other similar ones) coincides with and strengthens Merchant's critique of Modernity's understanding of nature as "dead". In addition to Merchant's critique from within the tradition, this critique from without also helps to locate Modern understandings of the world as but one understanding. Gunarti's view also includes a sense of the sacredness of nature, which is largely lost in the project of Modernity.

The word *bhumi* in Sanskrit and the Vedas scriptures is used to describe a goddess, the goddess of the earth. A personification of the earth, she is depicted as a dark-skinned woman with four arms who rides an elephant while carrying four pomegranates, a pitcher of water, a bowl of vegetables, and a bowl of spices (Nagaran 2011). She represents a source of food and fertility always ready to serve humanity. According to Gunarti, the water has a voice and can protest if humans arbitrarily exploit it. For her, the earth is one, organic, and inseparable, even when human ownership written on paper certificates exist. This is what encouraged farmers throughout the Kendeng Mountains to prevent themselves from selling land to anyone, except if that person truly understands the nature of the earth (*ngelmu lemah*). Specifically, this means that they will leave it in its natural condition, tend to it, and use it with good intentions in a way that blends human welfare with nature. From this perspective, mining and the poisonous pollution of factories are considered to be in opposition to *ngelmu lemah*. Gunarti is not the only one holding such a vision—entire movements are fuelled by such visions of nature in Indonesia.

One group enacting such a movement is the *Simbar Wareh* of the Kendeng Mountains. At the foot of the Kendeng Mountains live the Samin (or Sedulur Sikep) community, as they call themselves. They speak a local dialect of Javanese and preserve their traditions and culture (Maran 2000). The Samin community emerged in the nineteenth century as a social movement in opposition to Dutch colonization (Mumfangati 2009). This fight was a non-violent struggle, where independent agriculture and freedom was chosen over the pressures of the state (Sukmana 2003; Warsito 2001). Until now their relationship with nature has continued to be built upon by their thoughts and actions, which are both united and ecologically oriented. Since 2008 the Samin community has lived in struggle against the cement industry and the state. They are aware that the excavation of the Kendeng Mountains will mean the end of their livelihoods. Women play an important role in fighting for ecological integrity, through managing and tending to nature (Griffin 1978; Young 1990). Gunarti is part of the *Simbar Wareh*, a group of women concerned about the environment (Kelompok Perempuan Peduli Lingkungan—KPPL) who on February 13, 2009 joined the JMPPK. The Simbar Wareh was founded by Gunarti (the sister of head of the JMPPK, Gunretno). The name *Simbar Wareh* was inspired by two water springs, Simbarjoyo (Kecamatan Kayen) and Gua Wareh (Kecamatan Sukolilo). *Simbar* means to give water, and *wareh* means water itself. These names reflect the importance of water in local culture. Local analysis of the issues linking water, forest destruction, and cement production raise questions such as: Can water think? Does water, as a "living thing" have the most basic right to continue its cycle of life? As humans follow their cycle of life, they have a number of wishes including being able to survive. Are these two things not the same? Or are humans superior to water, and allowed to arbitrarily exploit water and determine its flow and cycle? Through this community Gunarti gathered and traveled from village to village to spread understanding about the importance of protecting the earth. According to Gunarti, women are those worst affected if cement factories are built, because women use more water than men in taking care of their households, farms, and livestock. This reinforces Merchant's argument (and the argument of ecofeminism more generally) that the oppression of women and the oppression of nature are inextricably linked.

The leadership of the JMPPK, headed by Gunarti's brother Gunretno, is organic. There is no organizational structure. They are transparent and do not receive donations or funding. The network they are building is based on beliefs about the protection of the Kendeng Mountains that extend across five *kabupaten* in Central Java: Rembang, Blora, Grobogan, Pati, and Kudus. Merchant states in *The Death of Nature* (hereafter *TDN*),

> Organic community ... growing out of peasant experience and village culture, was based on the leveling of differences and stressed, instead, the primacy of community, the collective will of the people, and the idea of internal self-regulation and consent. Here the communal whole was still greater and more important than the sum of the parts, but the parts were of equal or nearly equal value.
>
> *(Merchant 1980:76)*

This description holds true for the JMPKK. Members of JMPPK also include many Samin indigenous community members and individuals from Kecamatan Tambakromo and Kayen, as well as people from all throughout the Kendeng Mountains, the majority of whom are Muslim, including Sukinah and the other nine Kartini Kendeng women. Since the start of the conflict around mining and the protection of the environment, Gunretno has been traveling from village to village, conducting advocacy and meetings. He sows an awareness in surrounding communities about the importance of the Kendeng Mountain's richness as a source of water and protector of biodiversity. Gunretno's knowledge is not limited to matters of the karst, but also covers the issues of climate change and global warming. This knowledge is what encouraged Gunretno to inspire important women to become leaders throughout the Kendeng Mountains. He does not just care for Kendeng but encourages women to be seamstresses of knowledge among the villages and become the vanguard of the resistance movement against the destruction of nature. A few women who hold particular importance in the resistance are Paini dan Gunarti dari Pati, Sukinah dari Rembang dan Sutini, Giyem, Karsupi, Deni, Surani, Ambarwati, Murtini, and Ngadinah, who come from throughout the Kendeng Mountains. On April 13, 2016, it was they who encased their feet in cement in front of the presidential palace to attract widespread public attention for their cause.

In addition to direct action, in 2015 the JMPPK carried out litigation against the cement companies, and they were victorious for the people. Gunretno, as head of the JMPPK, stated that for the cement investors, "their minds only hold a narrow vision in the name of 'investment' which will clearly only lead to the suppression of the lives of all people and farmers in the Kendeng Mountains." He later expanded,

> The North Kendeng Mountains is a karst region which stretches across Kabupatens [administrative districts] Tuban, Rembang, Blora, Grobogan, Pati, and Kudus. The preservation of the North Kendeng Mountains is non-negotiable for us farmers. Not only for the preservation of our arable land,

which is also our identity, but also for the sake of protecting the ecosystem, which guarantees a supply of clean water and continues human life and the life of all creatures, not only in Central Java but throughout Java.

(Interview with Gunretno, June 6, 2016)

This movement that stretches across gender/sex, religious, and other boundaries models the type of organic community and action that Merchant writes of in *TDN* and that was common in Europe (and elsewhere) prior to the seventeenth century.

Ecofeminist Ethics in Indonesia: A Brief History

The strong presence of women in the fight to save the Kendeng Mountain region can be traced back genealogically over five centuries to a time when a woman was the sultan of the region. Queen Kalinyamat ruled the Kalinyamat Sultanate from 1546–1579. Ratu Kalinyamat was not a pacifist queen; she led battles against the Portuguese Armada on various occasions. The Portuguese writer, Diego de Couto, referred to her as *Rainha de Japara, senhora paderosa e rica* (Queen Kalinyamat, a rich and powerful woman). During the 30-year period between 1549 and 1579, the sultanate reached the height of its glory in the maritime world. She not only built ports but drove away a Portuguese Armada twice from the Maluku islands. In 1550 and 1574 she sent 4,000 soldiers from Jepara in 40 ships to assist the Sultan of Johor in freeing Maluku (the treasured "spice islands") from Europe (Hayati 2000). Even though they were forced to withdraw, the bravery of Queen Kalinyamat was impressive. This example of Queen Kalinyamat is always present in Sukinah's dreams. Leading attacks not only in Maluku, but once again against the Portuguese in Ambon in 1565, was *rainha de Japara, senhora poderosa e rica, de kranige Dame* (The queen of Jepara, a woman who is rich and strong, a brave woman). This was a time women sultanates were prominent not only in Aceh but also along the north coast of Java. The sultanate under the rule of Queen Kencana (maiden name Queen Kalinyamat) included Jepara, Kudus, Pati, Juwana, Rembang, and Mataram (Hayati 2000). Queen Kencana's strength and determination to protect is echoed by the women currently leading the protection movement of the Kendeng Mountains, their history deeply tied to the history of the northern coast of Java, particularly the coast of Jepara, Pati, and Rembang.

From a genealogical perspective, historical artefacts and manuscripts highlight many important women who had been leaders in this region, even before the arrival of the Dutch. In the latter half of the nineteenth century Kartini was born. In Indonesia, April 21 has been commemorated as Kartini Day since 1964. Her grave is located not far from Sukinah's tent. Kartini died at 25 years of age, after giving birth to her first child, and left behind the legacy of her struggle for women's literacy, education, and leadership. Her spirit in fighting for justice and equality for women is a historical narrative of Indonesian women who cannot be separated from the contemporary issues faced by Sukinah in resisting ecological inequality in the Cekungan

Air Tanah Watu Putih region, which will continue to be threatened if not preserved. The genealogical connection between Kartini and Sukinah is depicted in Kartini's resting place, which is in close proximity to the proposed site for the PT Semen Indonesia factory, and where Sukinah and hundreds of women from Kendeng raised tents as the protectors of the Kendeng people's livelihood.

Conclusion

This partial and brief explanation of the genealogy of women's leadership around the Kendeng Mountains, which actually extends back in recorded history at least as far as the sixteenth century, depicts the ethics of ecofeminism (Cuomo 1997; Shiva 1990). Ecofeminist ethics is not, then, a new phenomenon. Its roots can be traced back far into the long history of Indonesia (and other places to be sure). The struggle to defend ecological and human equality has been vigorously fought under the leadership of women. Merchant has been working hard to highlight and lift up such sources of eco-feminist ethics around the world, and this example could easily sit alongside those others she champions in her book *Earthcare: Women and the Environment* (Merchant 1986).

The connection of women with Kendeng ecology is bridged through their existen-tial identity as women via their bodies, the earth, their desire for reproductive morals, and their history. Merchant challenged the use of reproduction—hormones, men-struation, and pregnancy—as justification for the economic (and other) dependence of women upon men. She argues that economic dependency on the part of women was brought about in the seventeenth-century transition from subsistence to capitalist modes of production (Merchant 1980:163). This historical perspective can be used to empower the Kartini Kendeng women, who continue to grow even outside of the Kendeng Mountains. After the nine Kartini Kendeng cemented their feet in front of the palace in 2016, in the afternoon when the cement was broken, a rainbow appeared above the palace, emotionally moving the media and participants of the action.

Ecofeminism is rooted in feminist activism in opposing the institutionalized oppression and exploitation which is destroying ecosystems (Biehl 1991; Heller 1999). From a philosophical perspective, ecofeminism was born from previous forms of feminism, in particular those that focused on the value of caring (Mer-chant 1986). It also emerged from spiritual feminism that then politically manifested in movements to protect the forest, mountains, nature, animals, and biodiversity (Gaard 2010; Mallory 2010; Spretnak 1982). Environmental justice is a vital ele-ment of ecofeminism, which depicts an independent and sustainable life. Protectors and activists of ecofeminism are not only women, but also include among their number male feminists, as my research laid out in this chapter suggests. This brand of ecofeminism in Indonesia includes what Merchant calls "spiritual ecology."

> Spiritual ecology, like deep ecology, is a product of a profound sense of crisis in the ways that twentieth-century humans relate to the environment. Like deep ecology it focuses on the transformation of consciousness, especially

religious and spiritual consciousness. Recognizing the importance of some form of religious experience or worship in the lives of most people, spiritual ecologists attempt to develop new ways of relating to the planet that entail not an ethic of domination, but one of partnership with nature. Religious ideas create strong moods and motivations that act as an ecocentric ethic, guiding individuals and social movements toward new modes of behavior. The ideas of spiritual ecologists thus motivate individuals active in green ecological and ecofeminist social movements. Through rituals, a sense of reverence for nature can arise, thereby centering people for social action.

(Merchant 2005:118)

Accordingly, environmental protection should not (and perhaps cannot) only take the form of political action, but should also include everyday rituals and worship. The ecological preservation carried out by the people of the Kendeng Mountains has become a kind of spiritual practice and cannot be understood within the paradigm of modern advocacy, which relies too heavily on technocratic measures alone. In their opposition to the global cement industry, the ecofeminist activists of the Kendeng Mountains can be used as an instructive example of the ways spiritual ecology and partnership ethics might help promote the flourishing of life in the planetary future.

Note

1 Translated by Bryanna Wilson.

References

Alaimo, Stacy. 2000. *Undomesticated Ground: Recasting Nature as Feminist Space.* Ithaca, NY: Cornell University Press.

Biehl, Janet. 1991. *Rethinking Ecofeminist Politics.* Cambridge, MA: South End Press.

Cuomo, Christine J. 1997. *Feminism and Ecological Communities: An Ethic of Flourishing.* London: Routledge.

Dahrul, Fathiya and Harry Suhartono. 2016. "Indonesia's Biggest Cement Firm Looks Offshore Amid Glut at Home." Bloomberg.com. Last accessed September 22, 2017: www.bloomberg.com/news/articles/2016-06-21/indonesia-s-biggest-cement-firm-look s-offshore-amid-glut-at-home

Fitriani, Eva. 2016. "Industri Semen Kelebihan Kapasitas Produksi 30%." In *Berita Satu.* Last accessed September 22, 2017 www.beritasatu.com/ekonomi/349635-industri-sem en-kelebihan-kapasitas-produksi-30.html

Gaard, Greta. 2010. "New Directions for Ecofeminism: Toward a More Feminist Eco-Criticism." *ISLE: Interdisciplinary Studies in Literature and Environment* 17(4):1–23.

Global Cement Staff. 2016. "Semen Indonesia Net Profit Drops by 18.7% to US $337m in 2015." Last accessed September 22, 2017 www.globalcement.com/news/item/4653-semen-indonesia-net-profit-drops-by-18-7-to-us-337m-in-2015

Griffin, Susan. 1978. *Woman and Nature: The Roaring Inside Her.* New York: Harper & Row.

Hayati, dkk. 2000. *Peranan Ratu Kalinyamat di Jepara pada abad XVI.* Jakarta: Proyek.

Heller, Chaia. 1999. *Ecology of Everyday Life: Rethinking the Desire for Nature.* Montreal: Black Rose Books.

Kohn, Eduardo. 2013. *How Forests Think: Toward an Anthropology Beyond the Human.* Berkeley, CA: University of California Press.

Lismonto. 2016. "Breaking News: Pemkab Pati Menang di PTTUM Surabaya, Pabrik Semen Akan Berdiri." In MuriaNewsCom (August 2, 2016). Last accessed September 22, 2017 www.murianews.com/2016/08/02/89955/breaking-news-pemkab-pati-mena ng-di-pttun-surabaya-pabrik-semen-akan-berdiri.html

Luwih, Dalang Tri. 2016. Personal Interview. (August 5, 2016).

Mallory, Chaone. 2010. "The Spiritual Is Political: Gender, Spirituality, and Essentialism in Forest Defense." *Journal for the Study of Religion, Nature, and Culture* 4(1):48–71.

Maran, Rafael R. 2000. *Manusia dan Kebudayaan dalam Perspektif Ilmu Budaya Dasar.* Jakarta: PT Rineka.

Merchant, Carolyn. 1980. *The Death of Nature: Women, Ecology and the Scientific Revolution.* New York: Harper & Row.

Merchant, Carolyn. 1986. *Earthcare: Women and the Environment.* New York: Routledge.

Merchant, Carolyn. 2005. *Radical Ecology: The Search for a Liveable World.* New York: Routledge.

Merchant, Carolyn. 2016. *Autonomous Nature: Problems of Prediction and Control From Ancient Times to the Scientific Revolution.* New York: Routledge.

Mumfangati, Titi. 2009. *Kearifan Lokal di Lingkungan Masyarakat Samin Kabupaten Blora Jawa Tengah.* Yogyakarta: Kementrian Kebudayaan dan Pariwisata.

Nagaran, Vijaya Rettakudi. 2001. "Soil as the Goddess Bhudevi in a Tamil Women's Ritual." In *Women as Sacred Custodians of the Earth: Women, Spirituality and the Environment,* Alaine Low and Soraya Tremayne, eds. New York: Bergham Books.

Shiva, Vandana. 1990. "Development as a New Project of Western Patriarchy." Pp. 189–200 in *Reweaving the World: The Emergence of Ecofeminism,* ed. Irene Diamond and Gloria Feman Orenstein. San Francisco, CA: Sierra Club Books.

Spretnak, Charlene, ed. 1982. *The Politics of Women's Spirituality.* New York: Anchor/ Doubleday.

Sukmana, Oman. 2003. "Proses Perubahan Sosial Budaya Masyarakat Samin." In Nurudin dkk, ed. *Agama Tradisional: Potret Kearifan Hidup Masyarakat Samin dan Tengger.* Yogyakarta: LKIS.

Vaessen, Step. 2017. "Indonesians Take 'Concrete Stand' Against Cement Plant." Aljazeera.com. Last accessed September 22, 2017 www.aljazeera.com/video/news/2017/ 04/indonesian-farmers-oppose-cement-plant-construction-170405075148418.html

Warsito. 2001. *Pergeseran Sosial Budaya Masyarakat Samin.* Master's thesis, University of Muhammadiyah Malang.

Widodo, Amrih. 1997. "Samin in The New Order. The Politics of Encounter and Isolation." In *Imagining Indonesia: Cultural Politics and Political Culture.* Monographs in International Studies. Canberra: Australian National University (ANU).

Young, Iris Marion. 1990. "The Five Faces of Oppression." Pp. 39–65 in *Throwing Like a Girl and Other Essays in Feminist Philosophy and Social Theory.* Bloomington: Indiana University Press.

14

TOWARD A POLITICAL ECOLOGY OF ENVIRONMENTAL DISCOURSE

Yaakov Garb

Entry

In the early 80s, I wrote an undergraduate thesis on "The Uses and Misuses of the Whole Earth Image," a critical examination of the implications of the late 1960s color NASA photograph of the full earth that had become the iconic image of the environmental movement. This arose out of my puzzlement at the apparent disjunction between the environmentalist embrace of this image and its intrinsic features (a panoptic, distant, technologically-mediated rendition of the planet from the outside). My sense of epistemic problems intrinsic to this positioning was boosted by the explosion of non-environmental uses of the images in the media. Objectifying and often violent portrayals—the Earth controlled, straddled, squeezed, and trampled—swamped the compassionate icons of Earth embraced that appeared in environmentalist materials.

To better understand the epistemic disjuncture the NASA image offered and represented, I began thinking about and looking at premodern and alternative earth imagery, reading eclectically in ethnographic, literary, and philosophical literatures. Among these, of course, was Carolyn Merchant's *The Death of Nature: Women, Ecology, and the Scientific Revolution* (hereafter *TDN*), which examines the historical contexts of an earlier analogous shift of sensibility entailed by the emergence of a mechanical worldview.

At that time I lived only a couple of miles away from the Sausalito houseboat where Stewart Brand was running the *Whole Earth Catalog* and folding its spinoff magazine the *CoEvolution Quarterly* into the *Whole Earth Review*. The *Catalog* was a quintessential 1960s effort: a combination of counterculture magazine and product review catalog, specializing in self-sufficiency, ecology, DIY (Do It Yourself), whole systems, nomadics, and alternative education. Its title came from a public campaign Brand had initiated to have NASA release the "Whole Earth" image, which he sensed would galvanize a sense of wonderment, care, and shared destiny. This image would become the sole and central frontispiece on the large format first edition of the *Catalog*.[1] I was curious to pose my ideas about the icon's split impulses to the man who had launched the image into popular cul- ture, so introductions were somehow made, and I showed up on Brand's houseboat with my thesis and its accompanying binder of images. I emerged with his request that I write a version of the essay for the *Whole Earth Review*.[2]

Looking back at this now, over thirty years later, I see the editor, Kevin Kelly, describing this encounter in his introduction to the published essay (Garb 1985:18), as follows:

> A totem, as the Cree Indians named it, is an ally. As an ally the image of the whole Earth has served well, and seems to have enough medicine left in it to continue as our cover totem. "Pssssst," said an accented stranger in our office, "would you like to see my picture collection?" Sure. So we stood transfixed as he flipped through an album of battered whole Earth images, a selection of which is reproduced here. Evidences of our totem defiled? The curator of this exhibit is iconoclast Yaakov Garb, born in South Africa, raised in Jer- usalem, and recently graduated at World College West, Novato, CA, with something like this article as his thesis. He asks, "which department of a university should I apply to, to continue this type of research?" Good question.

Well, the answer to that question turned out to be Berkeley, and, specifically, the tutelage of Carolyn Merchant, who after seeing the same paper and binder of images, took me in and became my main doctoral advisor.

A generation later, the opportunity to look back at my work through the lens of an edited volume focused on Carolyn's *opus* makes clear to me how formative that decision was. I see the themes and sensibilities absorbed during my studies with Carolyn and in my training at Berkeley as a continuous thread through my work and academic preoccupations in the decades that followed. These tackled, in ever-widening circles, the political and material formation and influence of environmental (and environmentalist) imagery, with gender pervasively present as one of the key nodes for this co-constitution of imagery and social power. My chapter therefore maps these influences and preoccupations with the intent of contributing to a "Political Ecology of Environmental Discourse."

Berkeley Years

When I enrolled at Berkeley, Carolyn's appointment was in Conservation and Resource Studies, which did not offer a doctorate, but I was able to piece toge- ther an interdisciplinary thesis with Carolyn as my advisor, and her office became the center of my Berkeley studies. For someone with broad interests in both the scientific and social dimensions of environmental issues, this was a remarkable time to be at Berkeley. Just three minutes' walk east from Giannini Hall, where I was soaking up Carolyn's courses, was the Department of Geography, where I also took courses. A few minutes to the south I took courses in biology, and with faculty who introduced me to the emerging field of the sociology of science, a domain made accessible and intriguing to me through *TDN*. [3] Less accessible to me then, but still always in the background, were the field-based political ecologies being developed by people such as Michael Watts, Nancy Peluso, and Peter Taylor.

On the other side of the lectern, I was a teaching assistant in Carolyn's courses, as well as in Alan Miller's sweeping and fiery "Introduction to Environmental Issues." During the year when Carolyn was on sabbatical (gathering data for her New England book, I think) I taught her "Environmental Philosophy and Ethics" course. This tame title belied the course's much more complex social and political content. The course reader (in hindsight the template for *Radical Ecology*) began with the canonical works of environmental philosophers such as Baird Callicott,[4] Robin Attfield, John Passmore, Tom Regan, Holmes Rolston III,[5] Peter Singer, Christopher Stone, and Paul Taylor, who pushed the boundaries of a homocentric worldview within a conventional philosophical idiom. But then, after these frameworks were respectfully discussed, the course (at least in my mind) really took off, in both the thematic and ballistic senses of the phrase.

My intellectual identity for the coming decade was shaped by the terror and exhilaration of teaching this course as a graduate student, which demanded that I carefully work my way line-by-line through these course readings, and through Merchant's *TDN* (1980) and *Ecological Revolutions: Nature, Gender, and Science in New England* (1989). I owe much of (and imagine some of my students must now curse) the courage I gained from Carolyn's example in assigning rigorous but sometimes nigh indigestible foundational readings in her courses. My academic boot camp was, surely, sitting alone in front of thirty smart Berkeley undergraduates to explicate O'Connor's (O'Connor 1988) uncompromising and stern reworking of Marxist theory into his Second Contradiction of Capitalism (the forces and relations of production will undermine the conditions of production) or David Harvey's (Harvey 1979) comparison of the stances of Malthus, Ricardo, and Marx on the population and resources question as an example of a dialectical materialist critique of scientific neutrality.

Beyond the classroom, Carolyn herself exemplified the diverse and engaged ways in which academia could be expressed (and introduced me to others who did so, too). She steered me toward David Kubrin, a historian of science turned anti-nuclear protestor, who knew his Newton inside out (Kubrin 1981) but who would also put hexes on the nearby Livermore National Laboratory. And she introduced me to James O'Conner, a Marxist sociologist-economist who, alongside his grounded analyses of the fiscal crisis of the state, was involved in the minutiae of local environmental politics and protest, and established a vibrant journal and network of students who helped launch the field of Marxist or political ecology.

"Political ecology" had surfaced as a notion in the work of Eric Wolfe and Piers Blaikie, but it was in this period that O'Conner and others yoked the structural analysis offered by Marxism to the environmental domain. This allowed a principled analysis of how power structures drove environmental destruction by shaping (indeed, requiring) an uneven allocation of access, benefits, and harms involved in processes of extraction and production, and their evolution and expansion. The phrase rapidly grew into a field that was both punchy yet supple enough to bind together a range of work being done in development studies, geography, anthropology and sociology. This perspective began to inform my readings of environmentalist imagery and discourse, which had begun with my ambivalence about the "whole earth image" as an environmentalist icon.

Several kinds of training from Carolyn and at Berkeley shaped my approach to both parts of the equation embodied in this chapter's title, "the political ecology of environmentalist discourse." On the one hand, the trenchant critiques of liberal environmentalism that were becoming more common gave me vocabulary and courage to challenge environmentalist icons such as Rachel Carson's *Silent Spring*, for example, or the widely circulated caricatured portrayal of the Chipko movement. James O'Connor (1988) described Karl Polanyi's *The Great Transformation* (Polanyi [1944] 1957) as "a shining light in a heaven filled with dying stars and black holes of bourgeois naturalism, neo-Malthusianism, Club of Rome technocratism, romantic deep ecologyism, and United Nations one-worldism" (p. 13). Carolyn exposed her students in equal measure to both these dying stars and to the perspectives and tools that could illuminate their inadequacy.

At the same time, through *TDN* and then the sociology of science more broadly, and the work of Longino (1990) and Fox Keller (Keller and Mandelbrot 1984; Keller 1995) in particular, I understood with increasing rigor and nuance the social mediation of environmental knowledge (worldviews, images, discourses, models), and, in particular, how these both embody and shape material and social relations (such as gender and class location). And I learned the simultaneous importance of analyzing discourse as a self-contained universe of meaning structures, while, at the same time, placing environmental discourse and imaginaries firmly in their historical and material contexts. Thus, on the theoretical side my thinking was shaped by the recently published work on metaphor by George Lakoff (Lakoff and Johnson 2003) (then on the other side of campus), and by works on hermeneutics, discourse and narrative introduced to me by another of my thesis advisors, Martin Packer, in the Graduate School of Education, and by Cronon's essay "A Place for Stories: Nature, History, and Narrative" (Cronon 1992) in Carolyn's course. But it was from Carolyn that I understood the careful historical and material contextualization of discursive change. *TDN*'s portrayal of the seventeenth-century rise of the mechanical worldview emerged from its close reading of texts and circumstances of the period, and *Ecological Revolutions'* treatment of shifts in environmental consciousness in colonial New England was written after Carolyn and her partner Charlie had packed up their camper van and set out for many months of digging into local records of pelt exports, corn plots, and fertilizer use.

My doctoral thesis (Garb 1993) reflected these themes. While framed as a study in the role of emotion in scientific enquiry, it was, in effect, a historical-material analysis of how Loren Eiseley's narratives of plant evolution and the thematics of his popular nature writing more generally emerged from and functioned within his social world of Cold War America as well as within his personal world. Focusing on one of his essays in particular, I showed how Eiseley's portrayal of the evolution of flowering plants (Angiosperms) echoed in its claims and metaphors the preoccupations and givens of Cold War America in which and for which he wrote, in the same way that earlier and subsequent descriptions of the same topic by other writers reflected their milieu (Eiseley 1957).

To take one example, Eiseley identified and celebrated several Angiosperm traits as evolutionarily novel—pivots for not only the development of plant life but of animal evolution and, thus, human emergence as well. Those traits are perfectly aligned with the prevalent domestic ideology of Cold War America, which emphasized domestic containment and nurturance and the centrality of the mother–infant bond. As opposed to the "primitive" plants that preceded it, where the young must struggle up alone from nothing, in Angiosperms the seed is encased in a protective maternal coating, "packed in a little enclosed box stuffed full of nutritious food," "well fed" and "carefully cherished" in a way that allowed it to evolutionarily surpass its more primitive counterparts. This imagery echoed images and prevalent beliefs of a kind of domestic ideology that had rapidly become pervasive in other domains of the public sphere in the post war years of the 40s and 50s, whether as a backlash against the freedoms women had tasted during the war years, with men away at the front, a form of post-Hiroshima anxiety about the possible severance of human continuity, or a response to social forces that seemed to threaten the nuclear family and its values. This domestic ideology emphasized the same qualities of the protected seed that Eiseley's essay highlighted as the evolutionary novelty of the Angiosperms: a warm home filled with material abundance, and the role of the mother in providing a sheltering environment for the nurturance of the young.

In another chapter, I delved deeply into Eiseley's biography and the entire range of his writing to identify and explain his additional personal resonance with this imagery. As with much of his writing, Eiseley's account of Angiosperm evolution is colored by his own sense of abandonment by his mother and his troubled marriage to a second wife, who suffered a hearing loss and became increasingly paranoid and neurotic with time.

In addition to mapping out the mutual support and resonances between Eiseley's environmental imaginaries and his personal and historical location, I also examined the more formal structural appeal of these imaginaries using cognitive theories and formalist literary theory. Thus, I showed how Eiseley's narrative of Angiosperm and subsequent human emergence posed and resolved conflicts, actions that cognitive psychologists suggest are an important source of aesthetic pleasure. I then showed how Eiseley's cleavage of plant life into pre- and post-Angiosperm eras led to an account that revolved with remarkable consistency around a series of primal Levi-Straussian binary oppositions, at times even at the expense of fidelity to contemporary scientific understandings. Next, following the lead of paleontologist Missia Landau's analysis of scientific accounts of human evolution (Landau 1984), I showed how Eiseley's narratives closely followed the same sequential narrative functions of the heroic journey identified in Propp's (1928) *Morphology of the Folktale* (Propp 1968). Finally, and of necessity, I grappled with the methodological and epistemic challenge of showing why and how this multiplicity of (potentially exclusive) theoretical frameworks deepened our understanding of what made Eiseley's narratives appealing (penance, perhaps, for my unidimensional and barely theorized analysis of the whole earth image!)

Beyond Berkeley

Analyzing the formation and consequences of environmental imaginaries through a political-ecological sensibility became the focus of a series of essays I wrote in the years after I left Berkeley. The first of these was a careful reading (or, rather, re-reading) of another environmentalist icon, Rachel Carson's *Silent Spring*. Following a suggestion by Iain Boal, I compared the imagery and reception of this work with Lewis Herber's *Our Synthetic Environment*, which preceded it by a few months, and carried almost all of the same claims. Unlike Carson's acclaimed and movement-launching work, Herber's book was rapidly forgotten. While Carson was a more appealing writer for a popular audience, I suggested that the question of aesthetic appeal was inextricable from a deeper and more political appeal. What makes this comparison of reception interesting is that Herber was the pen name of the journalist and anarchist-theorist Murray Bookchin, who later became well known as the founder of social ecology. Carson (a woman scientist, though a "marginal" one in that she devoted her creative energies primarily to science writing) grounded her critique of pesticides on conceptions of natural balance and the web of life, and proposed reform and greater care in a way that made the book palatable to a wide audience. Bookchin, on the other hand, leveraged the pesticide issue toward a more sweeping critique.

> This range of assaults to human well-being and nature, claimed Bookchin, were of a piece, and originated in unviable social arrangements. They demanded a return to rural and agricultural communities of human scale though deindustrialization, decentralization, and a reining in of the profit motive, so that the "most pernicious laws of the market place" were not "given precedence over the most compelling laws of biology." Individual

action or even remedial legislation were not, in his mind, sufficient to get at the heart of these problems; a sound ecological practice was synonymous, for Bookchin, with shaping a satisfying social life. Bookchin's pill was clearly too big, bitter, and unfamiliar for most Americans to swallow at that time. His book was dismissed as "nice sentiments, only impossible," as "numbing" or "unmanageable" in its scope, and as offering only "incoherent," "intangible," or hopelessly utopian proposals.

(Garb 1995:540)

As opposed to Herber/Bookchin, Carson's book framed the entrenchment of pesticides and the call for their replacement as primarily an epistemic and moral problem, rather than a political-economic one. Her challenge to environmental practices was issued from within a deeply conventional, indeed, romantic, and implicitly gendered conception of nature, and energized by a familiar, simple, and powerful narrative: nature disturbed, wholeness undone.[6] This was its appeal, but, also, its limitation, in that it required her text to diffuse and evade political questions, of which, as her subsequent biography (Lear 1998) tells us, she was well aware. My essay traced how this evasion was accomplished at the level of the overall claims, of the anchoring imagery, and, even, at the micro level of sentence structure. And, also, how her avoidance of politics troubled the logic of her claims, which at critical moments was forced to veer away from naming names, and from making explicit the social choices underlying the destruction she portrayed, often in concrete detail.

In showing the limits and of what could and could not be said at that particular moment, and the consequences of this limit, I was not aiming to critique Carson, whom I admire, nor to minimize what her writing accomplished. Rather (and similar to my whole earth image analysis), I was trying to capture and reconcile the tensions between opportunity and constraint, determination and dynamism in the politics of environmentalism's cultural productions. My comparison with Bookchin's contemporaneous radical but forgotten book showed what lay beyond the extent of Carson's challenge to the status quo, but also underscores the likelihood that she was taking her audience just as far as they could go without her losing them. It was only later that I would encounter better and more forgiving ways to articulate this kind of achievement/failure through Gramsci's conception of hegemony as a slow cultural trench warfare through which the prevailing common sense is shifted, or in Williams' reworking of this conception, and his notion of "structures of feeling" (Williams 1976, 1977).

This critical rereading of a founding work of modern environmentalism continued my critique of the whole earth image as environmental icon, and my next essay (Garb 1997) continued to explore the intertwining of rhetorical form, imagery, and environmental politics in a more contemporary context, analyzing the Western reception of a widely circulated portrayal of India's Chipko as an ecofeminist movement. This essay was written during a year (1994–1995) spent as a Member of the Institute for Advanced Studies at Princeton as part of a group of scholars gathered under the theme of "Traveling Reform Movements: Feminism and Environmentalism." The essay contrasted historical accounts of the Chipko as a peasant protest movement, in all of its specific material and historical detail, with the iconified and abstract translations of it that circulated internationally, which cast it centrally as a non-violent feminist protest. In particular, I examined Vandana Shiva's prominent rendition of Chipko as a feminist movement, as part of her larger critique of the masculinism of Western development, science, and economics. Since Shiva's portrayal set the tone for other feminist treatments of Chipko, I wanted to see what the filtering left out and how and why this mattered. To generate parallax, I compared Shiva's account to Ramachandra Guha's (1989) *The Unquiet Woods: Ecological Change and Peasant Resistance in the Himalaya.* This work had rather different theoretical axes to grind (see Guha 1995, 2000; Ludden 2002), decentering Chipko as an important but small instance of peasant resistance movements more broadly. In Guha's account of the movement, the theme of what Western ecologists would call "ecological consciousness" is subdued, and women and gender are almost entirely absent.

While written some years before Carolyn's (1996) *Earthcare,* my Chipko essay (and the one on Progressive Era maternalist science following it, described below) engaged with many of the same themes, in particular the tensions associated with the discursive linkages of women and nature, and the ambivalent implications of translating this conjunction into the political sphere. I subtitled the Chipko essay (Garb 1997) "Lost in Translation," to reflect my argument that ecofeminist omission of what was going on around, and instead of, the iconic image of women hugging trees was important for both the Garhwali women in the originating context, as well as for the struggles of environmentalists in the West, to whom the image was (mis)translated. The version of Chipko shaped by Shiva figured as an anchoring icon in the form of ecofeminism she developed, which aimed to rectify the conjoined marginalizations of women, of subsistence activities, and of nature. But there were dangers in how she placed women and a valorized conception of the reproduction of everyday life at the heart of her analysis of environmental degradation. My essay tried to use other descriptions of the movement's context to underscore what seems to have been distorted and obscured by extremely tight essentialist systematicity of Shiva's linkage among women, subsistence, nature, the indigenous, the local, the traditional, the Hindu, the harmonious, and the just.

My conclusions on the political hazards of the woman/nature linkage were quite definite (and, in hindsight, a little risky for a male author at that point in time). I pointed to ways in which the selectivity of Shiva's (over)compensatory account could actually hamper the political ends she was trying to achieve, and that rather than her essentializing account of women's original empathy for nature, these ends would be better served by a more accurate rendition of the particular circumstances in which women's concern and efforts arose (or not). Referencing examples of the contexts and uses of this iconic version in the West and of the way its acclaim fed back to differentially intervene in its originating context, I suggested that both Western feminists and Garhwali women might be strengthened, not undermined, by retaining some of the less convenient details that Shiva's story omitted in order for her to portray a movement that was more superficially marketable as utopian feminist fable.

This analysis of a contemporary essentialist coupling of women to nature to achieve a political end was followed by a more historical essay on these themes, together with historian Jill Conway. We examined how feminists in critical periods in the nineteenth and twentieth centuries used an ideological coupling of women to nature as a political tool. Specifically, we examined how the American maternalist and domestic science traditions (from 1880 to 1950) achieved their proto-environmental agendas by feminizing concern for urban and domestic health and safety, and how cultural feminists of the 1970s were able to use an essentialist conflation of woman and nature as a galvanizing analytic and rhetoric for the critique of consumer society and the technological excesses of modern industry.

Our essay revolved around similar tensions between the productiveness and limitation of critique as had my earlier Chipko and Carson essays, though to some extent, approaching these from opposite directions. My Chipko analysis argued for materialist, political, and historicized explanations for the apparently greater commitment of women to the preservation of the environment, rather than essentialist ones. My essay with Conway, on the other hand, showed how women politically mobilized an essentialized women/nature linkage as a way of improving their own political and material conditions. The same could have been said of Carson's *Silent Spring*. While my analysis of this emphasized the limitations of its challenge to the status quo that remained embedded within a larger discursive conciliation to it, one could argue that Carson had also used familiar and widely resonant idioms of nature to energize political action. Conversely, I could have argued that despite their tactical effectiveness in progressive struggles, traditional maternalist claims about women's natural affinities re-inscribed potentially regressive gendered roles.[7] Thus, the essays shared this kind of ambivalence toward how environmentalist discourse balances change and continuity as it challenges hegemonic conceptions.

Before pivoting to the First World situation, our essay began its argument for materialist contextualization with reference to the apparently greater commitment of women to the protection of common property resources in Third World situations. Thus, we argued that:

> A linking of environmental behavior to gender as social location, rather than to the feminine as essential principle, means that women are not ahistorically linked to pro environmental behavior. Such linkages, when they exist, can

be a function of quite mundane and fragile circumstances. As Cecile Jackson (1993) demonstrates in her work on gender and development, women's social location can encourage environmental-destructive behaviors and attitudes, and struggles for gender equality (e.g., for full participation in development) can be at odds with efforts for environmental protection. Women may prefer gathering dead wood to cutting living trees not because of their reverential attitudes to nature and commitment to future generations, as some might claim, but because dead wood is lighter and easier to carry (400). Under systems of patrilineal inheritance women will be more mobile than men, have less of a stake in a particular place or property, and may therefore be less motivated to adopt conservation practices than men who hold primary land rights (406). Under conditions of stress it may be men who are in closer contact with the land, common property resources, and their care (408–411) and who exhibit the "conserving" characteristics seen by ecofeminists as inherently associated with women and female roles.

(p. 261)

Turning to the First World context, we examined the political use of emphasizing gender differences and essential traits. Whereas eighteenth-century women drew on Enlightenment rationalism and emphasized the *universality* of human reason as their basis for educating women and advancing their position, nineteenth-century feminists used the stress on the *differences* between male and female present in both Romanticism and evolutionary thought of that period to argue for complementary but equally important roles for men and women. Specifically, we looked at the impact of maternalist thought, on the one hand, and the "crisis of American masculinity," on the other, as respective shapers of female and male versions of (proto) environmentalism in the Progressive Era. The former legitimated the entry of women into feminized spheres of environmental action ("domestic science" and "industrial medicine"), while the latter energized the efforts of figures such as Roosevelt and Gifford Pinchot within masculinized spheres of wildlife and wilderness preservation.

While my Chipko essay saw little benefit from the environmental or feminist mobilization of essentialism, we posed the mobilization of maternalist tropes in the 1890s as strategically useful, at least implicitly and in hindsight. We argued that:

the "woman closer to nature" theme has been the basis on which feminist agitation for change has been most successful in modern societies, because it often permits the entry of women into new gendered social and political territories without disturbing traditional male/female power relationships. Thus maternalist thought in feminism is double-edged: accepting qualities assigned to women under patriarchy, even while providing a strategy that may open up, at least for the short term, new areas of social and intellectual life for women within a changing social and economic system.

(Conway and Garb 2000:263)

Our essay explored how this tension came to a head in a very pointed way for American feminists during the 1890s. Earlier nineteenth-century feminist thought had argued for the right to vote by appeal to Enlightenment ideas about the universality of human reason. But following the Civil War, when Black males received the vote while women's claims were denied, feminist leaders divided over whether to continue to argue for women's rights on the basis of equality or on the basis of their capacity to bring special sex-linked qualities to the political process. Social feminists chose the latter approach, drawing upon evolutionary thought to underscore qualities of nurturance, empathy, and altruism as essentially linked to the female biological role. They then leveraged this claim to forward protective legislation limiting exploitation of female and child labor, pacifism as an international policy, and for training for women in home economics and domestic science so that they could continue their role of caring for the health of their families within an urban and industrial society—a claim translated quite successfully into developing the feminized professions of domestic science and industrial medicine.

A major proponent of this approach, Alice Hamilton, developed her interest in industrial pollutants because she was shut out of more conventional forms of medical research. With obvious resonances with Carson's positioning two generations later, and to the tensions between various forms of ecofeminism discussed by Merchant a century later, Hamilton was clear sighted about how this essentialized positioning allowed her to forward concerns about the health of the working poor that were not available for men. "It seemed natural and right," she wrote, "that a woman should put the care of the producing workman ahead of the value of the thing he was producing. In a man it would have been seen as sentimentality or radicalism" (pp. 49–50).

Synthesis: Hindsight and Insights

I composed this chapter as tribute to the work of Carolyn Merchant, whose key ideas and commitments echo through my writing as described in the foregoing, and as well as through my subsequent work. This chapter also presents an opportunity for reflection on how an intuitive and perhaps simplistic reaction to the objectification implicit in and facilitated by NASA's whole earth image, and then my encounter with Carolyn's work, were further elaborated and grounded over the decades into a "Political Ecology of Environmental Discourse," and to synthesize the key contours and insights of this approach, as they emerged in the series of studies described here.

Many of the key tools and propositions of my approach to environmental and environmentalist discourse are now fairly standard to contemporary cultural studies and the fields that have become STS (Science and Technology Studies) and the sociology of knowledge. Knowledge of the natural world is mediated by discourse (images, metaphors, worldviews), and these embed and perpetuate social relations, often in the subtlest ways. Each of my case studies has deepened support for these claims with reference to environmentalist imagery. The whole earth analysis showed how a rapid transition in contemporary environmental worldview was facilitated by and embodied in the NASA image, whose implications were foreclosed to a large degree simply by its technical attributes and extraterrestrial vantage point. I wish I had been ready at that time to trace these themes in finer historical detail by studying the image's precursors, the technical particulars of its emergence, and the initial responses to it.

The Carson and Eiseley studies showed me the miraculous clarifying reading of a literary work that was possible—like the cleavage of a crystal hit at the right angle—once its key discursive/ideological "payload" had been identified. In both works, the core animating metaphors were felt at multiple reinforcing scales, their logic coercing the subject matter, always in flight from their inbuilt contradictions, and striving to hold off the collapse of hard-won opposites into one another. Still working my way through structuralist literary theory when I did that research, I lacked the deconstructionist tools that would have helped me better articulate these dynamics in the texts, the Marxist-literary vocabulary (*ala* Williams or Eagleton) that would have helped me better trace their ideological contexts and functions, or the New Historicist perspective that would help me ask better questions about audiences, genres, reception, and other cross-linked discourses.

The Carson essay raised for me the tension between facilitation and constraint in environmentalist mobilization of accepted discourses. But while Carson's mobilization of Romantic notions of nature, and the social feminist mobilization of maternalist tropes, both seemed to be ultimately progressive ones, Shiva's rendition of the Chipko movement seemed to me to be a more regressive essentialism, where the loss began to outweigh the gain. The Chipko study also alerted me to the very real consequences of the travel and recoil of simplifying myths in a globalized world. It showed how the generation and Western reception of one account of a local struggle can feed back to the originating context, channeling attention and resources to some efforts over others in ways that do not simply distort circulating depictions of an existing reality, but also rewrite it on the ground.

The material consequences of discourse and imagery became the explicit topic of further discourse-analytic papers, which moved from the examination of environmentalist imagery described above to the analysis of environmental policies and environmentally consequential projects. One paper, for example, examined how social narratives structure scenario-driven environmental modeling (Garb, Pulver, and Van Deever 2008), and another describes the discursive construction of "inevitability" in megaprojects (2005). Indeed, the latter essay traced four discursive-political ploys through which a proposed megaproject was propelled from tenuous concept to hundreds of kilometers of asphalt, demonstrating how the rhetorical and political were so infused so as to be inseparable. Through a series of discursive moves and framings problem definitions, past and future, and the scope of discussion were all defined/reworked in a way that implicitly narrowed the space of possibilities toward a single and apparently inevitable outcome: a new billion plus dollar highway running the length of Israel.

That decades of inquiry can be traced to what I absorbed from Carolyn, and that my research remains in constant dialog with her own core concerns at multiple levels, is testimony to the prescience, diversity, dynamism, and robustness of her work.

Notes

1 https://en.wikipedia.org/wiki/Whole_Earth_Catalog
2 Expanded versions of this essay appeared as Garb (1988, 1990).
3 In addition to Merchant's book, I was fortunate enough to be part of a class in which Helen Longino was testing the readings and ideas that formed the basis of her masterful *Science as Social Knowledge*, and to have Evelyn Fox-Keller read and even suggest the eventual title of my thesis.
4 See also J. Baird Callicott, "Carolyn Iltis: The Carolyn Merchant Few People Know," Chapter 1 in this volume.
5 See also Holmes Rolston III, "Leading and Misleading Metaphors: From Organism to Anthropocene," Chapter 6 in this volume.
6 In hindsight (an embarrassing admission for a student of Carolyn!), my essay did not give enough attention to the important gender valences of Carson's book and its impact. Who Carson was (both in her personal life as well as her professional location in a typically feminized role on the margins of science), what she said, how she said it, and the attacks on her were all gendered in ways that are subtly woven into the other discursive-political dynamics discussed in my essay's comparison.
7 Some of these themes are explored in Merchant's *Earthcare* (1996).

Bibliography

Conway, J. and Y. Garb. 2000. "Gender, Environment, and Nature: Two Episodes in Feminist Politics in Conway." Pp. 259–278 in Marx and Keniston, eds. *Earth, Air, Fire, Water: The Humanities and the Environment*. Amherst: University of Massachusetts Press.

Cronon, William. 1992. "A Place for Stories: Nature, History, and Narrative." *The Journal of American History* 78(4):1347–1376.

Eiseley, Loren. 1957. "How Flowers Changed the World." In *The Immense Journey: An Imaginative Naturalist Explores the Mysteries of Man and Nature*. New York: Random House.

Garb, Yaakov Jerome. 1985. "The Use and Misuse of the Whole Earth Image." *Whole Earth Review* 45:18–25.

Garb, Yaakov Jerome. 1988. "Attitudes Toward Nature: An Analysis of Modern Imagery." In Dianna DeLuca, ed. *Essays on Perceiving Nature*. Honolulu: Perceiving Nature Conference Committee, University of Hawaii.

Garb, Yaakov Jerome. 1990. "Perspective or Escape? Feminist Musings on Contemporary Earth Imagery." Pp. 264–278 in Irene Diamond and Gloria Feman Orenstein, eds. *Reweaving the World: The Emergence of Ecofeminism*. San Francisco, CA: Sierra Club Books.

Garb, Yaakov Jerome. 1993. *How Scientific Accounts Appeal to Their Authors and Readers: A Case Study in the Nature Writing of Loren Eisley*. Ph.D., University of California, Berkeley.

Garb, Yaakov Jerome. 1995. "Rachel Carson's *Silent Spring*." *Dissent* (Fall):539–546.

Garb, Yaakov Jerome. 1996. "Change and Continuity in Environmental World-View: The Politics of Nature in Rachel Carson's *Silent Spring*." Pp. 229–256 in David Macauley, ed. *Minding Nature: The Philosophers of Ecology*. New York: Guilford Press.

Garb, Yaakov Jerome. 1997. "Lost in Translation: Toward a Feminist Account of Chipko." Pp. 273–284 in Joan Scott, Cora Kaplan, and Debra Keates, eds. *Transitions, Environments, Translation: Feminism in International Politics*. New York: Routledge.

Garb, Yaakov Jerome. 2005. "Constructing the Trans-Israel Highway's Inevitability." *Israel Studies*, Summer.

Garb, Yaakov Jerome, Simone Pulver, and Stacy D. Van Deveer. 2008. "Scenarios in Society, Society in Scenarios: Toward a Social Scientific Analysis of Storyline-Driven Environmental Modeling." *Environmental Research Letters* 3(4).

Guha, Ramachandra. 1995. "Subaltern and Bhadralok Studies." Edited by David Arnold, David Hardiman, and Shahid Amin. *Economic and Political Weekly* 30(33):2056–2058.

Guha, Ramachandra. 2000. *The Unquiet Woods: Ecological Change and Peasant Resistance in the Himalaya*. Berkeley: University of California Press.

Harvey, David. 1979. "Population, Resources, and the Ideology of Science." Pp. 155–185 in *Philosophy in Geography*. Dordrecht: Springer.

Jackson, Cecile. 1993. "Women/Nature or Gender/History? A Critique of Ecofeminist 'Development'." *The Journal of Peasant Studies* 20(3):389–418.

Keller, Evelyn Fox and Benoit B. Mandelbrot. 1984. *A Feeling for the Organism: The Life and Work of Barbara McClintock*. New York: Henry Holt and Co.

Keller, Evelyn Fox. 1995. *Reflections on Gender and Science*. New Haven, CT: Yale University Press.

Kubrin, David. 1981. "Newton's Inside Out! Magic, Class Struggle, and the Rise of Mechanism in the West." Pp. 96–121 in Harry Woolf, ed. *The Analytic Spirit: Essays in the History of Science*. Ithaca, NY: Cornell University Press.

Lakoff, George, and Mark Johnson. 2003. *Metaphors We Live By*. Chicago: University of Chicago Press.

Landau, Misia. 1984. "Human Evolution as Narrative: Have Hero Myths and Folktales Influenced Our Interpretations of the Evolutionary Past?" *American Scientist* 72(3):262–268.

Lear, Linda. 1998. *Rachel Carson: Witness for Nature*. New York: Henry Holt & Co.

Longino, Helen E. 1990. *Science as Social Knowledge: Values and Objectivity in Scientific Inquiry*. Princeton, NJ: Princeton University Press.

Ludden, David, ed. 2002. *Reading Subaltern Studies: Critical History, Contested Meaning and the Globalization of South Asia*. London: Anthem Press.

O'Connor, James. 1988. "Capitalism, Nature, Socialism a Theoretical Introduction." *Capitalism Nature Socialism* 1(1):11–38.

Polanyi, Karl. [1944] 1957. *The Great Transformation: The Political and Economic Origin of Our Time*. Boston: Beacon Press.

Propp, Vladimir. 1968. *Morphology of the Folktale*. Revised edition. Reprinted by University of Texas in 2009. Austin: University of Texas Press.

Williams, Raymond. 1977. "Structures of Feeling." Pp. 128–135 in *Marxism and literature*. New York: Oxford University Press.

Williams, Raymond. 1983. *Keywords: A Vocabulary of Culture and Society*, revised edition. New York: Oxford University Press.

15

ENVIRONMENTAL HISTORY AND THE MATERIALIZATION OF BODIES

Whitney A. Bauman

> A narrative, whether Christian, environmental, or feminist, is an ideal form into which particular bits of content are poured. The form is the organizing principle; the content is the matter.
>
> *(Merchant 2003:37)*

Human beings, whatever else we are, are narrative-seeking and narrative-making creatures. We long to interlope ourselves with stories that make meaning of the various bits of data we experience and contribute to on a moment-by-moment basis. We don't only subject ourselves to these stories, but we also subject our friends, family members, all humans, our pets, other animals, mountains, rivers, forests, streams, the planet, and even the entire universe to these stories. Multiply your own story by over seven billion, and you get an idea of just how many stories there are floating around on the planet. Stories in themselves are not problematic. Whereas dolphins swim and birds fly, whatever else it means to be human, humans seem to make stories (though other species may as well).

The problem with stories begins when we try to collapse our own unique story into the only story. In other words, drawing from the language of Merchant's epigram to this chapter, when we force the material world into the form of our own story (our own image), we create violence for other earth bodies (Mazis 2002).[1] There is a long colonizing history of forcing the material world into a single story. We could talk about Plato's forms, the Christianizing mission, Locke's understanding of property, and the narrative of progress in science, among many others (Bauman 2009; Merchant 2003; Glacken 1967). Indeed many of Carolyn Merchant's works have been geared toward challenging these dominant stories and the ways in which they force bodies (human and non) into submission.

In this chapter I bring Merchant's work into dialogue with new conversation partners from the realm of Queer Theory (QT). In particular, I argue that her work in environmental history has done much to bring to light the ways in which dominant narratives of progress and decline are performed by earth-bodies (Merchant 2003). Second, I argue that Merchant's partnership ethic can be strengthened by dialogue with conversations around shared agency within queer theory. Shared agency refers to the idea that agency is relational, distributed within the systems that make up any given organism, between organisms, within and among ecosystems, and between biotic and abiotic life; it is a critique of the individualistic and uniquely human understanding of agency (Barad 2007:132–188). Third and finally, I argue that QT benefits from being read together with Merchant's partnership ethic, because this ethic extends the critique beyond the human to the rest of the natural world. I'm not arguing that Merchant is a queer theorist, but rather that her critical analysis of narrative and her partnership ethic can help lengthen the reach of queer theory beyond the human species.

Narratives and Performativity

Judith Butler (among others) has argued that our identities and our subjectivities are "performative." Performativity simply means that identities are not essential or set in stone by "Nature" or by "God"—whether we are talking about gender, sex, race, etc.—but identities are formed over time and these formations help shape the ways in which individuals "perform" their identities. For instance, she argues that phrases like "it's a boy" or "it's a girl" are tied to a whole host of scripts and rituals within different cultures that turn bodies into "boys" and "girls" (Butler 1990:151). This does not mean that we get to choose our own script for how we will become. Rather, it means we are born into worlds where we are subjected to dominant and alternative narratives, practices, and habits that are always and already co-creating bodies and ways of becoming in the world. These narratives and practices include languages, scientific understandings, ideas about genders (which are not always gender/sex dimorphic), art, religious and other traditions and beliefs, music, film, histories, and more. On the one hand, these narratives and practices shape the becoming of earth bodies, they help form habits of materialization in the world as certain narratives and practices are privileged over others. On the other hand, as Butler argues, bodies do matter (Butler 1993). Every embodiment is a unique manifestation of the flows of history, evolution, genetics, chemical elements, ecosystems, language, and culture. No body merely repeats itself in the image of the dominant or alternative narrative that it is subjected to.

The unique ways in which bodies become in the world, each a little differently, largely rely on the "repetitions" that form habits of becoming in an ongoing process of natural-cultural evolution (Deleuze 1994). Most of the underlying processes that make up life are repetitious: breathing, cell division, heart beats, seasons, the spinning of the earth, and the like. However, small differences can lead to the emergence of novelty and change. Evolutionary adaptations that lead to what we refer to as species, the development of the eye and the opposable thumb, the emergence of consciousness and language, are all part of a process by which small differences occur during repetitive processes. Our own individual lives depend upon these repetitive processes. Without them the difference that makes each of us unique would have no creative grounding to emerge out of. However, when we mistake repetitions for immutable laws and norms, this leads to parts of bodies and some entire bodies being "abjected" or left out of the system (Butler 1993:58–80). When these abjections are considered abnormal or aberrant, they are often discriminated against (think about how "natural" and "normal" are often used to discriminate based on race, gender, sexuality, etc.). However, it is also in the realm of these abjections, similar to what Derrida understood as *différance*, or "remainder," that possibilities for newness and change occur (Derrida 1974:x–xi). In other words, as enough of these abjections "pile up," they begin to lure bodies into different ways of becoming that acknowledge and pay attention to them. We might think here of various, ongoing movements: women's liberation, the civil rights movement, LGBTQ movements, Occupy Wall Street, Black Lives Matter, disability rights, animal liberation. All of these (and more) depend on some bodies that have been abjected by normative claims, laying claim to new narratives and systems that will account for their bodies. Or, we might think of this process in terms of how new scientific discoveries are made. A theory works as long as it makes sense of the most data, but there are always outlying data that cannot be accounted for in a given theory. If these outlying data begin to increase over time, similar to a Kuhnian revolution, then a new theory will come into place for accounting for more of the data (Kuhn 1962). This is a process that continues (in both examples) ad infinitum.

In her work, Carolyn Merchant has focused on the ways in which narratives can be violent toward human and earth bodies as they materialize in the world. Patriarchal narratives in science and religion, for example, have subordinated women's bodies and made the nonhuman world "dead stuff" for use toward human ends (Merchant 1980). This subordination and instrumentalization has in turn led to violence against women and environmental degradation (respectively). Whereas most queer theorists tend to focus on human subjects, engaging with Merchant's narrative might shed some light on how narratives also shape other earth bodies. Here I will look at some of her narrative critiques as found in the *Death of Nature: Women, Ecology, and the Scientific Revolution, Reinventing Eden: The Fate of Nature in Western Culture*, and *Autonomous Nature: Problems of Prediction and Control from Ancient Times to the Scientific Revolution*, and argue that her understanding of the relationship between language/epistemology and nature/ontology is not too far from the ideas found in Butler and others' understanding of Queer Theory (Merchant 1980, 2003, 2016).

The Death of Nature

One of Merchant's critiques has been that the narrative of modern science has subordinated all life to humanity. Further, that this subordination of life to humans does not understand all humans as equal: women and people of color are often not as valuable as elite, White males. Central to Merchant's understanding of the death of nature is the way in which nature shifts from being understood on the basis of organismic models—in which agency and value are distributed throughout the human and nonhuman world—toward being understood as machine. The ways in which the narratives of science begin to materialize the world are, she argues, learned and enforced over time. She notes the ways in which people had to learn to understand practices such as mining and animal experimentation as not infringing upon any spirits or value inhering in nature. In a long process, something like God or ultimate value was pushed further and further away from the material world rather than being something that inheres in the material world. Further, via Descartes, human beings as rational creatures became the only ensouled or valuable creatures; and even then, some more so than others: women and people of non-European descent would have to argue for their rationality and ensoulment for centuries to come. The only connection between God and the world was, then, through (some) human beings. All other life was made of dead matter that could be used toward human ends. Strengthening these more theoretical ideas and narrative assumptions was Newton's understanding of the mechanical cosmos. The mechanical model was then incarnated on the earth as sciences such as biology, geology, and zoology drew from Newtonian mechanics. These mechanical metaphors and models were even extended to the human body in the field of medicine suggesting, again, that the disembodied soul, or thinking-thing, is the only thing that is agential and has real value.

Added to this mechanical model was the idea that progress would be inevitable as science transformed nature. As Merchant argues, the culmination of such thought could be seen in Francis Bacon's *New Atlantis*. There, his utopian vision is of a world in which science displaces theology, and scientists displace priests (Merchant 1980:172–187). It was no longer the scripts and narratives of the church that would order bodies through ritual, doctrine, and discipline, but the scripts and narratives of science. Science now becomes more and more the realm in which health, sanity, and the future of life are explored: and bodies are divided and treated accordingly. Whereas the technologies of confession, the church hierarchy, and the sword once kept subjects in place, now reason, natural law, medicine, and nation-state sovereignty began to order subjects. The shifts in these narratives also led to a shift in the ways that bodies were disciplined according to gender, race, sex, sexuality, and nationality. As Foucault argued, identity, throughout the scientific revolution and the subsequent enlightenments, became less and less about religious and familial associations and more and more about biological understandings of race, sex, gender, and sexuality—though still under the banners of nationality (Foucault 1978). This linking of biological under-standings of identities and nationality would, of course, have disastrous con-sequences in the form of eugenics and genocide during the twentieth century, but space here does not permit me to take this detour.

As scientific technologies slowly but surely became more persuasive than any-thing religion had to offer, the industrial revolution got underway—but not without costs. Certain bodies (or aspects of certain bodies) were abjected by these new sciences: hence the incredible amount of social injustice and ecological ills that have arisen or endured since the time of the industrial revolution. As Mer-chant notes, following Horkheimer and Adorno, the problem with this largely mechanical model of Modern science is that the world is not organized according to the confines of human, instrumental reason (Horkheimer and Adorno 2002). Rather, we are a part of the rest of the natural world becoming: reason is part of—and thus not in a place to explain all of—nature. Forcing life into the con-fines of reason alone leads to violence against human and other earth bodies. The earth and its multitude of evolving forms of life can no more be contained in the "natural laws" of science than in theological or other religious doctrines: both enterprises are human, and forcing the world into either participates in a form of anthropocentrism. One only needs to look at how species evolve or how scien-tific ideas are constantly changing to understand this point. Species are merely a way of describing a "snapshot" of the current moment of evolution; the true nature of evolution, in the end, means that there really are no species, as all of life is constantly evolving, which is something Darwin hinted at in his metaphor of the evolution of life as a "tangled bank" (Darwin 1964:489). Likewise, the sci-ence of the nineteenth century is no longer the science of the twenty-first cen-tury, nor will today's science be the same as it will be in the twenty-second century. Mistaking our narratives and knowledge of reality with reality is akin to keeping the process of life from continually becoming. It just doesn't work, and it leads to reification and death.

Narratives of Progress and Decline

Another aspect of this anthropocentric approach to the world is the tendency for humans to project narratives of progress or decline upon the entire planet. In *Reinventing Eden*, Merchant follows the narratives of progress and decline from the biblical garden stories, to the scientific revolution, and on into contemporary environmental and feminist movements. The very idea of progress or decline depends upon a perspective that "backgrounds" information to the contrary (Plumwood 2002:27–30). These ideas favor events and facts that confirm their own narrative arc and downplay or ignore contrary facts and events. In other words, the history of cosmic expansion and geo-evolution and even the histories of human cultures show immense creativity *and* destruction, or what from a human perspec-tive we might call progress and decline. Forcing the world into just one of these narratives misses this ebb and flow of the natural-cultural processes. Furthermore, these are human narratives that only make sense from the perspective of certain peoples: the progress of science, for example, has also led to the environmental destruction of many places and the impoverishment of many peoples.

Because of the cost of "progress," many contemporary environmentalists have preferred an opposite narrative of decline. The world is getting worse and worse and eventually a human-induced apocalypse (climate catastrophe) will come. While climate "weirding,"[2] the current sixth mass extinction, and the gross eco-social inequities that persist as a result of anthropogenic forcings cannot be denied, there is little evidence that declensionist, apocalyptic narratives help us to adapt to and mitigate the problems of a changing planet. Rather, these narratives can contribute to a form of despair, which Joanna Macy has called "environmental despair," that actually stymies hope for a different possible future if it is not addressed and worked through (Macy 1995:240–262). And, again, such narratives of decline are indeed human projections as well: the climate is changing and the planet is facing a lot of problems that will likely only become more severe in the foreseeable future, but life on the planet will go on and rebound in ways that we can't yet imagine from this side of the transition. We need then to think about "hope" without being naïve. More recently, Joanna Macy has talked about the need for a type of radical, "active hope," in the face of insurmountable odds. This active hope neither gives in to despair, nor assumes that "all will be well" (Macy and Johnstone 2012). In other words, it troubles the certainty that narratives of progress and decline insist upon.

Reading a narrative arc of progress or decline into the "geo-history" (Latour 2017) of our planet shapes bodies into the performance of such narratives. How have the ideas that "technology will get us out of all of problems," or "it doesn't matter what we do, it's too late" materialized in the world, and what bodies and things are abjected by these materializations? How does the optimism of progress or the pessimism of declension play out in daily lives and ripple out through the rest of the natural world? Further, what blind spots does the zeal for either optimism or pessimism create in the world? If we look at the "slow violence" of progress, we will see that not all human bodies are affected equally by "progress" (Nixon 2013). Likewise, there are many bodies negatively affected by apocalyptic, declensionist, or apathetic narratives: inaction can be worse than action at times, and often comes from a privileged perspective. My point here is that narratives of "progress" and "decline" are always and only from particular embodied perspectives. Even if life has tended toward more and more biological complexity, this doesn't mean progress for all. The great die off of the dinosaurs allowed for the reign of the mammals, without which we would not be here. Is this decline or progress? The relatively stable climate over the past twenty or so thousand years which allowed for the emergence of civilizations that are now threatening that stability: progress or decline? The unimaginable advances in the technologies of medicine, production, communication, and transportation that have meant health and wealth progress for many has meant a decline in well-being for many earth others. From which perspective are we talking about progress or decline? Neither narrative gives enough weight to agency, embodiments, consequences, and complexity within the more than human world. How might we begin to "listen" deeply to the needs and concerns of the entire spectrum of planetary bodies?

Partnership and Agential Realism: Autonomous Nature

Part of the problem, according to Merchant, with a narrative that both makes humans somehow exceptional to the rest of the natural world (and again, some humans more than others), and that understands the arc of cultural evolution as progressive or declensionist, is that it gives all agency over to human beings. Human beings, then, are responsible for the entire future of the planetary community. Though this mechanical model is being challenged by recent developments and non-mechanical theories in many of the sciences (quantum physics, chaos and complexity theories, understandings of the microbiome, neurosciences, etc.), by postmodern theories, and by the "wicked" (Rittel and Webber 1973) and complex problems associated with global climate weirding and globalization, it still persists. As Merchant notes,

> Mechanism continues, however, in the everyday world of engineered bridges, skyscrapers, and airplanes in which we spend many of our waking moments. And mechanistic explanations are still the norm in molecular biology, genetics, neuroscience, parts of biochemistry, chemistry and physics, and parts of engineering and biophysics. But although Newtonian mechanics still describes the world in which we live and move, that world is a limited domain of the far larger, unpredictable, and dominant domain now characterized by chaos and complexity science. It is that world to which twenty-first century life must adapt.
>
> *(Merchant 2016:11)*

The ethic derived from such a mechanical understanding can only be a technoscientific managerialist model. Indeed, even the environmental ethics of "stewardship" maintain such a technoscientific managerialist model that assumes agency for the human species alone. Such a claim makes humans the dominant top to the rest of the natural world, in the same way that an omnipotent, all powerful God is the dominant power top to all of creation (Althaus-Reid 2000). In critiquing, deconstructing, and developing an alternative to this managerial, top-down model, Merchant argues for a "partnership ethic," rather than an ethic of stewardship. She writes,

> For the twenty-first century, I propose a new environmental ethic—a partnership ethic. It is an ethic based on the idea that people are helpers, partners,

and colleagues and that people and nature are equally important to each other. If both people and nature are acknowledged as actors, we have the possibility of a mutually beneficial situation.

A partnership ethic holds that the greatest good for the human and non-human communities is in their mutual living interdependence.

(Merchant 2003: 91)

In her more recent work, *Autonomous Nature*, which traces the history of "natura naturans" (nature naturing, or nature as alive) throughout the history of Western thought, she goes on to identify more specific precepts of this partnership ethic:

My ethic contains five precepts for a human community in a sustainable partnership with a nonhuman community: Equity between the human and nonhuman communities. Moral consideration for both humans and other species. Respect for both cultural diversity and biodiversity. Inclusion of women, minorities, and nonhuman nature in the code of ethical account-ability. An ecologically sound management that is consistent with the con-tinued health of both the human and the nonhuman communities.

(Merchant 2016:162)

Her partnership ethic, then, moves the model of relationality from a transcendent, top-down model, toward an immanent model in which we must cooperate with human and earth others. There are three components of this ethic that I would like to draw attention to. One is epistemic, one is agential, and the third is ontological. They are, of course, interrelated.

Epistemically, it is important to note that Merchant is maintaining the other-ness of earth others, unlike some deep ecologists who might argue that we can "think like a mountain," or become the universe thinking about itself (Leopold 1949:137–140; Berry and Swimme 1992). In order to be "partners" and "colla-borators" there must be more than one: indeed, in this case there is, for all intents and purposes, an infinite number of co-collaborators within the planetary com-munity. Acknowledging our difference while also recognizing our interrelated-ness with the rest of the natural world helps us to stay grounded in our embodied contexts. As Val Plumwood (2002) has argued, there is a huge difference between epistemic anthropocentrism (thinking from the human perspective) and ethical anthropocentrism (thinking only for human needs) (pp. 132–137). We need epistemic anthropocentrism because this simply acknowledges our positionality: bodies do matter and there is no objective position (Butler 1993; Harding 1991:138–163). Ethical anthropocentrism does not logically flow from epistemic anthropocentrism any more than my own socially-embodied location in the world would prevent me from understanding, sympathizing with, and having compassion for others who are different from me. We can acknowledge differ-ence without hierarchically valuing those differences, and we can acknowledge our relationality without obliterating difference. Merchant's partnership metaphor acknowledges this "multiplicity of becoming" that we call the planetary community (Keller and Schneider 2011).

Merchant's partnership ethic restores the agency to the rest of the natural world that was taken away through the long process of making nature dead stuff, known as the Scientific Revolution. Modern sciences, like modern philosophies, imagined only humans (only some and initially through God) to have agency in the world and all else was mere fodder to be used toward human ends. This was also true of women, children, and slaves for a large part of modern history: they were tools at the disposal of elite males. Ironically, the metaphysics that secured such a hierarchy would be undone by the very sciences that understood nature to be dead: evolutionary theory and physics in particular began to challenge the sharp divide between races, men and women, humans and animals, and matter and energy. Merchant draws from the sciences of chaos and complexity to argue for the agency of nature. She writes, "The new postmodern sciences of ecology, chaos, and complexity theory are consistent with the idea of nature as an actor ... Disorderly order, the world represented by chaos theory, becomes a component of the partnership ethic" (Merchant 2003:197). In other words, humans don't have the ability to predict and control once the rest of the natural world is seen from the sciences of chaos and complexity. The rest of the natural world, in a sense, has agency as well.

Restoring agency to the world (and to all humans) means that humans can no longer simply manage things, and that there is a certain amount of "freedom" and uncertainty at every level of reality. Karen Barad argues this as well in her book *Meeting the Universe Halfway*. Following the debates between Heisenberg and Bohr, she argues that reality is fundamentally indeterminate (not just that there is epistemic uncertainty) (Barad 2007:97–131). She then goes on to argue that such an understanding of the world suggests that even at the quantum level there is an element of contingency: reality becomes in certain directions not simply as a process of mere repetition, but in ways that create differences throughout. In other words, like the Deleuzian understanding of "difference and repetition" mentioned above, here the performance of repetitive processes and the small differences in those performances which lead to changes in the world, is extended to the quantum and subquantum level. This means, that even at the smallest levels we can imagine, there is some sort of "agency" or "freedom." The world is not just blindly determined (nor completely free as everything is subjected to relationality). This understanding suggests that what we understand as "natural laws" might better be thought of as habits of becoming rather than laws set in place for all time and all places. Performativity as the way in which entities are organized (in Butler's sense) extends to all levels of reality. Remember, performativity is not merely choosing to perform in certain ways and not others: rather it means that we are all subject to scripts for becoming, without which we would not be recognizable or understandable. Processes and histories of nature-culture becoming write these "scripts," through which all entities and things make their appearances in the cosmos. However, every performance of a given way of becoming is never exactly the same (Butler 1990:175–193; cf. Althaus-Reid 2000). This is why, over time, exceptions to what we understand to be theories and laws accrue, and we must shift our understandings to account for data that either goes unexplained or is left out of (or abjected from) current theories. Merchant's understanding of agency in the rest of the natural world might not go so far as Barad's, but it does support this understanding of reality. Such an understanding of reality is queer in that it immediately and by necessity sides with the argument that the fundamental nature of reality is not stable, but rather changes. Queer theory argues against the notion of stable identities and categories, and instead opts for an evolving, shifting, fluid reality in which no concepts, ideas, truths, or identity markers are stable. They are co-constructed over time in complex natural-cultural processes and thus can be changed. The boundaries between matter and energy (Einstein), species (Darwin), male and female (Magnus Hirschfeld, and later queer theory), race (critical race theory), and just about everything else are fluid and shifting. A partnership ethic recognizes the fluid and evolving nature of life and argues that we must work with, and not on behalf of or for, the rest of the natural world.[3]

The extension of agency throughout the rest of the natural world, something Merchant's partnership model has in common with animistic understandings of the world and which the so-called "new materialisms" have picked up on, does not by itself suggest that we ought to be partners with the rest of the natural world. One might, for instance, read the survival of the fittest into the world and hold on to a managerial, anthropocentric, or even egoistic ethic: in the battle between us (or me) versus them, I need to use all of my agency to protect us (or me). However, just as Merchant's understanding of nature and the world blurs boundaries between so many categories, so too it blurs the boundaries of what constitutes the self. Merchant draws from relational ontologies that are found in Native traditions, as well as other feminist and ecofeminist theories, to suggest that selves are only formed through relationships with human and earth others (Merchant 2005:83–87). Such an understanding works well with ideas of subject formation found in queer theory: viz., that selves are only formed in relationship to others and these selves are not stable over time (see, e.g., Rivera 2015). Such an ontology of the self—or lack of self—is also found in Buddhism, though Merchant doesn't deal with that. It is also the language that many biologists are beginning to use in terms of what the human individual is. Biologists and other scientists are beginning to understand that the human at the cellular, genetic, and organismal levels is really more like an ecosystem made up of bacteria, viruses, genomes, and other types of entities forming a permeable whole.[4] Furthermore, the plasticity of our neuronal structures suggests we are literally changed at the neuronal level on a daily basis by our interactions with human and earth others (Malibou 2008). The very fact of reading this text is changing the structure of your internal network, so in a sense it will always be a part of you.

Our languages, histories, and almost everything we hold to be "internal" to us are really not of our own doing but products of the history of biological evolution, ecological contexts, and histories of cultures. For this reason, the so-called "new materialists," such as William Connolly (2010), Karen Barad (2007), and Jane Bennett (2009), argue that our own agency depends on networks of other agencies acting upon us. We are part of a much larger system subsuming historical, biological, technological, and climatological flows. Latour argues that all of these actants together make up a larger system: what Lovelock and Margulius called Gaia (Latour 2017). Such systems are nonlinear and chaotic: hence a partnership ethic such as found in Merchant would do much more to account for this type of diffused agency than would a managerial ethic of stewardship. Indeed, we need new "queer" environmental narratives to address the problems we now face as a planetary community. The close of this chapter will move toward an argument for such queer narratives.

Queer Environmental Narratives: Beyond Progress and Decline

As I have argued throughout this chapter, Merchant's work in critically assessing environmental history and the narratives found therein could contribute to the queering of environmental discourse. By challenging the narratives of mechanical models of nature and humans as stewards and paying attention to the abjected earth bodies that accumulate around mechanical models and narratives of progress and decline, Merchant's work, like QT, helps to destabilize the patriarchal, and hierarchical relationships among different types of humans and between humans and the rest of the natural world. QT does this through challenging gender binarism, sexual dimorphism, and the heteronormativity dictated by the patriarchal, hierarchical ordering of earth bodies. Merchant's work, in addition to some of these similar critiques of sexism, also critiques anthropocentrism and returns agency to the world through her engagement with chaos and complexity theories in order to begin to look at how humans might live in partnership with the rest of the natural world. Merchant's more environmentally focused critique and QT's more human critique are both rattling the same structures that keep humans locked into binary thinking about the sex, gender, and sexuality, and hold humans over and above the rest of the natural world. Together they make a stronger critique.

Merchant's work does touch upon critiques of heteronormativity. She recognizes that the partnership model can extend beyond heteronormative models to include all types of partnerships: business, same sex, kinship, and human relationships with other species and organism and the more than human world (Merchant 2003:191–208). In this recognition alone, we might understand Merchant's narrative models as part of a larger project of queering environmental discourse. However, there are also some less obvious ways that Merchant's project could prove productive in dialogue with queering discourse surrounding religion and nature.

It is no accident that her work tends to deal with religious and scientific narratives: these are the two discursive areas that tend to lock identities in some sort of fixed place. For instance, science tells us what is "natural" and "unnatural" and religion tells us what is "God-given" or "against God's plan." I don't need to rehearse the atrocities done to the actual bodies of women, Native peoples, people of color, and LGBTQ peoples (among others) in the name of both Nature and God. Picking away at the narrative fray of what "Nature" is and how "God" functions, then, helps loosen our identities from these anchors. We are in a world of becoming in which unstable identities influence and change one another on a daily basis and toward an uncertain future. There are rules, but they are not the rules of mechanical nature, efficient causality, gender and sex binaries, or God-given realities. They are rules, rather, based upon habits of becoming in the world, and these habits of becoming can (and do) change.

What features might be needed for new narratives that pay close attention to this queer reality and to all the planetary agents that are continually interacting and co-creating our worlds on a moment-by-moment basis? First, and for reasons already discussed, we need precisely a narrative that is not based on progress or decline, and a narrative that understands agency as diffuse. Merchant's work, among others, does this. Second, and related, we need narratives that take unknowing seriously. As Catherine Keller notes, certainty often shuts down conversation: we get locked into our own perspectives and there can be no dialogue with an other (Keller 2015). The world's religious traditions have such narrative resources: from non-absolutism and multiperspectivalism in Jainism, to impermanence and change in Buddhism, to the concept of neti-neti in Hinduism,[5] to the mystical traditions of apophasis in Christianity, Judaism, and Islam, to name just a few. Idolatry is nothing more than equating something in flux and impermanent with an ultimate enduring reality. Alfred North Whitehead, who Keller draws from and who also knows a thing or two about chaos and complexity, called this the "fallacy of misplaced concreteness" (Whitehead 1925:51–58). Val Plumwood, whose work Merchant engages in developing her partnership ethic (Merchant 2003:196–205), also argued for something like a dialogical approach to human and earth others in which the other's influence on the self is not backgrounded but rather acknowledged and allowed to possibly change one's self (Plumwood 2002). Uncertainty in our knowing and relations with others is an important part of developing planetary narratives and ethics (rather than limiting such narratives and ethics to the boundaries of species, nation, or religion, for instance).

Third, we need stories, concepts, ideas, models, and theories (not necessarily grand over-arching narratives) that place us first and foremost within a planetary context, as creatures among creatures. Most of our extant religious narratives have a serious problem in that humans are identified first and foremost as special, and especially in some cases, the adherents to a given religion. Most of our extant philosophical systems also provide a special place for humans *vis a vis.* the rest of the natural world. And perhaps the worst "ism" the world has yet seen is the carving up of the world through much bloodshed and genocide, also oftentimes arbitrarily, into nation-states, also known as nationalism. These localized identities, helpful as they may have been at one point, are actually stumbling blocks when trying to deal with wicked problems such as climate change, acidification of oceans, and global species decline. The process of globalization—though not equal in its distribution of ecological goods and ills—means that we are all radically connected on a daily basis. Every solution, then, must keep this global network of human interactions in mind, not to mention the rest of the planetary community. Merchant's partnership ethic and understanding of nature's autonomy help us to think in this planetary direction.

There are many ways of working out such a narrative: one can get there through significant updates to extant religious narratives (for instance), one can get there through religious naturalisms and stories such as the "epic of evolution" (Goodenough 1998). Though one need not be explicitly "religious," I would argue that religion at its root is the practice of meaning-making (re-ligare/legere: to re-read, tie back). In this sense, narratives are meaning-making practices, so even secular environmentalism can be understood as "religious." Regardless of the narratives that gets us there, and whether we agree that they are "religious" or not, we must get to a place in which we first and foremost think of ourselves as planetary citizens and creatures among other creatures (Bauman 2014).

Fourth, and related, we need to be thinking of humans as evolving planetary creatures: we are evolving with humans, other animals, bacteria, viruses, and technologies. To really open ourselves to a future in which we become partners with the rest of the planetary community, we can no longer wall ourselves off as a species from all others: humans will evolve beyond *Homo sapiens* one way or another. Thinking imaginatively about how that happens could help us to create some new narratives for the planetary community. Trickster figures from many indigenous peoples might provide a model for how we might navigate between humans and other animals. Tricksters navigate, blur, and shift the boundaries between male/female, human/animal, the living and the dead, thereby opening us up for new kinds of relationships with human and earth others. Scholarship in trans- and post-humanism might help us navigate how we understand ourselves evolving technologically. The point is that if we open up ourselves toward evolving with the planetary community rather than remaining locked into our static understanding of humanity, then we can begin to create technologies for the planetary community and not just for the benefit of humans (Bauman 2017).

Fifth, and finally, we must begin to co-create narratives that keep us focused on how our narratives affect different earth bodies differently. In other words, how do our actions ripple out and effect earth-others in both anticipated and unanticipated ways. If narratives are living, they must be for the living and they must be adaptable to mitigate unforeseen negative consequences, present and future. Critical academic scholarship is constantly revising and/or replacing narratives so that narratives that were once sexist, racist, or homophobic are replaced with others that incorporate the critiques of these "isms" in an effort to acknowledge the value of a greater range of peoples and perspectives. This process of critique and change must continue ad infinitum as newly emerging "isms" always plague a given narrative. We need to continue revising and replacing always in a way that also addresses speciesism and presentism (Singer 1975). Speciesism is Peter Singer's word to describe the assumption that humans are ethically and/or morally more valuable than other life on the planet. Presentism is a word that I use to designate the myopic view of the future of life on the planet (on the one hand) and the priority and special location of the present in a given moment (on the other). Presentism means mistaking our own historically, culturally embodied location as the point at which we can narrate a universal perspective; again, this calls for a bit of apophasis or deconstruction of our self-understanding. As partners within an evolving planetary community, we will always be engaged in re-imagining our lives together and opening onto new and unexpected partners that arise in this process. This is yet another advantage of Merchant's partnership ethic.

Ursula LeGuin recently called for science fiction writers to help us to think of and imagine the world in new ways. Nothing could be a more appropriate way to end this chapter than with a quote from that speech. It sums up the ways in which Merchant's critical and creative narrative approach might help us to see the planetary community through new eyes, or in a word, queerly. She writes,

> Hard times are coming, when we'll be wanting the voices of writers who can see alternatives to how we live now, can see through our fear-stricken society and its obsessive technologies to other ways of being, and even imagine real grounds for hope. We'll need writers who can remember freedom—poets, visionaries—realists of a larger reality.
>
> *(Leguin 2014)*

I can't think of a better way to heed LeGuin's call than to imagine narratives for planetary partnerships of the kind that Merchant calls for.

Notes

1 By "earth bodies," I simply mean the distinct entities—human bodies, animals, plants, rivers, mountains—which are made up of combinations and flows of energy and elements on this planet.

2 The term is widely attributed to Hunter Lovins of the Rocky Mountain Institute. It gained more traction with an article by Thomas Friedman, "Global Weirding is Here" in *The New York Times*, February 17, 2010: www.nytimes.com/2010/02/17/opinion/17friedman.html. There is now a regular YouTube series with popular climate scientist Katharine Hayhoe called "Global Weirding": www.youtube.com/channel/UCi6Rkda EqgRVKi3AzidF4ow.

3 In this sense, Merchant's partnership ethic works well with Bruno Latour's notion of the collective in *Politics of Nature* (Latour 2004).

4 On this point, see the Human Microbiome Project: https://hmpdacc.org/.

5 Neti-neti or "not this, not that" is a way of understanding that we can never say what something is exactly, but only what it is not. It is similar to the apophatic traditions within Christianity that suggest we can never say what God is, only what god is not.

References

Althaus-Reid, Marcella. 2000. *Indecent Theology: Theological Perversions in Sex, Gender and Politics*. New York: Routledge.

Barad, Karen. 2007. *Meeting the Universe Halfway: Quantum Physics and the Entanglement of Matter and Meaning*. Durham, NC: Duke University Press.

Bauman, Whitney. 2009. *Theology, Creation and Environmental Ethics: From Creatio ex Nihilo to Terra Nullius*. New York: Routledge.

Bauman, Whitney. 2014. *Religion and Ecology: Developing a Planetary Ethic*. New York: Columbia University Press.

Bauman, Whitney. 2017. "Incarnating the Unknown: Planetary Technologies for a Planetary Community." *Religions* 8(65):1–10.

Bennett, Jane. 2009. *Vibrant Matter: A Political Ecology of Things*. Durham, NC: Duke University Press.

Berry, Thomas and Brian Swimme. 1992. *The Universe Story: From the Primordial Flaring Forth to the Ecozoic Era: A Celebration of the Unfolding of the Cosmos*. New York: HarperCollins.

Butler, Judith. 1990. *Gender Trouble: Feminism and the Subversion of Identity*. New York: Routledge.

Butler, Judith. 1993. *Bodies that Matter: On the Discursive Limits of Sex*. New York: Routledge.

Connolly, William. 2010. *A World of Becoming*. Durham, NC: Duke University Press.

Darwin, Charles. 1964 edition. *On the Origin of Species*. Boston, MA: Harvard University Press.

Deleuze, Gilles. 1994. *Difference and Repetition*. New York: Columbia University Press.

Derrida, Jacques. 1974. *Of Grammatology*. Baltimore, MD: Johns Hopkins University Press.

Foucault, Michel. 1978. *The History of Sexuality: Volume I, An Introduction*. New York: Random House.

Glacken, Clarence. 1967. *Traces on the Rhodian Shore: Nature and Culture in Western Thought From Ancient Times to the End of the Eighteenth Century*. Berkeley, CA: University of California Press.

Goodenough, Ursula. 1998. *The Sacred Depths of Nature*. New York: Oxford University Press.

Harding, Sandra. 1991. *Whose Science? Whose Knowledge? Thinking From Women's Lives*. Ithaca, NY: Cornell University Press.

Horkheimer, Max and Theodor Adorno. 2002 edition. *Dialectic of Enlightenment: Philosophical Fragments*. Palo Alto, CA: Stanford University Press.

Keller, Catherine, and Laurel Schneider. 2011. *Polydoxy: Theology of Multiplicity and Relation*. New York: Routledge.

Keller, Catherine. 2015. *Cloud of the Impossible: Negative Theology and Planetary Entanglement*. New York: Columbia University Press.

Kuhn, Thomas. 1962. *The Structure of Scientific Revolutions*. Chicago, IL: University of Chicago Press.

Latour, Bruno. 2004. *Politics of Nature: How to Bring the Sciences into Democracy*. Cambridge, MA: Harvard University Press.

Latour, Bruno. 2017. *Facing Gaia: Eight Lectures on the New Climactic Regime*. Cambridge: Polity Press.

Leguin, Ursula. 2014. "Speech in Acceptance of the National Book Foundation Medal." Found online at: www.ursulakleguin.com/NationalBookFoundationAward-Speech.html. (Last accessed October 9, 2017).

Leopold, Aldo. 1949. *A Sand County Almanac (Outdoor Essays and Reflections)*. Oxford: Oxford University Press.

Macy, Joanna. 1995. "Working Through Environmental Despair." In *Ecopsychology: Restoring the Earth, Healing the Mind*, edited by Theodor Roszak, Mary E. Gomes *et al.* New York, NY: Sierra Club Books.

Macy, Joanna. 2012. *Active Hope: How to Face the Mess We're in without Going Crazy*. Novato, CA: New World Library.

Macy, Joanna and Chris Johnstone (2012). *Active Hope: How to Face the Mess We're in without Going Crazy*. Novato, CA: New World Library.

Malabou, Catherine. 2008. *What Should we Do with Our Brain? (Perspectives in Continental Philosophy)*. New York, NY: Fordham University Press.

Mazis, Glen. 2002. *Earthbodies: Rediscovering our Planetary Senses*. Albany, NY: State University of New York.

Merchant, Carolyn. 1980. *The Death of Nature: Women, Ecology, and the Scientific Revolution*. New York, NY: HarperCollins.

Merchant, Carolyn. 2003. *Reinventing Eden: The Fate of Nature in Western Culture*. New York, NY: Routledge. Merchant, Carolyn. 2005. *Radical Ecology: The Search for a Livable World*. New York, NY: Routledge.

Merchant, Carolyn. 2016. *Autonomous Nature: Problems of Prediction and Control From Ancient Times to the Scientific Revolution*. New York, NY: Routledge.

Nixon, Rob. 2013. *Slow Violence and the Environmentalism of the Poor*. Cambridge, MA: Harvard University Press.

Plumwood, Val. 2002. *Environmental Culture: The Ecological Crisis of Reason*. New York, NY: Routeldge.

Rittel, Horst and Melvin Webber. 1973. "Dilemmas in a General Theory of Planning." *Sciences* 4:155–169.

Rivera, Mayra. 2015. *Poetics of the Flesh*. Durham, NC: Duke University Press.

Singer, Peter. 1975. *Animal Liberation*. New York, NY: HarperCollins.

Whitehead, Alfred North. 1925. *Science and the Modern World*. New York, NY: MacMillan.

16

A MIGHTY TREE IS CAROLYN MERCHANT

Patsy Hallen

The Death of Nature is a brilliant book.

It enabled me to comprehend the history and philosophy of science more deeply. It inspired me to dedicate my life as a teacher and researcher to "falling in love outwards" with the natural world and, as a consequence, to becoming more fully human.

In this chapter, I wish to show how Carolyn Merchant's original and provocative work, as well as her wonderful and grand presence, has expanded and enriched me and the thousands of students I have been fortunate enough to know over decades of university teaching.

The Background

In 1974, I was appointed a foundation member of staff at Murdoch University in Perth, Western Australia.

I was hired as a philosopher who could create interdisciplinary courses and apply the "accumulated wisdom of humans" to a broad range of topics. As a roving academic who was beholden to no specific program with its required courses, and who was free to develop elective options so long as they were well subscribed by students, I was in a privileged position to initiate new ventures.

For example, commencing in 1976, I co-coordinated a course with a theoretical chemist called "Science, Technology and Society." This course ran for over a decade, attracting students from a wide range of disciplines. It examined the assumptions of science, probed the limitations of a mechanistic world view, engaged with ethical issues in science such as genetic engineering, and deliberated on the social impacts of technology, such as computers.

In "Science, Technology and Society," I used the philosophical frameworks of Whitehead and Bergson to articulate science as process. I tried to show how the notion of detached neutrality can be dangerous in that it tends to camouflage how our personal, sexual, cultural, and species signatures inscribe the face of science. I used the metaphysics of Hegel and Heidegger to disclose how the "self" in science is often constructed as separate from and superior to nature and how "nature" is instrumentalized. I attempted to show how science can be incorporated into the military-industrial complex and how science contributes to various forms of domination, including sexual oppression. But I needed all the help I could get, as many of my students were training to be scientists and they viewed science as somehow sacrosanct.

So you can imagine how delighted I was when I discovered *The Death of Nature* (hereafter *TDN*) (Merchant 1980), which offered a radical and politically astute reinterpretation of the history of science. Being richly detailed and prodigiously researched, this colossal work provided me with priceless historical detail and compelling evidence.

The course materials of "Science, Technology and Society" contained a critique of the mechanical model of science where death, not life, begins to appear as the intelligible condition. Simultaneously, I had been developing a "living-earth ethics" whereby nature is seen as alive, full of self-generating complexity and resourcefulness. So to discover *TDN* was like finding gold. My "living-earth ethics" now had a powerful ally.

Reading *The Death of Nature*

I first read *TDN* in draft form in 1979. The proofs of the book were sent to Robert Cohen, an esteemed Professor of Physics at Boston University, in the hope that some of his review might be used on the cover.

I was a graduate student at Boston University from 1966–1969 where I studied Marx as well as Hegel's *Phenomenology of Mind* with Cohen. Cohen also supervised my Ph.D. thesis on "The Concept of Relation," in which I investigated how relationships are not just accidental, but substantial, constituting who we are. This model of interconnectedness was the nascent start of my involvement with radical ecology.

When I returned to Boston ten years later on study leave from Australia, Bob Cohen gave me the proofs of *TDN* to read.

I arrived at his office soon after to return the manuscript, full of praise for the book. I was overflowing with the joy one feels when someone expresses precisely one's developing ideas and backs them up with incisive evidence and cogent arguments.

I can vividly recall Bob Cohen's pithy response to my enthusiasm as he took the manuscript from me: "Brilliant but wrong!"

Even at that time, I knew who was wrong.

Cohen admired the founding fathers of modern science and contributors such as Francis Bacon. He could not see any significant connections between the images of women and nature constructed by Western culture. Nor could he accept the need to re-conceptualize the earth as a living organism. Fueled by a sedimented, and thus invisible, but nonetheless powerful, belief that physics was the bedrock of all science, he presumed inert matter (e.g. death!) to be the foundational keystone.

TDN challenges the hegemony of mechanistic science. It shows how this construction of science is implicated in the ecological crisis, how it contributes to the belief that we can and should control and dominate nature, and how this exacerbates the devaluation and inferiorization of women. With consummate skill, Merchant advances a sophisticated critique of mechanism, analyzes the ways in which the categories of women and nature are framed, reveals the crucial links between the subjugation of nature and women, and develops an alternative, organic view of nature.

TDN has been enormously influential. And not only was *TDN* a stunning tour de force of scholarship, it was prophetic. The final lines of the book, which call for a reassessment of the organic world view and for the integration of human and natural ecosystems, are as contemporary as landing a space probe on a comet.

Similar Interests

After *TDN*, Merchant went on to write many efficacious books, all with arresting titles. Each of them informed my own work. My academic interests are astonishingly similar to Carolyn's, so not only did *TDN* help me enormously, so did *Radical Ecology: The Search for a Livable World* (Merchant 2005). Let me explain.

In 1981, I developed a course in "Environmental Ethics," the first course of its kind in Australia. The state in which Perth is located, Western Australia, is approximately a million square miles (the land mass of India) with just 2.6 million people. Living in Australia brought me closer to the incredible wild world. It also educated me as to how easily such biodiversity, integrity, primal enchantment, and seeming inexhaustibility can be lost due to poorly regulated economic exploitation. Frontier ethics, boasting boundless expanses to be plundered and justifying human supremacy, rules in mineral-rich Western Australia. I hungered to expose the deficiencies of such a stance and to make philosophy more life-relevant by expanding my "living earth" ethics.

So I employed my knowledge as a philosopher, my passion for the bush, my experience as a backpacker in the outback, my involvement as an environmental activist and forest lover, and what skill I was gifted as a teacher to create a course that could help to heal the alienation of many modern people from the communicative presence of the "more-than-human" world and that could detail the political, economic and cultural transformations required to fulfill our deepest needs.

When *Radical Ecology* was published in 1992, eleven years after "Environmental Ethics" commenced, I used it as a textbook, with tremendous success. Students found it clear and succinct, offering them an excellent overview of the major metaphysical, ethical, scientific, and economic roots of the global ecological crisis. It also provided them with conceptual frameworks (such as the dialectical interplay between production and reproduction) for interpreting ecological revolutions, and it helped them to comprehend how environmental exploitation and social oppression are intertwined. As well, it gave them tools for creating pathways to a more just and livable world.

Inviting Carolyn to Australia

In 1991, a year before *Radical Ecology* was published, I invited Carolyn Merchant to be the first Visiting Ecofeminist Scholar at Murdoch University. I realized that ecofeminism was a vitally important and newly developing field. Guided by the insights of the early ecofeminists such as Françoise d'Eaubonne (1974, whose work *Le feminisme ou la mort* I read in French, as this work was not translated into English until 1989), I could see that the domination of nature and the domination of women are not only intimately connected but mutually reinforcing. The structures that keep women oppressed are the same structures that reduce living soil to barren sterility and poison fertile wetlands, making them toxic wastelands. I reckoned that the failure to identify these twin exploitations of women and nature would result in the further deterioration of both the human condition and that of non-human nature.

In 1990, I drew up a proposal to establish an elective course in ecofeminism, which would be open to undergraduates, graduates, and postgraduates. The proposal was acrimoniously received by Murdoch's administration and was within a hair's breath of being resoundingly rejected by Academic Council. To my delight, a person to whom I had shown the proposal supported the program with a very generous grant. With the money from this "fairy godmother," I was able to run the course for several fruitful years, inviting a series of respected ecofeminist academics: Carolyn Merchant, Chris Cuomo, Karen Warren and Noël Sturgeon from the United States; Sheila Mason from Canada; and Val Plumwood from Australia. The financial support was crucial. Not only did it open the way for the course to be approved, but it also enabled each scholar to be in residence for six months and to be responsible only for a single course. This allowed each recipient the time to participate fully in the life of the University, the space to work with and advise students, and the opportunity to think, research, reflect and write.

Each of these mentors subsequently contributed richly to ecofeminist scholarship through their publications and teaching efforts. The publications that followed from the ecofeminism residence of these scholars include Merchant's *Radical Ecology* (1992), which investigates the revolutionary thoughts and movements directed to sustaining life on earth and where she graciously acknowledges how my "ideas and enthusiasm greatly influenced her work"; Val Plumwood's *Feminism and the Mastery of Nature* (Plumwood 1993), which exposes the structures of oppression built into the master form of rationality; Noël Sturgeon's exposition *Ecofeminist Natures* (Sturgeon 1997), a wonderful antidote to those who would "essentialize" ecofeminism; Chris Cuomo's *Feminism and Ecological Communities* (Cuomo 1998) which argues the case for ecological feminism as an invaluable source of social and environmental ethics; and Karen Warren's *Ecofeminist Philosophy* (Warren 2000), which depicts the power and the promise of ecological feminism, and where in the Preface she generously thanks the patron and me for bestowing the opportunity and the support needed to write this book.

My First Choice

Carolyn Merchant was my first choice as the initial Visiting Ecofeminist Scholar. She was a professor at one of the most esteemed learning institutions in the world, a celebrated author and a leading luminary in the areas of the history and philosophy of science and ecofeminism. To my enchantment, Carolyn accepted my invitation, travelling to Perth for six months with her partner, Charlie Sellers. This choice was radiantly rewarded.

I first met Carolyn on the night of a Blue Moon. She arrived on foot, just as the full moon rose. My beloved and I were sitting on our porch overlooking Dolphin Lagoon and the Indian Ocean when she and Charlie materialized on the lawn before us, like magical apparitions. I was expecting Carolyn before the start of the semester (February, which is late summer "down under"), but I was not sure exactly when. An email she had courteously sent me containing this information went astray. So her appearance that night was a standout surprise, as splendiferous as the full moon.

During her tenure at Murdoch University, Carolyn contributed enormously to university life. Apart from her scintillating course on Ecofeminism, she gave guests lectures and talks to the community, assisted and advised Honors, Masters and Ph.D. students with their research, delivered seminars to staff and offered radio and television interviews. In these encounters, all the dimensions of her book *Earthcare* (Merchant 1996) were evident. Carolyn's communications were infused with a keen sense of history, a deep sensitivity to the "other," a marked appreciation of science as process, and a fine ability to articulate women's social and political agency.

Many people were impressed by Carolyn's measured presence and even skeptics, who previously had been dubious about how the unjustified domination of women could illuminate ecological damage and other forms of oppression, were won over.

It was during this period that the powerful theory of partnership ethics originated, developed and championed by Merchant, was born. This is an ethic of earthcare based on the dynamic partnership between human and nonhuman communities. This partnership ethic avoids the problematic gendering of nature as nurturing mother or goddess, and it has the potential to avoid the ecocentric dilemma of adjudicating between the rights of various life-forms. Even though the moral equality proposed by some versions of ecocentrism does not entail either identical treatment or actual equality, it is still an awkward principle to implement, and we tend to end up, like the pigs in *Animal Farm*, declaring that some living creatures are "more equal" than others. Partnership ethics has the potential to be based not on the problematic notion of equality but on the more vibrant concept of reciprocity, the reciprocity of interdependent living systems.

To paraphrase the remarkable author, Annie Dillard, I cannot cause light. The most I can do is to put myself and others in the path of its beam—in this case, in the path of Carolyn Merchant!

It is one thing to be dynamically informed by an author. It is quite another to admire, respect, and love that author as a person. Carolyn Merchant is a very special human being. She has a brilliant mind. She is loyal, caring, open, organized, hard-working, determined to help fashion a better world, and dedicated to the search for social and environmental justice. Carolyn is capable of moving mountains if her sense of fair play dictates. She also takes her teaching seriously and puts exceptional thoughtfulness into drawing the best out of each student. Carolyn even enrolled in an acting course to help improve her lecturing skills. This state of being-in-awe of Carolyn has endured and strengthened over the 26 years that I have known and worked with her.

Visiting California

In 1993, Carolyn invited me to teach at the University of California, Berkeley. I taught two courses, "Environmental Philosophy and Ethics" and "Ecofeminism." This was the first time ecofeminism was taught at UC Berkeley. In my course on ecofeminism, I investigated the complex, controversial yet fascinating relationship between women and nature. I tried to address the challenging question: Why focus on women when the diminishing of life's diversity and the undermining of the earth's life-support systems is a human concern?

Employing evidence from the history of science, I attempted to show why it is vital to explore the multi-layered association of women with nature in order for humans to make peace with nature. Scholars such as Brian Easlea (1981) in *Science and Sexual Oppression* document substantial connections between the birth of modern science and the burning of women healers. And as *TDN* reveals, Western science is permeated by images of an enticing but uncooperative female who must be penetrated by hard science, mastered into passive submission and rendered barren to reveal her secrets.

I strove to make my gender-based investigations throughout the course as inclusive and relational as possible, reaching out to complementary analyses of class, race, culture, and crucial eco-centered concerns. I also tried to demonstrate how the connections between women and nature are both unique and significant, and thus why a gender-sensitive analysis is irreplaceable. Eschewing essentialism, I neither gendered nature as female not privileged women as carers. But I drew upon women's nurturing experiences, their "cultures of resistance" and their ecological labor to illuminate human's life-debt to the earth.

I also tried to show how our culture is reluctant to acknowledge dependency, specifically our dependency on nature, and how this can lead to arrogance in believing that we can always improve on nature. Can we better natural ecosystems that have two-to-three billion years of research and development behind them?

Facing up to such questions does not mean that we abandon scientific endeavor, which, after all, is one of humanity's most precious possessions. Nor does it mean that we should not strive to improve human and nonhuman well-being through the power of applied science. But pondering these questions may help us to recognize the limitations of scientific inquiry and how our pathologies can play out in the systemic, systematic, and institutionalized exploitation of the natural world.

My classes buzzed with excitement. The classrooms were full to overflowing and students brought their boyfriends, parents, relatives, and mates. It was an experience of a lifetime. My students were overwhelmingly appreciative. They spontaneously declared that:

"Environmental Philosophy and Ethics was the best course that I have studied in my life."

"Environmental Philosophy will help me with my future work as a scientist and as a person living in the world."

"Ecofeminism was truly breath-taking, emboldening and life-changing."

"This unit has great depth and breath, and Patsy has an excellent way of inspiring students. I appreciated the various texts assigned in Ecofeminism as well as Patsy's own Reader and highly informative Study Guide."

"I was blown away by Patsy's energy, enthusiasm and wisdom."

I was (and still am) deeply moved and honored by these comments which many students sent me in letters and cards. But these tributes are not so much about me, but about them, my students, and their generosity, their ability to treasure and their willingness to be intimately touched by grand concepts. These testimonials are also not about me but about the ideas of my courses, ideals that we long for and yearn to live by.

I learned far more than I taught. I learned about the importance of humility and how to respectfully recognize and navigate the painful paradoxes and compromises involved in inhabiting our culture without becoming bitter or discouraged and how to select an arena for ethical action that brings joy.

Sailing and Ecofeminism

While at Berkeley, Carolyn's partner, Charlie, genially offered us accommodation on his sailboat moored in the Berkeley Marina. We had an unforgettable time outside the classroom, sailing in San Francisco Bay and the Pacific Ocean.

Curiously, sailing and ecofeminism inform each other. On a sailboat it is folly to believe that one can dominate nature. Such blind spots can endanger lives. The best sailors are Taoists. Sapient sailing involves understanding nature and fitting in with the dictates of weather, wind, swell, and tide. One learns to venerate the Taoist symbol of water, representing the qualities of openness, emptiness, receptivity, and humility. Such characteristics may be construed as "soft," but they can overwhelm and transform the strongest substances. Witness the Grand Canyon.

The feedback loops that underpin ecofeminist insights into the interconnections among oppressions are very evident on a boat. The results of pollution can be delayed for decades in normal society or displaced into less socially advantaged suburbs or countries. Whereas on a boat, if one forgets to secure a shackle or tie a rope properly, the mast will fall down.

We can also apply Val Plumwood's "logic of colonization" to sailing. This "logic," explored in Plumwood's work *Feminism and the Mastery of Nature*, exposes concealed agendas in the philosophical canon and, in doing so, uncovers the deep structures of oppression that are embedded in the master form of rationality of Western culture.

The master rationality makes "difference" the vehicle for hierarchy. Plumwood traces this logic of colonization in compelling detail. She rigorously illustrates the ways in which our oppositional and masculinized culture operates: backgrounding the other, denying dependency, incorporating or hyperseparating the other, instrumentalizing, homogenizing or stereotyping the other.

Being at sea clearly displays this "logic." Sailing makes plain that we cannot background nature; it is never peripheral or capable of being "improved" by patriarchal reason. Nor can we homogenize it; the sea is never uniform or one-dimensional. Furthermore, we cannot "hyper-separate" nature and humans, positioning nature in a dualistic way, as oppositional to humans. At sea, as on land, humans dwell within the wild world. And as sailors, we inferiorize the natural world to our peril. The ocean is not just a "standing reserve," an instrumental means in service of the master's ends. Nature is sovereign and unfathomable. Nature is not just more complex than we know; nature is more complex than we can know.

Merchant's book *Autonomous Nature* (Merchant 2016) develops this theme splendidly, investigating the idea of nature as an "active, sometimes disruptive and unruly entity" and the resulting tensions between order and chaos, stability and change, predictability and unpredictability. Carolyn also discloses how humans might live and in fact thrive within an autonomous, earthly nature, by respecting their "mutual living interdependence."

The Consequences of Carolyn: A Unique Course

In 2000, I commenced a novel course, "Ecophilosophy and Practice," in which I, an internationally-renowned visiting scholar, 15 students and my partner as navigator, spent 23 days (spread over three trips throughout the 16-week seme-ster) backpacking in the remote outback. The goals of this unique course, which ran for five years and was again magnanimously sponsored by my fairy god-mother, included recognizing that human flourishing is radically contingent on ecological well-being; linking one's discipline to the wider context of the wild world by ecologizing thought; and developing ways to help honor and restore the health, diversity, and complexity of natural and human communities.

We discovered that the pedagogical exuberance of the "more-than-human" world is enormous. There is no substitute for the lived experience of being in the bush, especially if we wish to relate ethically to it. To paraphrase the astute nat-uralist, Aldo Leopold, one can only be ethical in relation to something one knows, loves or believes in.

It was a risky venture, both in physical terms (potential snake bites and broken limbs) and metaphysical terms (in back-of-beyond places, there are fewer guard-rails to secure self-deception). But the course was premised on a kind of wild trust: the belief that the natural world is home, not some scary, hostile place, and that the most powerful educator is nature.

Together we wrapped the world in a web of songlines, those chorale pathways by which Aboriginal people navigate. Together we overcame biophobia, that pathological fear where the earth is imagined as fundamentally inhospitable, and developed biophilia, where we walked in a landscape of communicative pre-sences. Together we lessened our created wants and nourished our vital needs. Together we walked ourselves and the world into being.

The students (aspiring microbiologists, city planners, historians, environmental scientists and sustainable development policy-makers as well as philosophy stu-dents) were transformed from a disparate group into an intentional, fully func-tioning community.

Listen to their voices:

"The fullness I feel after a day immersed in the natural world contrasts harshly with the hollowness of a day shopping."

"This course is to environmental philosophy what laboratory experiments are to science. I find it an equally relevant, exciting and irreplaceable learning experience."

"The group is beyond a few superlatives…there is room to share your wildest thoughts…it's been a new experience in terms of honesty without needing to have a few beers beforehand…I am talking about things that profoundly move me, regularly, with different people, and without the slightest worry that the person listening wouldn't understand my feelings. What a gift to be amongst these people!"

"As far as the academic content of the course is concerned, I have a worrying feeling that I am going to learn more in four months at Murdoch [in Australia] than four years studying at St. Andrews [in Britain]."

Although I was the teacher, I also had to shuffle about a bit and engage in "world-travelling." I had to learn how (hard as it was) to abandon self-importance, how to be playful, how to be comfortable with uncertainty, how to be open to surprise. I had to recognize and try to overcome several temptations:

- The sergeant major (the value trap of needing to control);
- The burning martyr (the impulse to try and do everything myself);
- The worrywart (that form of bad faith where one does not allow grown people to take responsibility for themselves); and
- The tragic heroine (the urge to be rid of nagging, perplexing ambiguity, to sink into the comfort of neat, polarized dualisms and to construct total villains, e.g. those who formulate and follow bad policy and clear-cut old growth forests to make third-grade cardboard!).

Everyone contributed. Mark caught thirteen fish. Genelle created a palette of place. Jeremy reminded us of the importance of getting lost. Megan awakened lost worlds by her wondrous prose. Peter navigated us safely while I revealed how profoundly ignorant we are and how informative this Socratic ignorance is. Even the Vice Chancellor contributed—inadvertently. In a dramatic scene at Academic Council, he threw out the course when it was first to be offered. Possibly he was under pressure from certain government and corporate sectors to eradicate breeding grounds for conservationists. Of course, this instantly made the course famous. With the courageous support of the Dean and the Head of my Institute, "Ecophilosophy and Practice" began, with its instructive history.

And so, for five glorious years, with five wonderful tribes of students and five incredible visiting scholars (Jim Cheney, Stephan Harding, Leesa Fawcett, Kate Rawles, and Anthony Weston), we together recovered our ecological identities upon which our well-being is dependent.

So you see what Carolyn started!

The Karri Tree as Metaphor

In addition to the other metaphors I have employed to describe Carolyn in this chapter, my tribute to Carolyn Merchant (whose nickname is Carrie) can also be read through a Karri tree.

The Karri is a majestic, evergreen hardwood. This eucalyptus (*eucalyptus diversicolor*) is the tallest tree in Western Australia, growing to a height of 290 feet and reaching 20 feet in girth. It is the second tallest hardwood tree in Australia (after the Mountain Ash in Victoria and Tasmania, which grows 30 feet higher). And the Karri ranks in the top ten list of the largest living beings on the planet.

The Karri is found nowhere else on earth. The species is restricted to a small area in the south west of this Island continent. It grows on deep, loamy soils where the annual rainfall is in excess of 40 inches. Its trunk is smooth and billiard-cue straight for the first 190 feet, before it branches out into a full, balanced canopy. Its leaves are broadly lanceolate (shaped like a spearhead, tapering to each end), dark green above but paler underneath, leading to its name, "diversicolor."

To lie on the forest floor and look up into the dizzying heights of its branches with clouds sweeping past overhead is to risk vertigo. It is difficult to take in the beauty of such tall, straight trunks with their giddily high branches.

The bark of the Karri is shed each year and when the new bark appears, it varies in color from burnt sienna orange to wattle yellow to gleaming white. The platinum flowers produce a very high-grade honey, generally recognized as the best in Western Australia. The honey is harvested by honeyeaters such as the New Holland and by parrots like the Lorikeet. I have witnessed birds become so intoxicated by the honey that they cannot fly properly and have to rest for a considerable spell to sober up.

The Karri is also fabled for its straight roots that can penetrate rock and travel hundreds of feet into the earth to locate water. I have stood in a limestone cave, the roof of which was 100 feet below ground, and seen the tap root of a Karri plunge straight through the 90 foot cavern and disappear into the bedrock at my feet.

Like the Karri, Carolyn Merchant's life work has blossomed into a magnificent, intricate organism. Her books, like the trunk, stand tall and straight; her words, like the canopy, are full and balanced and her thoughts, like the leaves, are diverse and fecund. To put all of Carolyn's works together is to be dazzled. Just like being in a Karri forest, the reader risks vertigo contemplating her astonishing output. It is difficult to take in the volume of creative thought and meticulous research involved in producing such a splendid "forest" of ideas. Carolyn's thinking, like the bark of a Karri tree, is self-renewing with each of her readers, the offshoots helping to build compost where other notions can sprout and flourish. As with Karri honey, one can be nourished by Carolyn's enticing, delectable concepts. Like the roots of a Karri tree, Carolyn Merchant's ideas are formidable and penetrating, drilling into dogmatic assumptions and breaking up prejudices to locate life-giving meaning. Like the growth of a Karri tree, the richness of Carolyn Merchant's thought can only be won gradually through time, as a result of attentiveness and studiousness. The Karri, like so many hardwoods, has been extensively logged, often ending up not as a prized timber suitable for prestige furniture or craftwork but as an export to make third-grade cardboard. Like Carolyn, who is a highly literate scholar, steeped in historical documents, Karri is an endangered species.

The texts which inform Carolyn's research might seen antiquated, but actually they are startlingly contemporary. The ideas of thinkers such as Descartes, Bacon, and Newton shape our world as surely as bulldozers, guiding our behavior and formulating our policies. And unless we comprehend the ideologies which limit us, our remedies will only aggravate the life-threatening ills of modernity.

I planted Karri seedlings on our land at "Back Gate Gully" in 1978. The trees are now 100 feet high, just like the seminal ideas of Carolyn Merchant that have been sown and have prospered all over the world. With her theories firmly rooted in the earth, her ideas soar. Like the Karri, Carolyn Merchant's work is charged with power, offering vital gifts, sheltering novel hypotheses, protecting bold scholars, supporting transformative world-views and encouraging life-affirming actions.

Trees are crucial in maintaining life on our planet. So too is Carolyn Merchant's vision of a livable world. Through her writing and her person, Carolyn helps us to reconstruct, reimagine and reanimate our relationship with the "more-than-human" world.

No other work is more admirable.

References

Cuomo, Chris J. 1998. *Feminism and Ecological Communities: An Ethic of Flourishing*. London: Routledge.

Easlea, Brian. 1981. *Science and Sexual Oppression: Patriarchy's Confrontation with Woman and Nature*. London: Weidenfeld & Nicolson.

d'Eaubonne, Françoise. 1974. *Le féminisme ou la mort*. Paris: Horay.

Merchant, Carolyn. 1980. *The Death of Nature: Women, Ecology, and the Scientific Revolution*. San Francisco, CA: Harper & Row.

Merchant, Carolyn. 1996. *Earthcare: Women and the Environment*. New York: Routledge.

Merchant, Carolyn. 2005. *Radical Ecology: The Search for a Livable World*. New York: Routledge.

Merchant, Carolyn. 2016. *Autonomous Nature: Problems of Prediction and Control From Ancient Times to the Scientific Revolution*. New York: Routledge.

Plumwood, Val. 1993. *Feminism and the Mastery of Nature*. London: Routledge.

Sturgeon, Noël. 1997. *Ecofeminist Natures: Race, Gender, Feminist Theory, and Political Action*. New York: Routledge.

Warren, Karen J. 2000. *Ecofeminist Philosophy: A Western Perspective on What It is and Why It Matters*. Lanham, MD: Rowman & Littlefield.

AFTERWORD

Carolyn Merchant

In the foregoing chapters of *After the Death of Nature*, numerous scholars have praised, analyzed, and made suggestions for further work on my part. For all of these I am deeply grateful and have learned a great deal about the impact of my own work as well as ways to expand and enhance the argument made in my book *The Death of Nature: Women, Ecology, and the Scientific Revolution* (Merchant [1980] 1990). In the "Afterword" that follows, I discuss the historical changes that took place "after the death of nature" by looking at the eighteenth through the twenty-first centuries and the rise of a new age, now called the Anthropocene. In so doing, I include ideas from my other books and engage with ideas from the foregoing chapters, especially those by J. Baird Callicott, Holmes Rolston III, Mark Stoll, Norman Wirzba, Debora Hammond, Patsy Hallen, Shepard Krech III, Kenneth Worthy, Nancy Unger, Elizabeth Allison, and others. In the process I relate some of my own personal history as well as my own answers to the need for a new story, a new ethic, a new economy, new policies, and new spiritualities.

The "death of nature" as I conceptualized it in my book, *The Death of Nature* (hereafter *TDN*), dealt with the period in Western history from the Greco-Roman world to the end of the seventeenth and early eighteenth centuries. I focused in particular on the change between the Renaissance to what many have called the Scientific Revolution of the mid-sixteenth to the late seventeenth century, and how the worldview was transformed from an organism to a machine. I discussed the organic world as comprising a body, soul, and spirit in which the heavens were alive and the earth was viewed as a nurturing mother. The transformation of the earth-centered cosmos of Ptolemy to the sun-centered universe of Copernicus, Kepler, and Newton was reinforced by the terrestrial mechanics of Galileo, Boyle, and Newton who synthesized the two systems in his *Principia Mathematica* (*The Mathematical Principles of Natural Philosophy*) in 1687

(Newton 1960). In writing *TDN*, I incorporated ideas developed in my earliest publications under my former name Carolyn Iltis, and I am delighted that in Chapter 1 of this book, J. Baird Callicott has analyzed these contributions and placed them in the context of the ideas synthesized in *TDN*. His superb insights into my earliest work from the perspective of 2017 are both highly informative and deeply appreciated.[1]

In *TDN*, I argued that, in addition to the change in worldview from a living organism to a machine, God was now conceptualized a clockmaker, mathematician, and engineer. Simultaneously, society in the theories of Descartes, Hobbes, and Locke changed from an organic society of feudal manors and small farms in the Middle Ages and Renaissance to a mechanical model of individuals with machine-like bodies who competed like "atoms" fulfilling their own self-interests through ownership of land, factories, and industries.

In this "Afterword," I explore what happened historically after "the death of nature" during the period from the Enlightenment[2] of the eighteenth century through the mid-twenty-first century, an era named the Anthropocene by Paul Crutzen and Eugene Stoermer (Crutzen and Stoermer 2000). They argue that, as a result of the introduction of James Watt's steam engine in 1784, humans have dramatically altered the earth's climate. Although numerous scholars who have written on the Anthropocene have proposed new names and new starting points for the era (Haraway 2015; Moore 2014, 2016, 2017a, 2017b; Steffen, Crutzen, and McNeill 2007), I have chosen Crutzen and Stoermer's date because at that time the graph of greenhouse gases shows a major rise, followed by an acceleration in 1950s (Steffen et al. 2004). The late eighteenth and nineteenth centuries also introduced a full-scale industrial, capitalist society so that, by the middle of the twenty-first century, we might well experience a new "death of nature." This time, however, it puts at risk the human species itself which, as digital mechanist, data analyst, and environmental manipulator *par excellence*, has potentially set up the preconditions for its own extinction.

Indeed, climate change projections as of 2017 by the U.S. Environmental Protection Agency (EPA) say that by the year 2100 the average world temperature will increase by around 3–12°F (degrees Fahrenheit) and that the number of days with temperatures above 90 degrees will increase from around 5 percent in the years 1950–1979 to around 70 percent by 2035–2064. Projections of greenhouse gas emissions from the burning of fossil fuels range from a pessimistic high of over 1200 ppm (parts per million) of CO_2 (carbon dioxide) by 2100 to the most optimistic projection of a low of around 400 ppm. The organization 350.org[3] was formed in 2007 to pressure the nation to create policies to reduce the parts per million of CO_2 in the atmosphere from 400 ppm to 350 ppm as the safe upper limit for life on the planet (U.S. Environmental Protection Agency 2017; Raftery et al. 2017). These alarming projections would seem to herald the possibility of a new "death of nature" in the Age of the Anthropocene.

Advent of the Anthropocene

The eighteenth-century Enlightenment (*ca.* 1815–1889) that followed the Scientific Revolution was a period of great optimism. The advances in science that culminated in Isaac Newton's 1687 *Principia mathematica* (Newton 1960) led to a sense of the human ability to understand and control nature. The ideas of Jean Jacques Rousseau, Adam Smith, Voltaire, David Hume, Immanuel Kant, and other *philosophes* promoted scientific understanding, religious freedom, political independence, and equality. New compilations of human knowledge of the world appeared in the form of Rousseau's *Discourse on Inequality* (Rousseau 1983, 1992) and *The Social Contract* (Rousseau 1977, 1990), Adam Smith's *Wealth of Nations* (Smith 1776), and Denis Diderot and Jean d'Alembert's *Encyclopédie* (Diderot and d'Alembert 1754–1772). Academies, salons, and journals discussed and dispersed new knowledge of the natural world and its applications.

Especially important were the eighteenth-century scientific discoveries that would ultimately lead to the Age of the Anthropocene. These included the discovery of carbon dioxide (fixed air) by Joseph Black,[4] the chemical experiments of Antoine Lavoisier,[5] and the improvement of the steam engine by James Watt,[6] the results of which are the burning of enormous quantities of fossil fuels and the pumping of CO_2 and other greenhouse gases into the atmosphere. In 1754, Black discovered that by heating limestone (calcium carbonate) and treating it with acids he could produce a gas, which he called fixed air (CO_2), which would not support a flame or life itself. In 1762, he introduced the concept of latent heat— the idea that a substance such as water will remain at the same temperature until the entire volume evaporates, a concept critical to the workings of the steam engine (Fleming 1952). In 1775, Joseph Priestley showed that this "fixed air" could be made "respirable" again by growing plants in it. Lavoisier in 1778 coined the term oxygen, "an eminently respirable part of the air" and discovered that it would support combustion (MacLeod 1908:134). Most important to the concept of the Anthropocene, however, was James Watt's steam engine.

James Watt's Steam Engine

The task of moving objects other than by human (or animal) lifting, pushing, and pulling is an age-old problem. The five simple machines of the Greeks (the lever, the pulley, the wheel, the inclined plane, and the wedge) were force-maximizing devices, but needed to be powered by human or animal labor. In the Middle Ages, watermills used the force of gravity in the form of falling water to move objects, while windmills used moving air to accomplish similar tasks. Horses and mules were also used for comparable purposes. In the early eighteenth century (*ca.* 1712), Thomas Newcomen[7] (building on the work of Denis Papin and others) developed an engine[8] that by burning wood or coal in a furnace, water in a boiler was converted into steam[9] that would expand to push a piston in a cylinder upward. Then by condensing the steam with a shot of cold water, a vacuum was created in the cylinder, and external atmospheric pressure pushed it down, pulling the rocker arm upward. The rising and falling of the piston could then move the rocker arm that pushed, pulled, raised, or lowered external objects without the use of human or animal labor.

The Newcomen engine was immediately put into use all over England and greatly increased productivity, especially to pump water out of coal mines. The problem was that when the steam was cooled by injecting a shot of cold water to create the vacuum, it also cooled the cylinder. The cylinder then had to be reheated so that more steam could be created for the next motion of the piston, thereby wasting a lot of fuel.

In 1769, James Watt began to improve the efficiency of the Newcomen engine by working on a small model of the engine at Glasgow University. He discovered that by adding an exterior unit in which condensation could take place, he did not have to waste fuel by heating and cooling the same cylinder over and over again. Steam was created in a boiler and by expanding was pushed into the cylinder where the piston was located. The expanding steam pushed the top of the piston downward. Then a separate condenser filled with cold water sprayed water into the steam above the piston, reducing the air pressure and drawing the piston upward. With stopcocks placed both above and below the piston, the steam and low pressure could act alternately in a double action that enormously increased efficiency. In 1784, Watt and his partner Matthew Boulton patented a diagram of a double-acting steam engine that was used to construct steam engines throughout England. It was soon adapted beyond raising coal from mines to the development of steam-driven textile mills, steam boats, and steam trains.[10]

The Steam Engine and the Second Law of Thermodynamics

In the mid-nineteenth century, physicists Sadi Carnot (1796–1832) and Rudolph Clausius (1823–1888) addressed the problem of how to improve the amount of mechanical work obtained from the James Watt steam engine and in the process discovered that there can never be a perfect engine with no loss of heat—a discovery that by 1865 became the basis for the Second Law of Thermodynamics (Newburgh 2009; Mach 1986; Hiebert 1962). In 1824, Carnot published a short book titled *Reflections on the Motive Power of Fire*, in which he showed that the efficiency of the steam engine depends only on the temperatures of the two heat reservoirs in the cylinder and condenser, and that the ideal engine is frictionless and independent of the fluid used (Carnot 1824, 1890).

Then in 1850, Rudolf Clausius stated (without naming it as such) what became known as the second law of thermodynamics: "A transfer of heat from a hotter to a colder body always occurs in those cases in which work is done by heat, and in which also the condition is fulfilled that the working substance is in the same state at the end as at the beginning of the operation" (Magie 1899:89). An 1856 paper,

"On the Moving Force of Heat," stated the law as "heat can never pass from a colder to a warmer body without some other change occurring at the same time." In other words, for heat to be transferred from a cold to a hot body, work has to be expended. Then in 1865, he pulled it all together with his paper "On the Mechanical Theory of Heat—With Its Applications to the Steam Engine," naming the loss of energy available for work *entropy*. Here he stated the "first and second laws of thermodynamics" as (1) The energy of the universe is constant and (2) The entropy of the universe tends to a maximum (Clausius 1865, 1867:365; Clausius 1870:122–127). That is, the energy available for work (moving objects through space) is always decreasing because entropy, disorder, is always increasing. Disordered (high-entropy) matter such as burned ashes contains less energy than ordered (low-entropy) matter such as trees. The universe is running down to a higher-entropy state; order is turning to disorder; people grow older; rocks crumble. The cosmos seemed doomed to end in a heat death (a universe with no temperature differentials).

The second law of thermodynamics was of immense consequence in the historical period following the period described in my book, *TDN*. The optimism of the Enlightenment faded, exposing new limits to reality. But although what people could actually accomplish on earth was now severely compromised, the Watt steam engine nevertheless took off. It became the basis for the steamboat, the train, the factory, and the age of industrialization, spewing carbon dioxide from the burning of fossil fuels into the atmosphere. Ultimately, with the internal combustion engine in automobiles and airplanes, and then diesel-powered machines, more and more CO_2 was pumped into the air and oceans, resulting in global warming.

The Age of the Anthropocene in which humans are capable of causing a new "death of nature" on the planet is now our twenty-first-century nightmare. Do we need a new story, a new ethic, and a new type of economy that reverses the negative effects of the James Watt steam engine? Contributors to this volume argue that the answer is YES.

A New Story

Holmes Rolston III has written extensively about environmental ethics in books such as *Environmental Ethics: Duties to and Values in the Natural World* (Rolston 1988), *A New Environmental Ethics: The Next Millennium for Life on Earth* (Rolston 2012), and *Science and Religion: A Critical Survey* (Rolston 2006). I am honored that he has written a chapter for *After the Death of Nature*. In his chapter "Leading and Misleading Metaphors: From Organism to Anthropocene," Rolston writes:

> We need Carolyn Merchant today, more than ever … . She can make us much the wiser if we see that the twenty-first century is in even more danger than the sixteenth or seventeenth … . Facing an Anthropocene Epoch, we

need her insights into how ... the strictures of an ideology control us with controlling images of nature.

(Rolston, this volume, p. 103)

I appreciate the time that Rolston has taken to read my work so carefully and to comment on its value. I agree that we need a new ethic, worldview, and narrative. What would these look like in the Age of the Anthropocene? Should they criticize or incorporate the idea of the Anthropocene?

In my books, *Earthcare: Women and the Environment* (Merchant 1996), *Reinventing Eden: The Fate of Nature in Western Culture* (Merchant [2003] 2013), *Radical Ecology: The Search for a Livable World* (Merchant 2005:83–87), and *Autonomous Nature: Problems of Prediction and Control From Ancient Times to the Scientific Revolution* (Merchant 2016), I have proposed an ethic of partnership with nature and called nature a partner with humanity—ideas that can help form an antidote to human dominance in the Anthropocene. I have also given examples of how this ethic can be put into practice. Although partner is an anthropomorphic term, it implies a new relationship of give and take between humans and the planet. We take from the earth the basic food, clothing, shelter, and energy that keeps us alive as humans, but we also give back by composting and enriching the soil, replanting native species, recycling renewable resources, and leaving non-renewable resources in place as much as possible. We also learn from indigenous peoples around the world who have developed and used such practices over thousands of years. In this ethic, people of all genders are equal partners and all are partners with the earth. Partnership can form the basis of a new story and worldview (Merchant [2003] 2013).

My partnership ethic holds that the greatest good for the human and nonhuman communities is in their mutual living interdependence.

My partnership ethic has five precepts:

1. Equity between human and nonhuman communities;
2. Moral consideration for both humans and other species;
3. Respect for both cultural diversity and biodiversity;
4. Inclusion of women, minorities, and nonhuman nature in the code of ethical accountability;
5. An ecologically-sound management that is consistent with the continued health of both the human and the nonhuman communities. (Merchant [2003] 2013:224)

Rolston asks whether my partnership ethic could be adapted or extended to living in the Anthropocene? Or does there come with this new revolution "a fear of human domination of nature returning with a vengeance?" He quotes extensively from the "Ecomodernist Manifesto" that maintains that "future humans can fix these human-caused problems" created by the Anthropocene, an era named after ourselves in which there will be no limits on producing food. People will free up natural areas and the human impact on nature will "peak and decline this century." Rolston notes, "When human progress is progressively upscaled, ... the importance of ecosystem services is downscaled." He accurately concludes, "But none of this sounds like partnership." "There is nothing here of nature as active partner" (Rolston, this volume, p. 113).

In my view, this so-called "ecomodernism" is yet another form of human domination through technology and information theory, but this time it purports to save nature by moving people to ever more densely populated cities, freeing up so-called "wilderness" to be used for human recreation, not to be left alone. I do not believe that ecomodernism is the basis for a solution, a new story, or a new ethic.

Men and women are equally capable of reasoning and caring. As Rolston observes, "Merchant with her feminism anticipates the 'ethic of caring' as characteristic of her web-worked partnership ethic." In the past, women were perceived as being subordinate to men, but I do not think, as Rolston puts it, that "Merchant finds that what is distinctive about males ... is their capacity to reason compared to the caring, nurturing capacities of women." (Rolston, this volume, p. 107. Women have challenged this assumption ever since the seventeenth century. In *TDN* (Merchant [1980] 1990: preface, ch. 11) and in my writings on ecofeminism, I have provided a great deal of historical evidence about the reasoning power, writing ability, and mathematical and scientific capacities of women from Greco-Roman times to the present, especially feminist Betty Friedan (Merchant [1980] 1990; Friedan 1963), and environmentalist Rachel Carson (Merchant [1980] 1990; Carson 1962). Sherry Ortner (1972) explicitly challenged the dichotomy in her article "Is Female to Male as Nature Is to Culture?" I discuss these issues at length in my chapter on ecofeminism in *Radical Ecology: The Search for a Livable World* (Merchant [1992] 2005) and in my book *Earthcare: Women and the Environment* (Merchant 1996).

Rolston concludes his chapter with the following prescient statement: "'Welcome to the Anthropocene!'—seen as an Epoch in which the dominant species, humans, increasingly treasure their planet with promise" (Rolston, this volume, p. 115). He concludes with a view of God as divine and the earth as God's divine creation. I am not a religious person, but I agree that there is indeed much about the earth that is awe-inspiring, and it needs to be preserved and treasured.

The new story must be a Story of Sustainability rooted in the idea that humans take from the earth what they need for subsistence, give back what can be regrown and recycled, and leave non-renewable resources (especially fossil fuels) within the earth to the extent possible. My use of the term sustainability, however, should be distinguished from "Sustainable Development" as enunciated by Gro Harlem Bruntland in *Our Common Future*—also known as the Bruntland Report (World Commission on Environment and Development 1987). As I elaborated in *Radical Ecology*:

Rather than sustainable development, which reinforces dominant approaches to development, women's environmental groups, and many other NGOs, have substituted the term "sustainable livelihood." Sustainable livelihood is a people's oriented approach that emphasizes the fulfillment of basic needs, health, employment, and old-age security, the elimination of poverty, and women's control over their own bodies, methods of contraception, and resources. Such approaches are exemplified by localized sustainable agriculture, bioregionalism, and indigenous approaches to sustainability (Merchant [1992] 2005:23; see also Braidotti et al. 1994).

They include ecological methods that incorporate the wisdom of indigenous peoples and new forms of ecological management and restoration ecology that give back what is taken from the land.

My partnership ethic is based on a give and take between humans, and between humans and nature. In the last chapter of *Reinventing Eden*, I provide numerous examples of how to put this ethic into place. I include ways to work with business and within current ideas of capitalism while arguing that a sustainable system must move away from the exploitation of resources for the sake of profit. Implementing a partnership ethic is critical to the new Story of Sustainability as an alternative to the negative aspects of the Age of the Anthropocene.

Science and Religion

Mark Stoll takes up the question of religion, ecology, and the future of the Earth in his contribution to this book. I very much admire Mark Stoll's works *Protestantism, Capitalism, and Nature in America* (Stoll 1997) and *Inherit the Holy Mountain: Religion and the Rise of American Environmentalism* (Stoll 2015). I appreciate his Chapter 10 for this volume, "The Other Scientific Revolution: Calvinist Scientists and the Origins of Ecology," detailing the influence of Calvinism and reformed Presbyterianism on ecology. Stoll argues that John Calvin's theology was a major inspiration for the development of ecological science, which he refers to as one of the "trends overlooked by Merchant." Stoll provides a long list of Calvinist/Presbyterian men who appreciated nature and integrated nature into their faith, showing how they can be considered predecessors of an ecological science. Yet an appreciation for God's works in nature includes many complex intellectual, ethical, and religious dimensions as well as social contexts that go beyond what Stoll was able to discuss in this chapter.

Although my main emphasis in *TDN* was, as Stoll points out, on the rise of the mechanistic worldview, my work does include religious frameworks and individuals as well as the importance of gender, conservation, and stewardship for appreciating and preserving the environment. For example, in *TDN*, I include discussions of John Calvin, Robert Boyle, John Ray, William Derham, and others mentioned by Stoll who developed a stewardship approach to the care of nature.

Much of what was operative during the Scientific Revolution was directly tied to women's subordination through their perceived connections to nature. In the sixteenth and seventeenth centuries, women began to assert their right to equal religious opportunity. Stoll quotes some important passages from Calvin's writings regarding nature, for example: "Wherever you turn your eyes, there is no portion of the world that does not exhibit at least some sparks of beauty" (Stoll, this volume, p. 163), but does not quote Calvin's pronouncement that "the order of nature implies that the woman should be the helper of man." Although Calvin advocated that a woman had a right to divorce and that she should have equal responsibility in family worship and the education of children, he did not change his ideas about women's place in the natural world. Calvinist women, however, who read the Bible engaged in theological speculation—a form of liberation that was important before women could fully engage with the project of saving nature (Merchant [1980] 1990:146–147).

I appreciate Mark Stoll's effort to highlight the influence of figures such as John Ray and William Derham on the development of ecology, although he might be overlooking my chapter titled, "The Management of Nature," in *TDN* in which I discuss the philosophies of religious naturalists Ray and Derham who developed a philosophy of stewardship toward nature. Much that developed from a religious standpoint resulted from political compromises after the English Civil War as well as a perceived loss of forests, pollution of air and water, and loss of habitat that inspired the idea of religious stewardship over nature. If nature "could be used wisely and understood rationally," I wrote, "nature's abundance would not be exhausted" (Merchant [1980] 1990:252).

Concerning William Derham, I noted: "Derham's *Physico-Theology* (1713) might today be called an *ecotheology*. It embodied a number of ecologically sound principles, in a managerial framework of stewardship modeled on man's role as caretaker of God's creation." I also argued that

> Derham made use of not only the principle of ecological interdependence but also the concept of adaptation … . Each lake, pond, hill, and vale had its own group of trees, shrubs, plants, and animals … . Another ecological principle was that of population stability. Each valley, forest, or lake was kept in perfect balance so that the number of species in any one place remained constant, and there was sufficient room, food, and other necessaries.
>
> *(Merchant [1980] 1990:248, 251)*

Stoll's own elaboration of the ideas of these philosophers enriches his argument that Calvinism and reformed Presbyterianism contributed to the roots of ecological science.

Although my main thesis in *TDN* was that the Renaissance organic worldview was replaced by a mechanistic framework, I also elaborated on alternative approaches that resonated with organic and ecological assumptions. For example, in discussing small-scale utopian communities proposed in the sixteenth century, such as Tommaso Campanella's *City of the Sun* (1602), I wrote,

> Recognized today as keys to viable ecosystems in nature are the inter-relationships and organic unity among a system's parts and the maintenance of ecological diversity ... . In the *City of the Sun*, such principles subtly guided community norms and practices. Nature was an organic whole in which both natural and human cycles were integrated.
>
> *(Merchant [1980] 1990:83)*

In *TDN*, I also discussed the vitalism of Cambridge Platonists Henry More and Ralph Cudworth, as well as that of natural philosophers Anne Conway and Gottfried Wilhelm Leibniz who reasserted the fundamental organic unity of nature. "As a philosophy of nature," I wrote, "vitalism ... was inherently anti-exploitative" (Merchant [1980] 1990:253).

My other books likewise include substantive discussions of religion and nature. *Ecological Revolutions* (Merchant [1989] 2010) has a chapter on "The Animate Cosmos of the New England Farmer" that discusses the movement away from a strict Calvinist separation of God from nature and toward ways in which God showed his glory by his presence within the world of nature. *Radical Ecology* (Merchant [1992] 2005), which Stoll quotes in his opening statement, contains a chapter on "Spiritual Ecology" as well as an elaboration of the religious dimensions of several forms of environmental ethics. *Reinventing Eden* (Merchant [2003] 2013) has a major focus on the Garden of Eden story, while *Autonomous Nature* (Merchant 2016) has an entire chapter on "Christianity and Nature," as well as a chapter on Spinoza who developed what was later called pantheism.

In his Chapter 10 in this volume, Mark Stoll has contributed new insights and connections that advance the discussion of the Calvinist threads that nourished the development of the science of ecology in the twentieth century, for which I am very appreciative. Religion and spirituality are important because they can enhance the new Story of Sustainability critical to dealing with the Age of the Anthropocene.

Ecological Ethics

Norman Wirzba's excellent books on *The Paradise of God: Renewing Religion in an Ecological Age* (Wirzba 2007) and *From Nature to Creation: A Christian Vision for Understanding and Loving Our World* (Wirzba 2015) raise critical issues for spirituality and environmental ethics. In his chapter for this book, "From a Partnership to a Fidelity Ethic: Framing an Old Story for a New Time," Wirzba writes that my work shows "how the memory of Eden as the attainment of paradise has been used to underwrite the exploration and domination of nature (and women, and racial minorities, and indigenous peoples)." Moreover, "this philosophical story, along with the dualist metaphysic and epistemology it endorses, has been the dominant story for a long time, and it has made it is very difficult to read the Garden of Eden in ways that do not endorse dominion" (Wirzba, this volume, p. 72). Wirzba wants instead to reclaim the Eden story in new ways consistent with what he calls a fidelity ethic. An ethic of fidelity is an idea worth considering in light of the new Era of the Anthropocene. I will first discuss (1) the Eden story and then (2) the fidelity ethic.

(1) At the outset, I want to clarify the argument I made in my book *Reinventing Eden: The Fate of Nature in Western Culture* (Merchant [200] 2013). In the Bible, the ideas of dominion and the simultaneous creation of man and woman are presented in Genesis, chapter 1, while the Garden of Eden story and the sequential creation of Adam and then Eve are presented in Genesis, chapter 2. Genesis 1 becomes the basis for the domination of nature, while Genesis 2 becomes the inspiration for an ethic of stewardship based on the human management of nature (Bible, Chamberlin and Feldman 1961). How do the ideas of dominion and stewardship play out over time?

In the Bible's Genesis 2 story, God first created "man" from the dust. The name Adam derives from the Hebrew word, *adama*, meaning earth or arable land. *Adama* is a feminine noun, meaning an earth that gives birth to plants. God then created the Garden of Eden, the four rivers that flowed from it, and the trees for food (including the tree of life and the tree of the knowledge of good and evil in the center). He put "the man" in the garden "to dress and keep it," formed the birds and beasts from dust, and brought them to Adam to name. Only then did he create Eve from Adam's rib. Underlying this story is an ethic of stewardship and care for the land, points made by René Dubos in his "Conservation, Stewardship, and the Human Heart," (Dubos 1972) and his "Theology of the Earth" (Dubos 1973).

It was not until the seventeenth century in the hands of Francis Bacon that the idea of recovering Eden after "man's" fall from the garden was connected with the idea of dominion over nature. "Man by the Fall," Bacon wrote, "fell at the same time from his state of innocency and from his dominion over creation. Both of these losses can in this life be in some part repaired; the former by religion and faith, the latter by arts and science." He boldly asserted that "man" can "*recover* that right over nature which belongs to it by divine bequest" (Bacon 1870, 4:247–248, 114–115; Leiss 1972:48–52; Whitney 1986).

After the work of Francis Bacon, the Garden of Eden story takes on new meanings. The strong interventionist version in Genesis 1 validates the recovery of Eden through domination, while the softer Genesis 2 version advocates dressing and keeping the garden through human management (stewardship). Human labor could redeem the souls of men and women, while the earthly wilderness could be redeemed through cultivation and domestication—thereby recreating Eden on earth.

But Wirzba argues that we can rethink the Garden of Eden in a new way. He elaborates: "When read and retold in a new/old light [it] can play a powerful role in developing the ethic we need in a time of ecological degradation." It is a story of "human entanglements with the land, its diverse creaturely life, and with God." The gardening God loves the soil. He kisses it and breathes into it "divine, creating, nurturing, and sustaining life." He is "a creating God who does not ever want to be separated from creation." God wants to be with his creatures. He is not "a transcendent God who is distant from the world" (Wirzba, this volume, pp. 80–81).[11] I like and appreciate Wirzba's ideas of entanglement, nurturing, and sustaining life, but I am skeptical that a reclaimed Garden of Eden story is the best story for dealing with the problems of human domination in the Age of the Anthropocene.

(2) If we can rethink the Garden of Eden story, however, can we then move to what Wirzba calls a fidelity ethic? What exactly is a fidelity ethic and what are its underlying assumptions? What kinds of environmental problems can be solved by this ethic as opposed to my own partnership ethic? What might a fidelity ethic accomplish that a partnership ethic cannot?

Wirzba does not define the meaning of fidelity, but if we examine the roots of the term, we find that it comes from the Latin word "*fides*" meaning trust, faith, or belief; it is a word of the feminine gender. *Fides* was the goddess of trust.[12] Her symbol was the Turtle Dove. In Rome, she was worshipped as *Fides Publica Populi Romana*, the "trust" of the Roman people. *Bona fides* means "good faith." Faith (*fides*) as defined historically, therefore, seems to be at the root of what Wirzba calls a fidelity ethic, defining new human relations with God and the natural world. "A fidelity ethic," he writes, "offers us an invitation to develop the skill and sympathy, and discover the pain and joy a faithful life entails" (Wirzba, this volume, p. 83). I agree that skill and sympathy are critical to human relations with the natural world, but they are not inconsistent with a partnership ethic.

Drawing on the ideas of Tim Ingold concerning life and livelihood, Wirzba asserts that we need an ethic that treats all living things as relations in dynamic movement, embedded in entanglements and meshworks, "receiving from and giving to others." We need to appreciate the "countless ways in which humanity is entangled in the movements and lives of countless others." "Our activity and movement—our aliveness—are also the world's activity and movement in and through us."[13] Wirzba explains:

> If I have proposed that we speak in terms of a fidelity rather than a partner-ship ethic, it is because I think that the most fundamental task moving for-ward is to challenge the metaphysical picture and the epistemological stance that keeps us separate and in an oppositional frame of mind.
>
> *(Wirzba, this volume, p. 82)*

I like and accept Wirzba's ideas of "dynamic movement," "entanglement," and "receiving from and giving to others." But I ask: Fidelity to what? To humanity?

The Earth? God? Is a fidelity ethic fundamentally a religious ethic that depends on God?

My own approach is a *secular* ethic rooted in a form of process philosophy (as articulated by Alfred North Whitehead, John Cobb, and Charles Hartshorne) that sees change as dialectical, continuous, and interactive. Process is more fundamental than parts (atoms). My approach to ethics is grounded in the concept of relation, not in the self (egocentric ethics), society (homocentric ethics), or the cosmos (ecocentric ethics). Humans are dependent on all other forms of animate and inanimate nature and those forms are dependent on us (Merchant [1992] 2005:table 3.1). My partnership ethic depends on give and take, back and forth, collaboration and negotiation between humans and nonhuman nature.

In evaluating Wirzba's arguments, my questions are the following: Can the Garden of Eden story be rethought as a new story for the Age of the Anthropocene? And, second, can a fidelity ethic go beyond a partnership ethic? In brief, my answer to both questions is: We are not there yet. Until Wirzba shows by detailed examples how to put his fidelity ethic into practice and how a rethought Garden of Eden story can be applied to the real world, I'm sticking with partnership.

Ecofeminism

I am deeply amazed by the tribute paid to my ideas in my books *TDN, Earthcare*, and *Radical Ecology* by Patsy Hallen in Chapter 16 of this volume, "A Mighty Tree is Carolyn Merchant."[14] Patsy's invitation in 1991 to teach a course on "Ecofeminism" in Australia was exceptionally timely. At that moment, I was writing my 1992 book *Radical Ecology*. Its chapter on "Ecofeminism" was profoundly influenced by Patsy, the course, and the students that I taught at Murdoch University in Fremantle, Western Australia, as a result of Patsy's invitation. Not only did I write the chapter on ecofeminism while teaching at Murdoch, but as a result of giving visiting lectures at several Australian universities, I wrote an article on "The Ecological Self: Women and the Environment in Australia" that was published in my 1996 book, *Earthcare: Women and the Environment* (Merchant 1996). I had been deeply affected both by Rachel Carson's *Silent Spring* in 1962 (Carson 1962) on the devastating effects of pesticides on the environment, and by Betty Friedan's *The Feminine Mystique* (Frieden 1963) the following year that inspired the women's movement. But the two ideas did not come together until the early 1970s when books, courses, and the environmental movement began to connect the concepts of women and nature.

In 1974, while teaching a course at UC Berkeley[15] as a visiting lecturer, I met Geography Department graduate students Sandra Marburg and Lisa Watkins, who were organizing a conference titled "Women and Environment: A Gathering of Interested Persons Meeting and Discussing Solutions to the Most Urgent Threats to Life." At the conference, we explored the connections between women and nature and how women could work to save the planet. In 1978, Susan Griffin (author of the much-appreciated Foreword to this volume) published her earth-shattering book of poetic prose *Woman and Nature: The Roaring Inside Her*. I met her at a political meeting in a friend's living room in Berkeley as she was finalizing her book and I was working on the manuscript for *TDN*. We became friends, and she lectured in the classes I taught in my new position at UC Berkeley, which I began in 1979. Susan's book on *Woman and Nature* inspired a student-led class on "Women and Nature" that I sponsored in 1982.

I first heard the term ecofeminism in the year 1980 when *TDN* was published. People said, "Ok, nature is dead, now what?" The term "Ecofeminism" (*ecoféminisme*), as Patsy Hallen notes, was first used in print by Françoise d'Eaubonne in her book *Feminism or Death* (d'Eaubonne 1974). In 1972 she had founded the *ecologie-féminisme* center in Paris. D'Eaubonne called on women to lead an ecological revolution to save the planet and concluded her chapter on "The Time for Ecofeminism" with the prophetic phrase: "The planet placed in the feminine will flourish for all." A society recast in the "feminine," she asserted, would not mean power in the hands of women, but no power at all (d'Eaubonne 1974, in Merchant 2008:212). Around 1976, Ynestra King began teaching a course on "ecofeminism" at Murray Bookchin's Institute for Social Ecology in Plainfield, Vermont, and in 1980 she organized a conference in Amherst, Massachusetts on "Women and Life on Earth: Ecofeminism in the '80s." It was the advertisement for this conference on ecofeminism that gave me hope that feminism and ecology could come together to reverse "the death of nature."

In 1984, with the connections between women and nature being analyzed and conceptualized around the world, I was invited to be a Fulbright scholar at Umeå University in northern Sweden to teach two courses, one on "Nature and Culture" and the other on "Women and Nature." While there I researched and co-authored an article on "Making Peace with the Earth: Women and the Swedish Environment" with sociologist Abby Peterson (*Earthcare*, Ch. 8). In 1987, Irene Diamond and Gloria Orenstein organized a conference in honor of the 25th anniversary of Rachel Carson's *Silent Spring* on "Ecofeminist Perspectives: Nature, Culture, and Theory" at the University of Southern California that drew women and men from many countries. Out of that conference came their edited book *Reweaving the World: The Emergence of Ecofeminism* (Diamond and Orenstein 1990) in which I have a chapter titled "Ecofeminism and Feminist Theory."

During the 1980s and '90s, I published several articles (in addition to those mentioned above) articulating what women were doing to save the environment that were ultimately collected in my book *Earthcare* (Merchant 1996). In her chapter in this volume, Patsy Hallen goes on to relate how she sponsored several additional classes on ecofeminism at Murdoch during the 1990s and then how she came to UC Berkeley to teach "ecofeminism" in 1993 (Hallen, this volume, p. 270). Patsy was thus a great influence on my work not only through intense intellectual discussions, but also by giving me the opportunity to express and refine my theory of the differing forms of ecofeminism in chapter 8 and table 8.1 of *Radical Ecology* (Merchant [1992] 2005). It also made it possible to research and write the chapter mentioned above on "Women and the Environment in Australia" for my book *Earthcare* (Merchant 1996). Feminism and ecofeminism are both critical aspects of the New Story of Sustainability and partnership with the earth.

Systems Theory

Debora Hammond has done remarkable work on systems theory, publishing her outstanding book *The Science of Synthesis: Exploring the Social Implications of General Systems Theory* (Hammond 2003), and serving as president of the International Society for Systems Sciences (ISSS) in 2006. I have learned a great deal from her analysis of the roots of systems theory in the mid-twentieth century that has helped me articulate my own systems approach as a dialectical process and a new Story of Sustainability.

I became interested in systems theory when, soon after I began my job at UC Berkeley in 1979, I audited my colleague Arnold Schultz's course on "Ecosystemology." It was an eye-opening experience, not only for Arnold's insights into systems theory, but for his teaching style. His "Ecosystemology" course reader was a compilation of many articles on the systems approach with each article printed on large differently colored 11 × 17 sheets of paper. At the beginning of each lecture he would post a piece of colored paper on the blackboard. When students asked what the paper was for, he would say "Read an article in that color from the Ecosystemology reader." He used extra-large-sized paper so that people could not just shelve the reader, but had to leave it on their coffee table. In teaching, Arnold sometimes stood behind the podium and sometimes walked back and forth across the stage. He told the students that when he was behind the podium he was lecturing and when he was not behind the podium (which was most of the time) he was teaching. He always held his final examination in the Berkeley Rose Garden where part of it was written (as then required by UC Berkeley) and part of it was held in small groups. Arnold's introductions to each chapter of his "Ecosystemology" reader can now be found on the Conservation and Resource Studies website.[16]

Arnold Schultz's systems theory influenced both my teaching and my approach to history in my second book *Ecological Revolutions: Nature, Gender, and Science in New England* (Merchant [1989] 2010), which I had just published when Debora Hammond arrived at Berkeley as a graduate student. My theoretical approach in that book was a synthesis of the dialectics of Karl Marx (Parsons 1977) as an interaction between systems of production and ideology into which I integrated Arnold's approach to ecological systems and Abby Peterson's approach to gender and reproduction. But rather than using boxes and arrows as was the method of systems theory, I used a diagram of interacting circles that reflected a feminist and process-oriented approach. I also incorporated Thomas Kuhn's *Structure of Scientific Revolutions* (Kuhn 1962) in delineating two major Ecological Revolutions—a colonial ecological revolution that transformed native peoples' ways of life by way of external ecological inputs and European settlements, and a capitalist ecological revolution that occurred internally as colonial subsistence lifestyles were transformed by capitalist industrialization. This second revolution drew on and was shaped by my partner and husband Charles Sellers's theories in *The Market Revolution: Jacksonian America, 1815–1846* (Sellers 1991). Charlie's work has been a major influence on my thinking since the early 1970s when I was writing *TDN*, and especially on my theoretical approach in *Ecological Revolutions*.

Building on Debora Hammond's outstanding insights into systems theory, I believe that a dialectical systems approach and a critique of capitalist forms of economics can contribute to a new earth that uses resources both sustainably and economically as an integral part of a new Story of Sustainability.

The Ecological Indian

Shepard Krech III, long-time colleague through three summer seminars taught at the National Humanities Center (NHC) between 1996 and 2000, and co-research fellow in the NHC class of 2001, has written a gracious and provocative chapter for this volume titled "Carolyn Merchant and *The Ecological Indian*." Krech's books *The Ecological Indian: Myth and History* (Krech 1999) and his subsequent *Spirits of the Air: Birds and American Indians in the South* (Krech 2009) bring together our shared interests in the changing ecology of the American landscape and bird life throughout the Americas. I have benefitted from Krech's well-crafted critiques of approaches to environmental history that tend to idealize Native American relations with animals and the land prior to European intervention. I learned a great deal from his contributions to the summer seminars at the NHC as well as our work together on the three-volume *Encyclopedia of World Environmental History* while we were fellows at the Center in 2001 (Krech, McNeill, and Merchant 2004).

In his Chapter 8 for this volume, Krech notes that in some places "Merchant and I are [not] in perfect lockstep" and points to what he calls "differences in our reading of the history of ecology and conservation in Native North America." One example of this problem, he states in his chapter, "was an essay by historian Calvin Martin called 'Micmacs and French in the Northeast'" (Krech, this volume, p. 139), which I included in all three editions of my edited book *Major Problems in American Environmental History* (Merchant [1993] 2012). I did this even after reading the excellent arguments in *The Ecological Indian* because I wanted students to learn to analyze historical documents and essays and develop their own interpretations of history.

Calvin Martin's essay in *Major Problems* (Merchant [1993] 2012:ch. 2) was excerpted from his 1974 article, "The European Impact on the Culture of a

Northeastern Algonquin Tribe: An Ecological Interpretation," published in the *William and Mary Quarterly* (Martin 1974). Martin followed this article with his book *Keepers of the Game: Indian–Animal Relationships and the Fur Trade* (Martin 1978). Krech then challenged Martin's interpretation of the ways in which native peoples related to other animals and the environment in his edited book *Indians, Animals, and the Fur Trade: A Critique of "Keepers of the Game"* (Krech 1981).

The *Major Problems* series, in which Calvin Martin's essay is included, was designed to present documents and essays with differing perspectives so that students can learn to evaluate critically the evidence and arguments presented. Chapter 2 on "Native American Ecology and European Contact" included a comparison of the transformation processes initiated by the arrival of Europeans on three different Indian cultures (Pueblos in the Southwest, Micmacs in the Northeast, and Indians on the Great Plains). My goal was to present two or three primary source documents for each case along with an interpretive essay, asking the students to compare the three cases and to critically assess the documents in relation to the arguments in the essays. The documents for the Micmacs included a description from Jesuit Nicolas Denys from 1672, discussing Micmac life before and after the fur trade, and another from 1691, featuring the recollections of Father Chrestien Le Clercq on the ways in which hunters imitated the habits of their prey and adhered to rituals for disposing of their remains (Merchant [1993] 2012:ch. 2). The "Introduction" to chapter 2 states the following:

> Encounters between Pueblos and Spanish in the Southwest and between Micmacs and French in the Northeast and the introduction of horses on the Great Plains altered the ecological habitats and cultures of Native Americans. Although the transformation processes in the three cases had similarities, they were also different … . These three examples [cover] three different ecosystems: deserts, forests, and grasslands.
>
> *(Merchant [1993] 2012:33–34)*

Martin's emphasis is on Indian–animal spiritual relationships and the consequences of European introductions into the Micmac environment. Critics of Martin argued that the fur trade was established in the 1580s through 1640s, but the epidemics that Martin claimed changed the Micmacs' spirituality occurred *after* the fur trade began (Merchant [1993] 2012). In my lectures I drew on Krech's examples showing that the Pueblo and Great Plains Indians, as well as the Micmac, were not "ecological" as Martin and others had cast them (Krech 1999:chs. 2, 5, 7).

My objective was to engage students in a discussion of the pros and cons of Martin's, Krech's, and other historians' explanations. I asked: What is at stake here? A materialist or idealist interpretation of history or something far more complex? Is materialism (e.g., Jared Diamond's thesis that the "guns, germs, and steel" introduced by Europeans were the causes of change) or ideas (such as Martin's argument that emphasized spiritual change) the driver of history? Or is there a much more complex process of change involving many factors, such as those pointed out by Krech? My goal was to teach students to question the underlying assumptions behind the arguments of environmental historians, to go to the sources for evidence of their thesis, and to give them confidence in their own abilities to read, analyze, and evaluate history.

I am grateful to Shepard Krech III for his insights and analysis of many North American Indian cultures in *The Ecological Indian* and his critical perspectives on the numerous factors operating in historical and environmental change which I integrated into my courses and lectures. I have learned a great deal from knowing him over the past two decades.

Enriching *TDN*

Kenneth Worthy's book *Invisible Nature: Healing the Destructive Divide Between People and the Environment* (Worthy 2013) is a brilliant analysis of the intellectual, social, and psychological consequences of humanity's disconnection from the natural world over the past two millennia and ways to restore lost relationships and connections. In his stimulating Chapter 2 for this book, "*The Death of Nature* or Divorce from Nature?", he shows how "the mechanistic cosmology advanced the project of divorce from nature … and perhaps more important, [how] it intensified the adoption of an organizing principle that [he calls] dissociation—various forms of disconnection, separation, isolation, and alienation—running through structures of Western thought." "The concept of dissociation," he writes, "deepens and enhances the understanding of mechanistic cosmology elaborated in *TDN* by elucidating the effects of mechanism on relations of all kinds" (Worthy, this volume, p. 43). Worthy especially focuses on Greek philosophy as background to the concept of dissociation. Dissociations alienate people from nature and from the consequences of each person's own actions on other people, the living world, and the natural environment. Restoring the lost wholeness will require a major reset in human/nature relations. I greatly appreciate his extension and elaboration of the personal and social effects of the "divorce" from nature. They contribute significantly to a new Story of Sustainability that must heal the divisions created by the divorce and dissociation of humanity from the natural world.

Nancy Unger's highly complimentary Chapter 7 in this volume, titled "Personal, Political, and Professional: The Impact of Carolyn Merchant's Life and Leadership" elaborates on the ways her own scholarship has been influenced by my work on gender. Examples include her superb book *Beyond Nature's Housekeepers: American Women in Environmental History* (Unger 2012), her first-rate article "Women and Gender: Useful Categories of Analysis in Environmental History" (Unger 2014) and her wonderful co-authored essay, "'Mother Nature is Getting Angrier': Turning Sacred Navajo Land into a Toxic Environment (Unger and Bolton 2015)." Nancy is a great public speaker, doing interviews and broadcasts for NPR, KQED, CNN, and C-Span. Her work includes the role of

LGBTQ in history, an enrichment that gives me great pleasure and admiration for her. I am deeply grateful to Nancy for detailing the ways in which her own work on gender has been enriched by mine. In turn, my own ideas have been enhanced by hers. Recognition of LGBTQ rights and responsibilities must become part of an ethic of partnership between people and the earth.

Elizabeth Allison's eloquently written Chapter 5, "Bewitching Nature," offers another road to "after the death of nature." Allison proposes an "ethic of flourishing," emerging from her studies in the Himalayas and especially of Buddhism. Her excellent dissertation *Enspirited Places, Material Traces: The Sanctified and the Sacrificed in Modernizing Bhutan* (Allison 2009) (and book in progress with the working title *Enchanted Earth: Ecology, Religion, and Development in Modernizing Bhutan*), reveals an array of ecological insights developed over many years by indigenous communities in Bhutan. Such approaches contribute to a revision of ideas of mechanism rooted in Western epistemology and ontology in directions that can enhance partnerships with nature. She advocates greater emphasis on justice, receptive listening, openmindedness, and recognizing that other peoples and life forms are active agents in a world that is polyfocal and polyvocal. By listening to indigenous peoples and marginalized groups, as well as the voice of the nonhuman world, we can move forward toward liberatory policies that can make "their way into national and international policy discourses." The contributions of indigenous peoples to listening, justice, partnerships, and an ethic of flourishing are critical to a sustainable earth. Moreover, her recent article, "Toward a Feminist Care Ethic for Climate Change" (Allison 2017), that draws on traditional ecological knowledge (TEK) is a profound addition to her ethic of flourishing that dovetails with my own partnership ethic. These approaches are well-argued, significant approaches to environmental history and ways to advance human partnerships with nature.

In addition to the chapters discussed above, I am honored by the admirable contributions made by Heather Eaton, Sverker Sörlin, Dewi Candraningrum, Laura Alice Watt, Yaakov Garb, and Whitney Bauman. Each has contributed significant insights into my work, enriched its implications, and extended it in new directions. Together, the contributors to this volume have produced pathways to a better future for both humanity and the earth.

Conclusion

The chapters in *After the Death of Nature* have helped me to rethink the ideas and assumptions on which my intellectual work has been based. I believe that we need a new story and a new ethic for the Age of the Anthropocene, as we are in danger of experiencing another "death of nature" that may include the human species as well as much of the physical and biological world as it exists today.

That new story is a Story of Sustainability in which humans and the earth are in dynamic interaction, and there is a give and take between humans and nonhuman nature. It recognizes that nature is autonomous and not always predictable—a nature described not only by mechanistic science but also by chaos and complexity theories. As humans, we can learn from what is now happening to the oceans and atmosphere as a result of the anthropogenic accumulation of greenhouse gases that is disrupting life as we know it today. We can use our knowledge of science, technology, and society, along with our spiritual and ethical relations with each other and the nonhuman world, to create that new story. The New Ethic that accompanies the New Story is a Partnership Ethic. It states: *The greatest good for the human and nonhuman communities is in their mutual living interdependence.*

My mantra is

> Solar panels on every roof;
> Bicycles in every garage;
> And
> Vegetables in every backyard.

Policies, ethics, and individual actions can restore, reclaim, and reinvigorate the earth.

Notes

1 Carolyn Iltis was the name I took in 1961 when I married Hugh Iltis, a professor of Botany at the University of Wisconsin, Madison, where I did my graduate work and wrote my doctoral dissertation on "The Controversy over Living Force: Leibniz to d'Alembert" (Iltis [Merchant] 1967). As Shepard Krech III relates in Chapter 8 of this book, on my first date with Hugh we went out and burned a prairie. The Botany Department's teaching prairie north of Madison had become overgrown with invasive plants and aspens and burning was the time-honored method of restoring native prairie plants. Hugh took me out to see the prairie and while we were walking through it, he took out some matches and tossed them into the overgrown vegetation. As we drove along the road below, fire engines arrived and put out the flames. The following spring the rejuvenated prairie was a mass of beautiful flowers. During our marriage we burned several other prairies that we helped to purchase for the Nature Conservancy. I learned much about ecology and conservation from Hugh during my years in Madison. In 1967 after completing my doctoral dissertation, I left Hugh Iltis and moved to Berkeley, California where I obtained a position at the University of San Francisco and helped to found the Natural Sciences Interdisciplinary Program, sponsored by the Physics Department. When I began my position at the University of California, Berkeley in 1979, I took back my maiden name, Carolyn Merchant under which all my subsequent writings have been published. See Merchant ... /carolyn-merchant. For more on my early history and a collection of publications that characterize my academic work over the past decades, see Merchant, 2018.
2 Enlightenment (n.d.) In *Wikipedia*. Retrieved November 10, 2017, from https://en.wikipedia.org/wiki/Age_of_Enlightenment
3 350.org. (n.d.). In *Wikipedia*. Retrieved November 10, 2017, from https://en.wikipedia.org/wiki/350.org
4 Joseph Black (n.d.) In *Wikipedia*. Retrieved November 10, 2017, from https://en.wikipedia.org/wiki/Joseph_Black

5   Antoine Lavoisier (n.d.) In *Wikipedia*. Retrieved November 10, 2017, from https://en. wikipedia.org/wiki/Antoine_Lavoisier

6   James Watt (n.d.). In *Wikipedia*. Retrieved November 10, 2017, from https://en. wikipedia.org/wiki/James_Watt

7   Newcomen (n.d.). In *Wikipedia*. Retrieved November 10, 2017, from http://technology.niagarac.on.ca/people/mcsele/newcomen.htm

8   Newcomen Engine (n.d.) *Wikipedia*. Retrieved November 10, 2017, from https://en. wikipedia.org/wiki/Newcomen_atmospheric_engine

9   Steam. www.egr.msu.edu/~lira/supp/steam/

10 Steam Engine (n.d.). In *Wikipedia*. Retrieved November 10, 2017, from www.deutsches-museum.de/en/information/young-people/inventors-trail/drivetrains/steam-engine/

11 Wirzba's approach resonates with the idea of panentheism (as opposed to pantheism): The universe is a manifestation of God; God and the world are interrelated. God interpenetrates the world and is actively present in it. Panentheism ... /panentheism/ citation may not be needed here.

12 Fides. (n.d.) In *Wikipedia*. Retrieved November 10, 2017, from https://en.wikipedia. org/wiki/Fides_(deity).

13 Wirzba's ethic also seems to resonate with the ideas of John Cobb and David Ray Griffin that grew out of Alfred North Whitehead's process philosophy—a theory in which everything is in constant change and based on relations.

14 Regarding Patsy Hallen's comment on Robert S. Cohen (Hallen, this volume, p. 000), I first met Bob Cohen at the Enrico Fermi Summer Institute on the History of Twentieth Century Physics in Varenna, Italy in the summer of 1972 and we have been friends ever since. Cohen introduced me to the work of Boris Hessen (Hessen [1931] 1968). This essay played a formative role in my analysis in *TDN* (Merchant [1980] 1990). I believe that Cohen grew to appreciate the argument of *TDN*. When I saw him in June 2016 at the conference on Emile du Châtelet held at Boston University he made very complimentary comments about my work.

15 Merchant, Carolyn. https://ourenvironment.berkeley.edu/people/carolyn-merchant.

16 Conservation and Resource Studies website: https://nature.berkeley.edu/advising/majors/conservation-and-resource-studies

References

Allison, Elizabeth. 2009. *Enchanted Earth: Ecology, Religion, and Development in Modernizing Bhutan, Enspirited Places, Material Traces: The Sanctified and the Sacrificed in Modernizing Bhutan*. Doctoral Dissertation, University of California Berkeley.

Allison, Elizabeth. 2017. "Toward a Feminist Care Ethic for Climate Change." *Journal of Feminist Studies in Religion* 33(2):152–158.

Bacon, Francis. 1870. *Works*. Ed. James Spedding, Robert Leslie Ellis, and Douglas Devon Heath. 14 vols. London: Longmans Green.

Bible, King James Version. See Chamberlin and Feldman, *Dartmouth Bible*.

Braidotti, Rosi, et al. 1994. *Women, the Environment and Sustainable Development: Towards a Theoretical Synthesis*. London: Zed Books.

Carnot, Sadi. 1824. *Réflexions sur la puissance motrice du feu et sur les machines propres à développer cette puissance*. Paris: Bachelier.

Carnot, Sadi. 1890. *Reflections on the Motive Power of Heat and on Machines Fitted to Develop This Power*. Trans. R. H. Thurston. New York: Wiley. Carson, Rachel. 1962. *Silent Spring*. Boston: Houghton Mifflin.

Chamberlin, Roy B. and Herman Feldman. 1961. *The Dartmouth Bible, An Abridgment of the King James Version, with Aids to Its Understanding as History and Literature, and as a Source of Religious Experience*. Boston: Houghton Mifflin.

Clausius, Rudolf. 1865. "Über vershiedene für Anwendung bequeme Formen der Hauptgleichungen der mechanishen Wärmetheorie." *Annalen der Physik* 125:353–400.

Clausius, Rudolf. 1867. *The Mechanical Theory of Heat: With Its Applications to the Steam Engine and to the Physical Properties of Bodies*. London: J. Van Voorst.

Clausius, Rudolf. 1870. "On a Mechanical Theorem Applicable to Heat." *Philosophical Magazine* ser. 4, 40:122–127.

Crutzen, Paul J. and Eugene F. Stoermer. 2000. "The Anthropocene." *IGPB (International Geosphere-Biosphere Programme) Newsletter* 41:17.

d'Eaubonne, Françoise. 1974. *Le Féminisme ou la Mort*. Paris: Pierre Horay.

d'Eaubonne, Françoise. 1994. "The Time for Ecofeminism." Trans. by Ruth Hottel. Pp. 174–197 in *Key Concepts in Critical Theory: Ecology*, Carolyn Merchant, ed. Atlantic Highlands, NJ: Humanities Press.

Diamond, Irene and Gloria Orenstein, eds. 1990. *Reweaving the World: The Emergence of Ecofeminism*. San Francisco, CA: Sierra Club Books.

Diderot, Denis and Jean d'Alembert. 1754–1772. *Encyclopédie*. Paris: Neufchastel.

Dubos, René. 1972. "Conservation, Stewardship, and the Human Heart." *Audubon Magazine* (September):21–28.

Dubos, René. 1973. "A Theology of the Earth." Pp. 43–54 in *Western Man and Environmental Ethics: Attitudes Toward Nature and Technology*, Ian Barbour, ed. Reading, MA: Addison Wesley. Fleming, Donald. 1952. "Latent Heat and the Invention of the Watt Engine." *Isis* 43(1, April):3–5.

Friedan, Betty. 1963. *The Feminine Mystique*. New York: Dell.

Hammond, Debora. 2003. *The Science of Synthesis: Exploring the Social Implications of General Systems Theory*. Boulder, CO: University Press of Colorado.

Haraway, Donna. 2015. "Anthropocene, Capitaloscene, Plantationocene, and Chthulucene: Making Kin." *Environmental Humanities* 6:159–165.

Hessen, Boris. 1968. "The Social and Economic Roots of Newton's Principa" (1931). In *The Rise of Modern Science: Internal or External Factors*, George Basalla, ed. Lexington, MA: DC Heath.

Hiebert, Erwin. 1962. *Historical Roots of the Principle of the Conservation of Energy*. Madison, WI: Wisconsin State Historical Society.

Iltis [Merchant], Carolyn. 1967. "The Controversy Over Living Force: Leibniz to d'Alembert." Doctoral Dissertation, University of Wisconsin, Madison.

Krech, Shepard, III. 1981. *Indians, Animals and the Fur Trade: A Critique of "Keepers of the Game"*. Athens, GA: University of Georgia Press.

Krech, Shepard, III. 1999. *The Ecological Indian: Myth and History*. New York: Norton.

Krech, Shepard, III, John McNeill, and Carolyn Merchant, eds. 2004. *Encyclopedia of World Environmental History*. 3 vols. New York: Routledge.

Krech, Shepard, III. 2009. *Spirits of the Air: Birds and American Indians in the South*. Athens, GA: University of Georgia Press.

Kuhn, Thomas. 1962. *Structure of Scientific Revolutions*. Chicago: University of Chicago Press.

Leiss, William. 1972. *The Domination of Nature*. New York: George Braziller.

Mach, Ernst. 1986. *Principles of the Theory of Heat*. Trans. T. J. McCormack. Dordrecht: Reidel.

MacLeod, J. J. R. 1908. "A Brief Survey of the Development of Physiological Knowledge from the time of the Reformation to the beginning of the Nineteenth Century." *Cleveland Medical Journal* 7(3) (March):121–135.

Magie, William F. 1899. Trans. and ed. *The Second Law of Thermodynamics: Memoirs by Carnot, Clausius, and Thomson.* New York: Harper.

Martin, Calvin. 1974. "The European Impact on the Culture of a Northeastern Algonquin Tribe: An Ecological Interpretation." *William and Mary Quarterly* 31(January):7–26.

Martin, Calvin. 1978. *Keepers of the Game: Indian–Animal Relationships and the Fur Trade.* Berkeley, CA: University of California Press.

Merchant, Carolyn. [1980] 1990. *The Death of Nature: Women, Ecology, and the Scientific Revolution.* San Francisco, CA: HarperCollins (2nd ed.).

Merchant, Carolyn. [1992] 2005. *Radical Ecology: The Search for a Livable World.* New York: Routledge (2nd ed.).

Merchant, Carolyn. 2008. *Key Concepts in Critical Theory: Ecology.* Amherst, NY: Prometheus Books (2nd ed.).

Merchant, Carolyn. [1989] 2010. *Ecological Revolutions.* Chapel Hill, NC: University of North Carolina Press (2nd ed.).

Merchant, Carolyn, ed. [1993] 2012. *Major Problems in American Environmental History: Documents and Essays.* Lexington, MA: D.C. Heath (2nd ed., Boston: Houghton Mifflin, 2004; 3rd ed., Boston: Wadsworth Cengage, 2012).

Merchant, Carolyn. 1996. *Earthcare: Women and the Environment.* New York: Routledge.

Merchant, Carolyn. 2005. *Radical Ecology: The Search for a Livable World.* New York: Routledge (2nd ed).

Merchant, Carolyn. [2003] 2013. *Reinventing Eden: The Fate of Nature in Western Culture.* New York: Routledge (2nd ed., 2013).

Merchant, Carolyn. 2016. *Autonomous Nature: Problems of Prediction and Control From Ancient Times to the Scientific Revolution.* New York: Routledge.

Merchant, Carolyn. 2018. *Science and Nature: Past, Present, and Future.* New York: Routledge.

Moore, Jason. 2014. "The End of Cheap Nature or: How I Learned to Stop Worrying about 'the' Environment and Love the Crisis of Capitalism." Pp. 285–314 in Christian Suter and Christopher Chase-Dunn, eds. *Structures of the World Political Economy and the Future of Global Conflict and Cooperation.* Berlin and London: LIT Verlag.

Moore, Jason, ed. 2016. *Anthropocene or Capitalocene? Nature, History, and the Crisis of Capitalism.* Oakland, CA: PM Press, Kairos Books.

Moore, Jason. 2017a. "The Capitalocene: On the Nature and Origins of Our Ecological Crisis, Pt. I." *Journal of Peasant Studies* 44(3):594–630.

Moore, Jason. 2017b. "The Capitalocene: Accumulation by Appropriation and the Centrality of UnPaid Work/Energy, Pt. II." *Journal of Peasant Studies.* Published online, March 24.

Newburgh, Ronald. 2009. "Carnot to Clausius: Caloric to Entropy." *European Journal of Physics* 30:713–728.

Newton, Isaac. 1960. *Mathematical Principles of Natural Philosophy.* Trans. A. Motte and F. Cajori. Berkeley, CA: University of California Press.

Ortner, Sherry B. 1972. *Feminist Studies* 1(2, Autumn):5–31.

Panentheism. https://plato.stanford.edu/entries/panentheism

Parsons, Howard, ed. 1977. *Marx and Engels on Ecology.* Westport, CT: Greenwood Press.

Raftery, Adrian E. et al. 2017. "Less than 2°C Warming by 2100 Unlikely." *Nature Climate Change* 7(September):637–641.

Rolston, Holmes, III. 1988. *Environmental Ethics: Duties to and Values in the Natural World.* Philadelphia: Temple University Press.

Rolston, Holmes, III. 2006. *Science and Religion: A Critical Survey.* West Conshohocken, PA: Templeton Press, originally published 1986.

Rolston, Holmes, III. 2012. *A New Environmental Ethics: The Next Millennium for Life on Earth.* New York: Routledge.

Rousseau, Jean Jacques. 1977. *Du Contrat Social.* Paris: Editiones du Seuil, originally published 1762. Rousseau, Jean Jacques. 1983. *Discours sur l'origine et les fondements de l'iné-galité parmi les homes.* Paris: Editiones Sociales, originally published 1754.

Rousseau, Jean Jacques. 1990. *The Social Contract.* London: Dent.

Rousseau, Jean Jacques. 1992. *Discourse on the Origin and Basis of Inequality Among Men.* Indianapolis: Hackett.

Sellers, Charles. 1991. *The Market Revolution: Jacksonian America, 1815–1846.* New York: Oxford University Press.

Smith, Adam. 1776. *An Inquiry into the Nature and Causes of the Wealth of Nations.* London: W. Strathan and T. Cadell.

Steffen, Will et al. 2004. *Global Change and the Earth System: A Planet Under Pressure.* Berlin: Springer.

Steffen, Will, Paul Crutzen, and John McNeill. 2007. "The Anthropocene: Are Humans Now Overwhelming the Great Forces of Nature?" *Ambio* 6(8, December):614–671.

Stoll, Mark. 1997. *Protestantism, Capitalism, and Nature in America.* Albuquerque: University of New Mexico Press.

Stoll, Mark. 2015. *Inherit the Holy Mountain: Religion and the Rise of American Environmentalism.* New York: Oxford University Press.

Unger, Nancy. 2012. *Beyond Nature's Housekeepers: American Women in Environmental History.* New York: Oxford University Press.

Unger, Nancy. 2014. "Women and Gender: Useful Categories of Analysis in Environmental History." Pp. 600–643 in *Oxford Handbook of Environmental History.* Andrew Isenberg, ed. New York: Oxford University Press.

Unger, Nancy and Marie Bolton. 2015. "'Mother Nature is Getting Angrier': Turning Sacred Navajo Land into a Toxic Environment." Pp. 31–45 in *Environmental Crisis and Human Costs.* Ufuk Özdağ and François Gavillon, eds. Madrid: Universidad de Alcalá.

U.S. Environmental Protection Agency. 2017. Washington, DC. https://19janua ry2017snapshot.epa.gov/climate-change-science/future-climate-change_.html

Whitney, Charles. 1986. *Francis Bacon and Modernity.* New Haven, CT: Yale University Press.

Wirzba, Norman. 2007. *The Paradise of God: Renewing Religion in an Ecological Age.* Oxford: Oxford University Press.

Wirzba, Norman. 2015. *From Nature to Creation: A Christian Vision for Understanding and Loving Our World.* Grand Rapids, MI: Baker Academic.

World Commission on Environment and Development. 1987. *Our Common Future.* [*Bruntland Report.*] New York: Oxford University Press.

Worthy, Kenneth. 2013. *Invisible Nature: Healing the Destructive Divide Between People and the Environment.* Amherst, NY: Prometheus Books.

INDEX